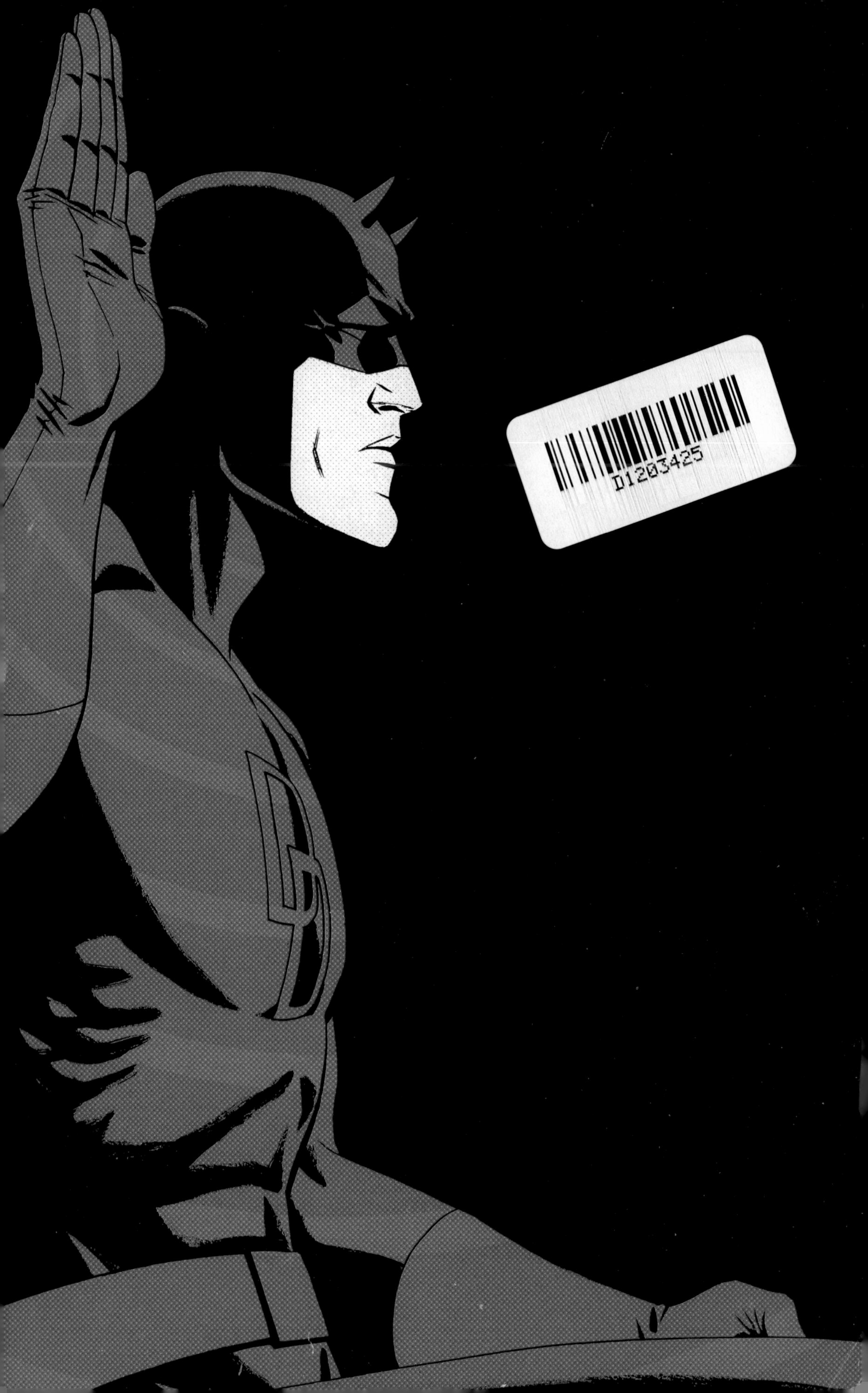

WHEN MATT MURDOCK WAS A KID, HE LOST HIS SIGHT IN AN ACCIDENT INVOLVING A TRUCK CARRYING RADIOACTIVE CHEMICALS. THOUGH HE COULD NO LONGER SEE, THE CHEMICALS HEIGHTENED MURDOCK'S OTHER SENSES AND IMBUED HIM WITH AN AMAZING 360-RADAR SENSE. NOW MATT USES HIS ABILITIES TO FIGHT FOR HIS CITY. HE IS THE *MAN WITHOUT FEAR*. HE IS... *DAREDEVIL*!

AFTER DAREDEVIL SAVED THE PURPLE CHILDREN FROM BEING USED IN A PLANET-ALTERING SCHEME RUN BY THEIR FATHER, ZEBEDIAH KILLGRAVE, THE KIDS REPAID THEIR HERO BY USING THEIR MIND-INFLUENCING POWERS TO MAKE THE WORLD FORGET DAREDEVIL'S TRUE IDENTITY IS MATT MURDOCK. SHOCKED BY THEIR ACTIONS, BUT NOT WANTING TO SQUANDER THIS FRESH START, MATT RETURNED TO NEW YORK, WAS READMITTED TO THE BAR, AND IS TAKING THE FIRST STEPS TOWARDS A PLAN THAT WILL CHANGE EVERYTHING...

DAREDEVIL
SUPREME

CHARLES SOULE
WRITER

GORAN SUDŽUKA *(Nos. 21-23)*,
ALEC MORGAN *(Nos. 24-25)* &
RON GARNEY *(Nos. 26-28)*
ARTISTS

MATT MILLA
COLOR ARTIST

VC's CLAYTON COWLES
LETTERER

DAN PANOSIAN *(No. 21)*, **MIKE DEODATO JR.** & **FRANK MARTIN** *(No. 22)*,
DAVID LOPEZ *(Nos. 23-24)*, **RON GARNEY** & **MATT MILLA** *(Nos. 25-26)* AND
MIKE DEODATO JR. & **MATT MILLA** *(Nos. 27-28)*
COVER ART

MARK BASSO
ASSOCIATE EDITOR

MARK PANICCIA
EDITOR

COLLECTION EDITOR **MARK D. BEAZLEY**
ASSISTANT EDITOR **CAITLIN O'CONNELL**
ASSOCIATE MANAGING EDITOR **KATERI WOODY**
SENIOR EDITOR, SPECIAL PROJECTS **JENNIFER GRÜNWALD**

VP PRODUCTION & SPECIAL PROJECTS **JEFF YOUNGQUIST**
SVP PRINT, SALES & MARKETING **DAVID GABRIEL**
BOOK DESIGNER **ADAM DEL RE**

EDITOR IN CHIEF **AXEL ALONSO**
CHIEF CREATIVE OFFICER **JOE QUESADA**
PRESIDENT **DAN BUCKLEY**
EXECUTIVE PRODUCER **ALAN FINE**

DAREDEVIL: BAC... OL. 5 — SUPREME. Contains material originally published in magazine form as DAREDEVIL #21-28. First printing 2017. ISBN# 978-1-302-90563-7. Published ... subsidiary of MARVEL ENTERTAINMENT, LLC. OFFICE OF PUBLICATION: 135 West 50th Street, New York, NY 10020. Copyright © 2017 MARVEL No similarity ...cters, persons, and/or institutions in this magazine with those of any living or dead person or institution is intended, and any such similarity which may exist ... **the U.S.A.** DAN BUCKLEY, President, Marvel Entertainment; JOE QUESADA, Chief Creative Officer; TOM BREVOORT, SVP of Publishing; DAVID BOGART, SVP of ...lishing & Partnership; C.B. CEBULSKI, VP of Brand Management & Development, Asia; DAVID GABRIEL, SVP of Sales & Marketing, Publishing; JEFF YOUNGQUIST, ...s; DAN CARR, Executive Director of Publishing Technology; ALEX MORALES, Director of Publishing Operations; SUSAN CRESPI, Production Manager; STAN ...rtus. For information regarding advertising in Marvel Comics or on Marvel.com, please contact Vit DeBellis, Integrated Sales Manager, at vdebellis@marvel.com. For Marvel subscription inquiries, please call 888-511-5480. **Manufactured between 10/6/2017 and 11/6/2017 by QUAD/GRAPHICS WASECA, WASECA, MN, USA.**

10 9 8 7 6 5 4 3 2 1

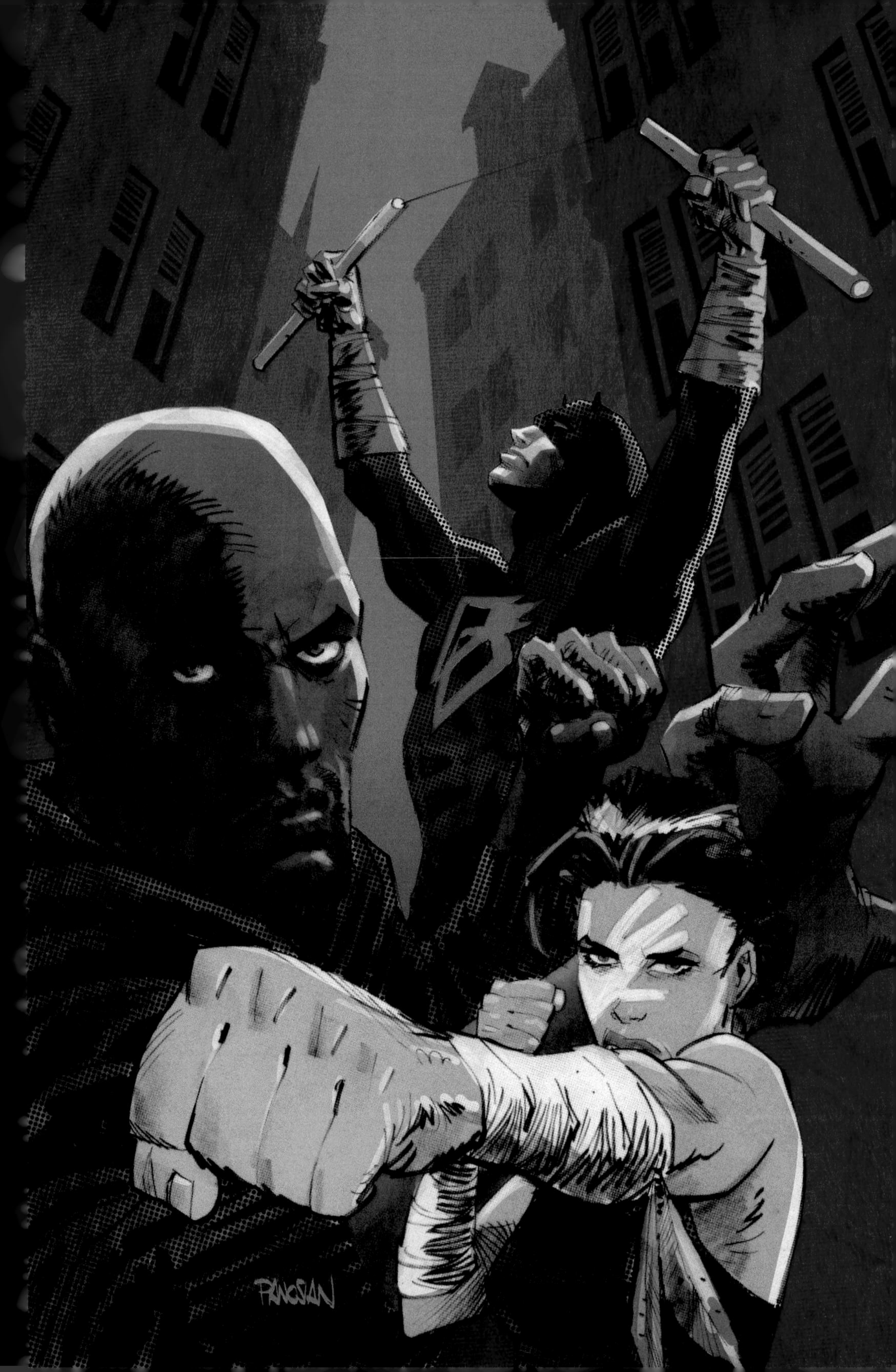
PANOSIAN

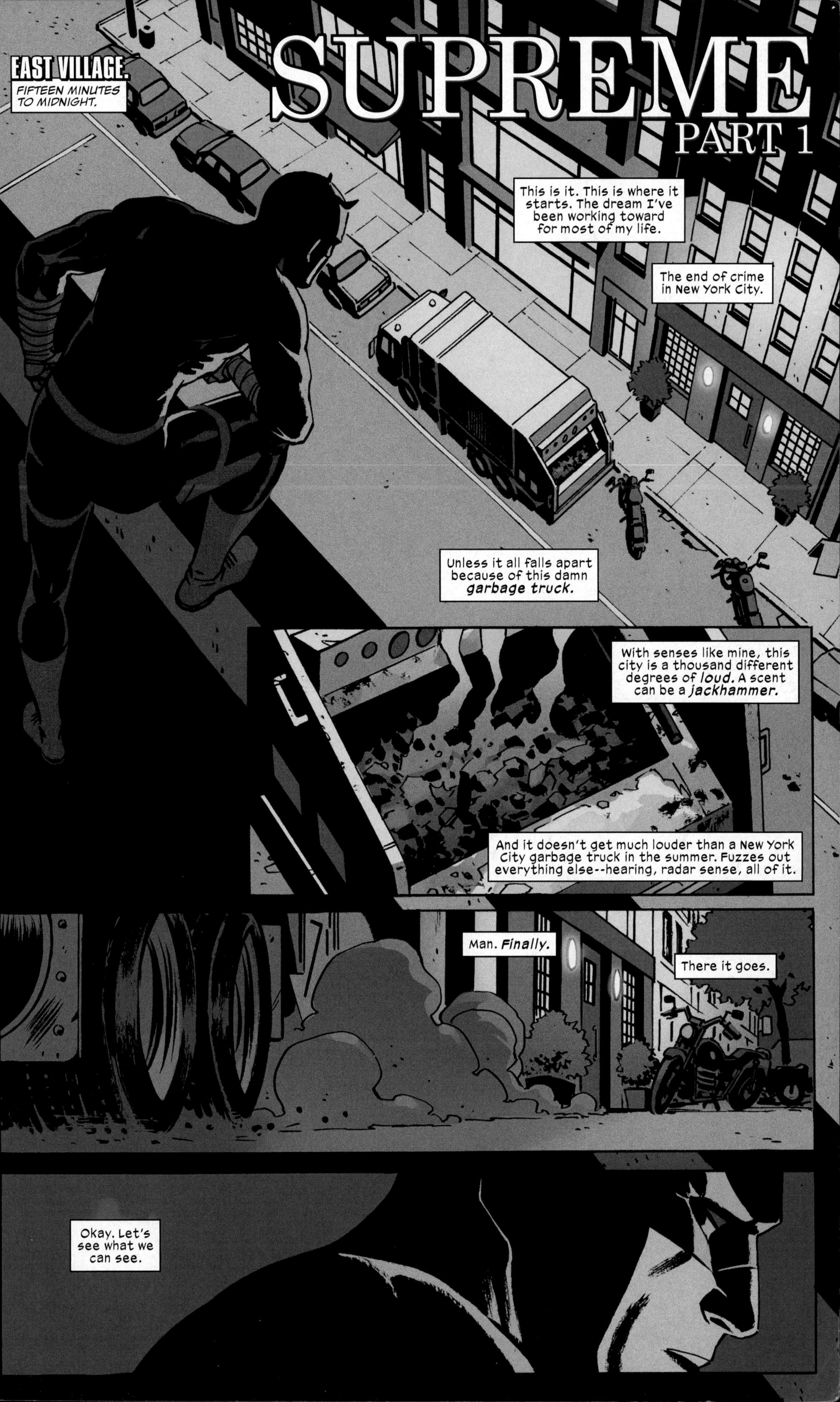
SUPREME
PART 1
EAST VILLAGE.
FIFTEEN MINUTES TO MIDNIGHT.
This is it. This is where it starts. The dream I've been working toward for most of my life.
The end of crime in New York City.
Unless it all falls apart because of this damn garbage truck.
With senses like mine, this city is a thousand different degrees of loud. A scent can be a jackhammer.
And it doesn't get much louder than a New York City garbage truck in the summer. Fuzzes out everything else--hearing, radar sense, all of it.
Man. Finally.
There it goes.
Okay. Let's see what we can see.

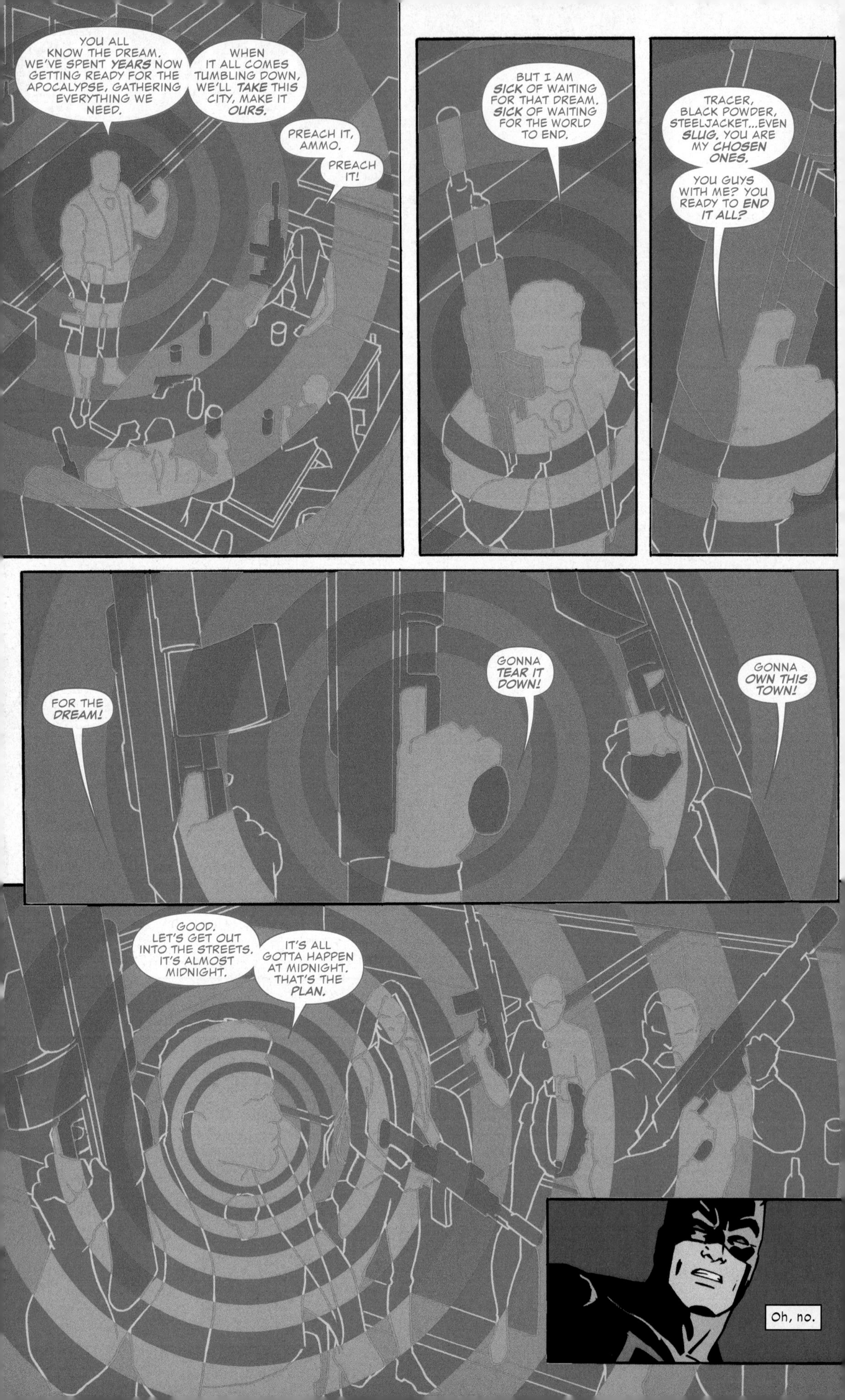

YOU ALL KNOW THE DREAM. WE'VE SPENT YEARS NOW GETTING READY FOR THE APOCALYPSE, GATHERING EVERYTHING WE NEED.
WHEN IT ALL COMES TUMBLING DOWN, WE'LL TAKE THIS CITY, MAKE IT OURS.
PREACH IT, AMMO.
PREACH IT!
BUT I AM SICK OF WAITING FOR THAT DREAM. SICK OF WAITING FOR THE WORLD TO END.
TRACER, BLACK POWDER, STEELJACKET...EVEN SLUG. YOU ARE MY CHOSEN ONES.
YOU GUYS WITH ME? YOU READY TO END IT ALL?
FOR THE DREAM!
GONNA TEAR IT DOWN!
GONNA OWN THIS TOWN!
GOOD. LET'S GET OUT INTO THE STREETS. IT'S ALMOST MIDNIGHT.
IT'S ALL GOTTA HAPPEN AT MIDNIGHT. THAT'S THE PLAN.
Oh, no.

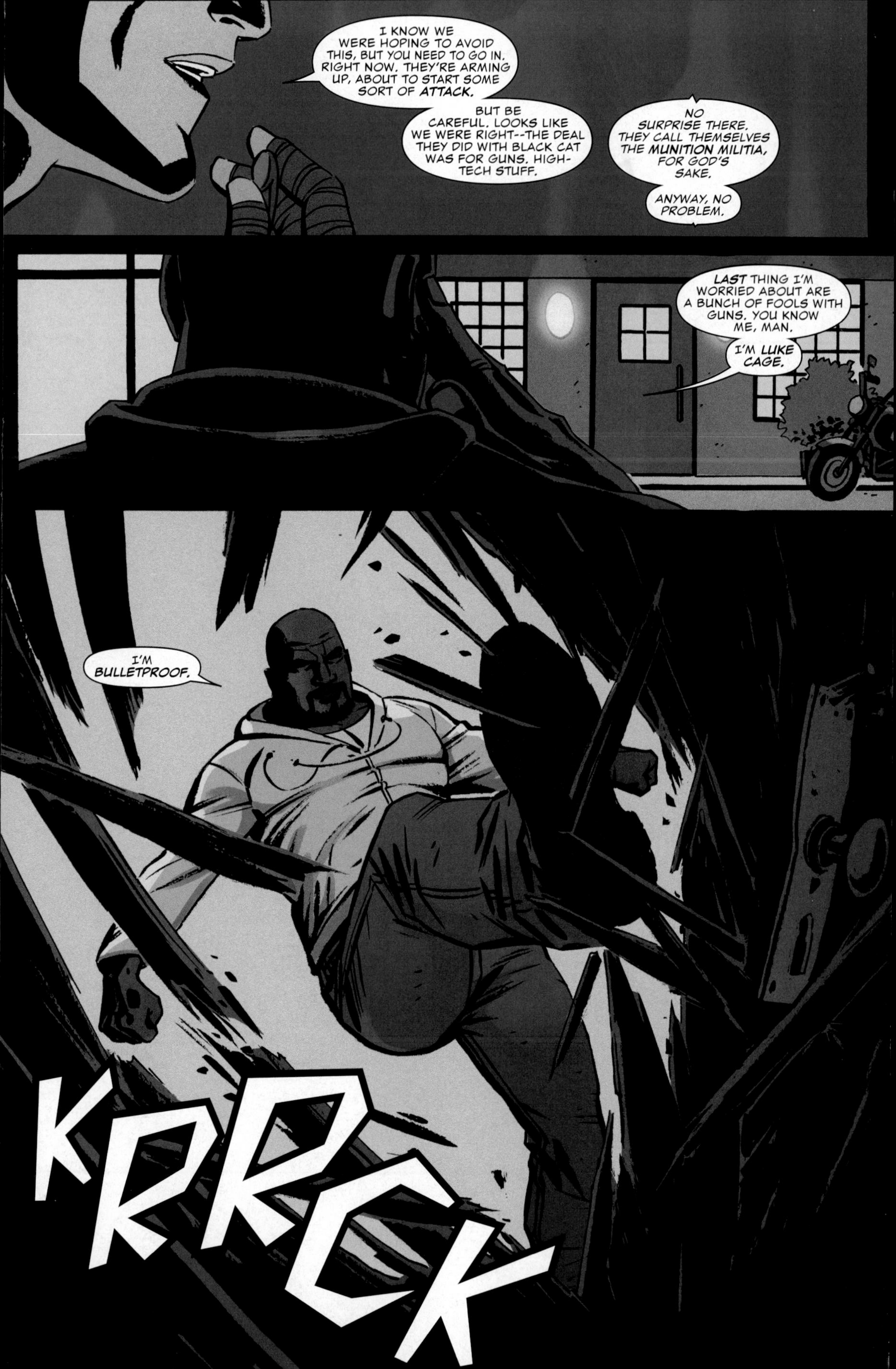
I KNOW WE WERE HOPING TO AVOID THIS, BUT YOU NEED TO GO IN. RIGHT NOW. THEY'RE ARMING UP, ABOUT TO START SOME SORT OF ATTACK.
BUT BE CAREFUL. LOOKS LIKE WE WERE RIGHT--THE DEAL THEY DID WITH BLACK CAT WAS FOR GUNS. HIGH-TECH STUFF.
NO SURPRISE THERE. THEY CALL THEMSELVES THE MUNITION MILITIA, FOR GOD'S SAKE.
ANYWAY, NO PROBLEM.
LAST THING I'M WORRIED ABOUT ARE A BUNCH OF FOOLS WITH GUNS. YOU KNOW ME, MAN.
I'M LUKE CAGE.
I'M BULLETPROOF.
KRRCK

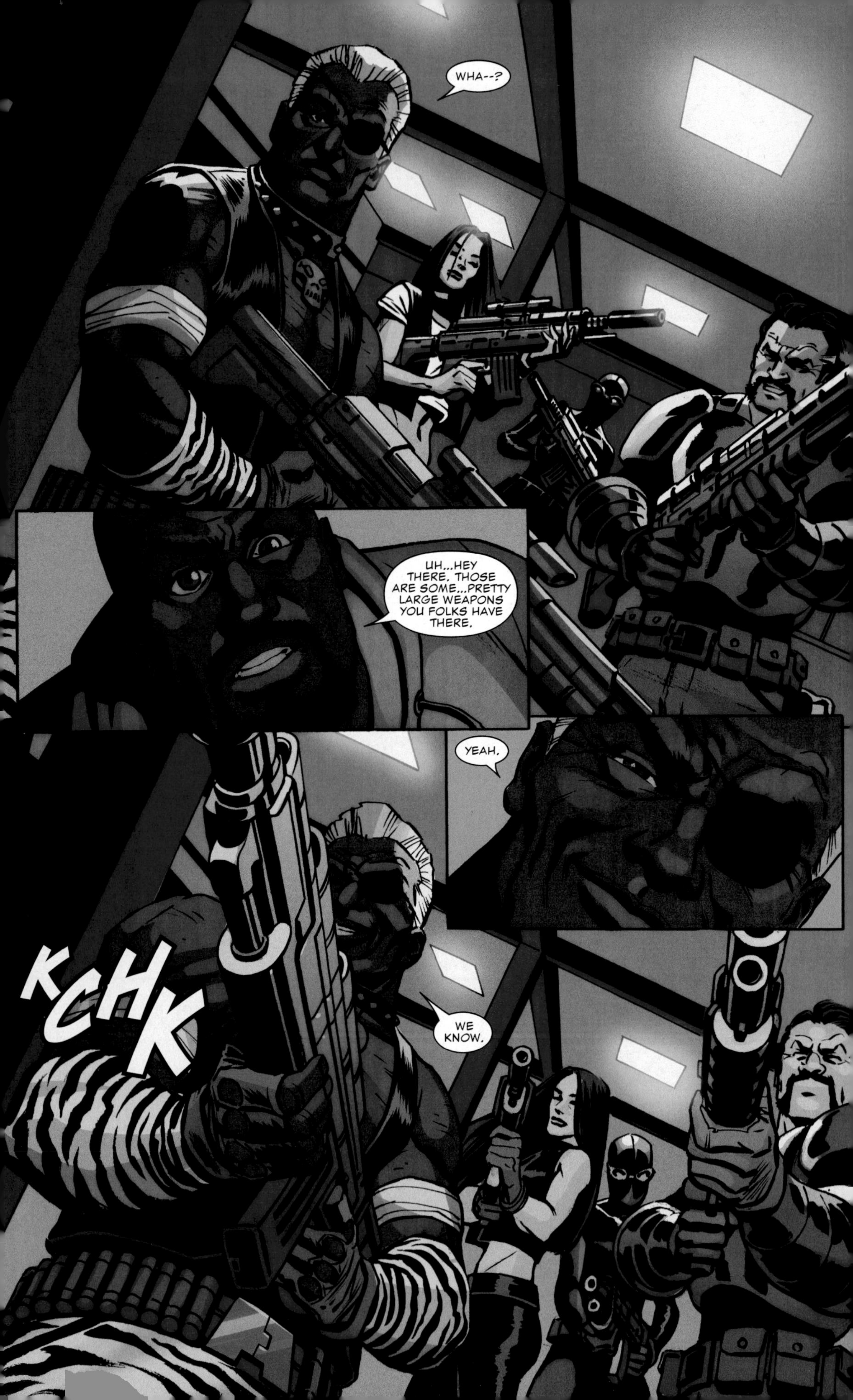
WHA--?
UH...HEY THERE. THOSE ARE SOME...PRETTY LARGE WEAPONS YOU FOLKS HAVE THERE.
YEAH.
KCHK
WE KNOW.

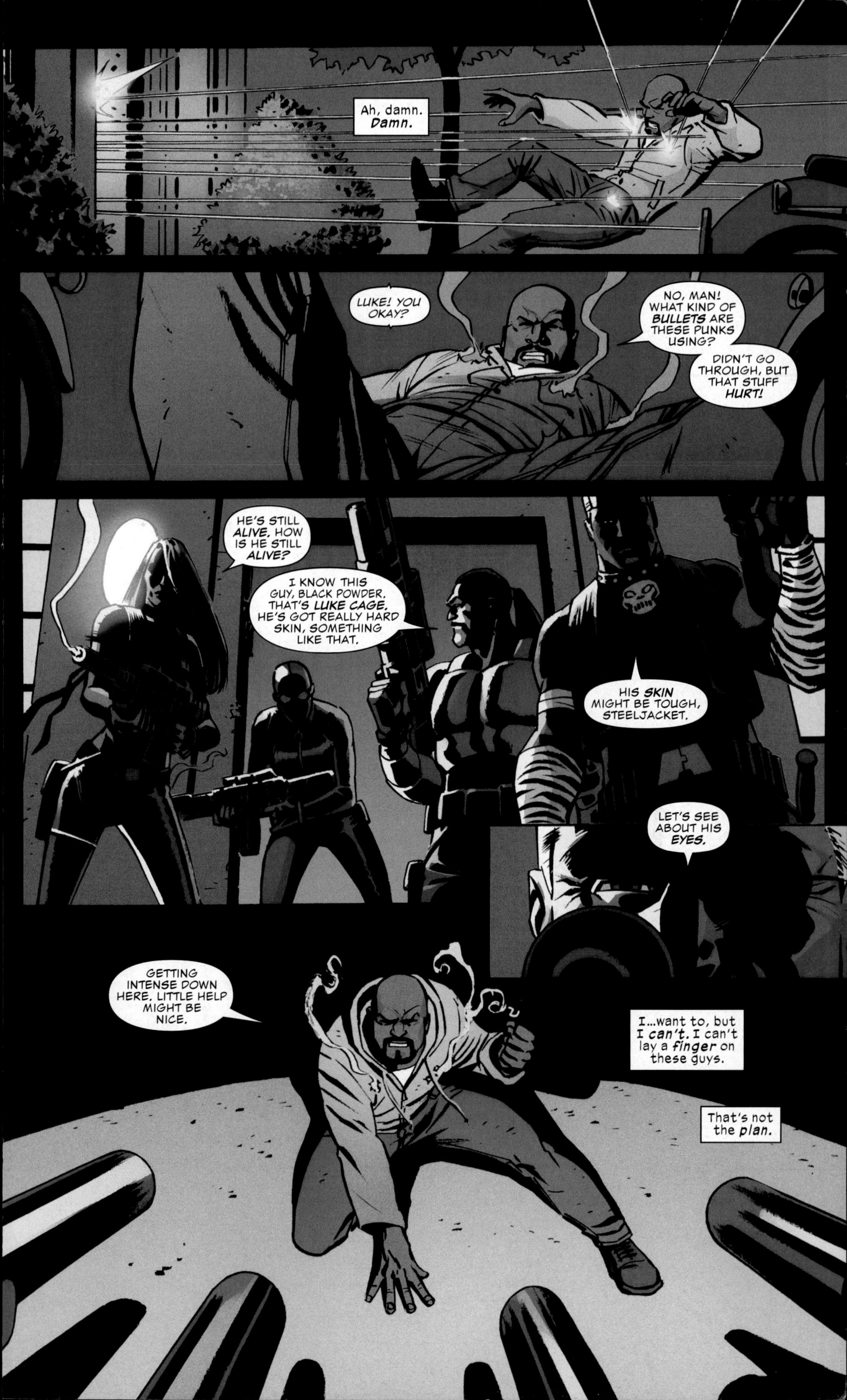

Ah, damn. Damn.
LUKE! YOU OKAY?
NO, MAN! WHAT KIND OF BULLETS ARE THESE PUNKS USING?
DIDN'T GO THROUGH, BUT THAT STUFF HURT!
HE'S STILL ALIVE. HOW IS HE STILL ALIVE?
I KNOW THIS GUY, BLACK POWDER. THAT'S LUKE CAGE. HE'S GOT REALLY HARD SKIN, SOMETHING LIKE THAT.
HIS SKIN MIGHT BE TOUGH, STEELJACKET.
LET'S SEE ABOUT HIS EYES.
GETTING INTENSE DOWN HERE. LITTLE HELP MIGHT BE NICE.
I...want to, but I can't. I can't lay a finger on these guys.
That's not the plan.

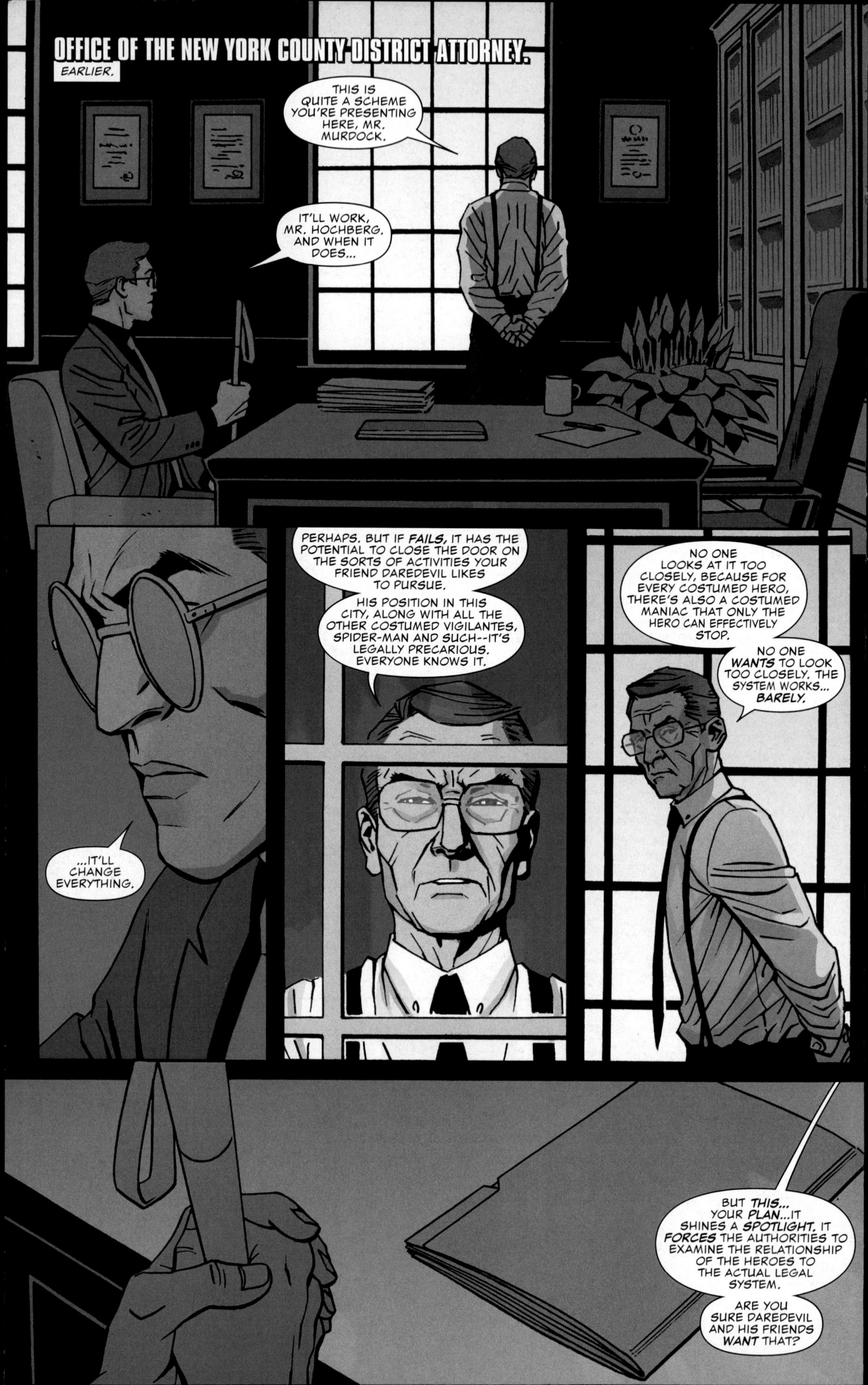
OFFICE OF THE NEW YORK COUNTY DISTRICT ATTORNEY.
EARLIER.
THIS IS QUITE A SCHEME YOU'RE PRESENTING HERE, MR. MURDOCK.
IT'LL WORK, MR. HOCHBERG. AND WHEN IT DOES...
...IT'LL CHANGE EVERYTHING.
PERHAPS. BUT IF FAILS, IT HAS THE POTENTIAL TO CLOSE THE DOOR ON THE SORTS OF ACTIVITIES YOUR FRIEND DAREDEVIL LIKES TO PURSUE.
HIS POSITION IN THIS CITY, ALONG WITH ALL THE OTHER COSTUMED VIGILANTES, SPIDER-MAN AND SUCH--IT'S LEGALLY PRECARIOUS. EVERYONE KNOWS IT.
NO ONE LOOKS AT IT TOO CLOSELY, BECAUSE FOR EVERY COSTUMED HERO, THERE'S ALSO A COSTUMED MANIAC THAT ONLY THE HERO CAN EFFECTIVELY STOP.
NO ONE WANTS TO LOOK TOO CLOSELY. THE SYSTEM WORKS... BARELY.
BUT THIS... YOUR PLAN...IT SHINES A SPOTLIGHT. IT FORCES THE AUTHORITIES TO EXAMINE THE RELATIONSHIP OF THE HEROES TO THE ACTUAL LEGAL SYSTEM.
ARE YOU SURE DAREDEVIL AND HIS FRIENDS WANT THAT?

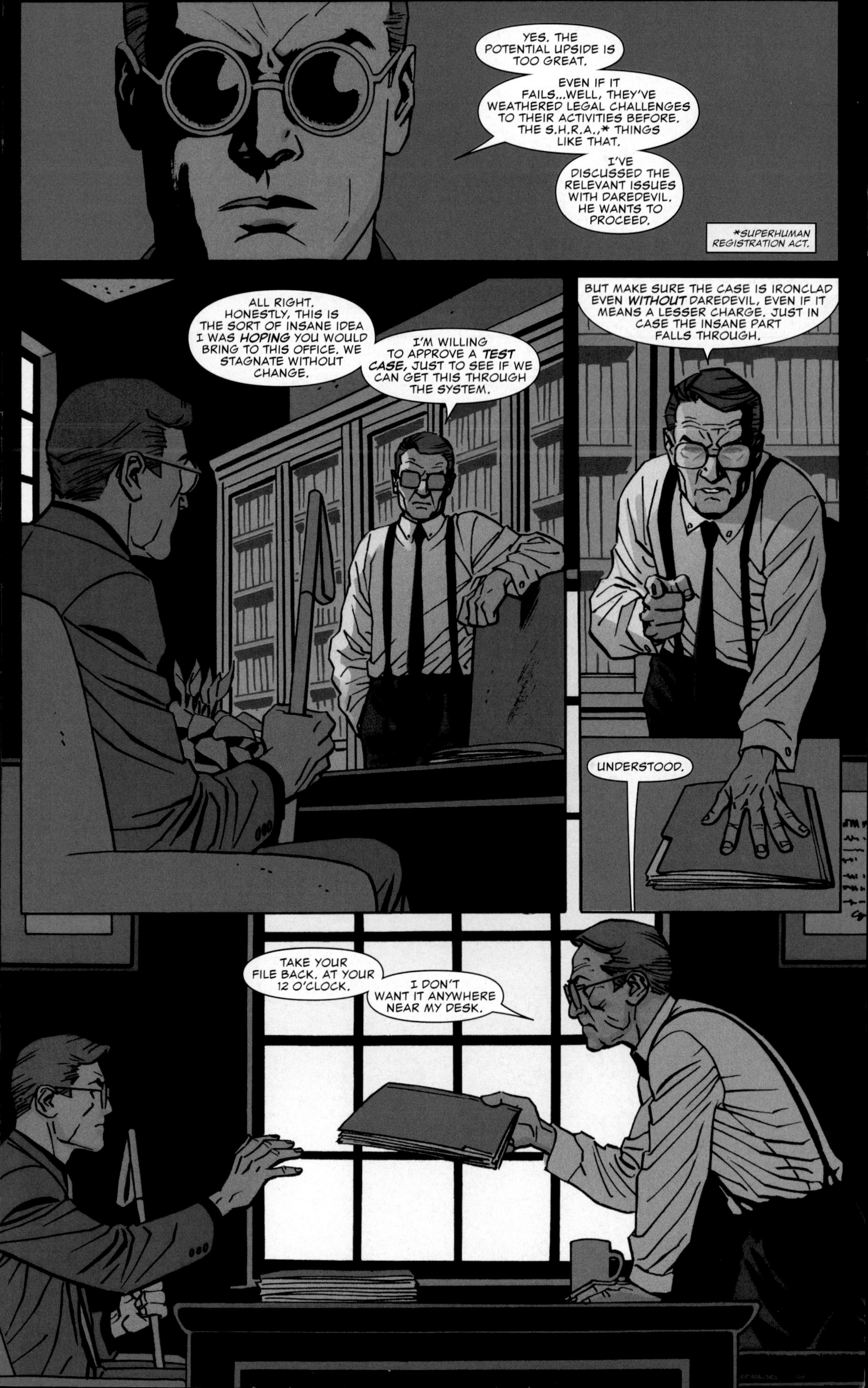
YES. THE POTENTIAL UPSIDE IS TOO GREAT.
EVEN IF IT FAILS...WELL, THEY'VE WEATHERED LEGAL CHALLENGES TO THEIR ACTIVITIES BEFORE. THE S.H.R.A.,* THINGS LIKE THAT.
I'VE DISCUSSED THE RELEVANT ISSUES WITH DAREDEVIL. HE WANTS TO PROCEED.
*SUPERHUMAN REGISTRATION ACT.
ALL RIGHT. HONESTLY, THIS IS THE SORT OF INSANE IDEA I WAS HOPING YOU WOULD BRING TO THIS OFFICE. WE STAGNATE WITHOUT CHANGE.
I'M WILLING TO APPROVE A TEST CASE, JUST TO SEE IF WE CAN GET THIS THROUGH THE SYSTEM.
BUT MAKE SURE THE CASE IS IRONCLAD EVEN WITHOUT DAREDEVIL, EVEN IF IT MEANS A LESSER CHARGE. JUST IN CASE THE INSANE PART FALLS THROUGH.
UNDERSTOOD.
TAKE YOUR FILE BACK. AT YOUR 12 O'CLOCK.
I DON'T WANT IT ANYWHERE NEAR MY DESK.

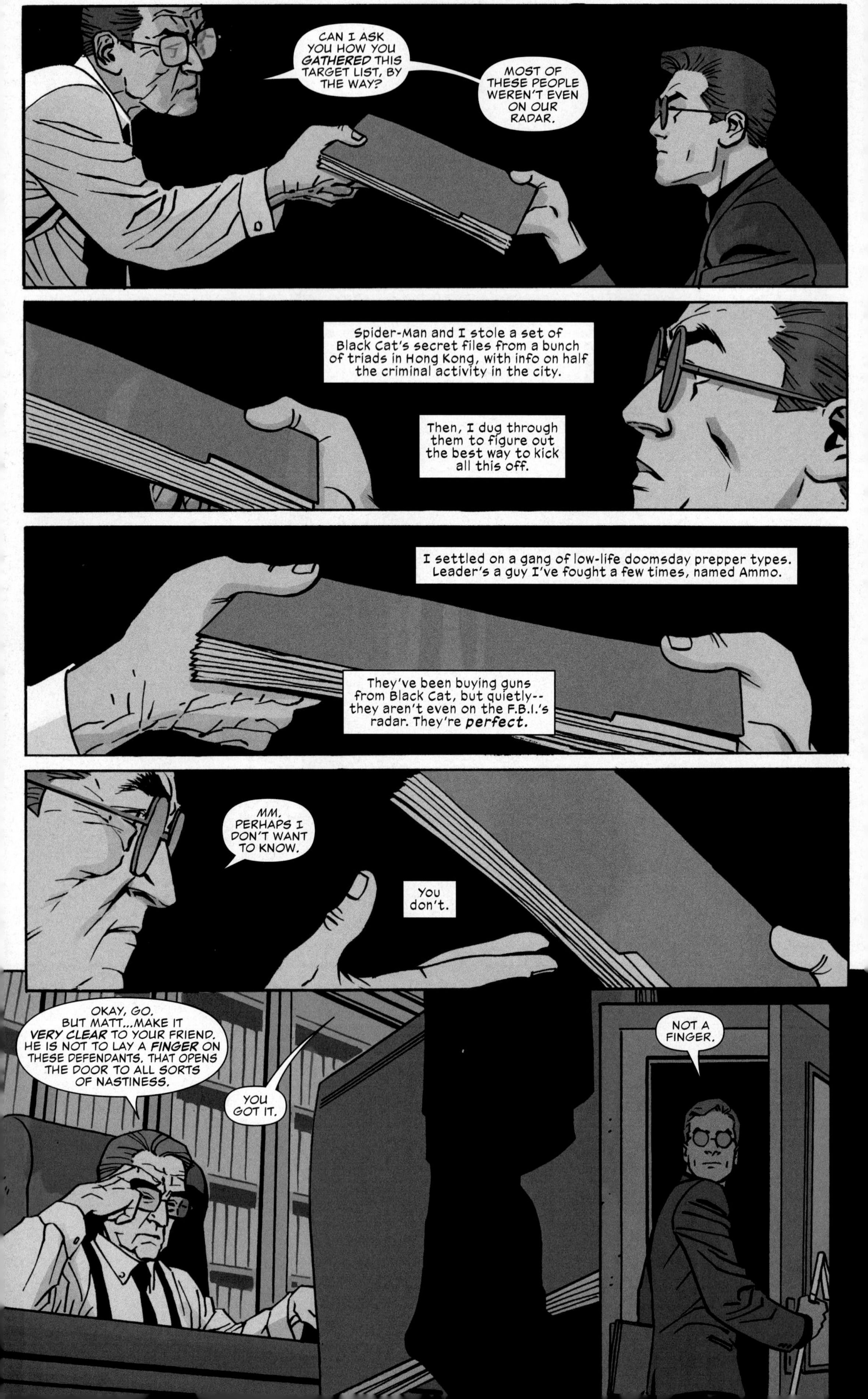
CAN I ASK YOU HOW YOU GATHERED THIS TARGET LIST, BY THE WAY?
MOST OF THESE PEOPLE WEREN'T EVEN ON OUR RADAR.
Spider-Man and I stole a set of Black Cat's secret files from a bunch of triads in Hong Kong, with info on half the criminal activity in the city.
Then, I dug through them to figure out the best way to kick all this off.
I settled on a gang of low-life doomsday prepper types. Leader's a guy I've fought a few times, named Ammo.
They've been buying guns from Black Cat, but quietly-- they aren't even on the F.B.I.'s radar. They're perfect.
MM. PERHAPS I DON'T WANT TO KNOW.
You don't.
OKAY, GO. BUT MATT...MAKE IT VERY CLEAR TO YOUR FRIEND. HE IS NOT TO LAY A FINGER ON THESE DEFENDANTS. THAT OPENS THE DOOR TO ALL SORTS OF NASTINESS.
YOU GOT IT.
NOT A FINGER.

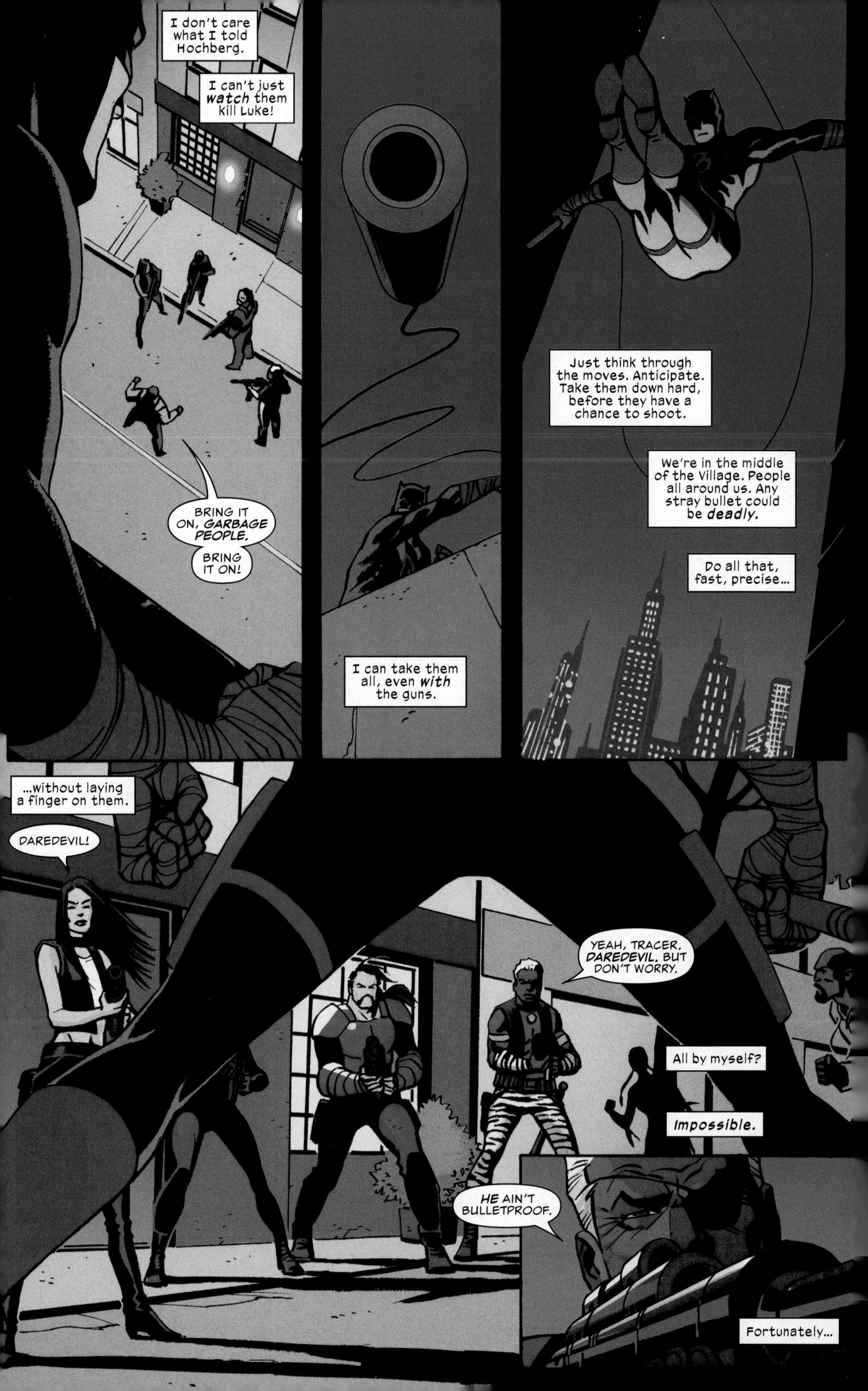
I don't care what I told Hochberg.
I can't just *watch* them kill Luke!
BRING IT ON, *GARBAGE PEOPLE.*
BRING IT ON!
I can take them all, even *with* the guns.
Just think through the moves. Anticipate. Take them down hard, before they have a chance to shoot.
We're in the middle of the Village. People all around us. Any stray bullet could be *deadly.*
Do all that, fast, precise...
...without laying a finger on them.
DAREDEVIL!
YEAH, TRACER. *DAREDEVIL.* BUT DON'T WORRY.
HE AIN'T BULLETPROOF.
All by myself?
Impossible.
Fortunately...

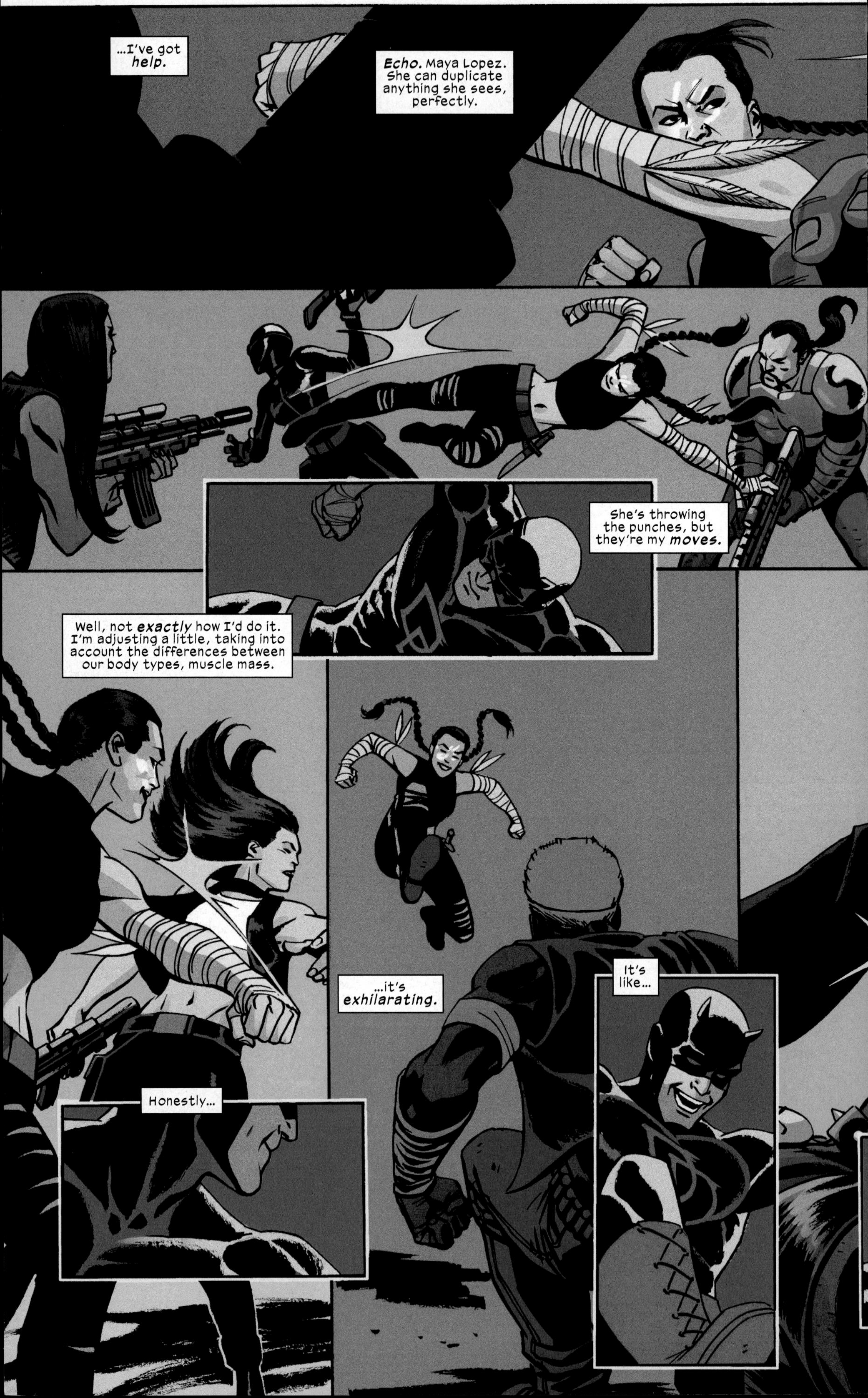
...I've got *help.*
Echo. Maya Lopez. She can duplicate anything she sees, perfectly.
She's throwing the punches, but they're my *moves.*
Well, not *exactly* how I'd do it. I'm adjusting a little, taking into account the differences between our body types, muscle mass.
Honestly...
...it's *exhilarating.*
It's like...

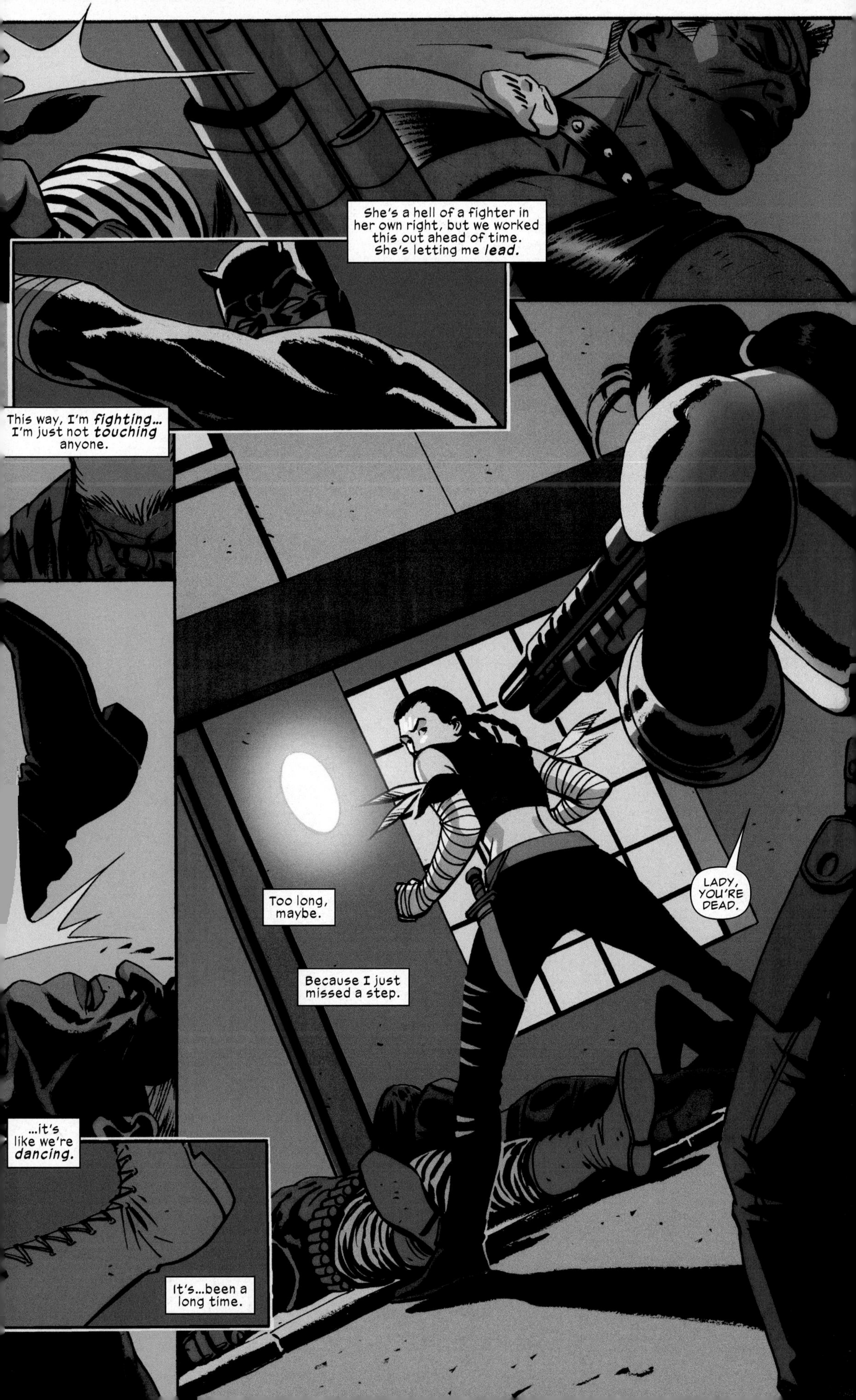
She's a hell of a fighter in her own right, but we worked this out ahead of time. She's letting me *lead.*
This way, I'm *fighting*... I'm just not *touching* anyone.
...it's like we're *dancing*.
Too long, maybe.
Because I just missed a step.
LADY, YOU'RE DEAD.
It's...been a long time.

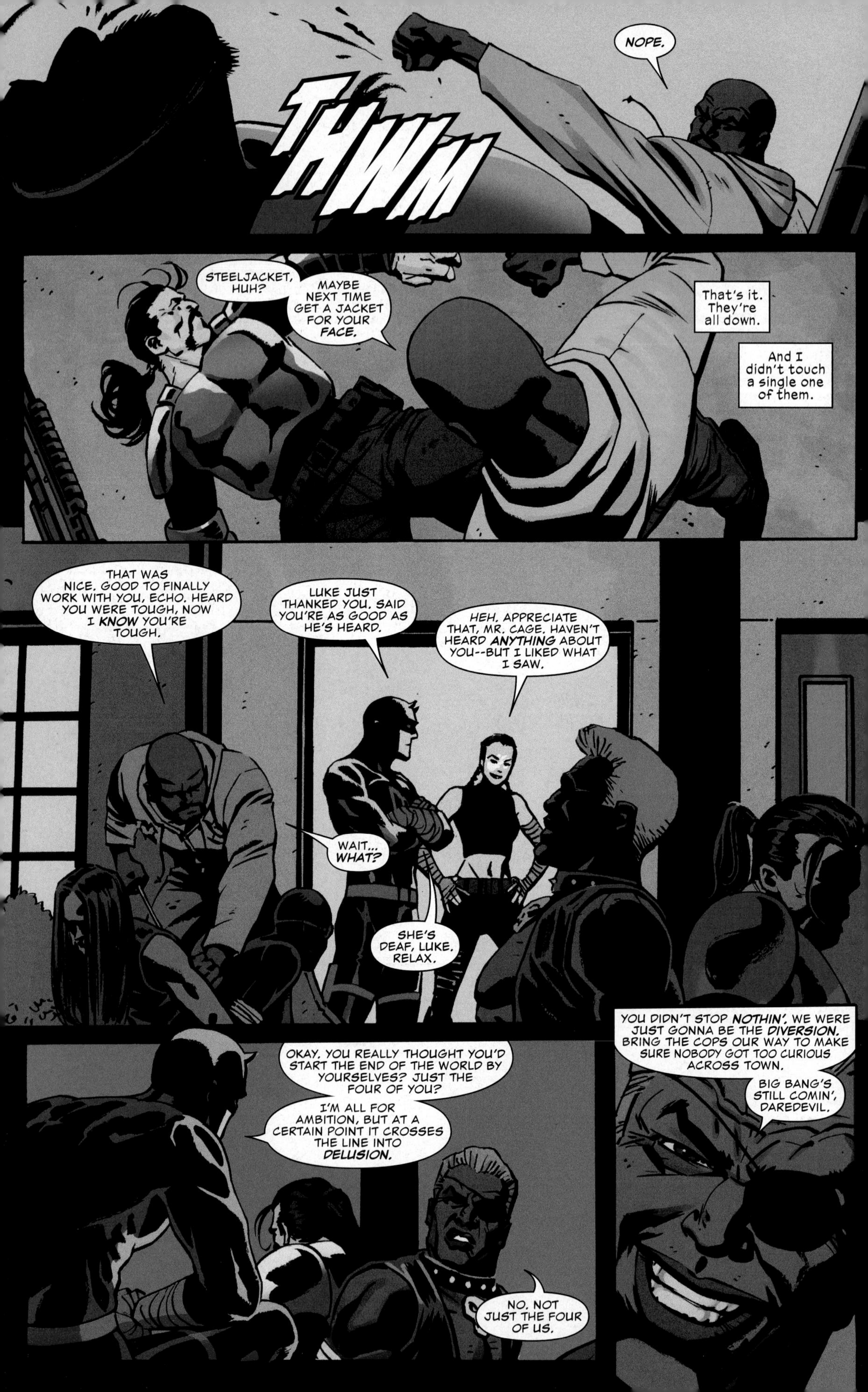
THWM
NOPE.
STEELJACKET, HUH?
MAYBE NEXT TIME GET A JACKET FOR YOUR FACE.
That's it. They're all down.
And I didn't touch a single one of them.
THAT WAS NICE. GOOD TO FINALLY WORK WITH YOU, ECHO. HEARD YOU WERE TOUGH, NOW I KNOW YOU'RE TOUGH.
LUKE JUST THANKED YOU. SAID YOU'RE AS GOOD AS HE'S HEARD.
HEH. APPRECIATE THAT, MR. CAGE. HAVEN'T HEARD ANYTHING ABOUT YOU--BUT I LIKED WHAT I SAW.
WAIT... WHAT?
SHE'S DEAF, LUKE. RELAX.
OKAY. YOU REALLY THOUGHT YOU'D START THE END OF THE WORLD BY YOURSELVES? JUST THE FOUR OF YOU?
I'M ALL FOR AMBITION, BUT AT A CERTAIN POINT IT CROSSES THE LINE INTO DELUSION.
NO. NOT JUST THE FOUR OF US.
YOU DIDN'T STOP NOTHIN'. WE WERE JUST GONNA BE THE DIVERSION. BRING THE COPS OUR WAY TO MAKE SURE NOBODY GOT TOO CURIOUS ACROSS TOWN.
BIG BANG'S STILL COMIN', DAREDEVIL.

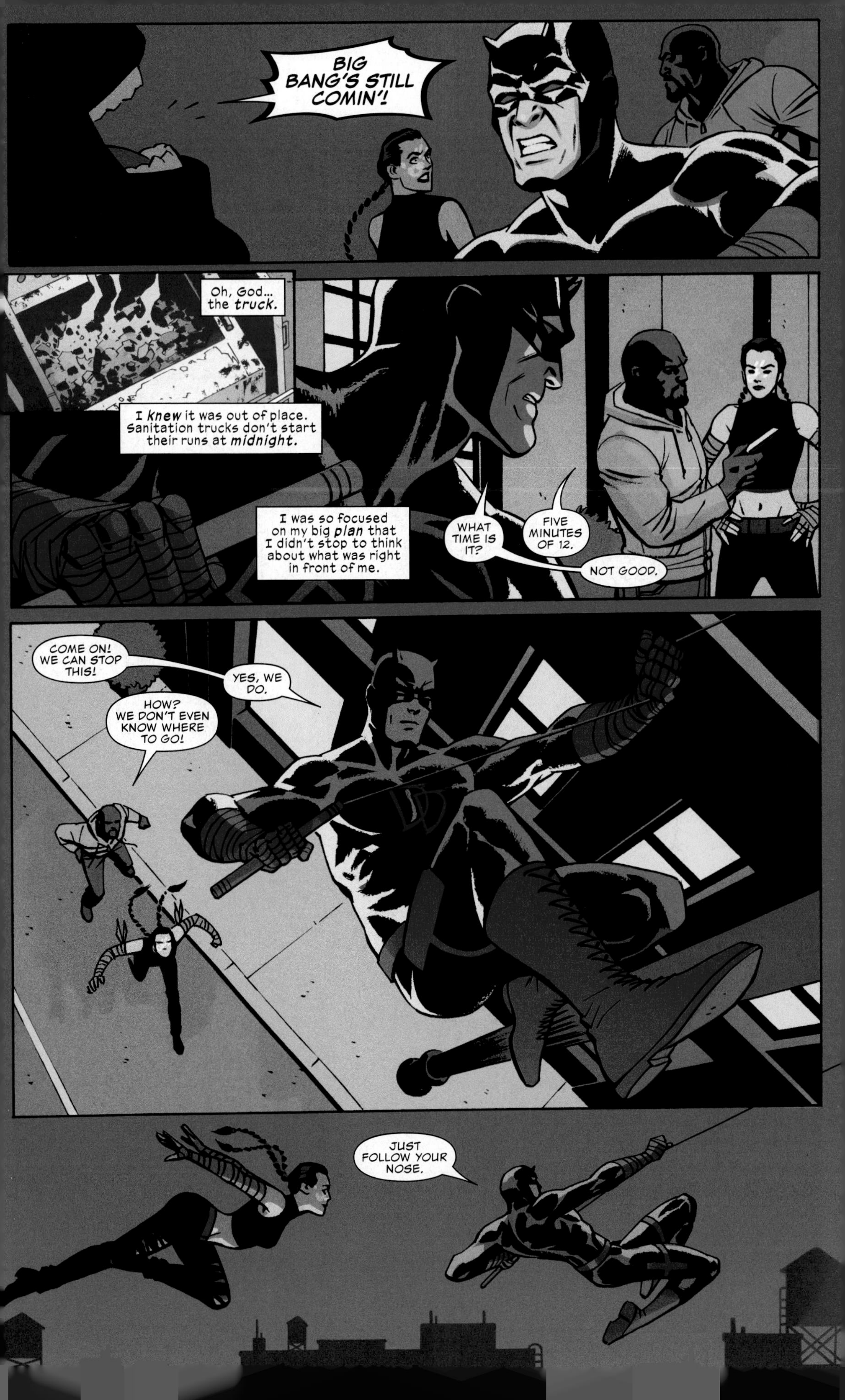
BIG BANG'S STILL COMIN'!
Oh, God... the truck.
I knew it was out of place. Sanitation trucks don't start their runs at midnight.
I was so focused on my big plan that I didn't stop to think about what was right in front of me.
WHAT TIME IS IT?
FIVE MINUTES OF 12.
NOT GOOD.
COME ON! WE CAN STOP THIS!
YES, WE DO.
HOW? WE DON'T EVEN KNOW WHERE TO GO!
JUST FOLLOW YOUR NOSE.

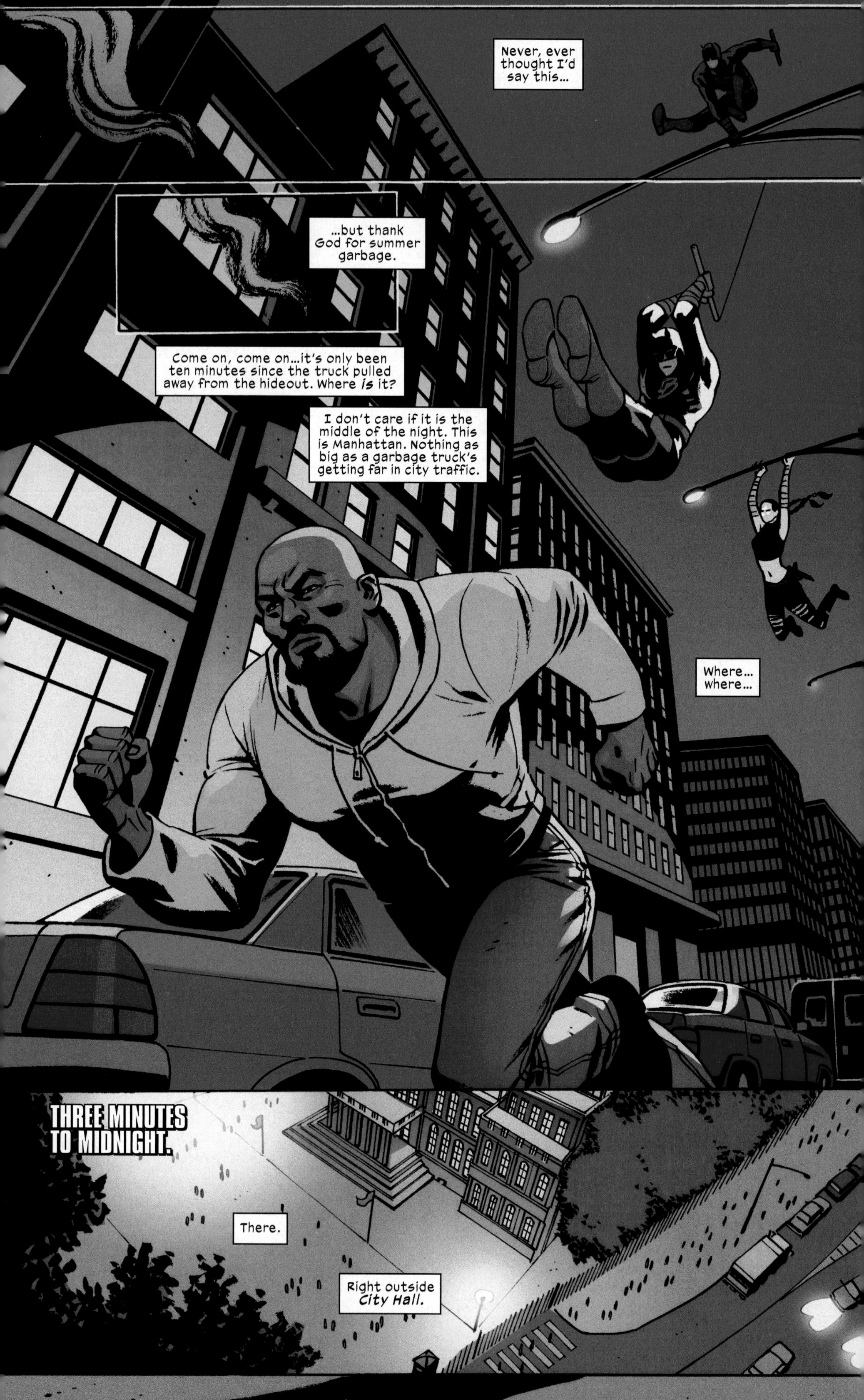
Never, ever thought I'd say this...
...but thank God for summer garbage.
Come on, come on...it's only been ten minutes since the truck pulled away from the hideout. Where *is* it?
I don't care if it is the middle of the night. This is Manhattan. Nothing as big as a garbage truck's getting far in city traffic.
Where... where...
THREE MINUTES TO MIDNIGHT.
There.
Right outside *City Hall.*

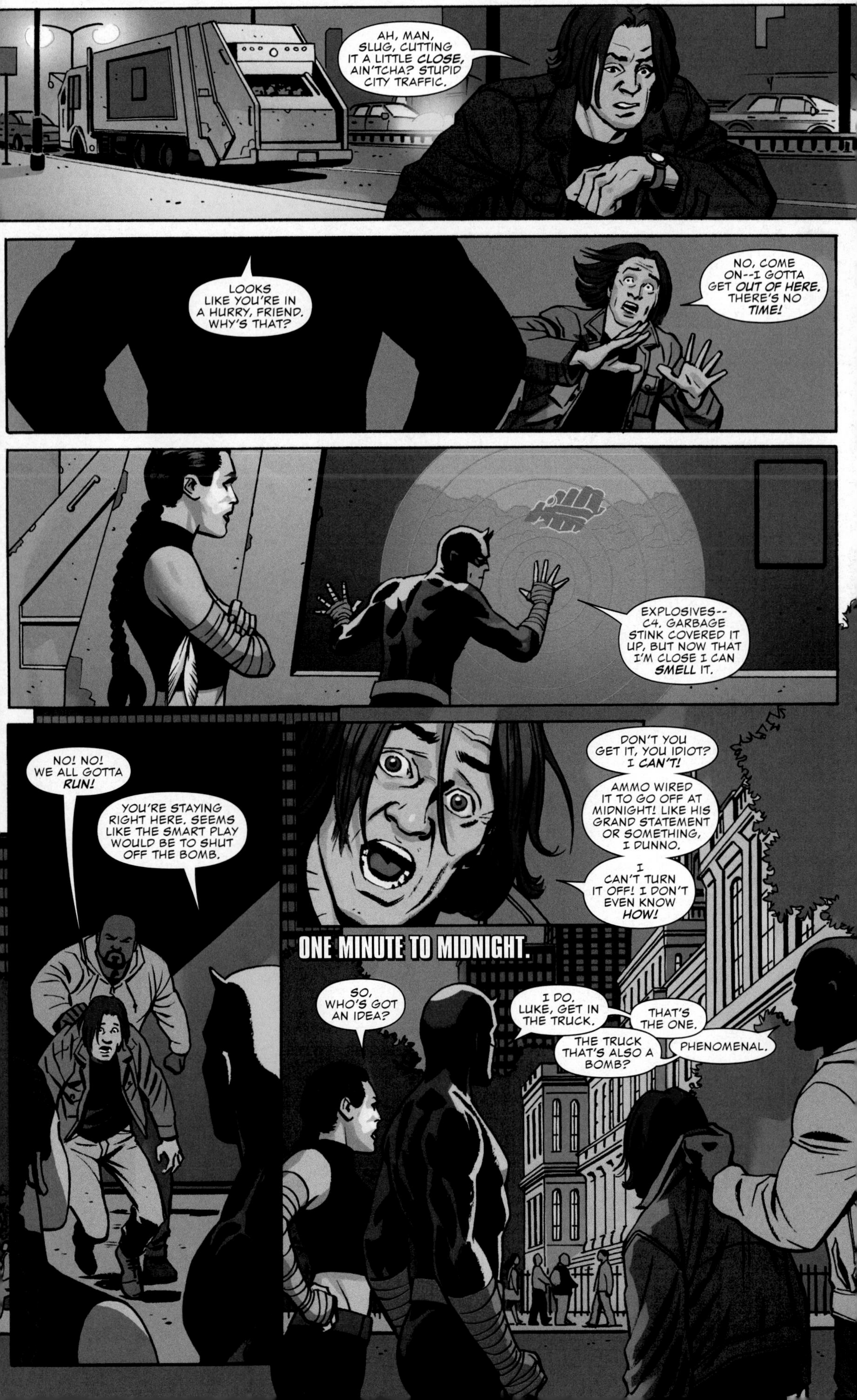
AH, MAN, SLUG, CUTTING IT A LITTLE CLOSE, AIN'TCHA? STUPID CITY TRAFFIC.
LOOKS LIKE YOU'RE IN A HURRY, FRIEND. WHY'S THAT?
NO, COME ON--I GOTTA GET OUT OF HERE. THERE'S NO TIME!
EXPLOSIVES--C4. GARBAGE STINK COVERED IT UP, BUT NOW THAT I'M CLOSE I CAN SMELL IT.
NO! NO! WE ALL GOTTA RUN!
YOU'RE STAYING RIGHT HERE. SEEMS LIKE THE SMART PLAY WOULD BE TO SHUT OFF THE BOMB.
DON'T YOU GET IT, YOU IDIOT? I CAN'T!
AMMO WIRED IT TO GO OFF AT MIDNIGHT! LIKE HIS GRAND STATEMENT OR SOMETHING, I DUNNO.
I CAN'T TURN IT OFF! I DON'T EVEN KNOW HOW!
ONE MINUTE TO MIDNIGHT.
SO, WHO'S GOT AN IDEA?
I DO. LUKE, GET IN THE TRUCK.
THAT'S THE ONE.
THE TRUCK THAT'S ALSO A BOMB?
PHENOMENAL.

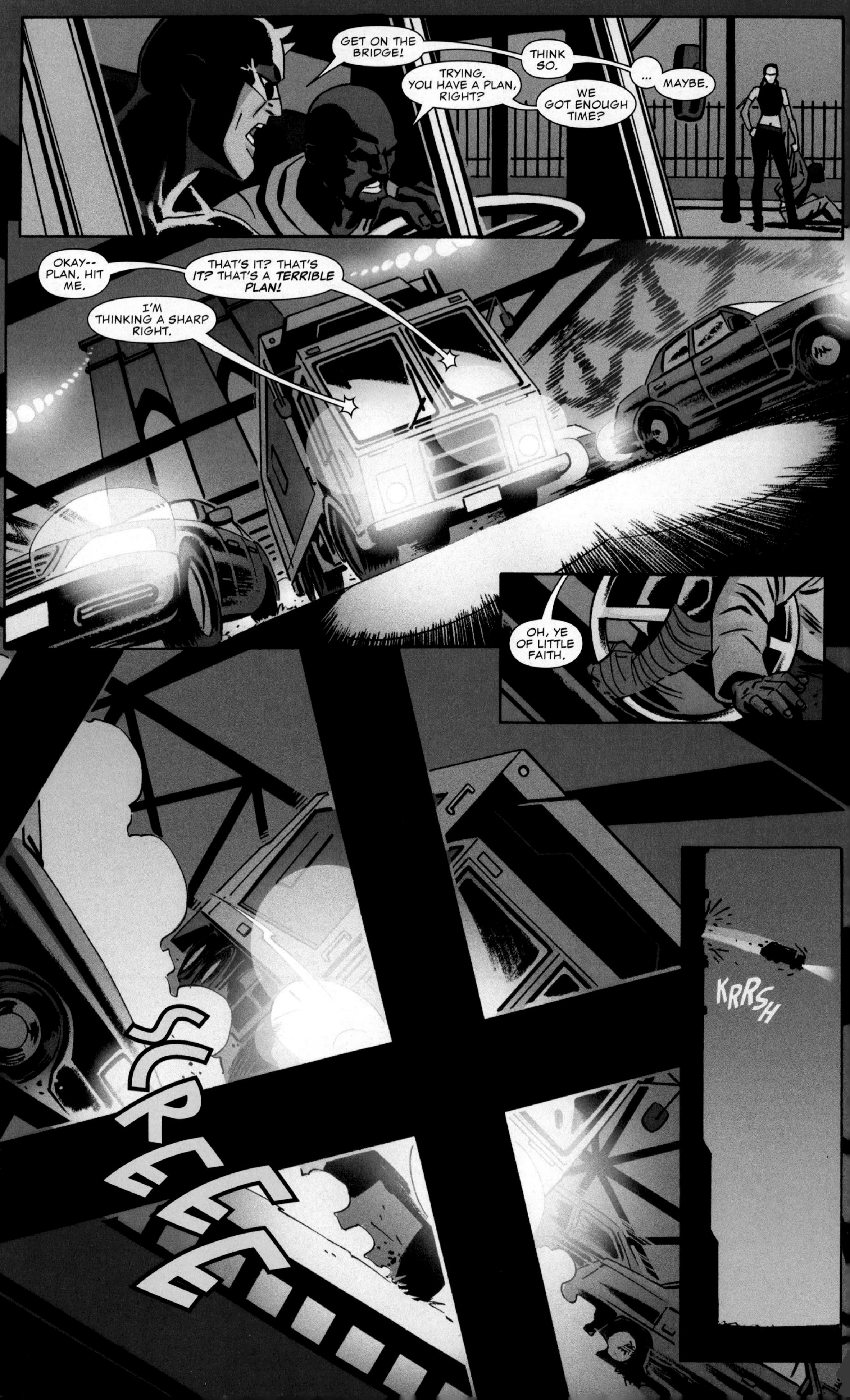
GET ON THE BRIDGE!
TRYING. YOU HAVE A PLAN, RIGHT?
THINK SO.
WE GOT ENOUGH TIME?
... MAYBE.
OKAY--PLAN. HIT ME.
I'M THINKING A SHARP RIGHT.
THAT'S IT? THAT'S IT? THAT'S A TERRIBLE PLAN!
OH, YE OF LITTLE FAITH.
SCREEEE...
KRRSH

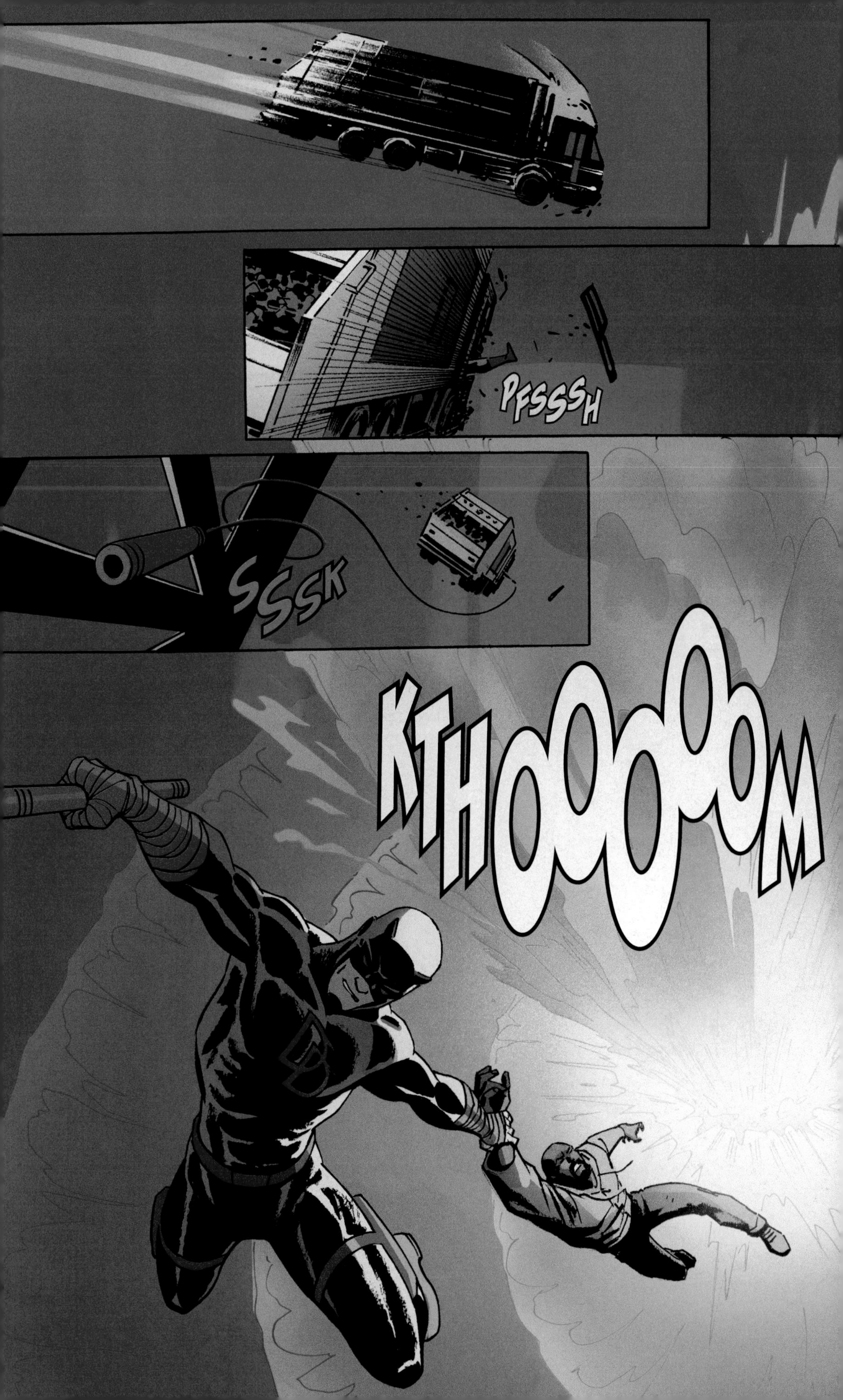
PFSSSH
SSSK
KTHOOOOOOM

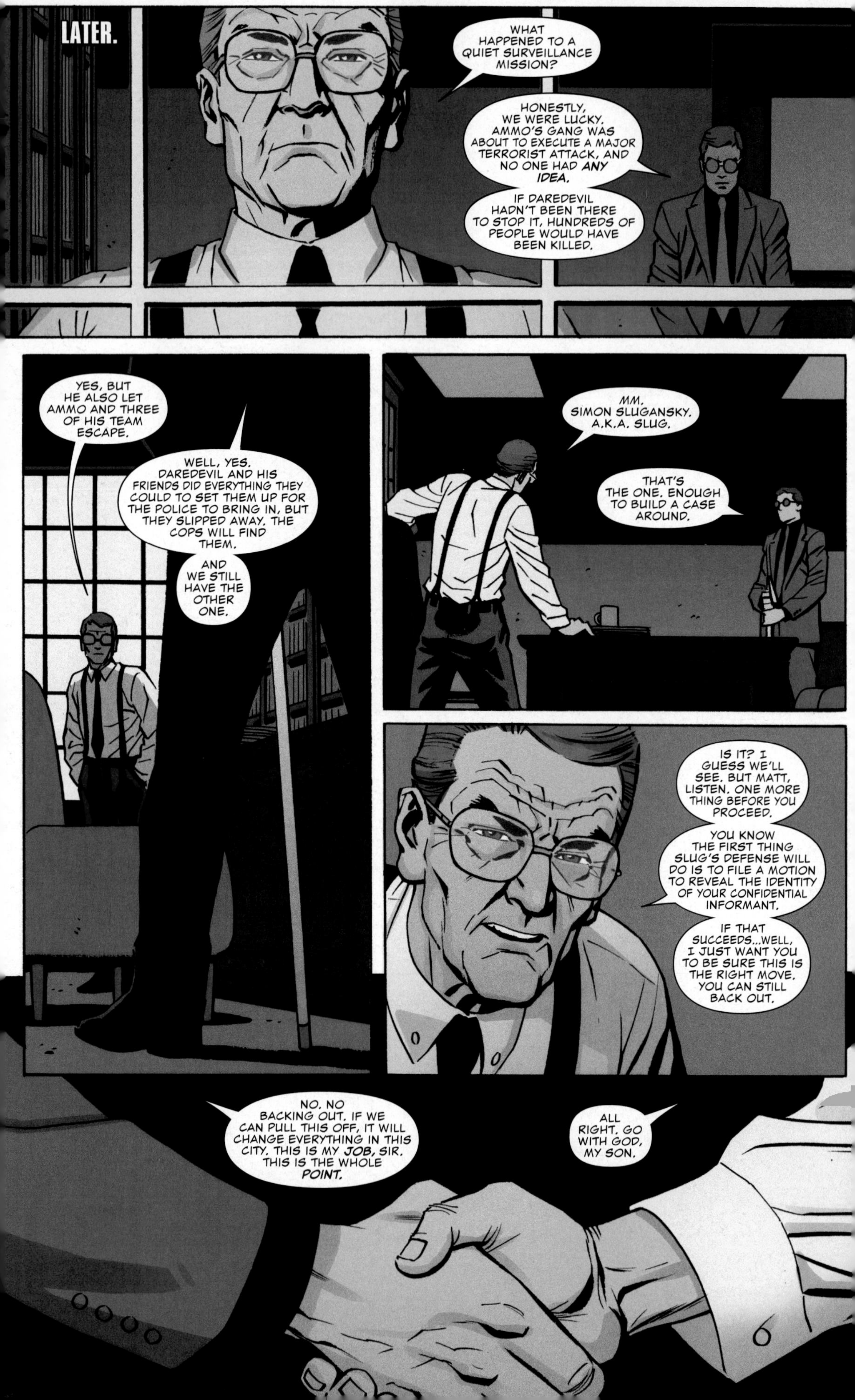

LATER.
WHAT HAPPENED TO A QUIET SURVEILLANCE MISSION?
HONESTLY, WE WERE LUCKY. AMMO'S GANG WAS ABOUT TO EXECUTE A MAJOR TERRORIST ATTACK, AND NO ONE HAD ANY IDEA.
IF DAREDEVIL HADN'T BEEN THERE TO STOP IT, HUNDREDS OF PEOPLE WOULD HAVE BEEN KILLED.
YES, BUT HE ALSO LET AMMO AND THREE OF HIS TEAM ESCAPE.
WELL, YES. DAREDEVIL AND HIS FRIENDS DID EVERYTHING THEY COULD TO SET THEM UP FOR THE POLICE TO BRING IN, BUT THEY SLIPPED AWAY. THE COPS WILL FIND THEM.
AND WE STILL HAVE THE OTHER ONE.
MM. SIMON SLUGANSKY. A.K.A. SLUG.
THAT'S THE ONE. ENOUGH TO BUILD A CASE AROUND.
IS IT? I GUESS WE'LL SEE. BUT MATT, LISTEN. ONE MORE THING BEFORE YOU PROCEED.
YOU KNOW THE FIRST THING SLUG'S DEFENSE WILL DO IS TO FILE A MOTION TO REVEAL THE IDENTITY OF YOUR CONFIDENTIAL INFORMANT.
IF THAT SUCCEEDS...WELL, I JUST WANT YOU TO BE SURE THIS IS THE RIGHT MOVE. YOU CAN STILL BACK OUT.
NO. NO BACKING OUT. IF WE CAN PULL THIS OFF, IT WILL CHANGE EVERYTHING IN THIS CITY. THIS IS MY JOB, SIR. THIS IS THE WHOLE POINT.
ALL RIGHT. GO WITH GOD, MY SON.

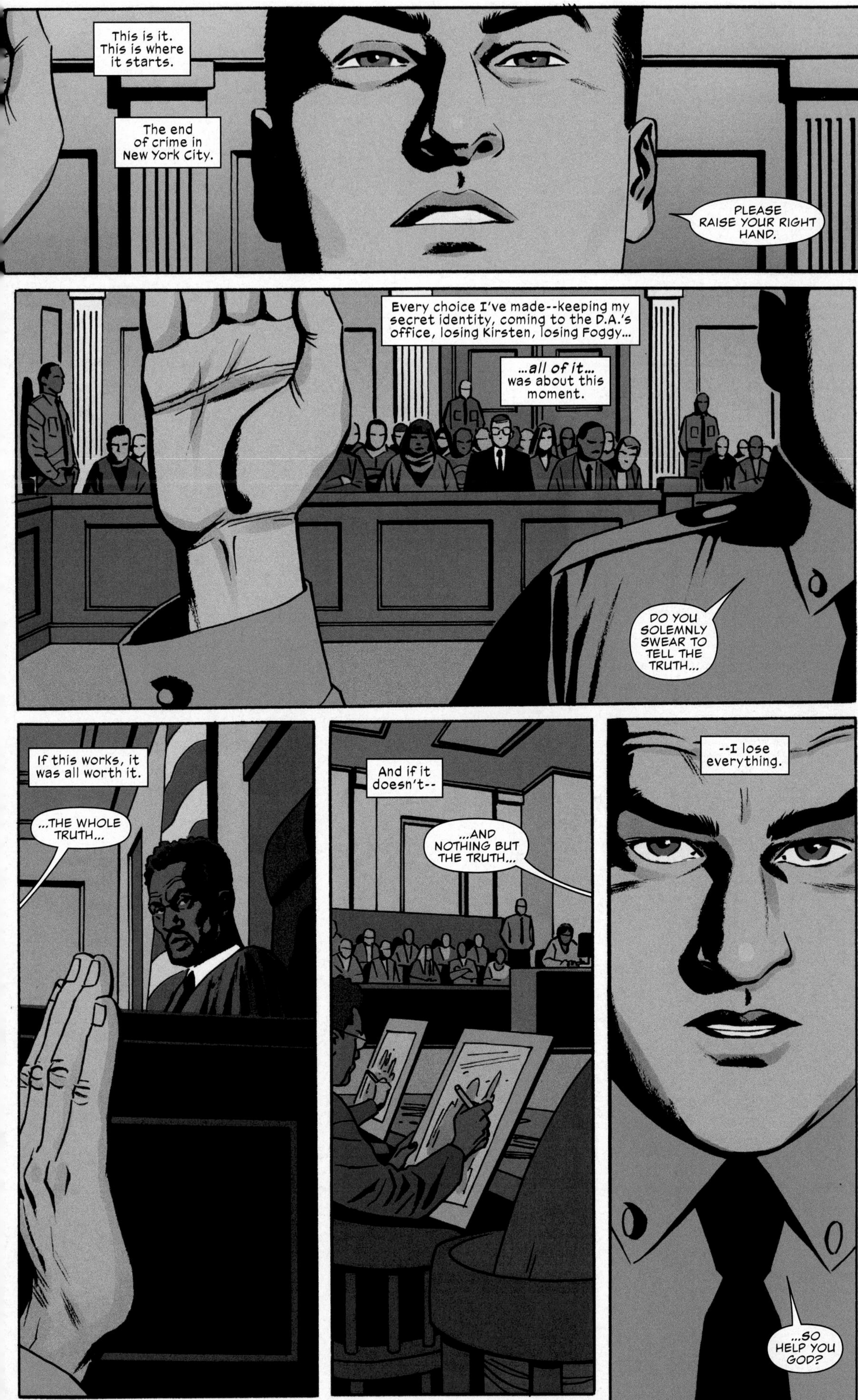
This is it. This is where it starts.
The end of crime in New York City.
PLEASE RAISE YOUR RIGHT HAND.
Every choice I've made--keeping my secret identity, coming to the D.A.'s office, losing Kirsten, losing Foggy...
...all of it... was about this moment.
DO YOU SOLEMNLY SWEAR TO TELL THE TRUTH...
If this works, it was all worth it.
...THE WHOLE TRUTH...
And if it doesn't--
...AND NOTHING BUT THE TRUTH...
--I lose everything.
...SO HELP YOU GOD?

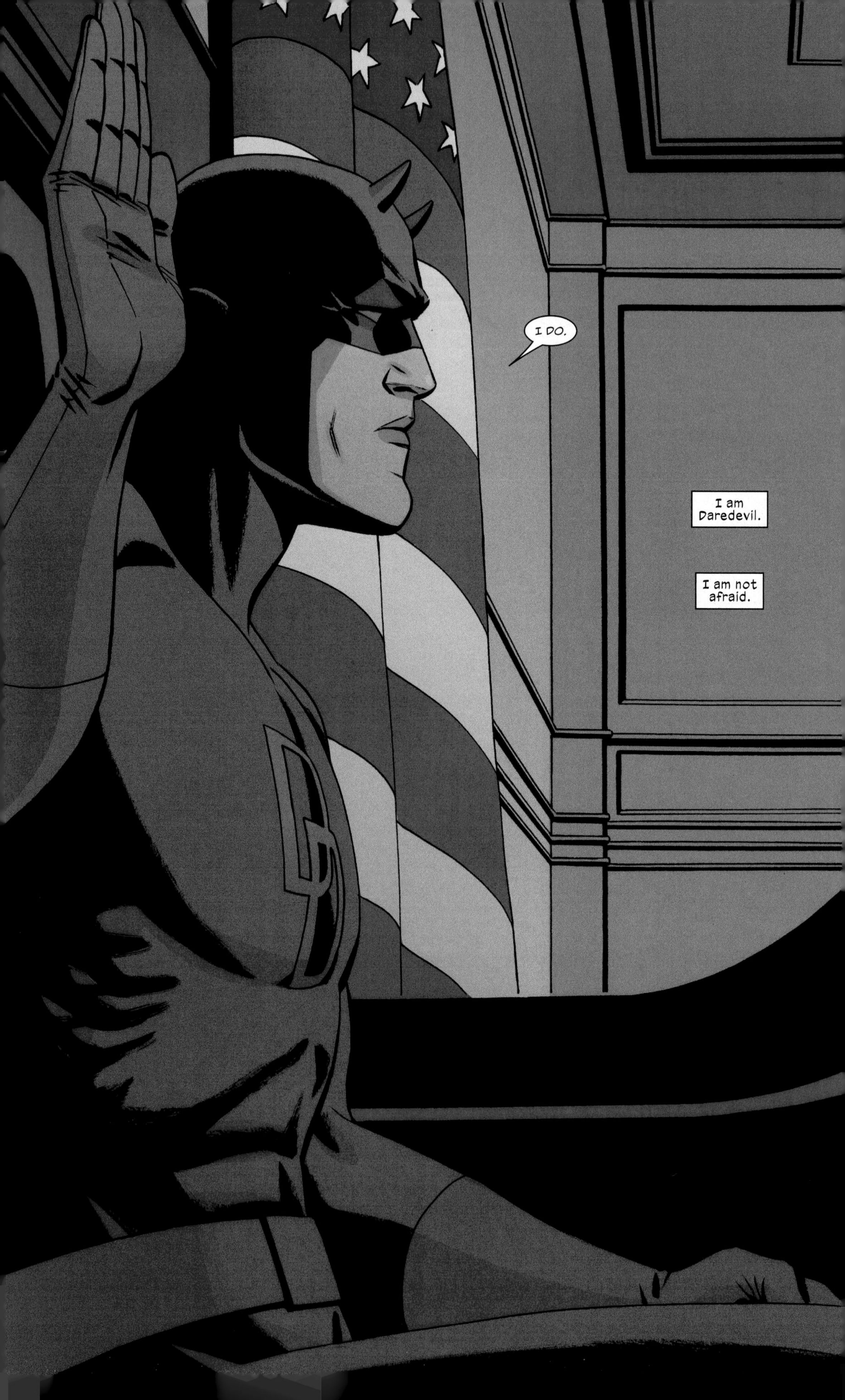
I DO.
I am Daredevil.
I am not afraid.

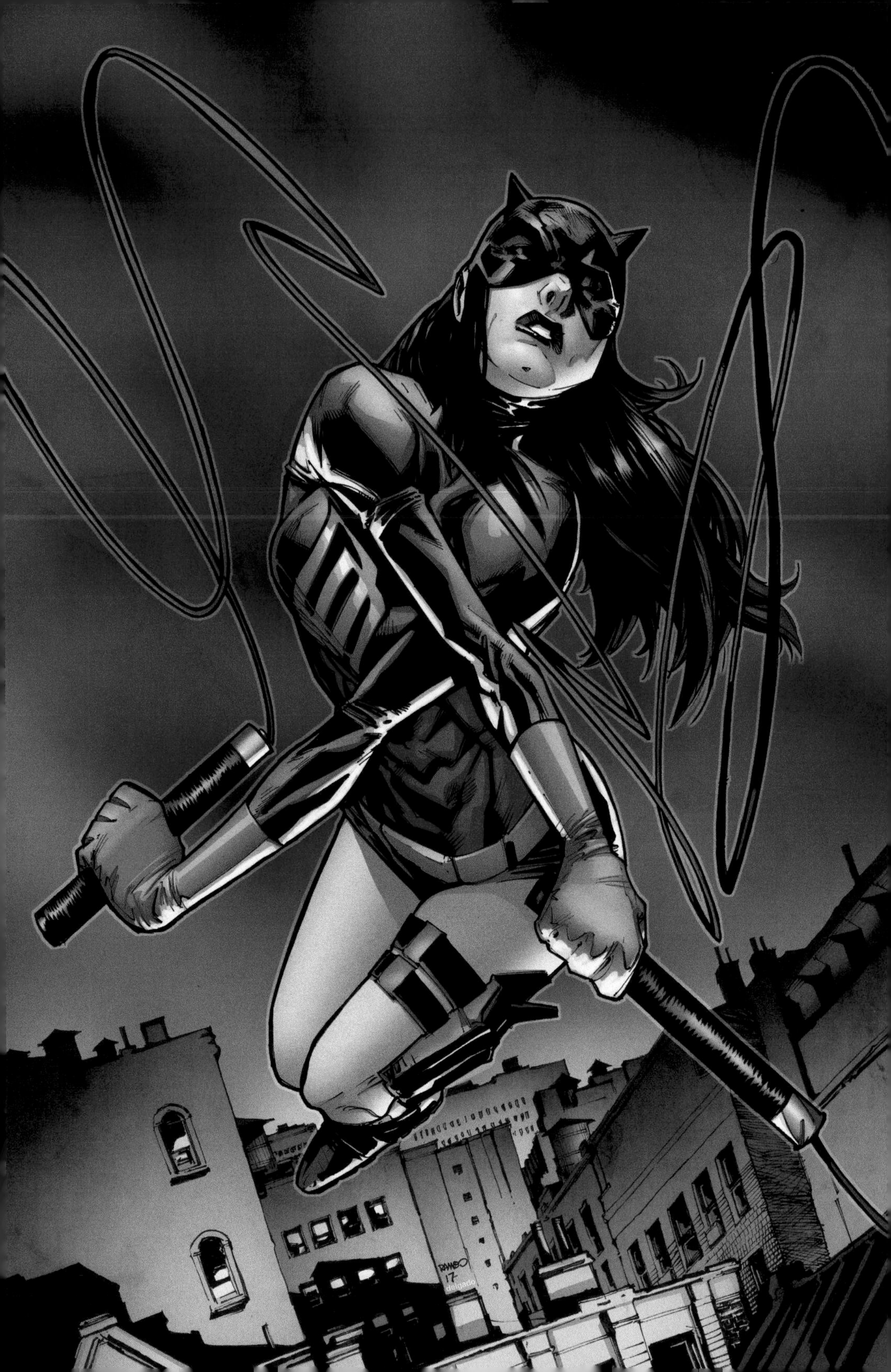
RAMOS 17
delgado

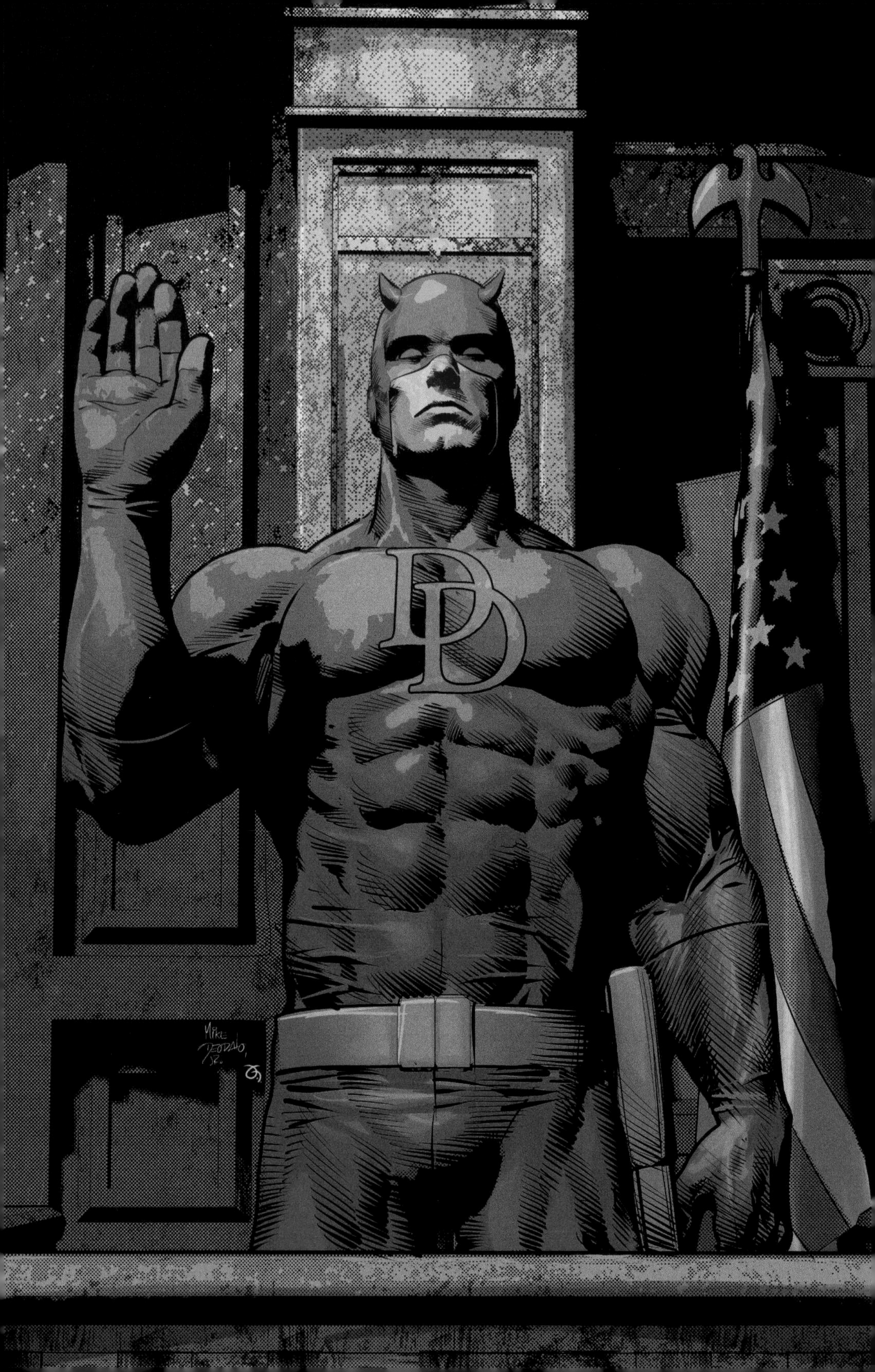

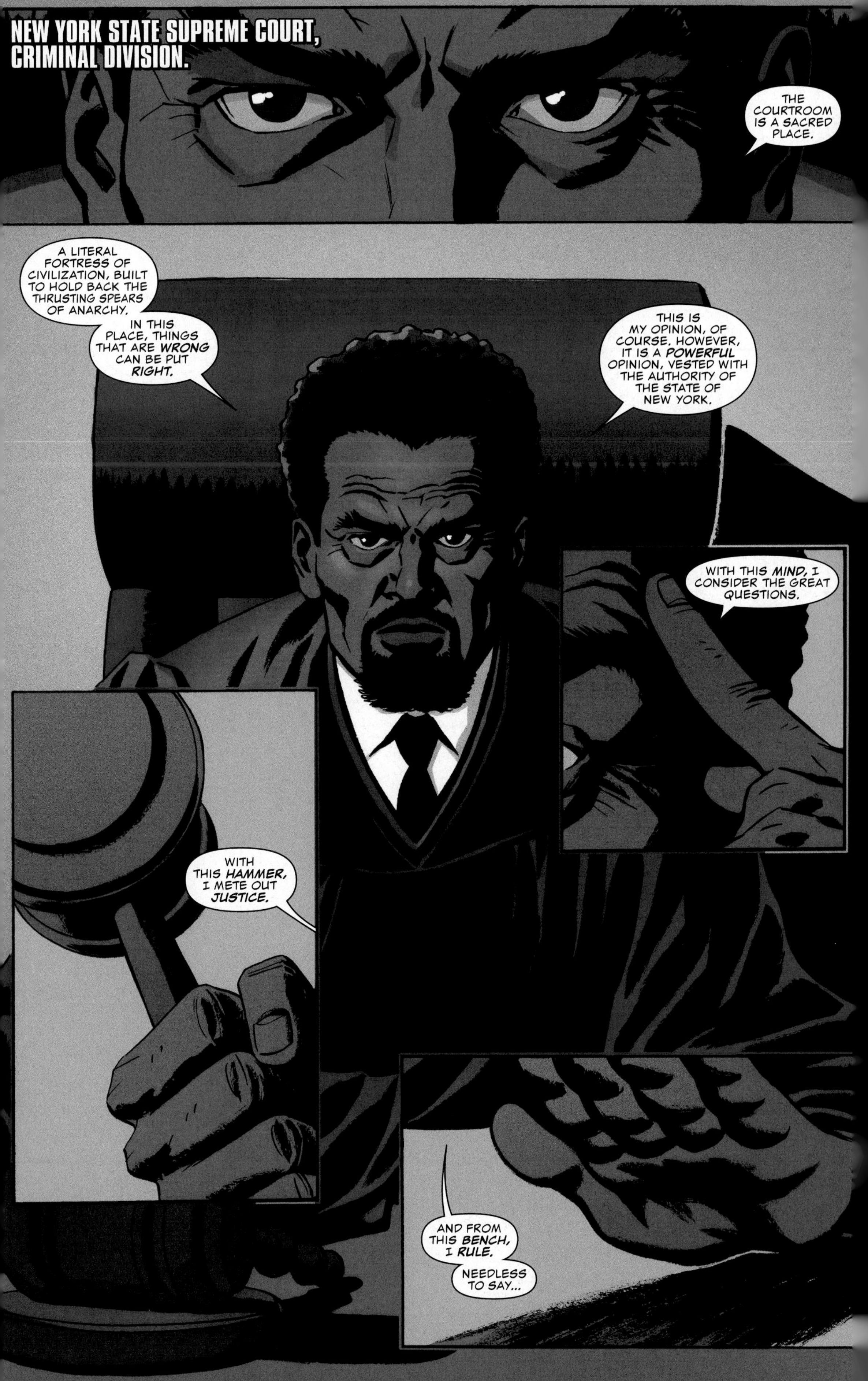
NEW YORK STATE SUPREME COURT, CRIMINAL DIVISION.
THE COURTROOM IS A SACRED PLACE.
A LITERAL FORTRESS OF CIVILIZATION, BUILT TO HOLD BACK THE THRUSTING SPEARS OF ANARCHY.
IN THIS PLACE, THINGS THAT ARE WRONG CAN BE PUT RIGHT.
THIS IS MY OPINION, OF COURSE. HOWEVER, IT IS A POWERFUL OPINION, VESTED WITH THE AUTHORITY OF THE STATE OF NEW YORK.
WITH THIS MIND, I CONSIDER THE GREAT QUESTIONS.
WITH THIS HAMMER, I METE OUT JUSTICE.
AND FROM THIS BENCH, I RULE.
NEEDLESS TO SAY...

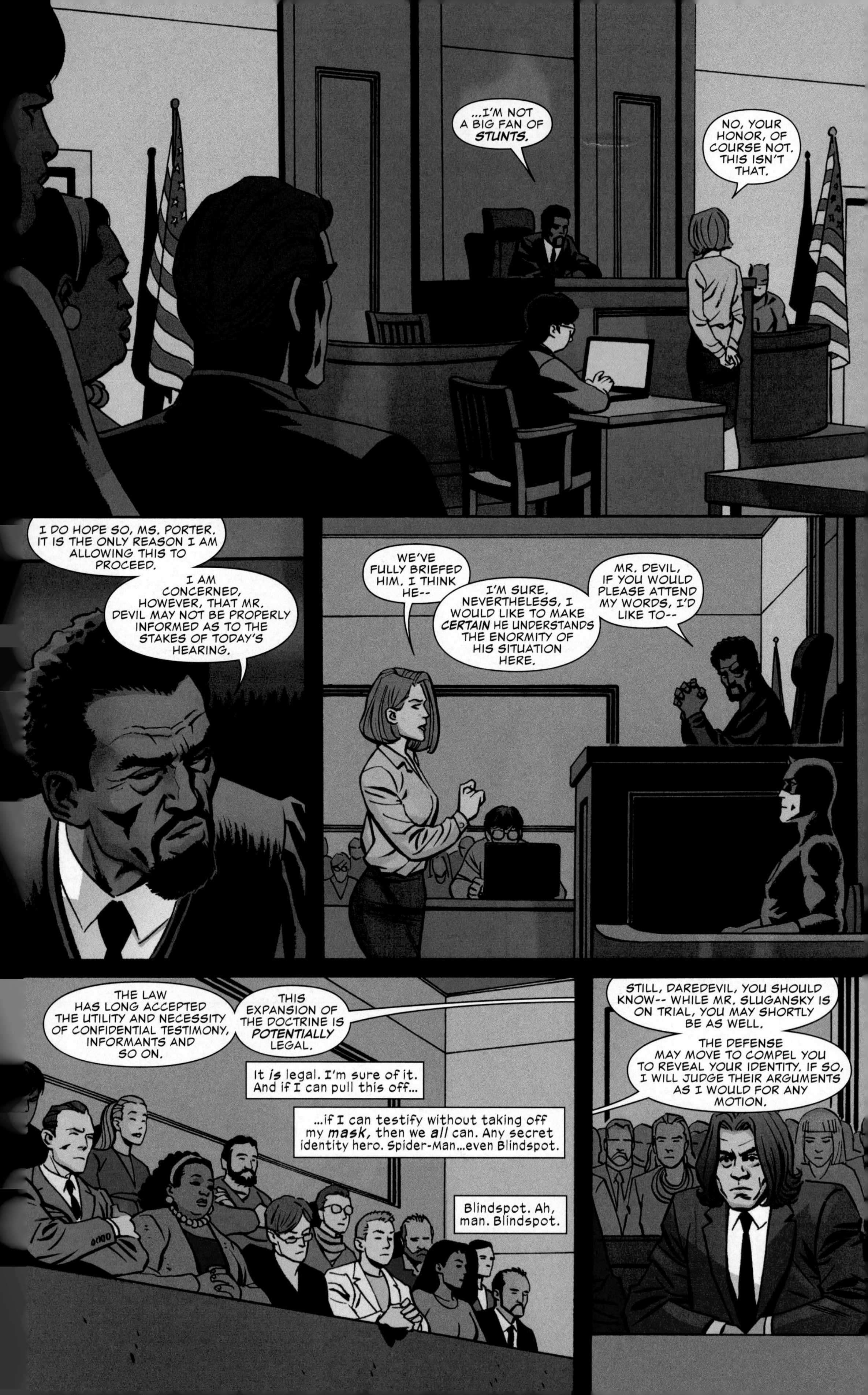
...I'M NOT A BIG FAN OF STUNTS.
NO, YOUR HONOR, OF COURSE NOT. THIS ISN'T THAT.
I DO HOPE SO, MS. PORTER. IT IS THE ONLY REASON I AM ALLOWING THIS TO PROCEED.
I AM CONCERNED, HOWEVER, THAT MR. DEVIL MAY NOT BE PROPERLY INFORMED AS TO THE STAKES OF TODAY'S HEARING.
WE'VE FULLY BRIEFED HIM. I THINK HE--
I'M SURE. NEVERTHELESS, I WOULD LIKE TO MAKE CERTAIN HE UNDERSTANDS THE ENORMITY OF HIS SITUATION HERE.
MR. DEVIL, IF YOU WOULD PLEASE ATTEND MY WORDS, I'D LIKE TO--
THE LAW HAS LONG ACCEPTED THE UTILITY AND NECESSITY OF CONFIDENTIAL TESTIMONY, INFORMANTS AND SO ON.
THIS EXPANSION OF THE DOCTRINE IS POTENTIALLY LEGAL.
It is legal. I'm sure of it. And if I can pull this off...
...if I can testify without taking off my mask, then we all can. Any secret identity hero. Spider-Man...even Blindspot.
Blindspot. Ah, man. Blindspot.
STILL, DAREDEVIL, YOU SHOULD KNOW-- WHILE MR. SLUGANSKY IS ON TRIAL, YOU MAY SHORTLY BE AS WELL.
THE DEFENSE MAY MOVE TO COMPEL YOU TO REVEAL YOUR IDENTITY. IF SO, I WILL JUDGE THEIR ARGUMENTS AS I WOULD FOR ANY MOTION.

SUPREME
PART 2

Well...it sort of is. That's why I put the red suit back on. Go for the razzle-dazzle.

IT'S DAREDEVIL, YOUR HONOR.

PARDON ME?

ONE WORD.

NOTED.

THE STATE HAS CALLED YOU, DAREDEVIL, TO TESTIFY AT THE TRIAL OF SIMON SLUGANSKY.

HE STANDS ACCUSED OF CRIMINAL CONSPIRACY, TERRORIST ACTS AND OTHER CHARGES THAT HAVE ALREADY BEEN COVERED IN DETAIL.

Correct. Slug's part of a gang called the Clip, and they tried to blow up City Hall in an attempt to kick-start the collapse of civilization.

I'm not sure it even made sense to them.

YOU ARE HERE AS DAREDEVIL, NOT IN YOUR CIVILIAN PERSONA.

YOU WISH TO TESTIFY ANONYMOUSLY.

Slug's gang escaped, but we got him, and I picked up plenty of evidence with my super-senses.

If the judge lets me testify, I can put him away, and maybe get him to turn over on his crew.

It could change *everything.* Our powers let us gather evidence the cops just can't. If we can present it in court, *legally...*

IF SUCH A MOTION WERE SUCCESSFUL, I WOULD REQUIRE YOU TO REMOVE YOUR MASK HERE, IN FRONT OF ALL AND SUNDRY ASSEMBLED.

YES, I KNOW. MR. MURDOCK LAID ALL OF THIS OUT TO ME.

AND KNOWING ALL OF THIS, YOU CHOOSE TO PROCEED?

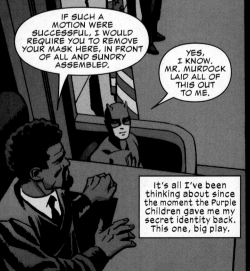

...no more tying up bad guys, leaving them for the police and praying the system can get a conviction. We can be part of the process from start to finish.

It's all I've been thinking about since the moment the Purple Children gave me my secret identity back. This one, big play.

It all comes down to this. Here. Today.

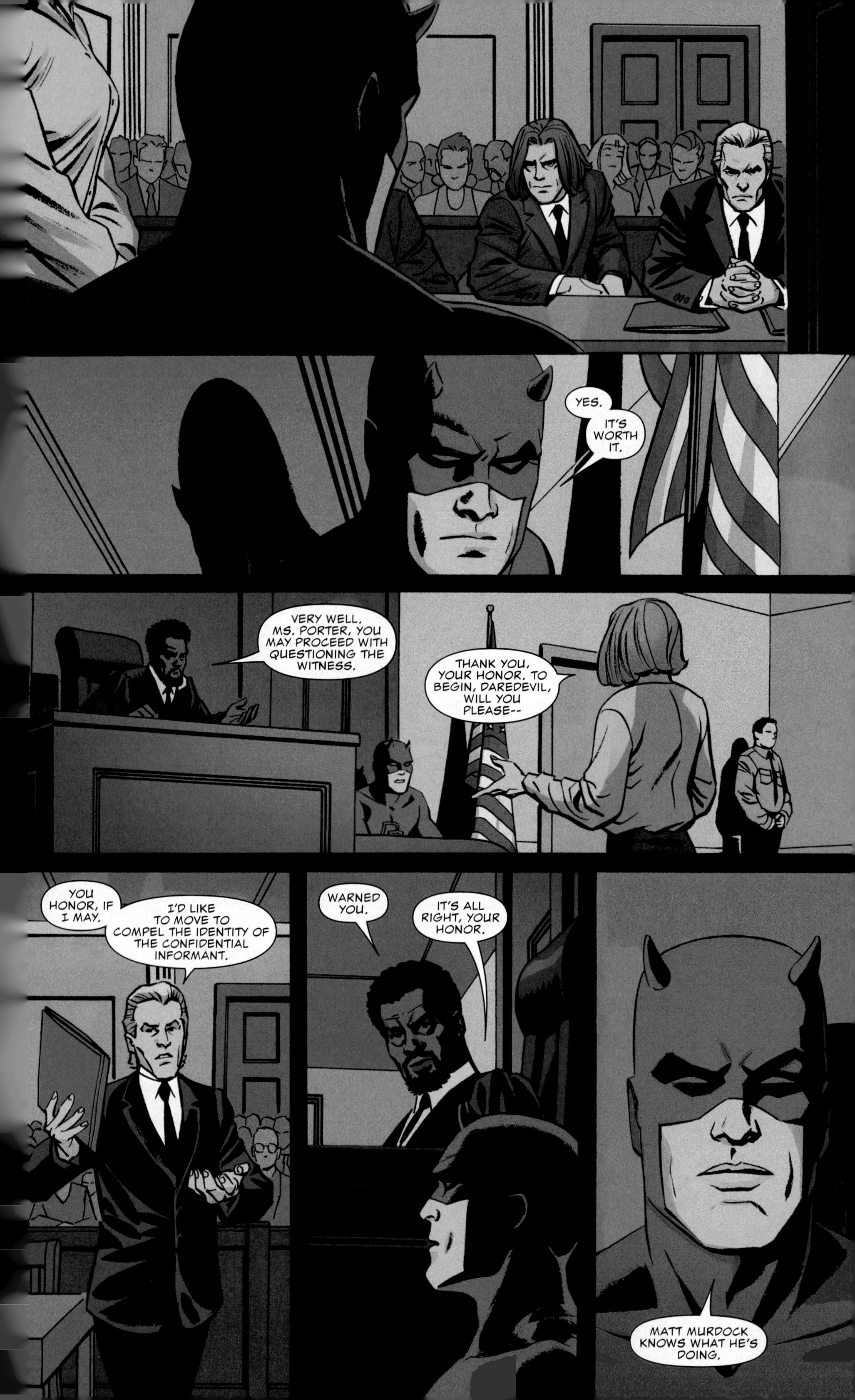
YES.
IT'S WORTH IT.
VERY WELL. MS. PORTER, YOU MAY PROCEED WITH QUESTIONING THE WITNESS.
THANK YOU, YOUR HONOR. TO BEGIN, DAREDEVIL, WILL YOU PLEASE--
YOU HONOR, IF I MAY.
I'D LIKE TO MOVE TO COMPEL THE IDENTITY OF THE CONFIDENTIAL INFORMANT.
WARNED YOU.
IT'S ALL RIGHT, YOUR HONOR.
MATT MURDOCK KNOWS WHAT HE'S DOING.

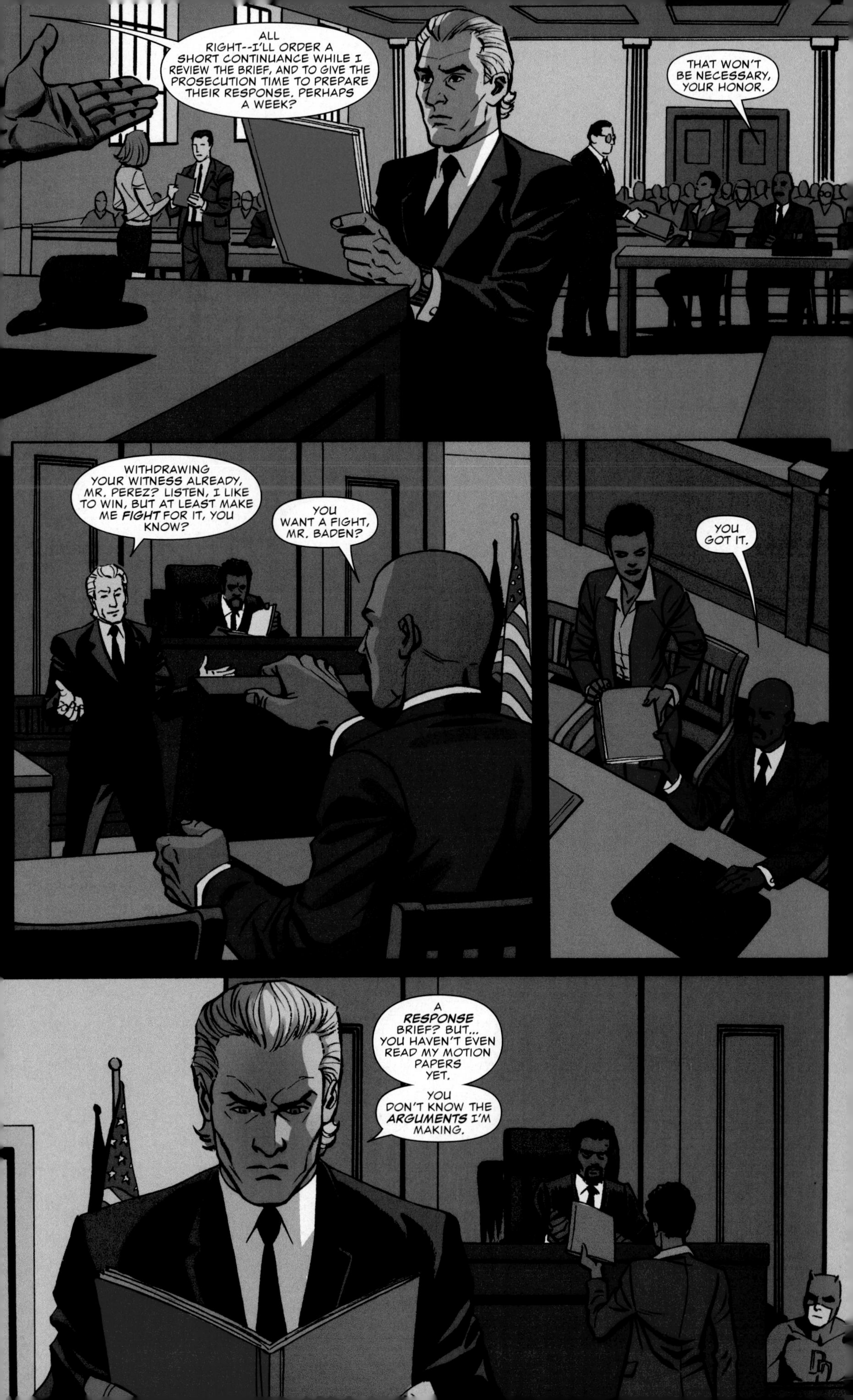
ALL RIGHT--I'LL ORDER A SHORT CONTINUANCE WHILE I REVIEW THE BRIEF, AND TO GIVE THE PROSECUTION TIME TO PREPARE THEIR RESPONSE. PERHAPS A WEEK?
THAT WON'T BE NECESSARY, YOUR HONOR.
WITHDRAWING YOUR WITNESS ALREADY, MR. PEREZ? LISTEN, I LIKE TO WIN, BUT AT LEAST MAKE ME FIGHT FOR IT, YOU KNOW?
YOU WANT A FIGHT, MR. BADEN?
YOU GOT IT.
A RESPONSE BRIEF? BUT... YOU HAVEN'T EVEN READ MY MOTION PAPERS YET.
YOU DON'T KNOW THE ARGUMENTS I'M MAKING.

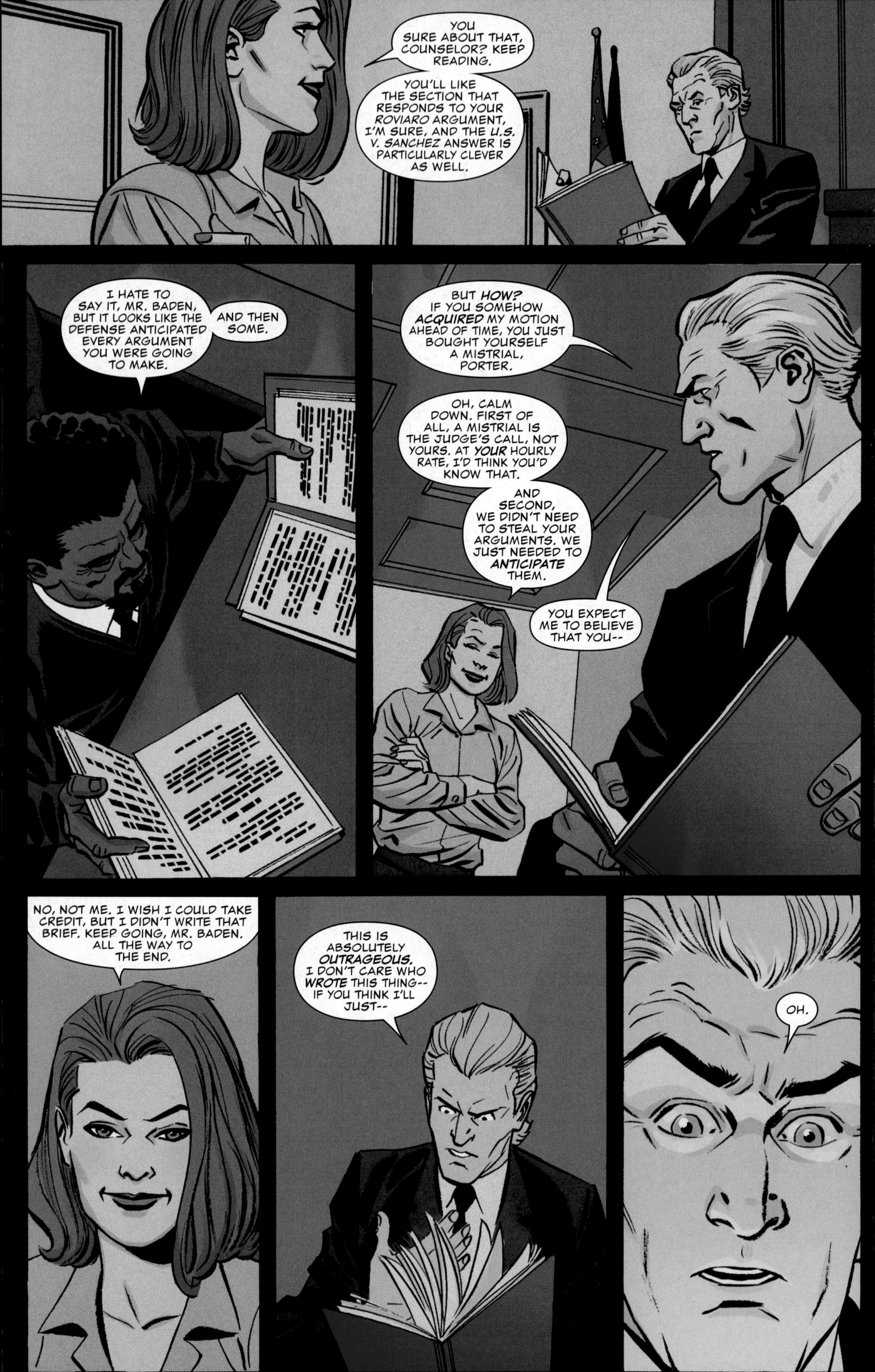
YOU SURE ABOUT THAT, COUNSELOR? KEEP READING.
YOU'LL LIKE THE SECTION THAT RESPONDS TO YOUR ROVIARO ARGUMENT, I'M SURE, AND THE U.S. V. SANCHEZ ANSWER IS PARTICULARLY CLEVER AS WELL.
I HATE TO SAY IT, MR. BADEN, BUT IT LOOKS LIKE THE DEFENSE ANTICIPATED EVERY ARGUMENT YOU WERE GOING TO MAKE.
AND THEN SOME.
BUT HOW? IF YOU SOMEHOW ACQUIRED MY MOTION AHEAD OF TIME, YOU JUST BOUGHT YOURSELF A MISTRIAL, PORTER.
OH, CALM DOWN. FIRST OF ALL, A MISTRIAL IS THE JUDGE'S CALL, NOT YOURS. AT YOUR HOURLY RATE, I'D THINK YOU'D KNOW THAT.
AND SECOND, WE DIDN'T NEED TO STEAL YOUR ARGUMENTS. WE JUST NEEDED TO ANTICIPATE THEM.
YOU EXPECT ME TO BELIEVE THAT YOU--
NO, NOT ME. I WISH I COULD TAKE CREDIT, BUT I DIDN'T WRITE THAT BRIEF. KEEP GOING, MR. BADEN. ALL THE WAY TO THE END.
THIS IS ABSOLUTELY OUTRAGEOUS. I DON'T CARE WHO WROTE THIS THING-- IF YOU THINK I'LL JUST--
OH.

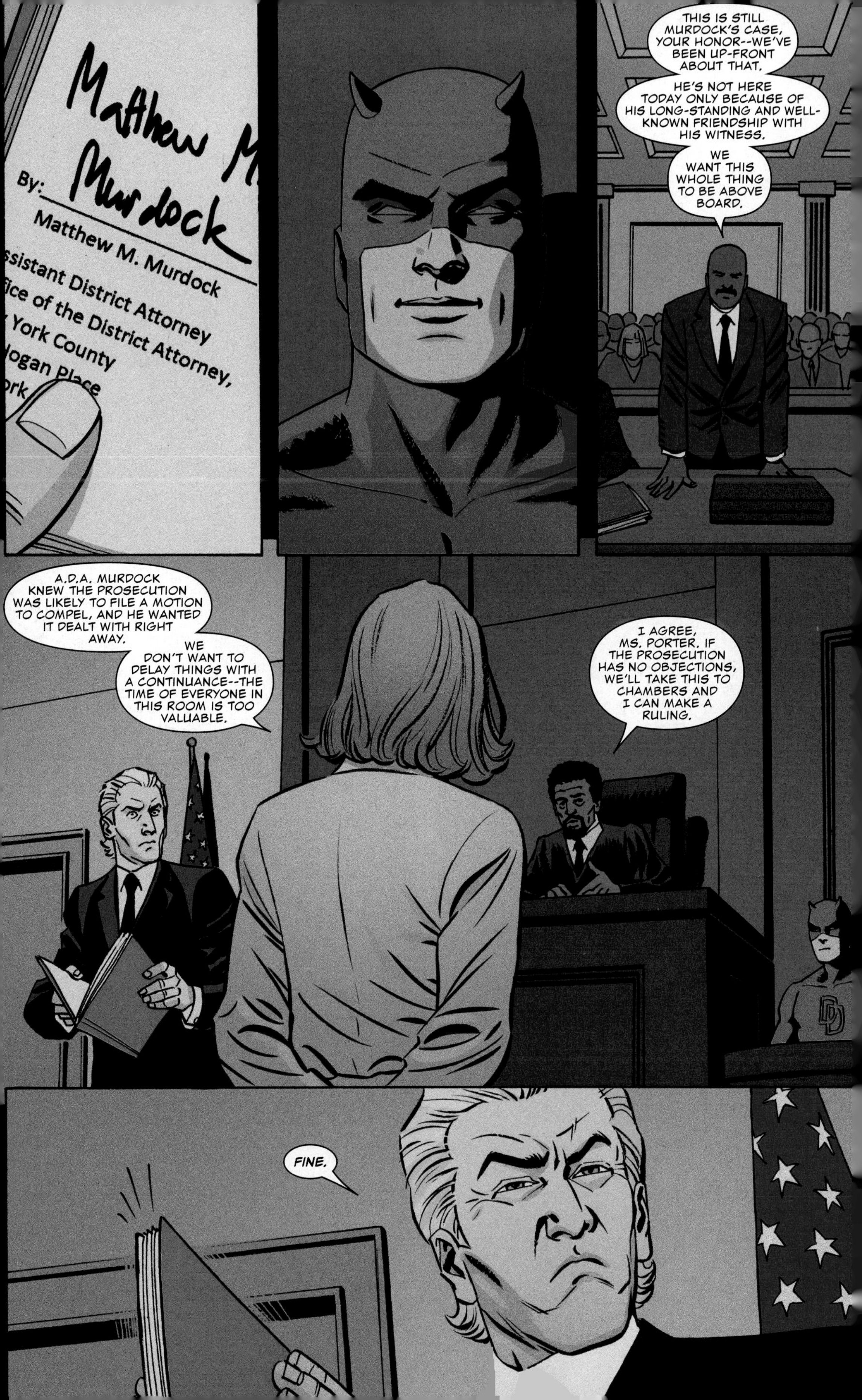
Matthew M. Murdock
By:
Matthew M. Murdock
ssistant District Attorney
fice of the District Attorney,
York County
Hogan Place
ork
THIS IS STILL MURDOCK'S CASE, YOUR HONOR--WE'VE BEEN UP-FRONT ABOUT THAT.
HE'S NOT HERE TODAY ONLY BECAUSE OF HIS LONG-STANDING AND WELL-KNOWN FRIENDSHIP WITH HIS WITNESS.
WE WANT THIS WHOLE THING TO BE ABOVE BOARD.
A.D.A. MURDOCK KNEW THE PROSECUTION WAS LIKELY TO FILE A MOTION TO COMPEL, AND HE WANTED IT DEALT WITH RIGHT AWAY.
WE DON'T WANT TO DELAY THINGS WITH A CONTINUANCE--THE TIME OF EVERYONE IN THIS ROOM IS TOO VALUABLE.
I AGREE, MS. PORTER. IF THE PROSECUTION HAS NO OBJECTIONS, WE'LL TAKE THIS TO CHAMBERS AND I CAN MAKE A RULING.
FINE.

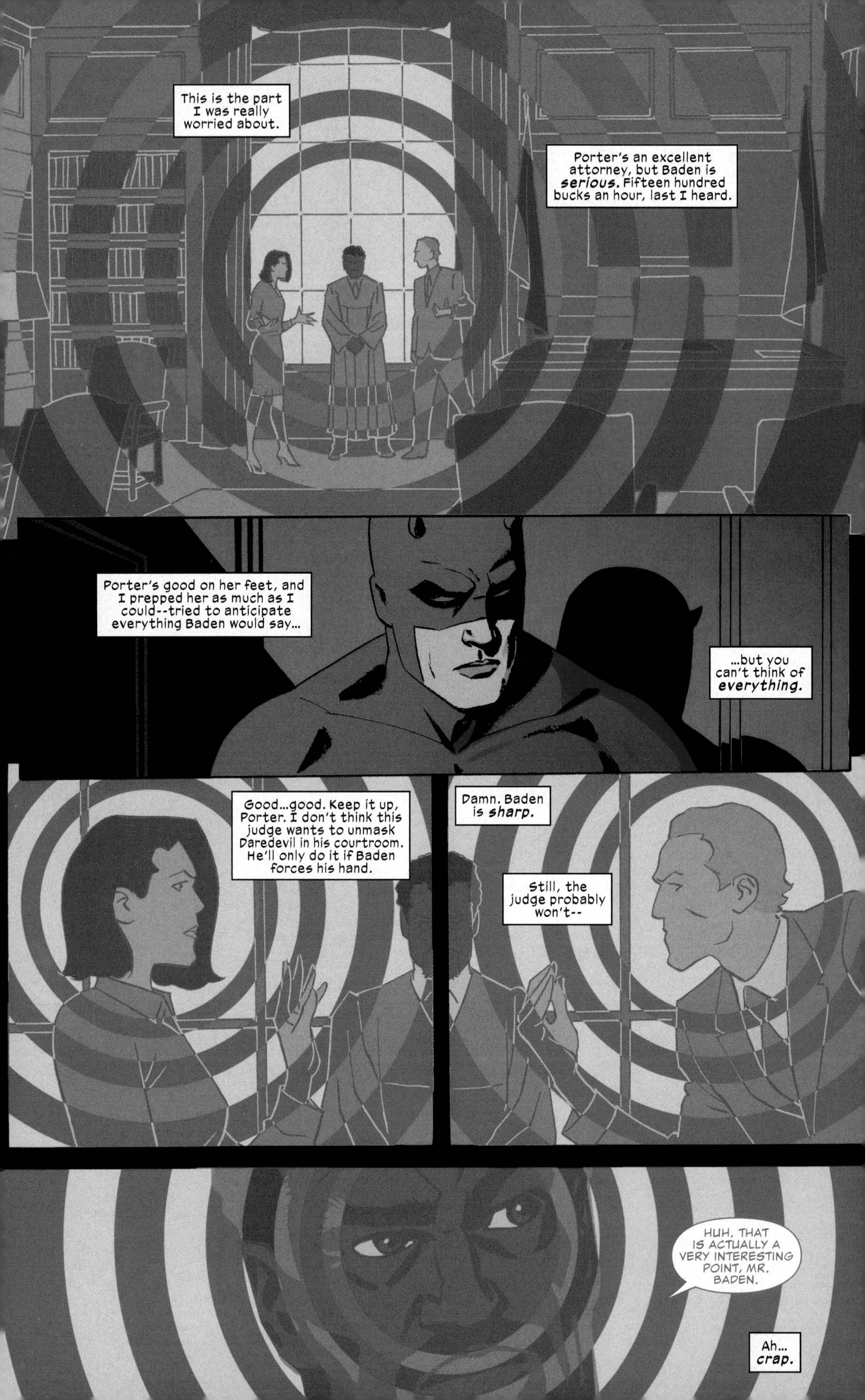
This is the part I was really worried about.
Porter's an excellent attorney, but Baden is *serious.* Fifteen hundred bucks an hour, last I heard.
Porter's good on her feet, and I prepped her as much as I could--tried to anticipate everything Baden would say...
...but you can't think of *everything.*
Good...good. Keep it up, Porter. I don't think this judge wants to unmask Daredevil in his courtroom. He'll only do it if Baden forces his hand.
Damn. Baden is *sharp.*
Still, the judge probably won't--
HUH. THAT IS ACTUALLY A VERY INTERESTING POINT, MR. BADEN.
Ah... *crap.*

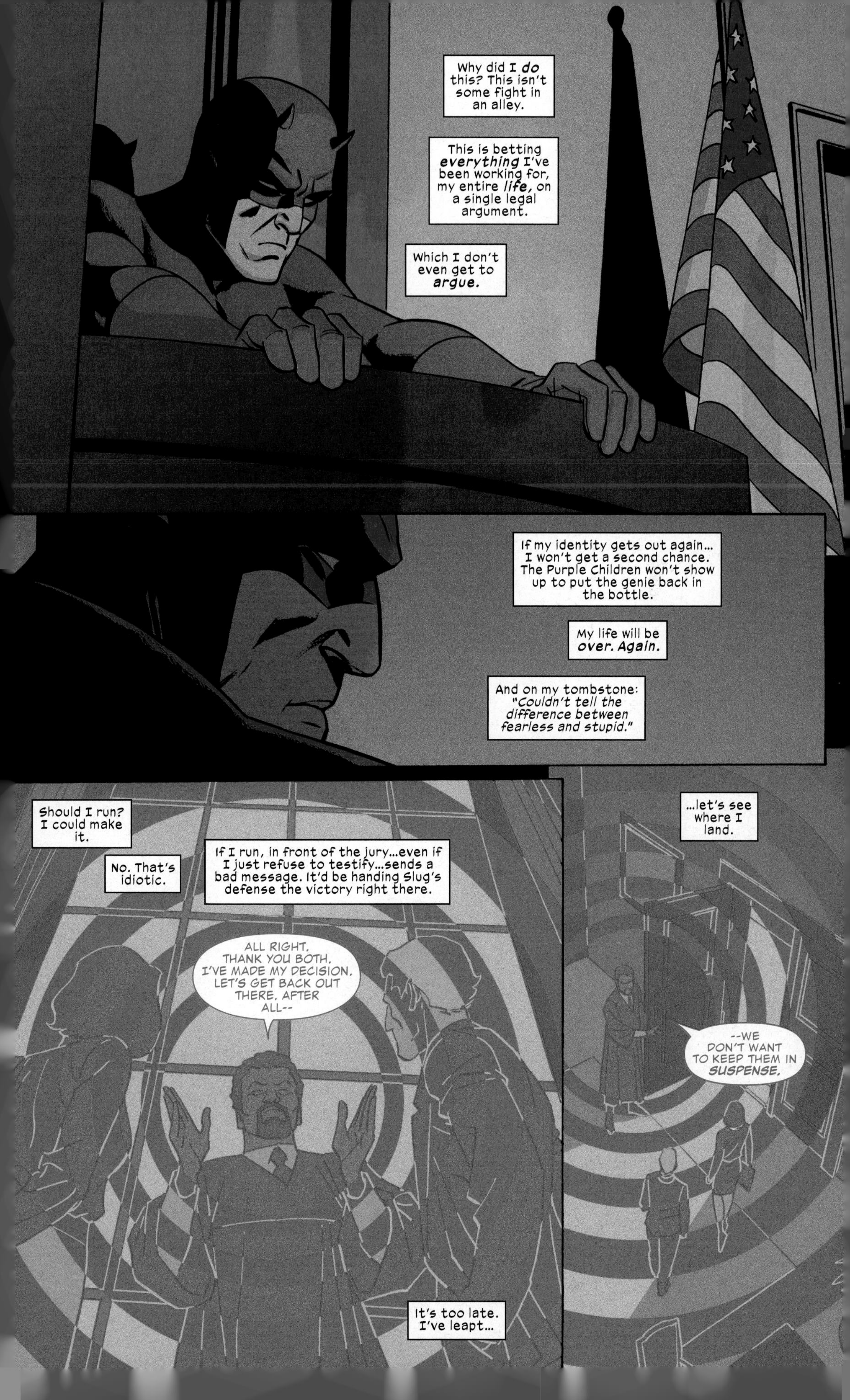
Why did I do this? This isn't some fight in an alley.
This is betting everything I've been working for, my entire life, on a single legal argument.
Which I don't even get to argue.
If my identity gets out again... I won't get a second chance. The Purple Children won't show up to put the genie back in the bottle.
My life will be over. Again.
And on my tombstone: "Couldn't tell the difference between fearless and stupid."
Should I run? I could make it.
No. That's idiotic.
If I run, in front of the jury...even if I just refuse to testify...sends a bad message. It'd be handing Slug's defense the victory right there.
ALL RIGHT. THANK YOU BOTH. I'VE MADE MY DECISION. LET'S GET BACK OUT THERE, AFTER ALL--
It's too late. I've leapt...
...let's see where I land.
--WE DON'T WANT TO KEEP THEM IN SUSPENSE.

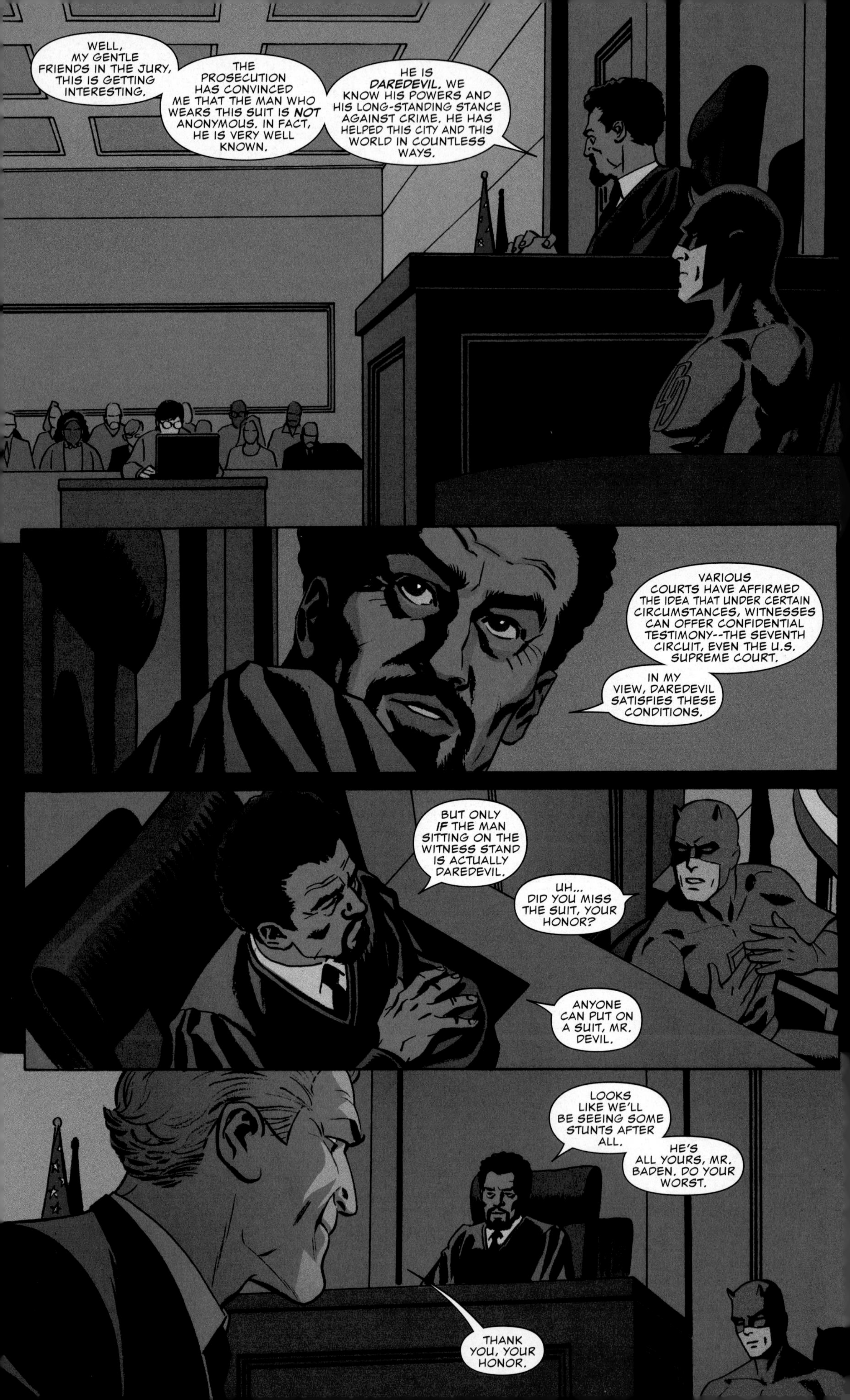
WELL, MY GENTLE FRIENDS IN THE JURY, THIS IS GETTING INTERESTING.
THE PROSECUTION HAS CONVINCED ME THAT THE MAN WHO WEARS THIS SUIT IS *NOT* ANONYMOUS. IN FACT, HE IS VERY WELL KNOWN.
HE IS *DAREDEVIL*. WE KNOW HIS POWERS AND HIS LONG-STANDING STANCE AGAINST CRIME. HE HAS HELPED THIS CITY AND THIS WORLD IN COUNTLESS WAYS.
VARIOUS COURTS HAVE AFFIRMED THE IDEA THAT UNDER CERTAIN CIRCUMSTANCES, WITNESSES CAN OFFER CONFIDENTIAL TESTIMONY--THE SEVENTH CIRCUIT, EVEN THE U.S. SUPREME COURT.
IN MY VIEW, DAREDEVIL SATISFIES THESE CONDITIONS.
BUT ONLY *IF* THE MAN SITTING ON THE WITNESS STAND IS ACTUALLY DAREDEVIL.
UH... DID YOU MISS THE SUIT, YOUR HONOR?
ANYONE CAN PUT ON A SUIT, MR. DEVIL.
LOOKS LIKE WE'LL BE SEEING SOME STUNTS AFTER ALL.
HE'S ALL YOURS, MR. BADEN. DO YOUR WORST.
THANK YOU, YOUR HONOR.

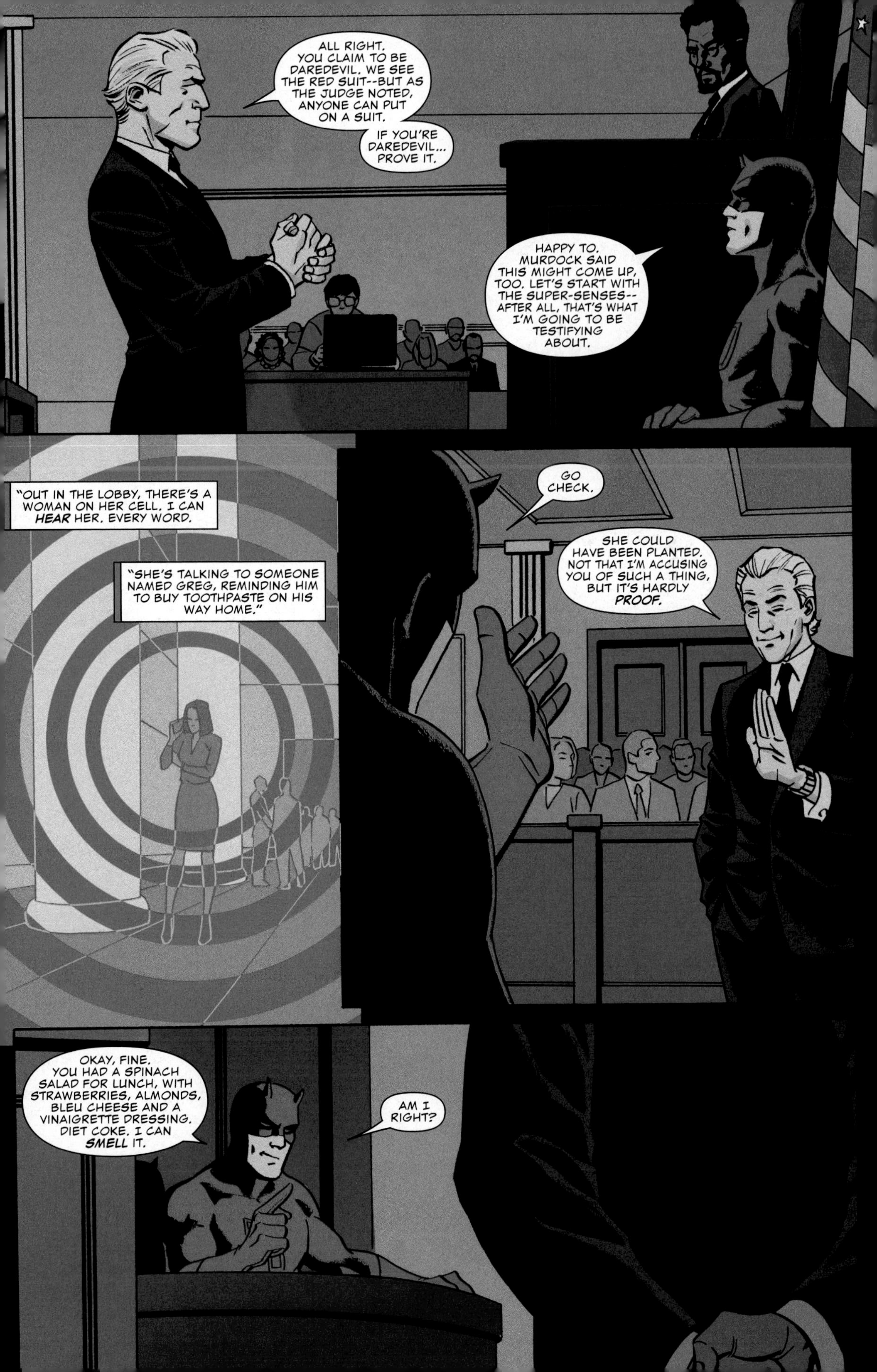
ALL RIGHT. YOU CLAIM TO BE DAREDEVIL. WE SEE THE RED SUIT--BUT AS THE JUDGE NOTED, ANYONE CAN PUT ON A SUIT.
IF YOU'RE DAREDEVIL... PROVE IT.
HAPPY TO. MURDOCK SAID THIS MIGHT COME UP, TOO. LET'S START WITH THE SUPER-SENSES--AFTER ALL, THAT'S WHAT I'M GOING TO BE TESTIFYING ABOUT.
"OUT IN THE LOBBY, THERE'S A WOMAN ON HER CELL. I CAN HEAR HER. EVERY WORD.
"SHE'S TALKING TO SOMEONE NAMED GREG, REMINDING HIM TO BUY TOOTHPASTE ON HIS WAY HOME."
GO CHECK.
SHE COULD HAVE BEEN PLANTED. NOT THAT I'M ACCUSING YOU OF SUCH A THING, BUT IT'S HARDLY PROOF.
OKAY, FINE. YOU HAD A SPINACH SALAD FOR LUNCH, WITH STRAWBERRIES, ALMONDS, BLEU CHEESE AND A VINAIGRETTE DRESSING. DIET COKE. I CAN SMELL IT.
AM I RIGHT?

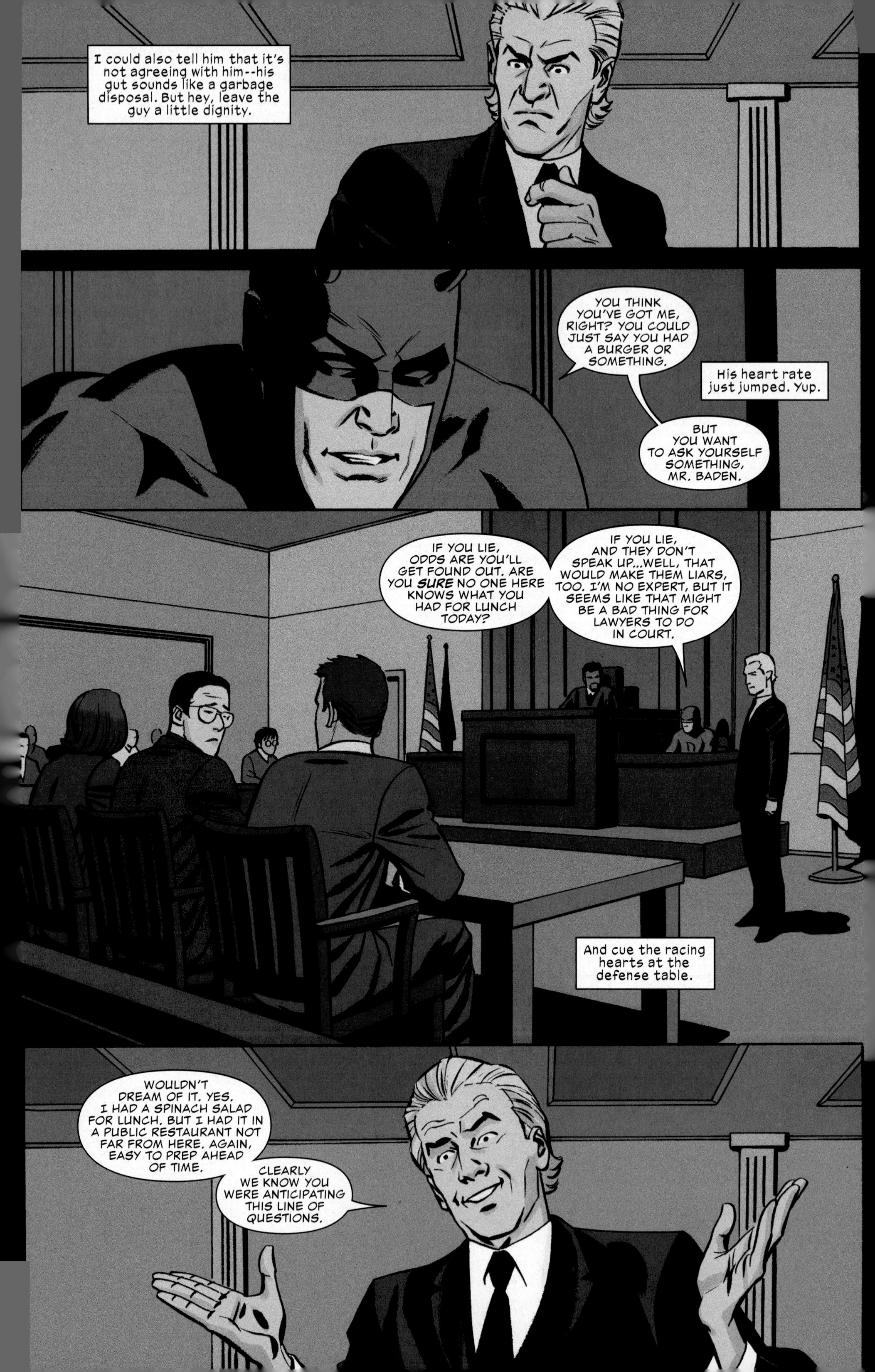
I could also tell him that it's not agreeing with him--his gut sounds like a garbage disposal. But hey, leave the guy a little dignity.
YOU THINK YOU'VE GOT ME, RIGHT? YOU COULD JUST SAY YOU HAD A BURGER OR SOMETHING.
His heart rate just jumped. Yup.
BUT YOU WANT TO ASK YOURSELF SOMETHING, MR. BADEN.
IF YOU LIE, ODDS ARE YOU'LL GET FOUND OUT. ARE YOU SURE NO ONE HERE KNOWS WHAT YOU HAD FOR LUNCH TODAY?
IF YOU LIE, AND THEY DON'T SPEAK UP...WELL, THAT WOULD MAKE THEM LIARS, TOO. I'M NO EXPERT, BUT IT SEEMS LIKE THAT MIGHT BE A BAD THING FOR LAWYERS TO DO IN COURT.
And cue the racing hearts at the defense table.
WOULDN'T DREAM OF IT. YES, I HAD A SPINACH SALAD FOR LUNCH. BUT I HAD IT IN A PUBLIC RESTAURANT NOT FAR FROM HERE. AGAIN, EASY TO PREP AHEAD OF TIME.
CLEARLY WE KNOW YOU WERE ANTICIPATING THIS LINE OF QUESTIONS.

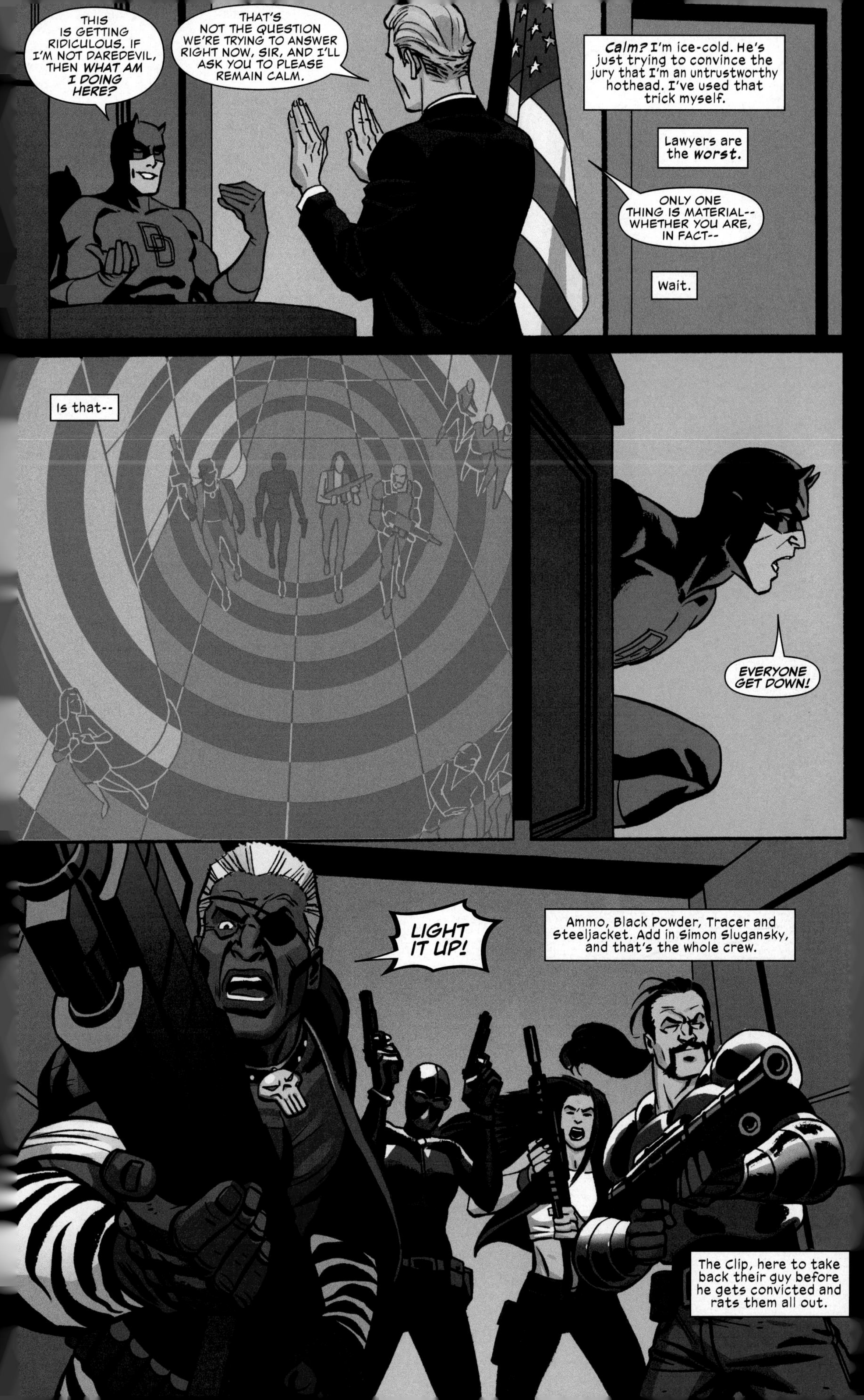
THIS IS GETTING RIDICULOUS. IF I'M NOT DAREDEVIL, THEN WHAT AM I DOING HERE?
THAT'S NOT THE QUESTION WE'RE TRYING TO ANSWER RIGHT NOW, SIR, AND I'LL ASK YOU TO PLEASE REMAIN CALM.
Calm? I'm ice-cold. He's just trying to convince the jury that I'm an untrustworthy hothead. I've used that trick myself.
Lawyers are the worst.
ONLY ONE THING IS MATERIAL--WHETHER YOU ARE, IN FACT--
Wait.
Is that--
EVERYONE GET DOWN!
LIGHT IT UP!
Ammo, Black Powder, Tracer and Steeljacket. Add in Simon Slugansky, and that's the whole crew.
The Clip, here to take back their guy before he gets convicted and rats them all out.

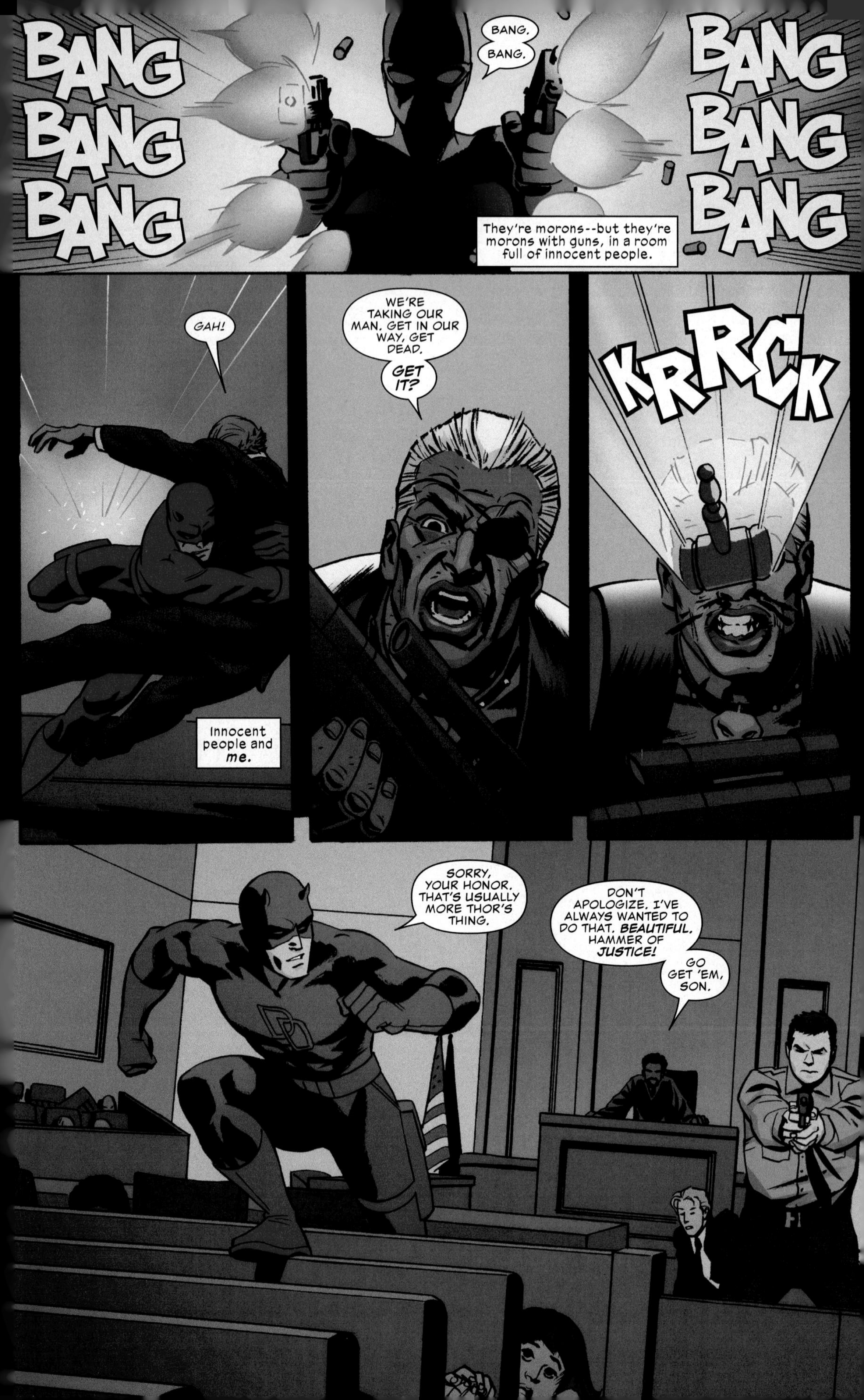
BANG
BANG
BANG
BANG.
BANG.
BANG
BANG
BANG
They're morons--but they're morons with guns, in a room full of innocent people.
GAH!
Innocent people and *me.*
WE'RE TAKING OUR MAN. GET IN OUR WAY, GET DEAD.
GET IT?
KRRCK
SORRY, YOUR HONOR. THAT'S USUALLY MORE THOR'S THING.
DON'T APOLOGIZE. I'VE ALWAYS WANTED TO DO THAT. *BEAUTIFUL.* HAMMER OF *JUSTICE!*
GO GET 'EM, SON.

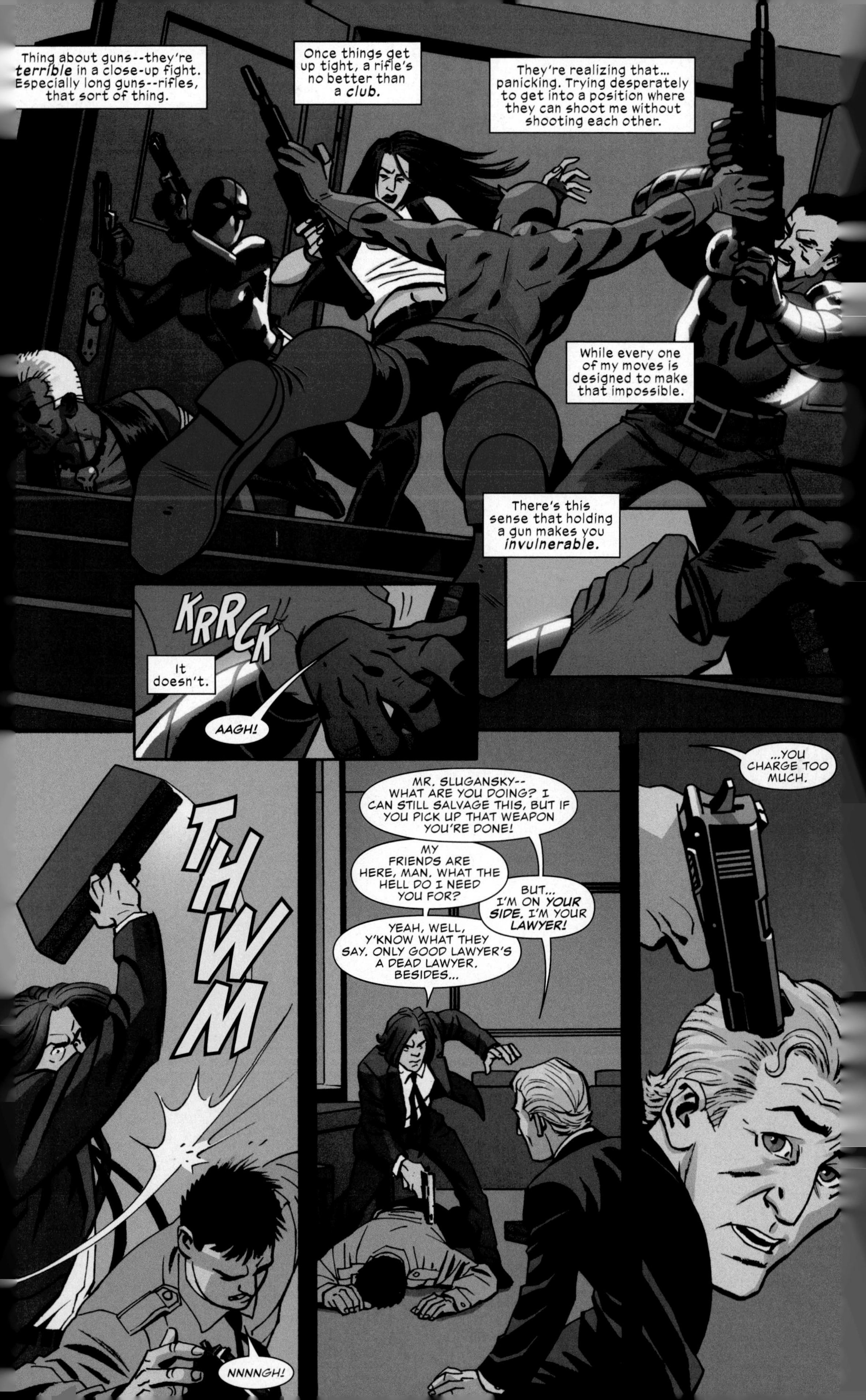
Thing about guns--they're *terrible* in a close-up fight. Especially long guns--rifles, that sort of thing.
Once things get up tight, a rifle's no better than a *club.*
They're realizing that... panicking. Trying desperately to get into a position where they can shoot me without shooting each other.
While every one of my moves is designed to make that impossible.
There's this sense that holding a gun makes you *invulnerable.*
KRRCK
It doesn't.
AAGH!
THWM
NNNNGH!
MR. SLUGANSKY-- WHAT ARE YOU DOING? I CAN STILL SALVAGE THIS, BUT IF YOU PICK UP THAT WEAPON YOU'RE DONE!
MY FRIENDS ARE HERE, MAN. WHAT THE HELL DO I NEED YOU FOR?
BUT... I'M ON *YOUR SIDE.* I'M YOUR *LAWYER!*
YEAH, WELL, Y'KNOW WHAT THEY SAY. ONLY GOOD LAWYER'S A DEAD LAWYER. BESIDES...
...YOU CHARGE TOO MUCH.

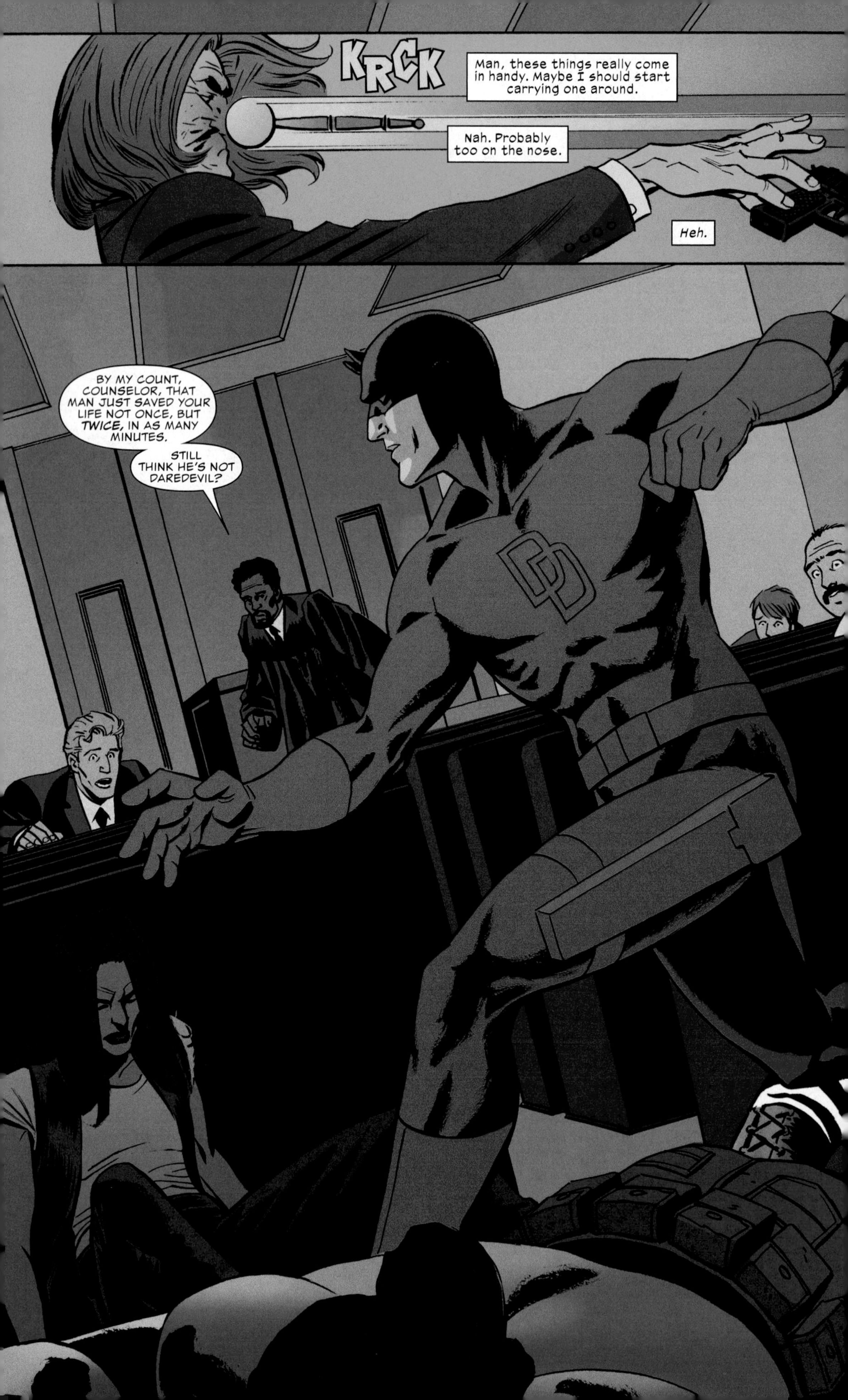
KRCK
Man, these things really come in handy. Maybe I should start carrying one around.
Nah. Probably too on the nose.
Heh.
BY MY COUNT, COUNSELOR, THAT MAN JUST SAVED YOUR LIFE NOT ONCE, BUT TWICE, IN AS MANY MINUTES.
STILL THINK HE'S NOT DAREDEVIL?

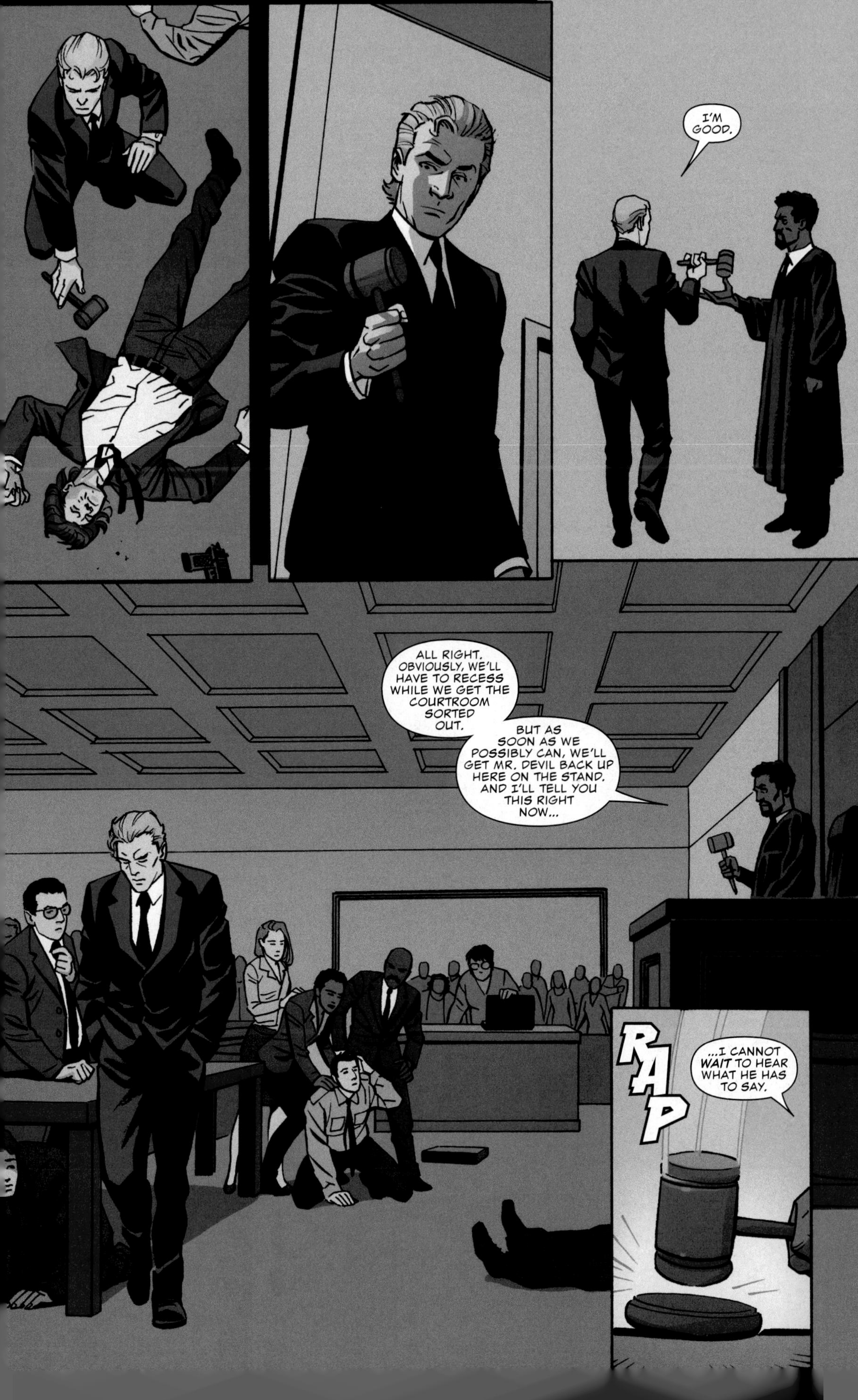
I'M GOOD.
ALL RIGHT. OBVIOUSLY, WE'LL HAVE TO RECESS WHILE WE GET THE COURTROOM SORTED OUT.
BUT AS SOON AS WE POSSIBLY CAN, WE'LL GET MR. DEVIL BACK UP HERE ON THE STAND, AND I'LL TELL YOU THIS RIGHT NOW...
RAP
...I CANNOT WAIT TO HEAR WHAT HE HAS TO SAY.

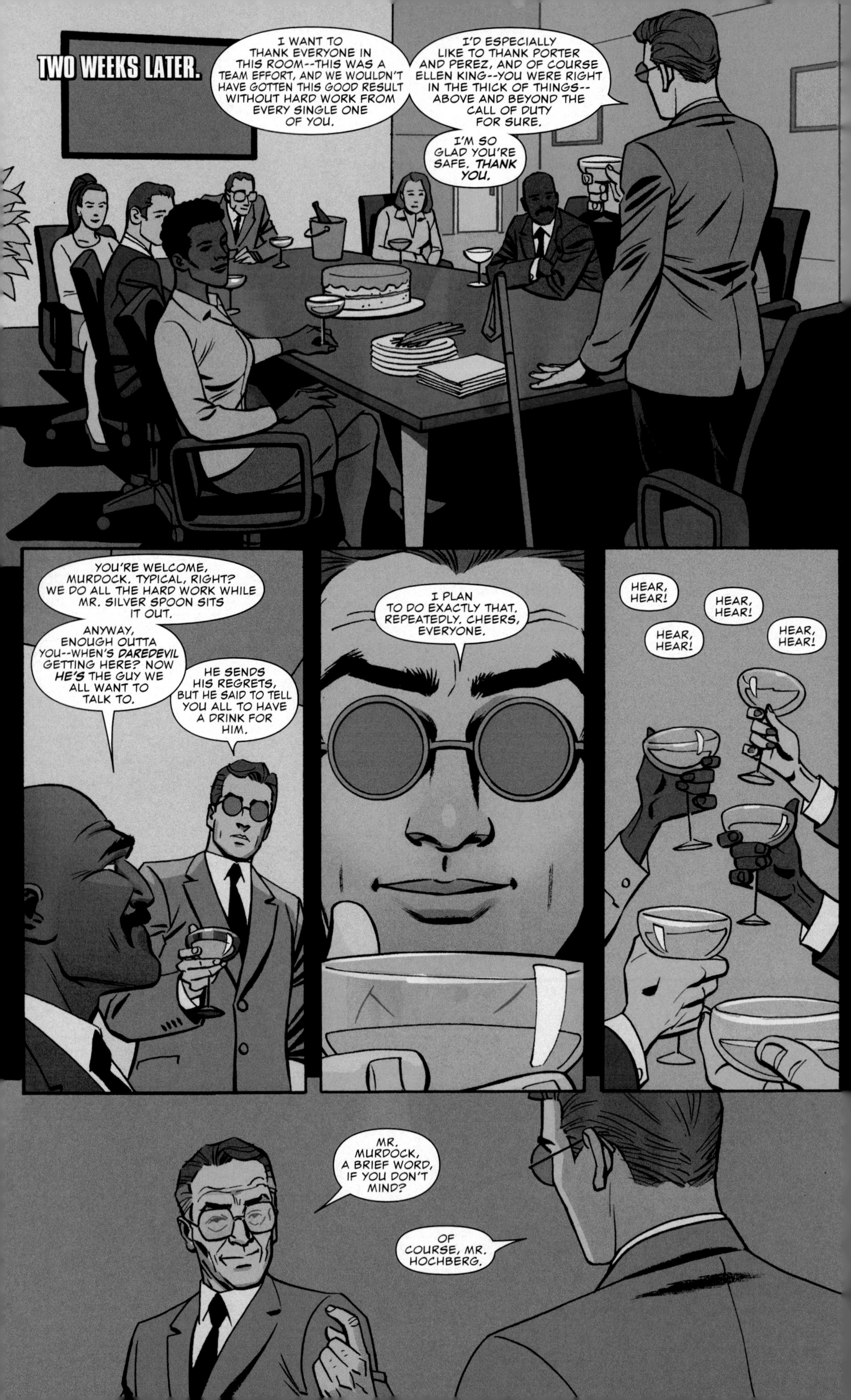
TWO WEEKS LATER.
I WANT TO THANK EVERYONE IN THIS ROOM--THIS WAS A TEAM EFFORT, AND WE WOULDN'T HAVE GOTTEN THIS GOOD RESULT WITHOUT HARD WORK FROM EVERY SINGLE ONE OF YOU.
I'D ESPECIALLY LIKE TO THANK PORTER AND PEREZ, AND OF COURSE ELLEN KING--YOU WERE RIGHT IN THE THICK OF THINGS--ABOVE AND BEYOND THE CALL OF DUTY FOR SURE.
I'M SO GLAD YOU'RE SAFE. *THANK YOU.*
YOU'RE WELCOME, MURDOCK. TYPICAL, RIGHT? WE DO ALL THE HARD WORK WHILE MR. SILVER SPOON SITS IT OUT.
ANYWAY, ENOUGH OUTTA YOU--WHEN'S *DAREDEVIL* GETTING HERE? NOW *HE'S* THE GUY WE ALL WANT TO TALK TO.
HE SENDS HIS REGRETS, BUT HE SAID TO TELL YOU ALL TO HAVE A DRINK FOR HIM.
I PLAN TO DO EXACTLY THAT. REPEATEDLY. CHEERS, EVERYONE.
HEAR, HEAR!
HEAR, HEAR!
HEAR, HEAR!
HEAR, HEAR!
MR. MURDOCK, A BRIEF WORD, IF YOU DON'T MIND?
OF COURSE, MR. HOCHBERG.

YOU GOT A NEW YORK STATE JUDGE TO ALLOW A SUPER HERO TO OFFER TESTIMONY WITHOUT REMOVING HIS MASK. WELL DONE.

THANK YOU. I CAN'T BELIEVE THINGS GOT AS DANGEROUS AS THEY DID...BUT AT LEAST NO ONE WAS HURT. ON OUR SIDE, ANYWAY, AND NOW THAT WE'VE SET A PRECEDENT...

"...IT'S REALLY JUST THE *BEGINNING.*"

FINAL ☆☆☆☆
DAILY 📢 BUGLE
$1.00 (in NYC)
$1.50 (outside city)
NEW YORK'S FINEST DAILY NEWSPAPER

THE DEVIL YOU (DON'T) KNOW

Super-powered vigilante Daredevil testifies in [N]ork State Supreme Court.

[MAN]HATTAN: In an unprecedented [expansi]on of existing law, the hero was not [requi]r[ed] to disclose his actual identity before

attacked by members of the apocalyptic street gang known as the Clip, who were attempting to remove Slugansky from the trial. Daredevil was able to dispatch the cri[minals befor]e they could comp[lete their missio]n, and all five [members of] the Clip in police cu[st]ody. Daredevil th[e]n proceeded to offer detailed testimony abo[ut] the earlier incident in which

HMM. YOU SEE...IT'S THIS KIND OF THING.

MY POINT EXACTLY. SLUGANSKY AND THE REST OF THAT STUPID GANG OF HIS ARE GOING AWAY FOR A LONG TIME--BUT WHAT YOU DID HERE...PEOPLE WON'T LET IT LIE.

IT'S JUST A MATTER OF TIME BEFORE SOMEONE CHALLENGES THAT PART OF THE CASE. THE FOURTH AMENDMENT IMPLICATIONS-- THIS COULD GO ALL THE WAY UP.

I KNOW. I KNEW THAT WHEN I STARTED. I'M READY, THOUGH.

"ANYONE WHO WANTS TO FIGHT ME ON THIS... THEY CAN BRING IT ON."

FINAL ☆☆☆☆
DAILY 📢 BUGLE
SINCE 1897
$1.00 (in NYC)
$1.50 (outside city)
NEW YORK'S FINEST DAILY NEWSPAPER

THE DEVIL YOU (DON'T) KNOW

Super-powered vigilante Daredevil testifies in New York State Supreme Court.

MANHATTAN: In an unprecedented expansion of existing law, the hero was not required to disclose his actual identity before

THIS SORT OF THING. *THIS* IS NOT PLAYING FAIR, AND YOU KNOW WHAT?

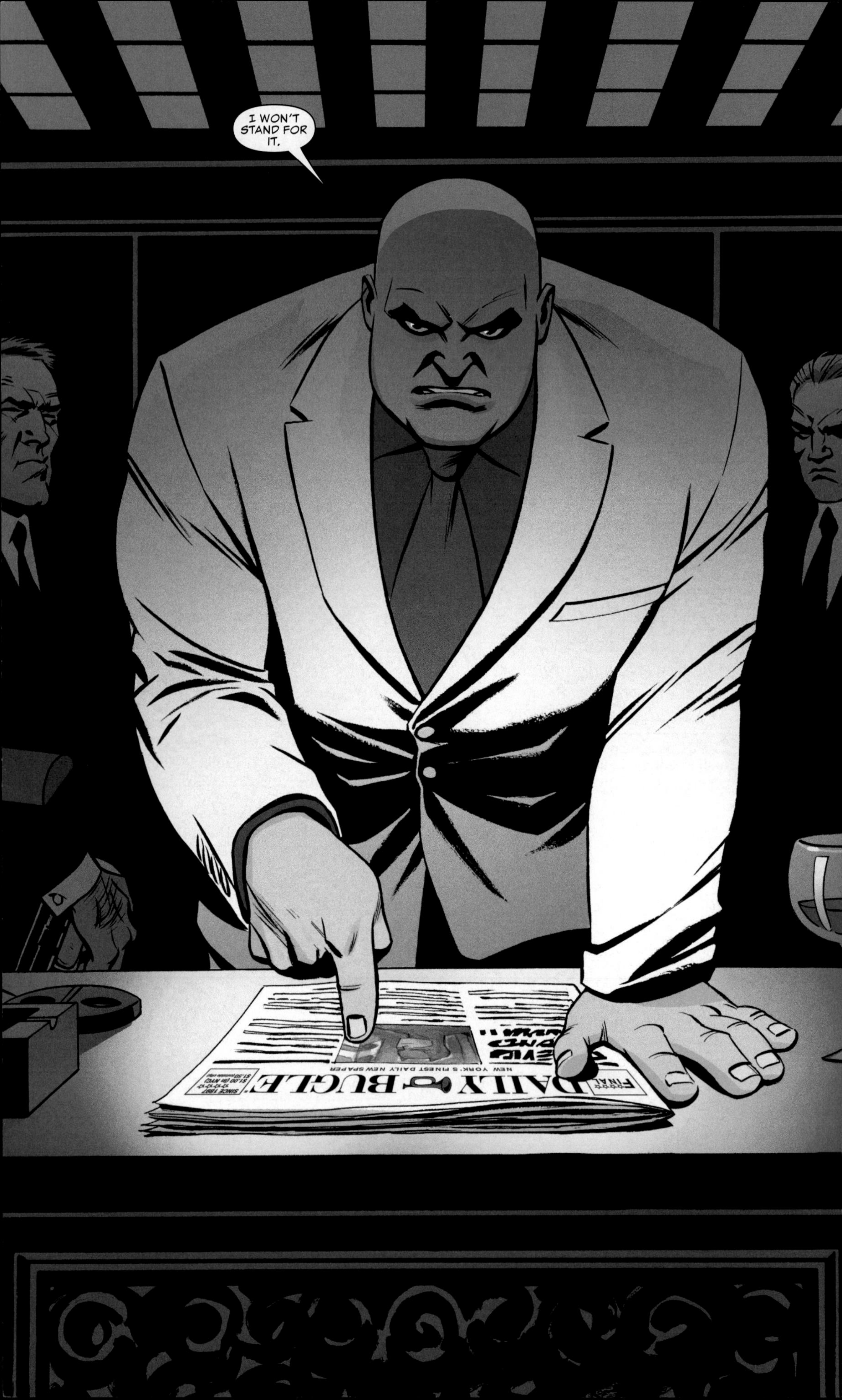
I WON'T STAND FOR IT.
DAILY BUGLE
NEW YORK'S FINEST DAILY NEWSPAPER

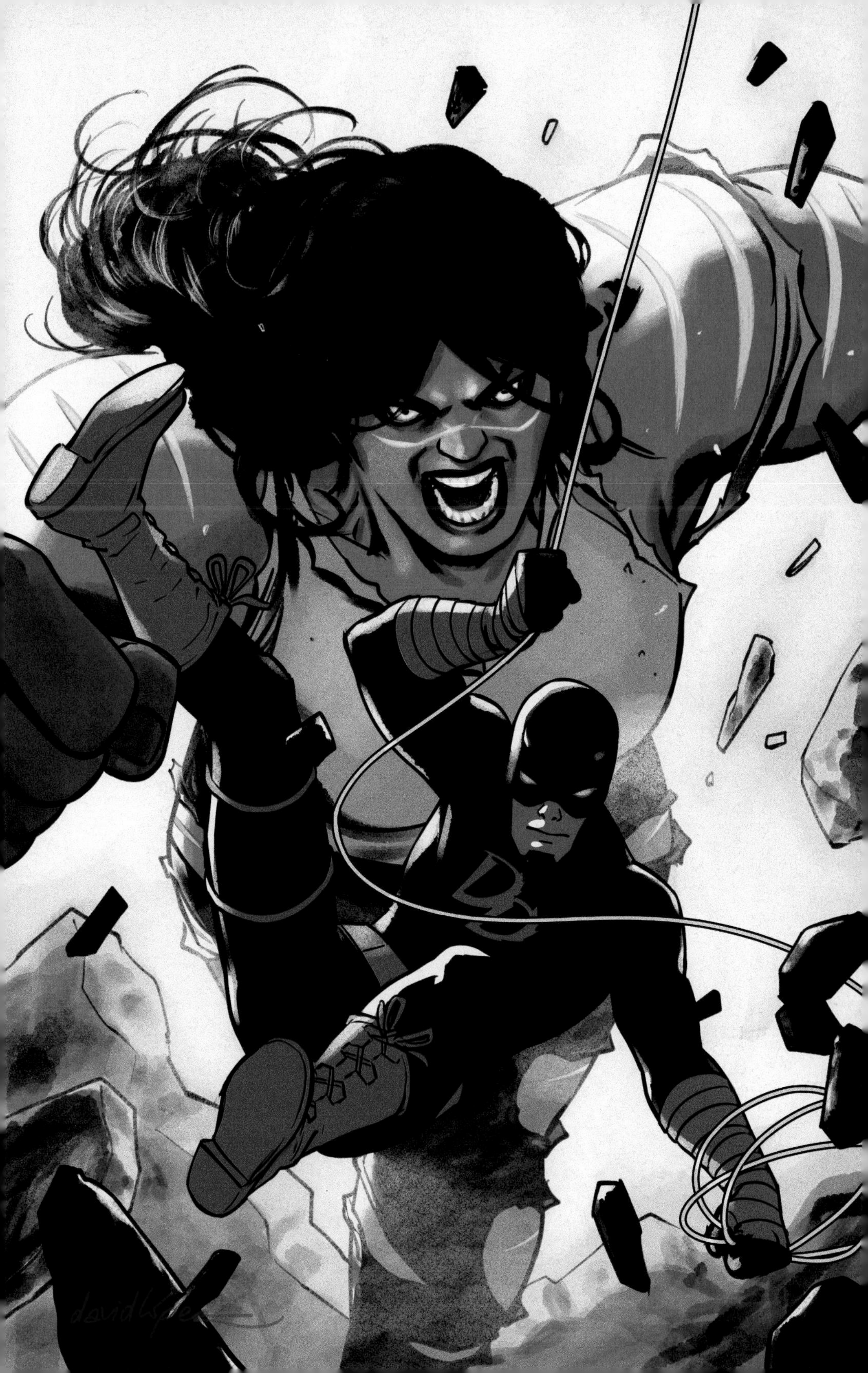

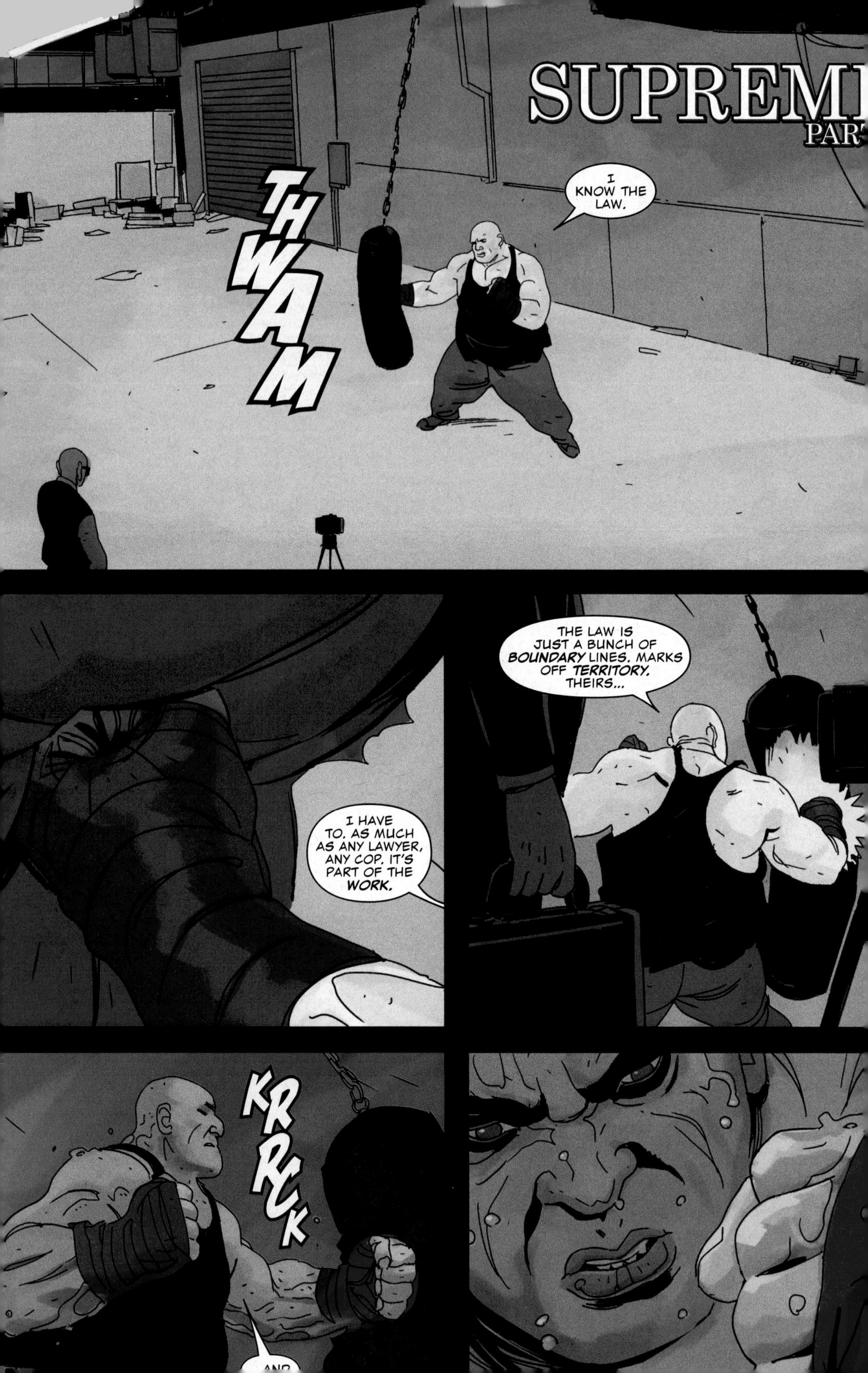
SUPREM
PAR
THWAM
I KNOW THE LAW.
THE LAW IS JUST A BUNCH OF BOUNDARY LINES. MARKS OFF TERRITORY. THEIRS...
I HAVE TO. AS MUCH AS ANY LAWYER, ANY COP. IT'S PART OF THE WORK.
KRRCK

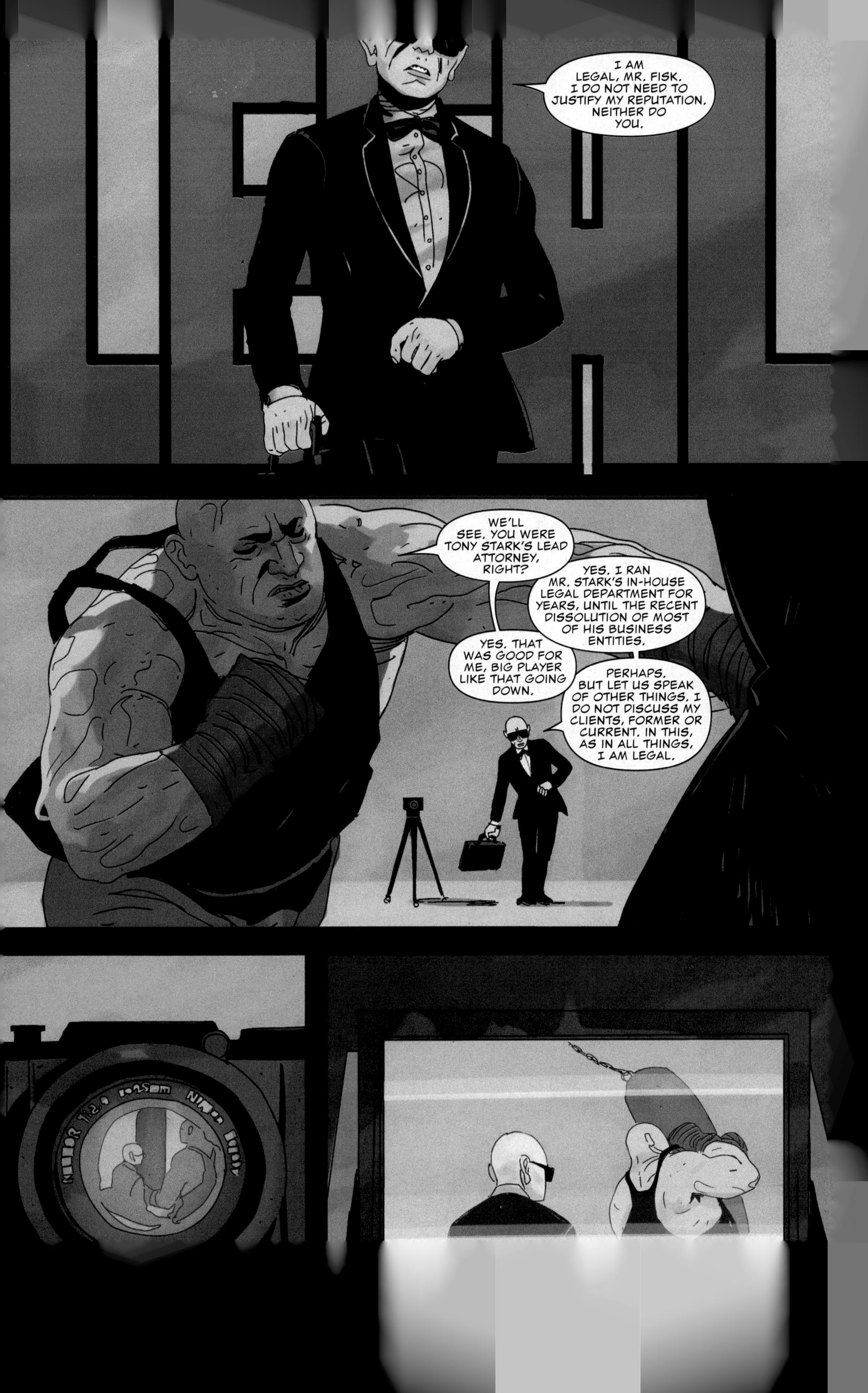
I AM LEGAL, MR. FISK. I DO NOT NEED TO JUSTIFY MY REPUTATION. NEITHER DO YOU.
WE'LL SEE. YOU WERE TONY STARK'S LEAD ATTORNEY, RIGHT?
YES. I RAN MR. STARK'S IN-HOUSE LEGAL DEPARTMENT FOR YEARS, UNTIL THE RECENT DISSOLUTION OF MOST OF HIS BUSINESS ENTITIES.
YES. THAT WAS GOOD FOR ME, BIG PLAYER LIKE THAT GOING DOWN.
PERHAPS. BUT LET US SPEAK OF OTHER THINGS. I DO NOT DISCUSS MY CLIENTS, FORMER OR CURRENT. IN THIS, AS IN ALL THINGS, I AM LEGAL.

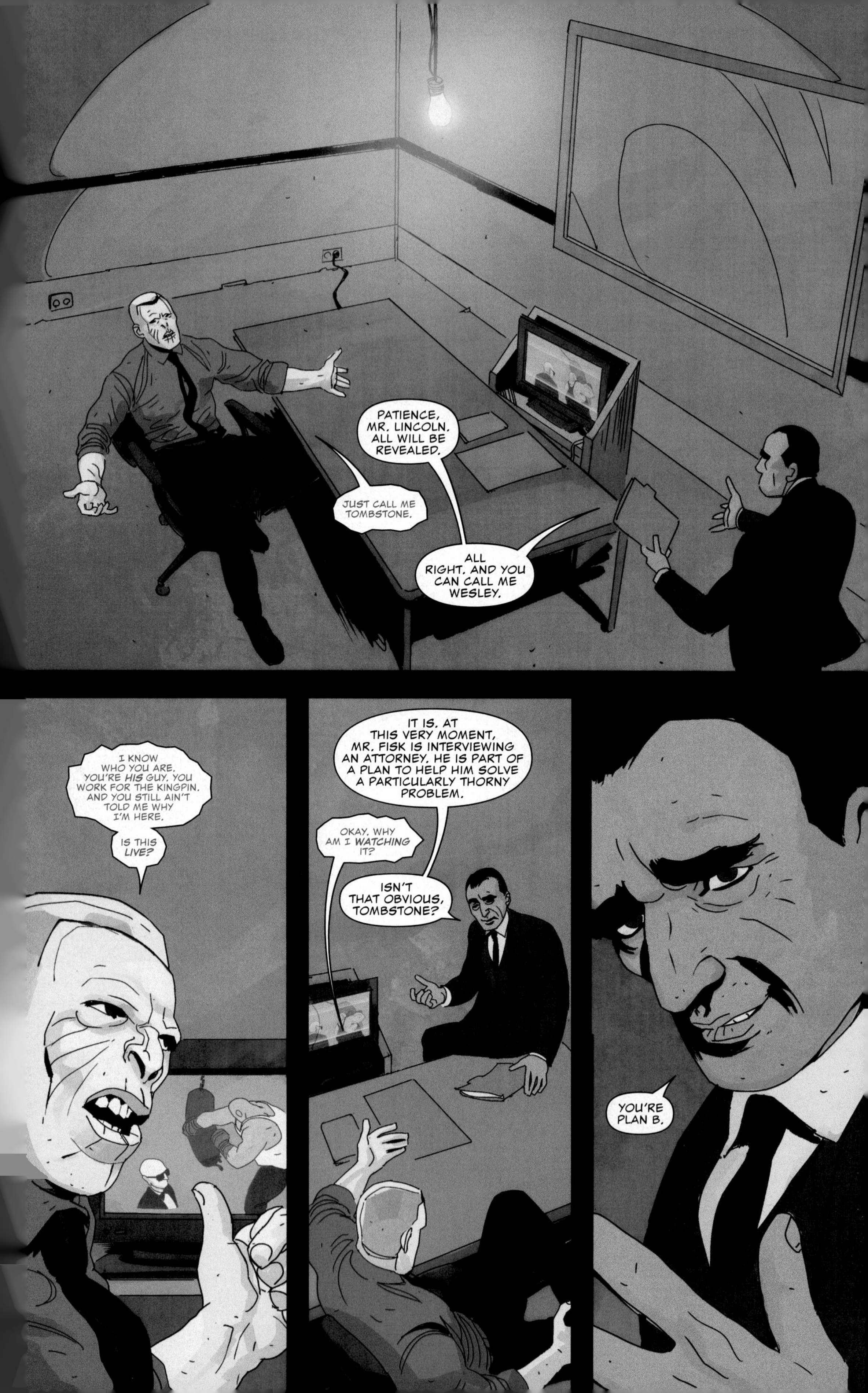
PATIENCE, MR. LINCOLN. ALL WILL BE REVEALED.
JUST CALL ME TOMBSTONE.
ALL RIGHT. AND YOU CAN CALL ME WESLEY.
I KNOW WHO YOU ARE. YOU'RE *HIS* GUY. YOU WORK FOR THE KINGPIN. AND YOU STILL AIN'T TOLD ME WHY I'M HERE.
IS THIS *LIVE?*
IT IS. AT THIS VERY MOMENT, MR. FISK IS INTERVIEWING AN ATTORNEY. HE IS PART OF A PLAN TO HELP HIM SOLVE A PARTICULARLY THORNY PROBLEM.
OKAY. WHY AM I *WATCHING* IT?
ISN'T THAT OBVIOUS, TOMBSTONE?
YOU'RE PLAN B.

THE MANHATTAN DISTRICT ATTORNEY'S OFFICE IS PURSUING A CRIMINAL CASE AGAINST A MAN NAMED SIMON SLUGANSKY.

THE CHARGES VARY--THE MOST SIGNIFICANT BEING CERTAIN ALLEGED TERRORIST ACTIONS.

THIS, IN ITSELF, IS NOT UNUSUAL. IT IS THE D.A.'S JOB. WHAT IS A BIT MORE UNORTHODOX HERE, HOWEVER, IS--

WHM

DAREDEVIL.

JUST SO. THE LEAD ATTORNEY FOR THE CITY IS A MAN NAMED MATTHEW MURDOCK.

HE IS VERY GOOD. I'M SURE HE COULD HAVE SUCCESSFULLY PROSECUTED MR. SLUGANSKY IN THE TRADITIONAL MANNER.

INSTEAD, HE CALLED *DAREDEVIL* AS HIS LEAD WITNESS.

THIS CREATED A HOST OF COMPLICATIONS, BECAUSE THE PROSECUTION INSISTED THAT DAREDEVIL DID NOT HAVE TO REVEAL HIS ACTUAL IDENTITY IN ORDER TO TESTIFY.

THEY TREATED HIM AS A CONFIDENTIAL WITNESS, AND WHEN THE DEFENSE MOVED TO COMPEL THE RELEASE OF HIS TRUE NAME, THE TRIAL COURT JUDGE RULED AGAINST THEM.

THE DEFENSE APPEALED, BUT THAT RULING WAS UPHELD AT THE APPELLATE LEVEL. THEY APPEALED *AGAIN*, WHICH BRINGS US TO NOW.

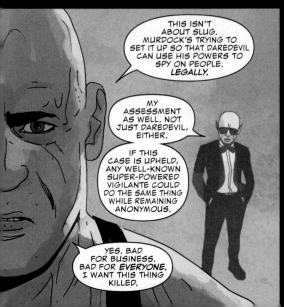

THIS ISN'T ABOUT SLUG. MURDOCK'S TRYING TO SET IT UP SO THAT DAREDEVIL CAN USE HIS POWERS TO SPY ON PEOPLE. *LEGALLY.*

MY ASSESSMENT AS WELL. NOT JUST DAREDEVIL, EITHER.

IF THIS CASE IS UPHELD, ANY WELL-KNOWN SUPER-POWERED VIGILANTE COULD DO THE SAME THING WHILE REMAINING ANONYMOUS.

YES. BAD FOR BUSINESS. BAD FOR *EVERYONE.* I WANT THIS THING KILLED.

ONE WAY OR THE OTHER.

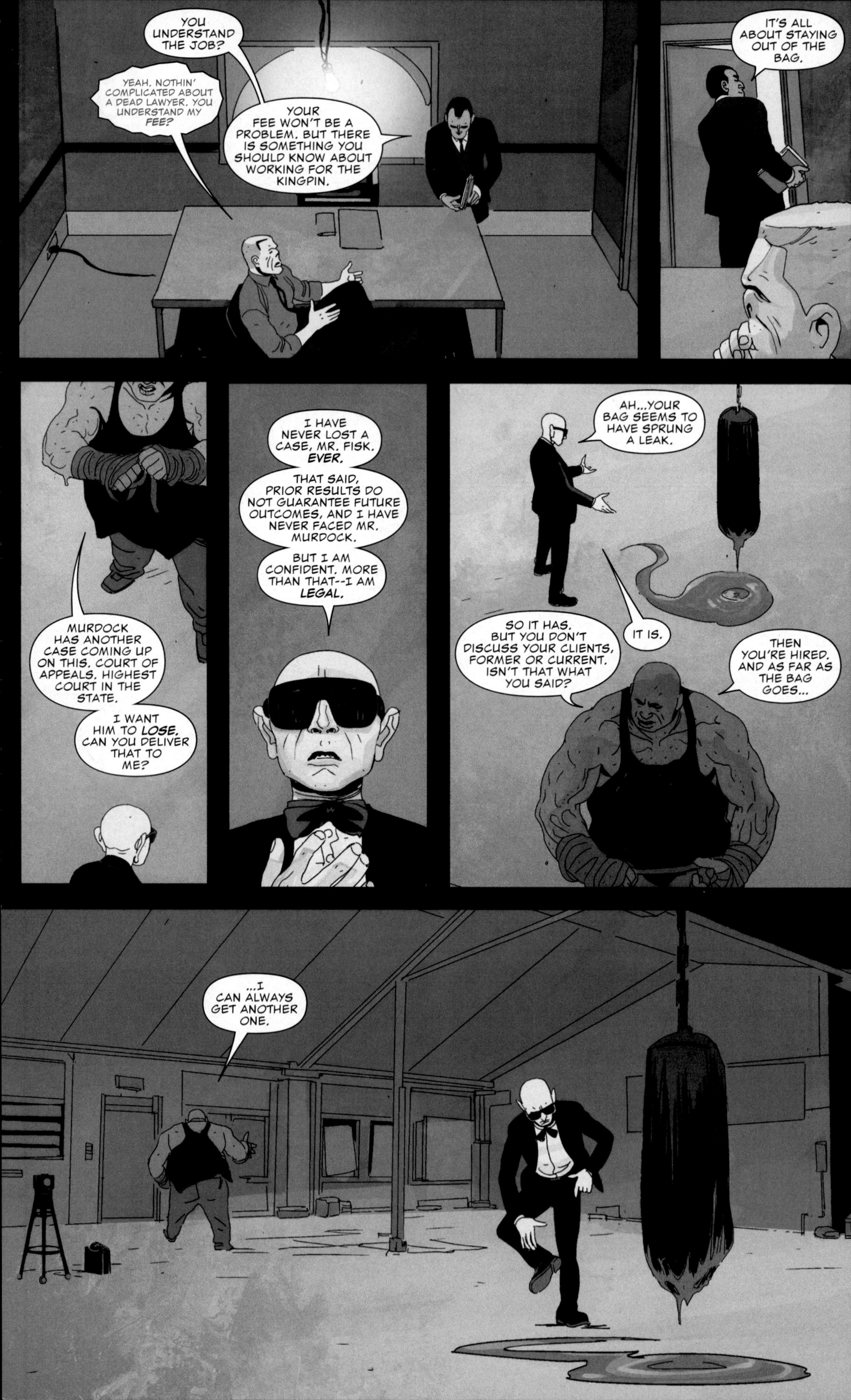

YOU UNDERSTAND THE JOB?
YEAH. NOTHIN' COMPLICATED ABOUT A DEAD LAWYER. YOU UNDERSTAND MY FEE?
YOUR FEE WON'T BE A PROBLEM. BUT THERE IS SOMETHING YOU SHOULD KNOW ABOUT WORKING FOR THE KINGPIN.
IT'S ALL ABOUT STAYING OUT OF THE BAG.
MURDOCK HAS ANOTHER CASE COMING UP ON THIS. COURT OF APPEALS. HIGHEST COURT IN THE STATE.
I WANT HIM TO LOSE. CAN YOU DELIVER THAT TO ME?
I HAVE NEVER LOST A CASE, MR. FISK. EVER.
THAT SAID, PRIOR RESULTS DO NOT GUARANTEE FUTURE OUTCOMES, AND I HAVE NEVER FACED MR. MURDOCK.
BUT I AM CONFIDENT. MORE THAN THAT--I AM LEGAL.
AH...YOUR BAG SEEMS TO HAVE SPRUNG A LEAK.
IT IS.
SO IT HAS. BUT YOU DON'T DISCUSS YOUR CLIENTS, FORMER OR CURRENT. ISN'T THAT WHAT YOU SAID?
THEN YOU'RE HIRED. AND AS FAR AS THE BAG GOES...
...I CAN ALWAYS GET ANOTHER ONE.

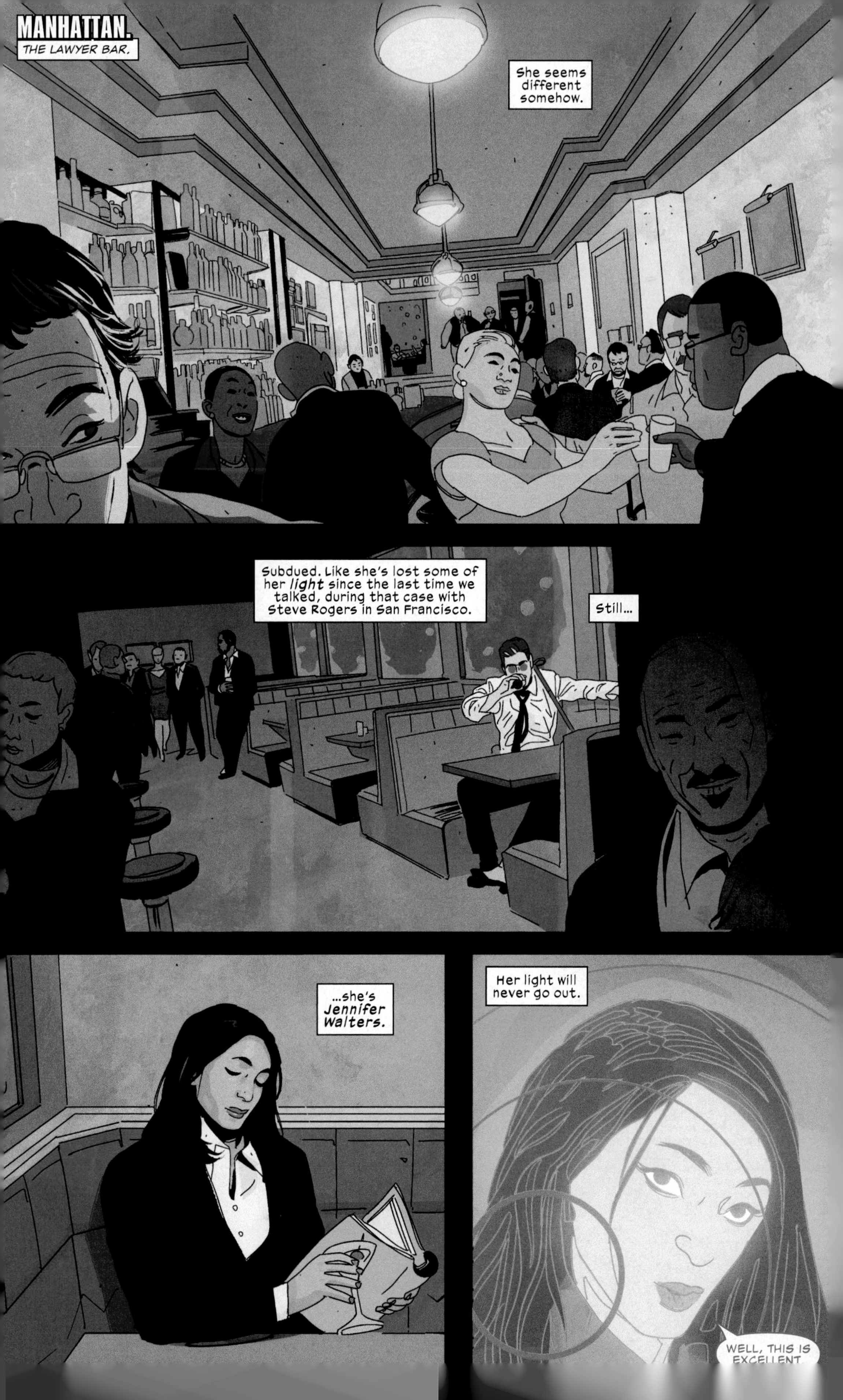

MANHATTAN.
THE LAWYER BAR.
She seems different somehow.
Subdued. Like she's lost some of her *light* since the last time we talked, during that case with Steve Rogers in San Francisco.
Still...
...she's *Jennifer Walters.*
Her light will never go out.
WELL, THIS IS

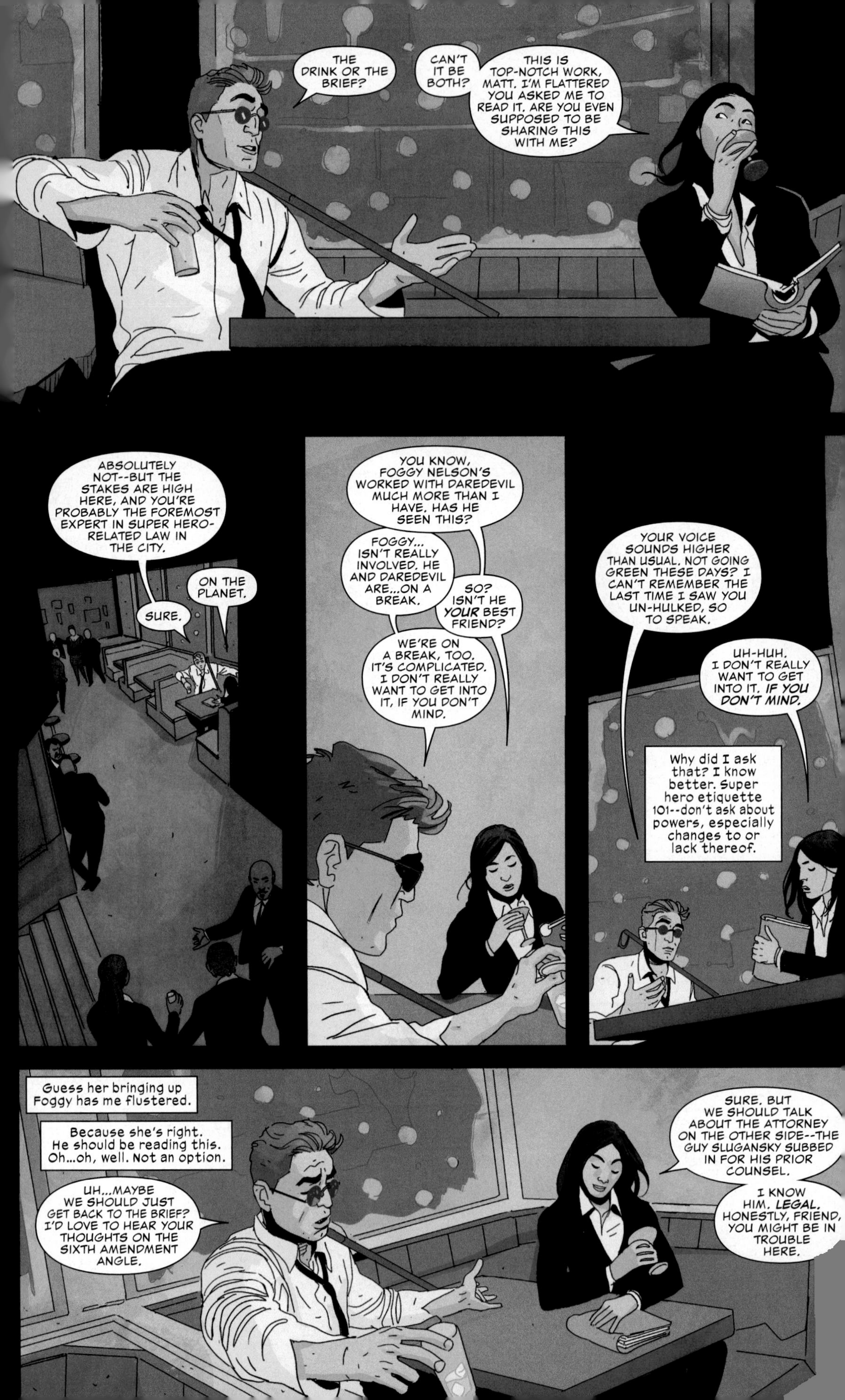
THE DRINK OR THE BRIEF?
CAN'T IT BE BOTH?
THIS IS TOP-NOTCH WORK, MATT. I'M FLATTERED YOU ASKED ME TO READ IT. ARE YOU EVEN SUPPOSED TO BE SHARING THIS WITH ME?
ABSOLUTELY NOT--BUT THE STAKES ARE HIGH HERE, AND YOU'RE PROBABLY THE FOREMOST EXPERT IN SUPER HERO-RELATED LAW IN THE CITY.
SURE.
ON THE PLANET.
YOU KNOW, FOGGY NELSON'S WORKED WITH DAREDEVIL MUCH MORE THAN I HAVE. HAS HE SEEN THIS?
FOGGY... ISN'T REALLY INVOLVED. HE AND DAREDEVIL ARE...ON A BREAK.
SO? ISN'T HE *YOUR* BEST FRIEND?
WE'RE ON A BREAK, TOO. IT'S COMPLICATED. I DON'T REALLY WANT TO GET INTO IT, IF YOU DON'T MIND.
YOUR VOICE SOUNDS HIGHER THAN USUAL. NOT GOING GREEN THESE DAYS? I CAN'T REMEMBER THE LAST TIME I SAW YOU UN-HULKED, SO TO SPEAK.
UH-HUH. I DON'T REALLY WANT TO GET INTO IT. *IF YOU DON'T MIND.*
Why did I ask that? I know better. Super hero etiquette 101--don't ask about powers, especially changes to or lack thereof.
Guess her bringing up Foggy has me flustered.
Because she's right. He should be reading this. Oh...oh, well. Not an option.
UH...MAYBE WE SHOULD JUST GET BACK TO THE BRIEF? I'D LOVE TO HEAR YOUR THOUGHTS ON THE SIXTH AMENDMENT ANGLE.
SURE. BUT WE SHOULD TALK ABOUT THE ATTORNEY ON THE OTHER SIDE--THE GUY SLUGANSKY SUBBED IN FOR HIS PRIOR COUNSEL.
I KNOW HIM. *LEGAL.* HONESTLY, FRIEND, YOU MIGHT BE IN TROUBLE HERE.

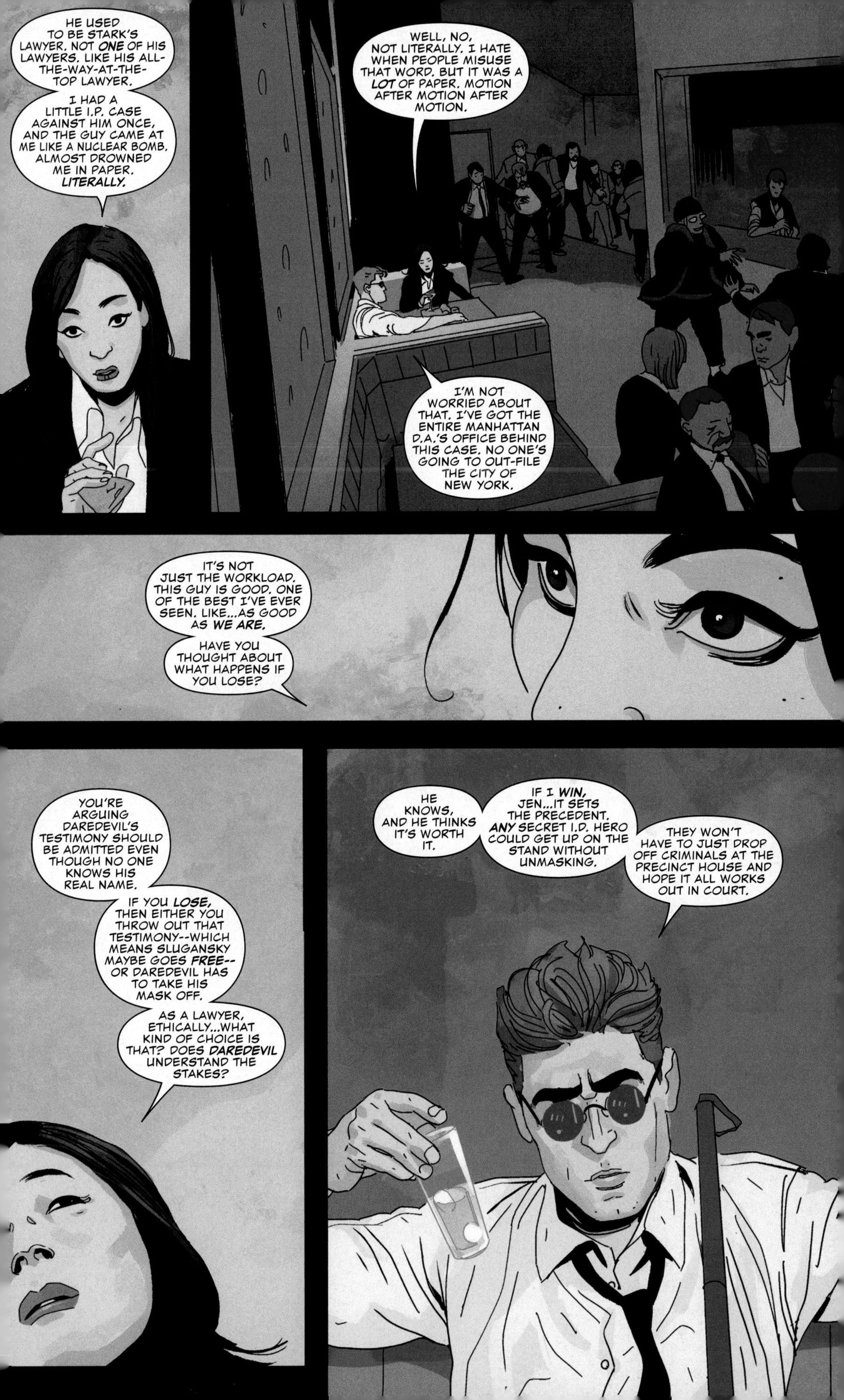
HE USED TO BE STARK'S LAWYER. NOT ONE OF HIS LAWYERS. LIKE HIS ALL-THE-WAY-AT-THE-TOP LAWYER.
I HAD A LITTLE I.P. CASE AGAINST HIM ONCE, AND THE GUY CAME AT ME LIKE A NUCLEAR BOMB. ALMOST DROWNED ME IN PAPER. LITERALLY.
WELL, NO, NOT LITERALLY. I HATE WHEN PEOPLE MISUSE THAT WORD. BUT IT WAS A LOT OF PAPER. MOTION AFTER MOTION AFTER MOTION.
I'M NOT WORRIED ABOUT THAT. I'VE GOT THE ENTIRE MANHATTAN D.A.'S OFFICE BEHIND THIS CASE. NO ONE'S GOING TO OUT-FILE THE CITY OF NEW YORK.
IT'S NOT JUST THE WORKLOAD. THIS GUY IS GOOD. ONE OF THE BEST I'VE EVER SEEN. LIKE...AS GOOD AS WE ARE.
HAVE YOU THOUGHT ABOUT WHAT HAPPENS IF YOU LOSE?
YOU'RE ARGUING DAREDEVIL'S TESTIMONY SHOULD BE ADMITTED EVEN THOUGH NO ONE KNOWS HIS REAL NAME.
IF YOU LOSE, THEN EITHER YOU THROW OUT THAT TESTIMONY--WHICH MEANS SLUGANSKY MAYBE GOES FREE--OR DAREDEVIL HAS TO TAKE HIS MASK OFF.
AS A LAWYER, ETHICALLY...WHAT KIND OF CHOICE IS THAT? DOES DAREDEVIL UNDERSTAND THE STAKES?
HE KNOWS, AND HE THINKS IT'S WORTH IT.
IF I WIN, JEN...IT SETS THE PRECEDENT. ANY SECRET I.D. HERO COULD GET UP ON THE STAND WITHOUT UNMASKING.
THEY WON'T HAVE TO JUST DROP OFF CRIMINALS AT THE PRECINCT HOUSE AND HOPE IT ALL WORKS OUT IN COURT.

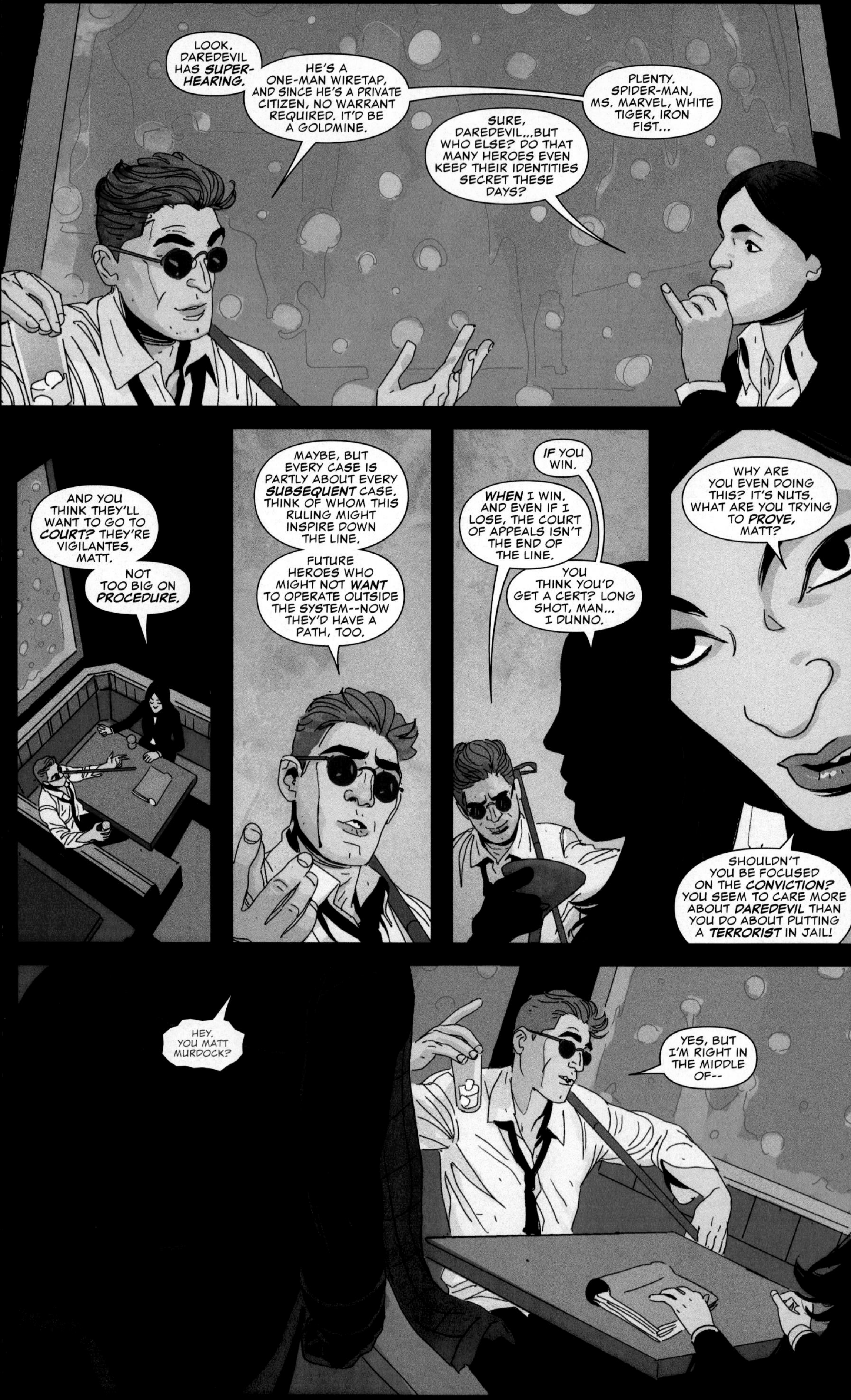

LOOK. DAREDEVIL HAS SUPER-HEARING.
HE'S A ONE-MAN WIRETAP, AND SINCE HE'S A PRIVATE CITIZEN, NO WARRANT REQUIRED. IT'D BE A GOLDMINE.
SURE, DAREDEVIL...BUT WHO ELSE? DO THAT MANY HEROES EVEN KEEP THEIR IDENTITIES SECRET THESE DAYS?
PLENTY. SPIDER-MAN, MS. MARVEL, WHITE TIGER, IRON FIST...
AND YOU THINK THEY'LL WANT TO GO TO COURT? THEY'RE VIGILANTES, MATT.
NOT TOO BIG ON PROCEDURE.
MAYBE, BUT EVERY CASE IS PARTLY ABOUT EVERY SUBSEQUENT CASE. THINK OF WHOM THIS RULING MIGHT INSPIRE DOWN THE LINE.
FUTURE HEROES WHO MIGHT NOT WANT TO OPERATE OUTSIDE THE SYSTEM--NOW THEY'D HAVE A PATH, TOO.
IF YOU WIN.
WHEN I WIN. AND EVEN IF I LOSE, THE COURT OF APPEALS ISN'T THE END OF THE LINE.
YOU THINK YOU'D GET A CERT? LONG SHOT, MAN... I DUNNO.
WHY ARE YOU EVEN DOING THIS? IT'S NUTS. WHAT ARE YOU TRYING TO PROVE, MATT?
SHOULDN'T YOU BE FOCUSED ON THE CONVICTION? YOU SEEM TO CARE MORE ABOUT DAREDEVIL THAN YOU DO ABOUT PUTTING A TERRORIST IN JAIL!
HEY. YOU MATT MURDOCK?
YES, BUT I'M RIGHT IN THE MIDDLE OF--

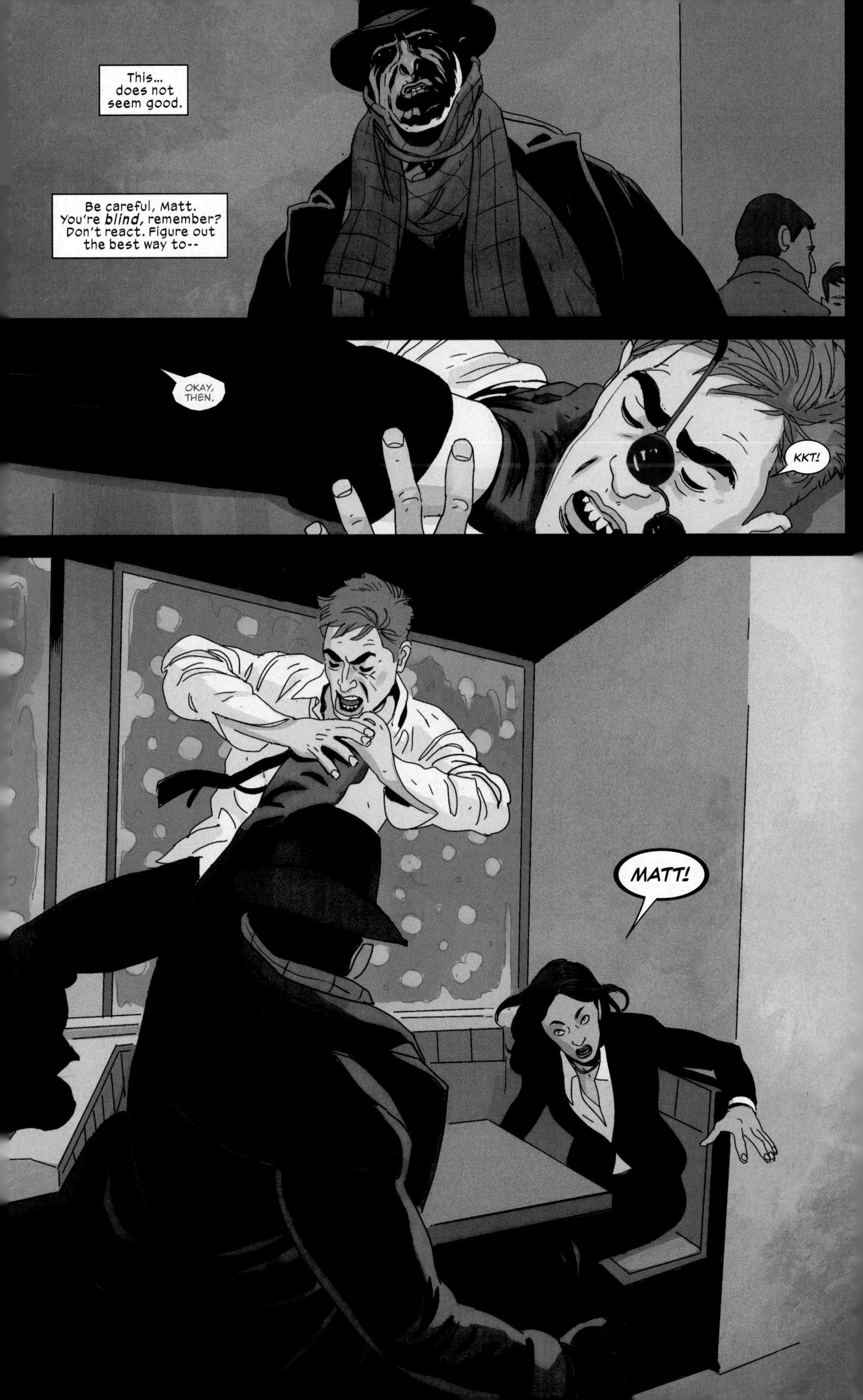
This... does not seem good.
Be careful, Matt. You're *blind*, remember? Don't react. Figure out the best way to--
OKAY, THEN.
KKT!
MATT!

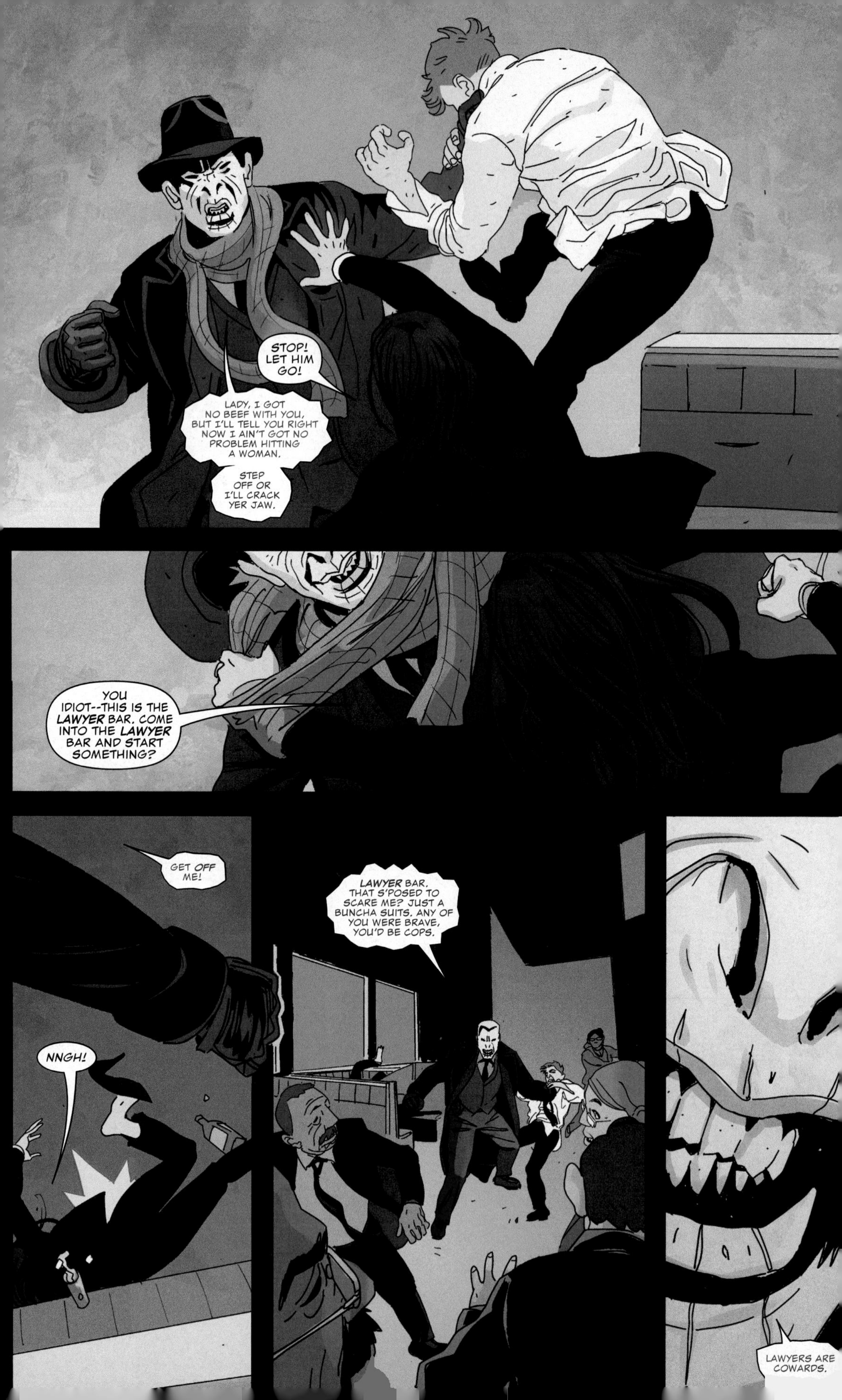
STOP! LET HIM GO!
LADY, I GOT NO BEEF WITH YOU, BUT I'LL TELL YOU RIGHT NOW I AIN'T GOT NO PROBLEM HITTING A WOMAN.
STEP OFF OR I'LL CRACK YER JAW.
YOU IDIOT--THIS IS THE LAWYER BAR. COME INTO THE LAWYER BAR AND START SOMETHING?
GET OFF ME!
NNGH!
LAWYER BAR. THAT S'POSED TO SCARE ME? JUST A BUNCHA SUITS. ANY OF YOU WERE BRAVE, YOU'D BE COPS.
LAWYERS ARE COWARDS.

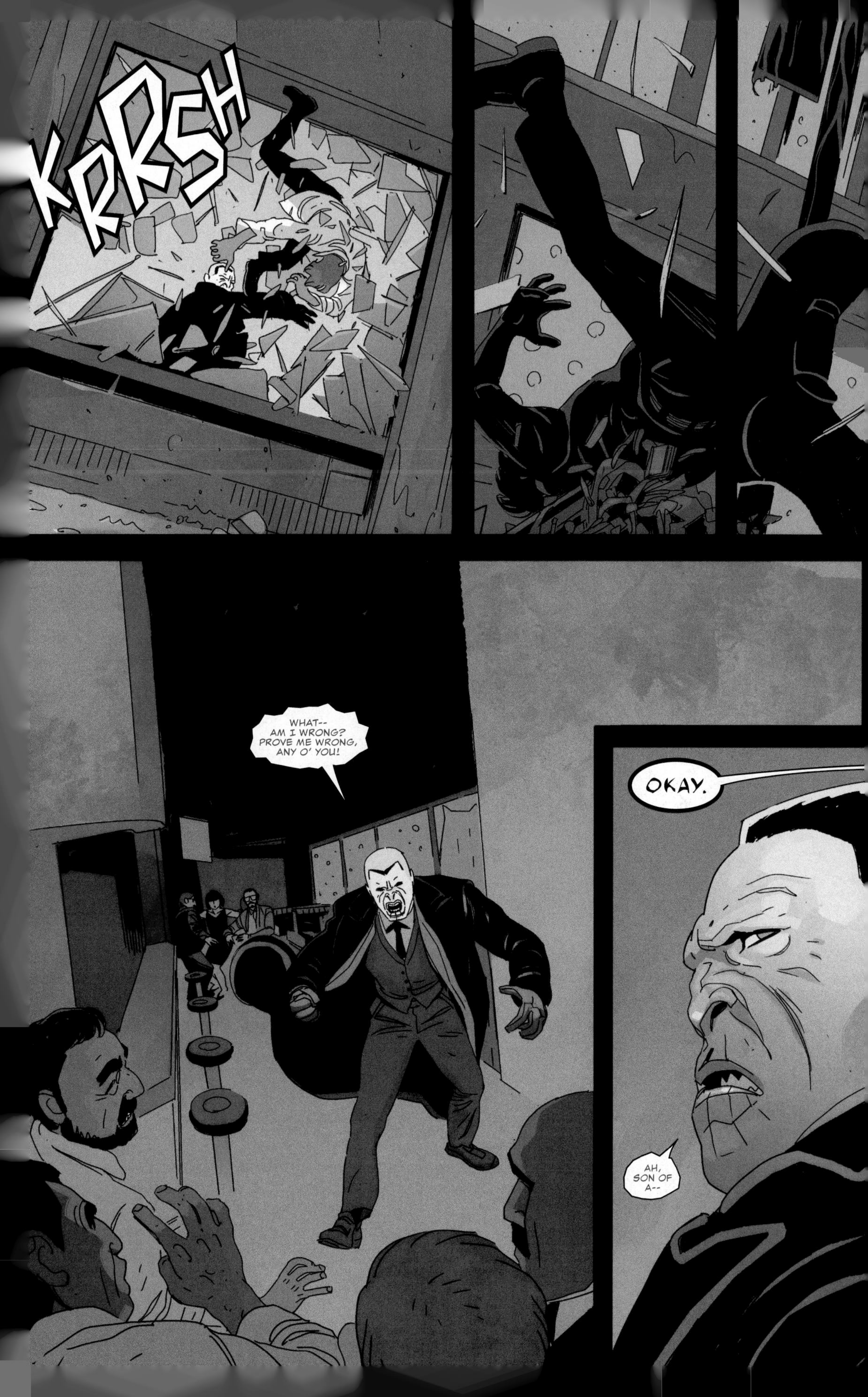
KRRSH
WHAT-- AM I WRONG? PROVE ME WRONG, ANY O' YOU!
OKAY.
AH, SON OF A--

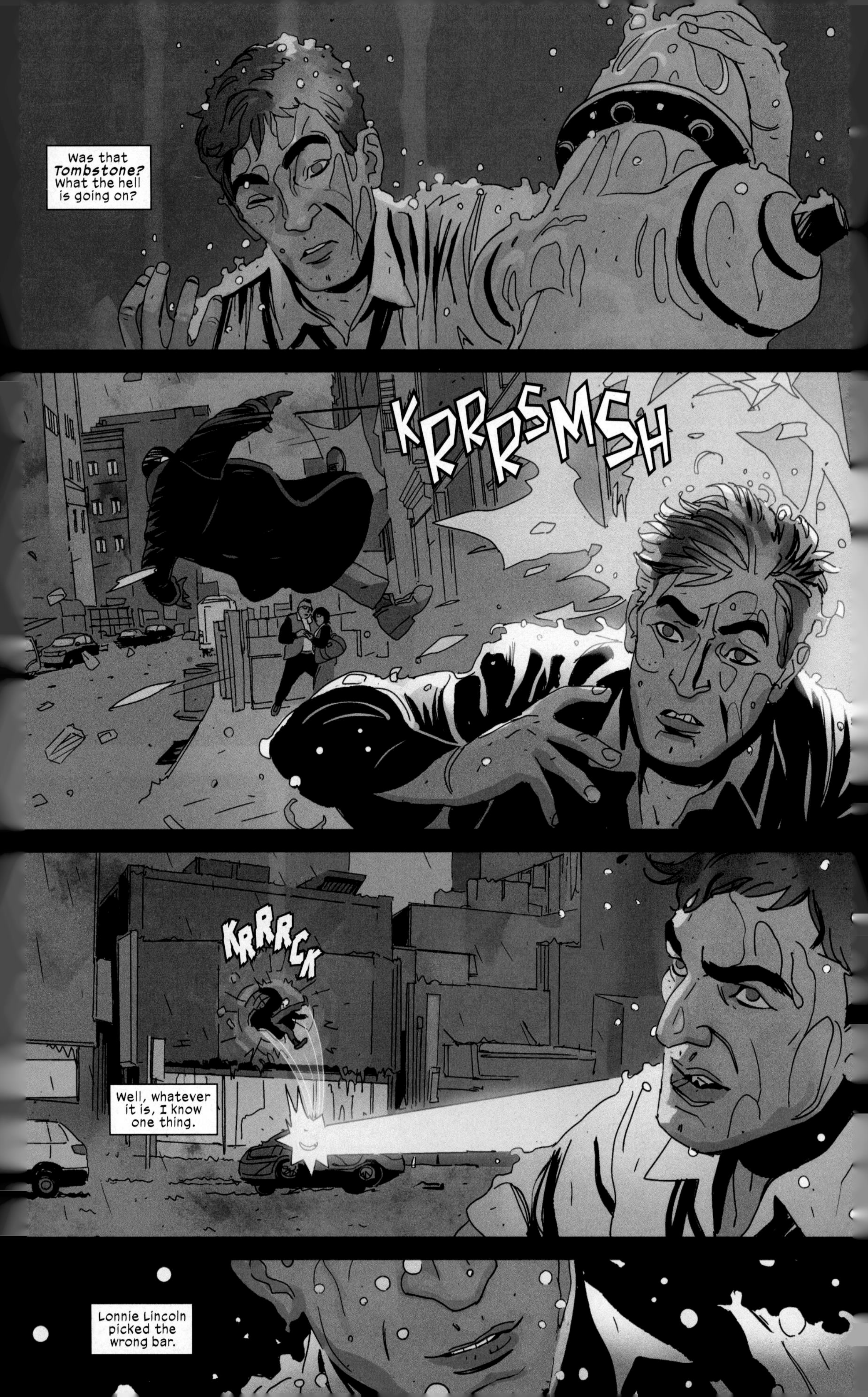
Was that Tombstone? What the hell is going on?
KRRRSMSH
KRRRCK
Well, whatever it is, I know one thing.
Lonnie Lincoln picked the wrong bar.

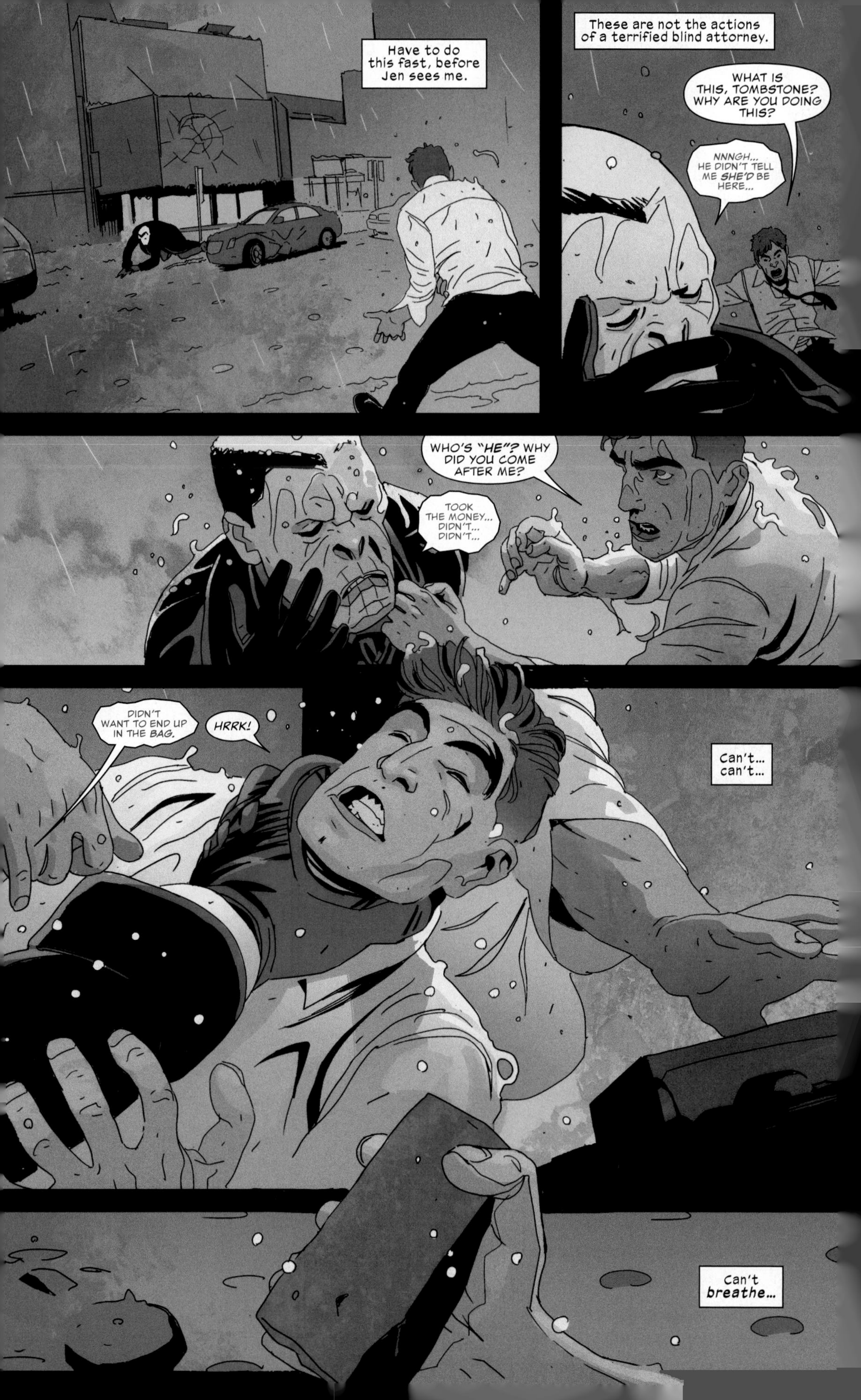
Have to do this fast, before Jen sees me.
These are not the actions of a terrified blind attorney.
WHAT IS THIS, TOMBSTONE? WHY ARE YOU DOING THIS?
NNNGH... HE DIDN'T TELL ME SHE'D BE HERE...
WHO'S "HE"? WHY DID YOU COME AFTER ME?
TOOK THE MONEY... DIDN'T... DIDN'T...
DIDN'T WANT TO END UP IN THE BAG.
HRRK!
Can't... can't...
Can't breathe...

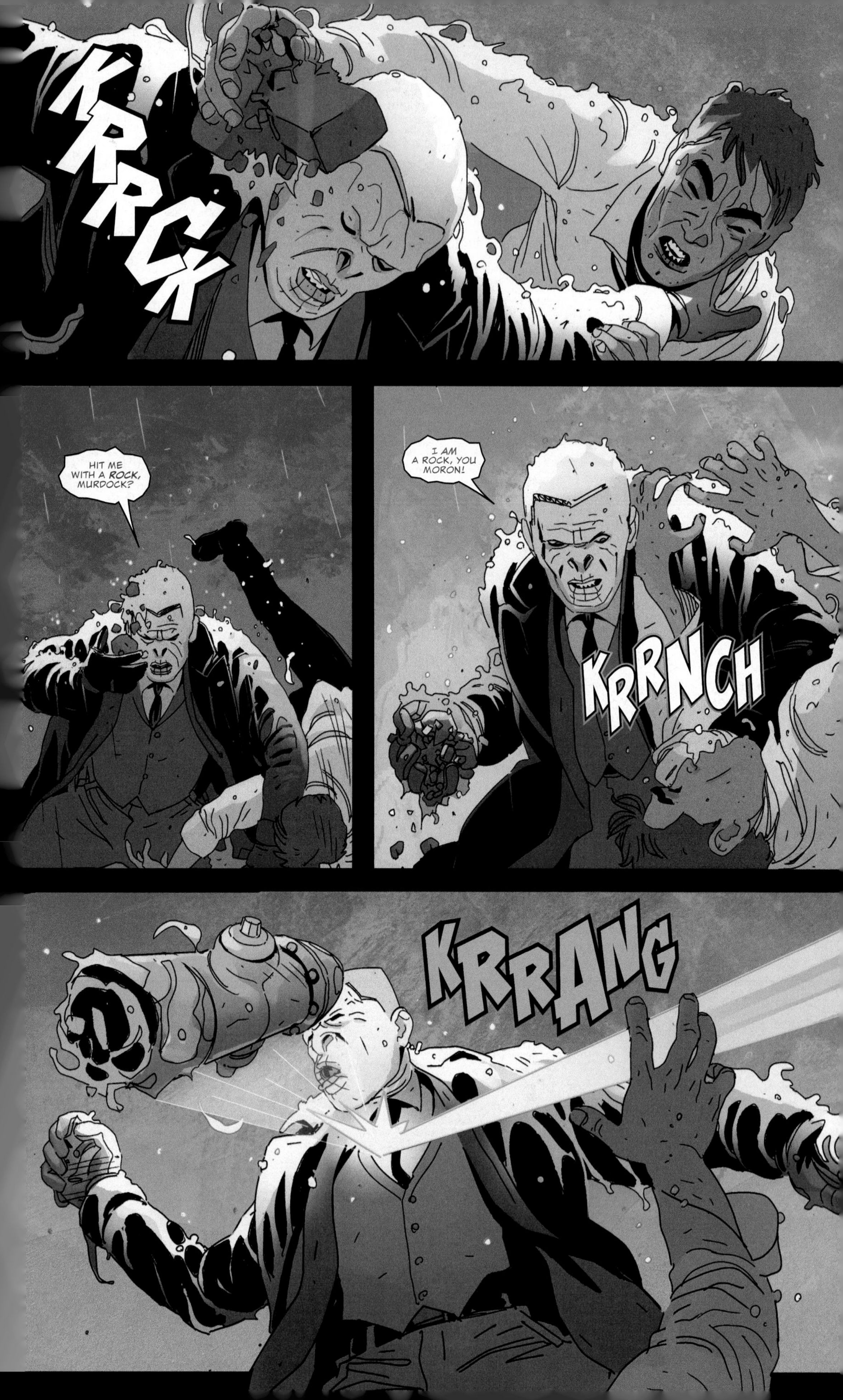
KRRCK
HIT ME WITH A ROCK, MURDOCK?
I AM A ROCK, YOU MORON!
KRRNCH
KRRANG

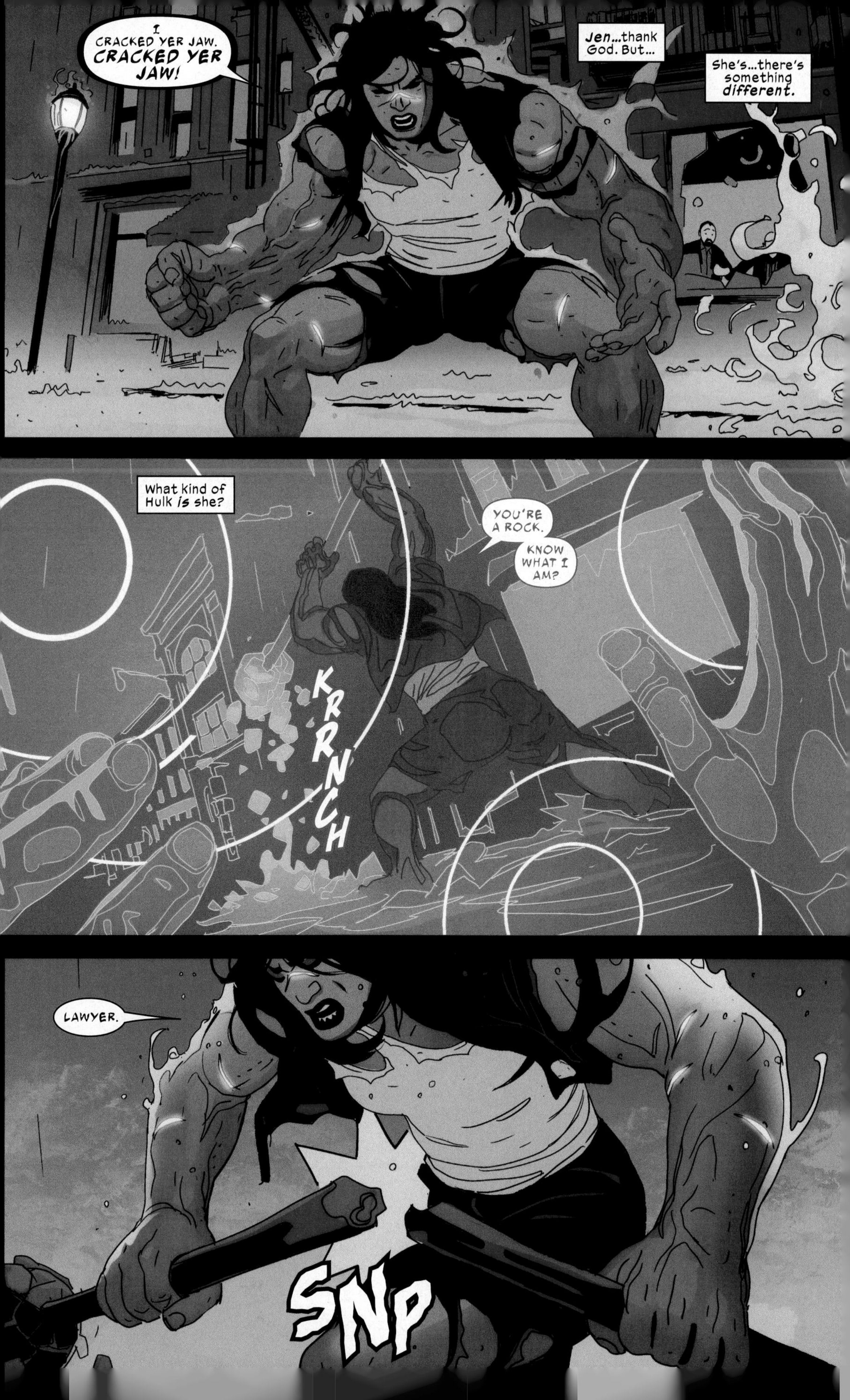
I CRACKED YER JAW. CRACKED YER JAW!
Jen...thank God. But...
She's...there's something different.
What kind of Hulk is she?
YOU'RE A ROCK.
KNOW WHAT I AM?
KRRNCH
LAWYER.
SNP

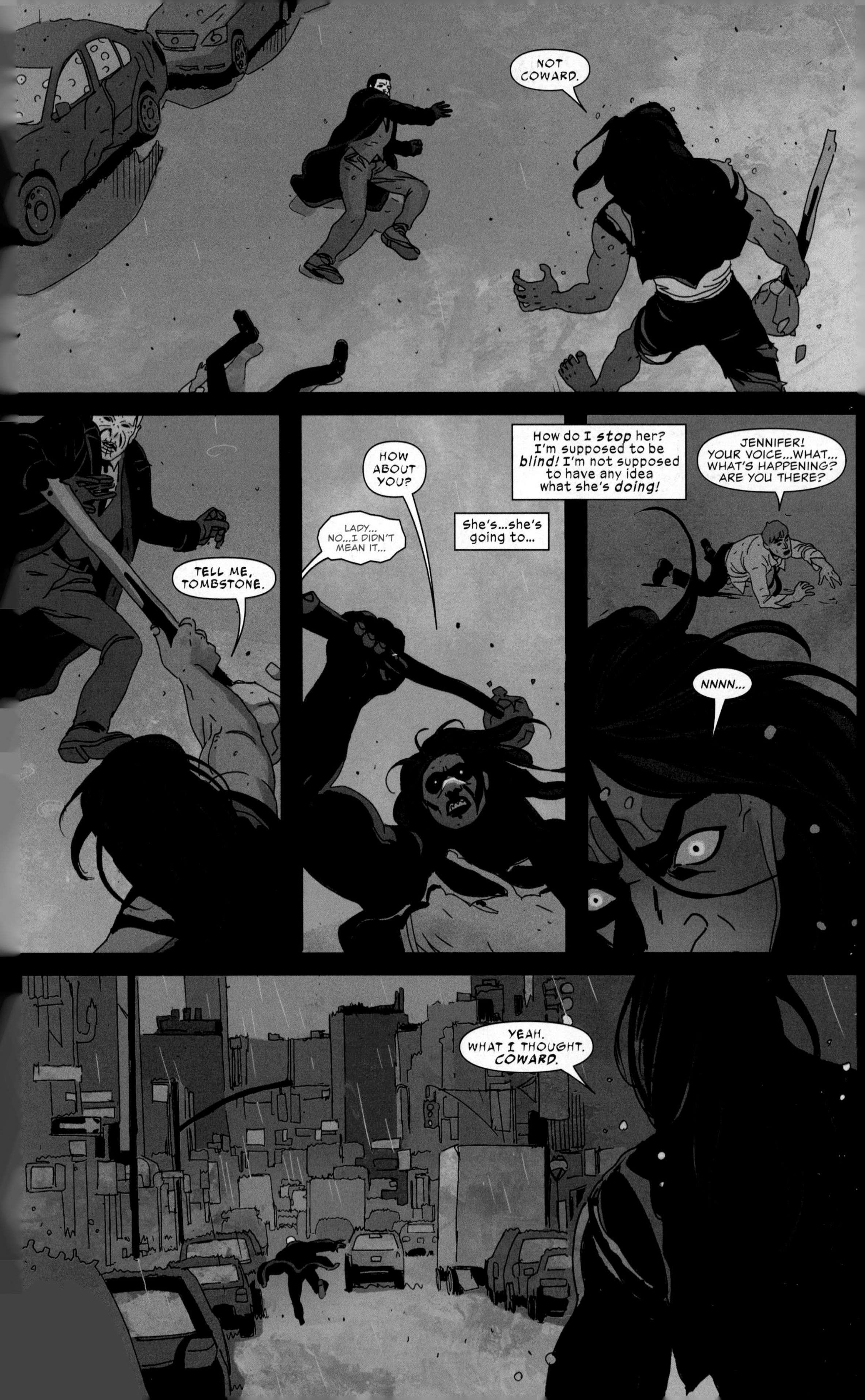
NOT COWARD.
TELL ME, TOMBSTONE.
HOW ABOUT YOU?
LADY... NO...I DIDN'T MEAN IT...
She's...she's going to...
How do I *stop* her? I'm supposed to be *blind!* I'm not supposed to have any idea what she's *doing!*
JENNIFER! YOUR VOICE...WHAT... WHAT'S HAPPENING? ARE YOU THERE?
NNNN...
YEAH. WHAT I THOUGHT. **COWARD.**

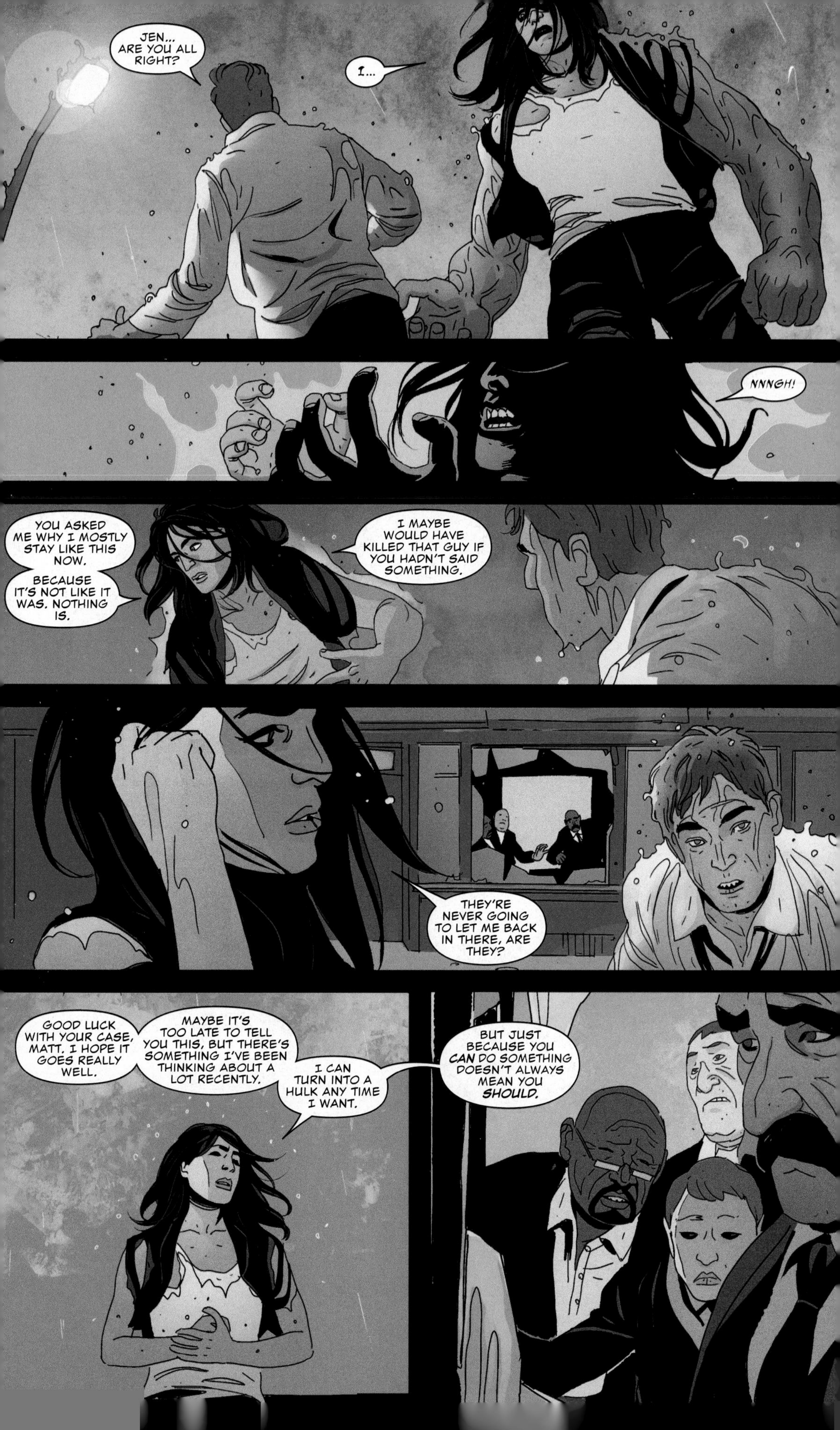
JEN... ARE YOU ALL RIGHT?
I...
NNNGH!
YOU ASKED ME WHY I MOSTLY STAY LIKE THIS NOW.
BECAUSE IT'S NOT LIKE IT WAS. NOTHING IS.
I MAYBE WOULD HAVE KILLED THAT GUY IF YOU HADN'T SAID SOMETHING.
THEY'RE NEVER GOING TO LET ME BACK IN THERE, ARE THEY?
GOOD LUCK WITH YOUR CASE, MATT. I HOPE IT GOES REALLY WELL.
MAYBE IT'S TOO LATE TO TELL YOU THIS, BUT THERE'S SOMETHING I'VE BEEN THINKING ABOUT A LOT RECENTLY.
I CAN TURN INTO A HULK ANY TIME I WANT.
BUT JUST BECAUSE YOU CAN DO SOMETHING DOESN'T ALWAYS MEAN YOU SHOULD.

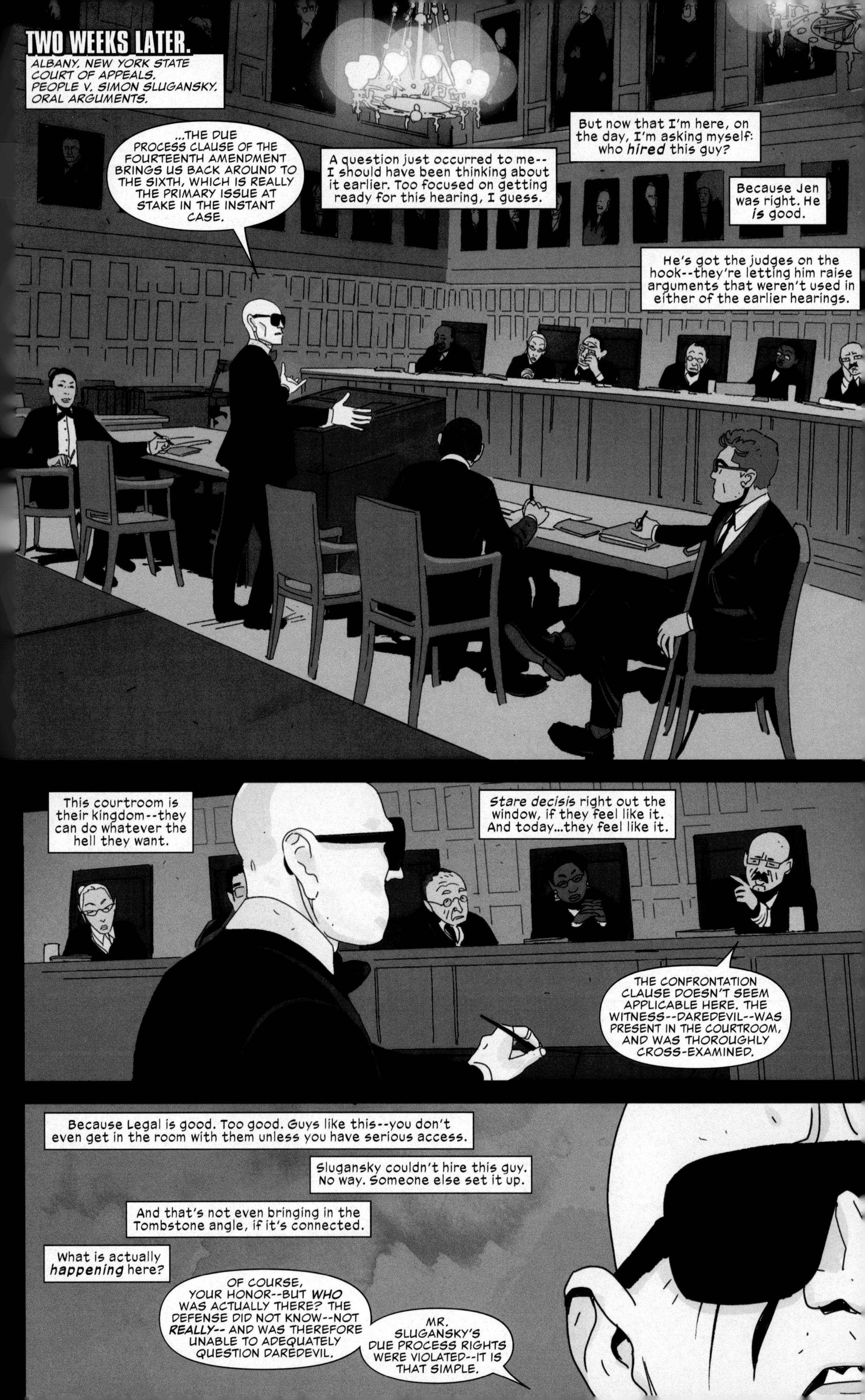
TWO WEEKS LATER.
ALBANY, NEW YORK STATE COURT OF APPEALS. PEOPLE V. SIMON SLUGANSKY. ORAL ARGUMENTS.
...THE DUE PROCESS CLAUSE OF THE FOURTEENTH AMENDMENT BRINGS US BACK AROUND TO THE SIXTH, WHICH IS REALLY THE PRIMARY ISSUE AT STAKE IN THE INSTANT CASE.
A question just occurred to me--I should have been thinking about it earlier. Too focused on getting ready for this hearing, I guess.
But now that I'm here, on the day, I'm asking myself: who *hired* this guy?
Because Jen was right. He *is* good.
He's got the judges on the hook--they're letting him raise arguments that weren't used in either of the earlier hearings.
This courtroom is their kingdom--they can do whatever the hell they want.
Stare decisis right out the window, if they feel like it. And today...they feel like it.
THE CONFRONTATION CLAUSE DOESN'T SEEM APPLICABLE HERE. THE WITNESS--DAREDEVIL--WAS PRESENT IN THE COURTROOM, AND WAS THOROUGHLY CROSS-EXAMINED.
Because Legal is good. Too good. Guys like this--you don't even get in the room with them unless you have serious access.
Slugansky couldn't hire this guy. No way. Someone else set it up.
And that's not even bringing in the Tombstone angle, if it's connected.
What is actually *happening* here?
OF COURSE, YOUR HONOR--BUT *WHO* WAS ACTUALLY THERE? THE DEFENSE DID NOT KNOW--NOT *REALLY*-- AND WAS THEREFORE UNABLE TO ADEQUATELY QUESTION DAREDEVIL.
MR. SLUGANSKY'S DUE PROCESS RIGHTS WERE VIOLATED--IT IS THAT SIMPLE.

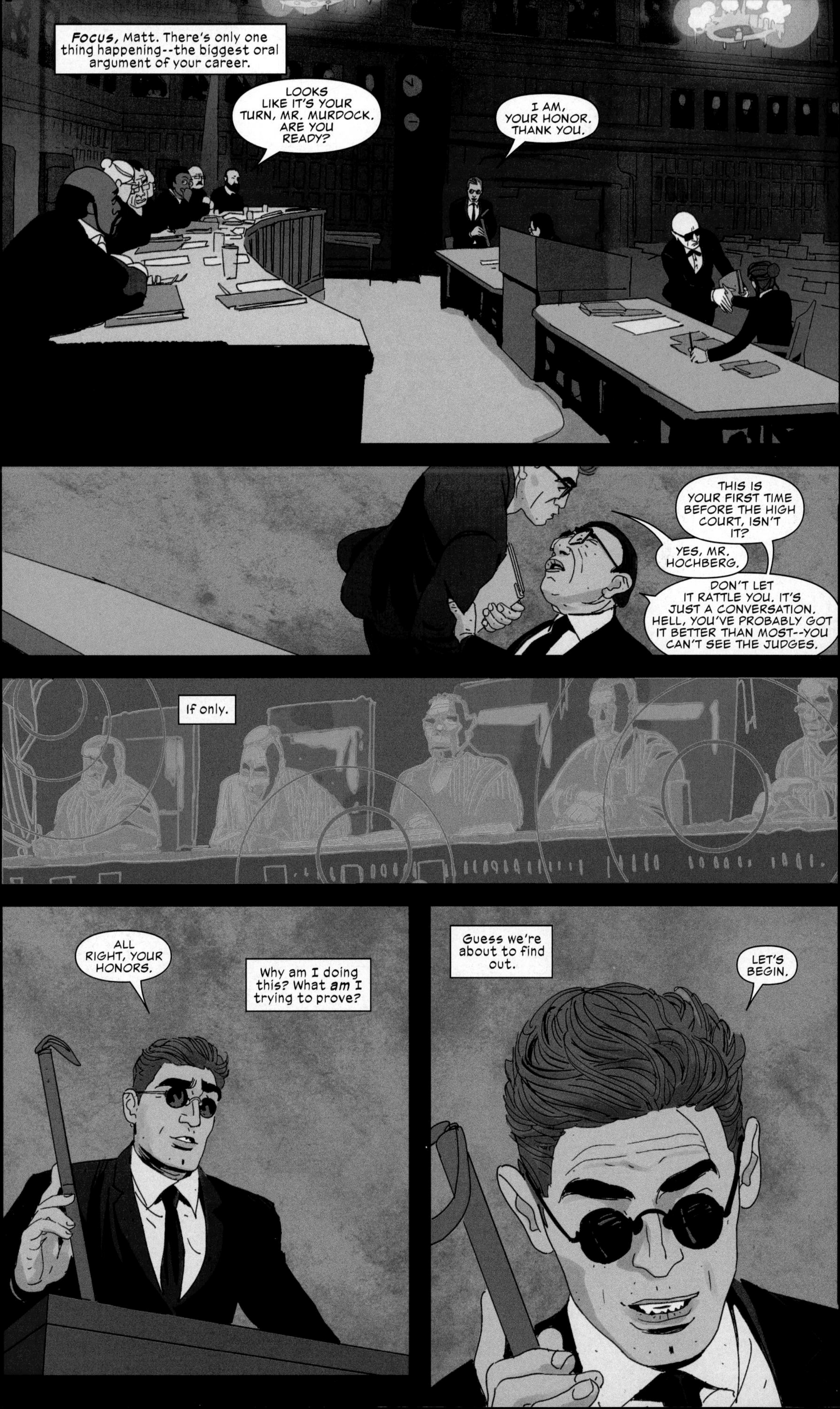

Focus, Matt. There's only one thing happening--the biggest oral argument of your career.
LOOKS LIKE IT'S YOUR TURN, MR. MURDOCK. ARE YOU READY?
I AM, YOUR HONOR. THANK YOU.
THIS IS YOUR FIRST TIME BEFORE THE HIGH COURT, ISN'T IT?
YES, MR. HOCHBERG.
DON'T LET IT RATTLE YOU. IT'S JUST A CONVERSATION. HELL, YOU'VE PROBABLY GOT IT BETTER THAN MOST--YOU CAN'T SEE THE JUDGES.
If only.
ALL RIGHT, YOUR HONORS.
Why am I doing this? What *am* I trying to prove?
Guess we're about to find out.
LET'S BEGIN.

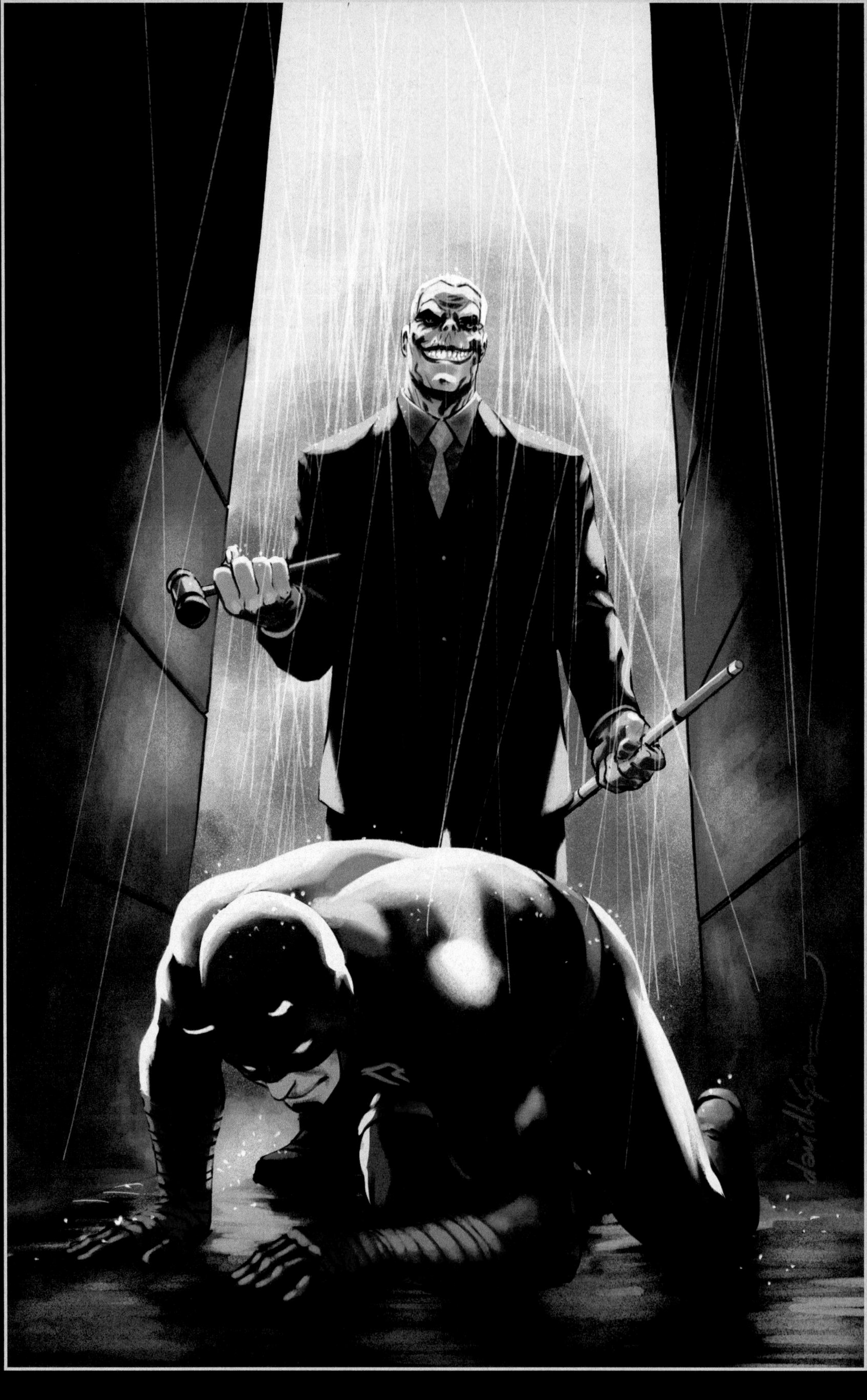

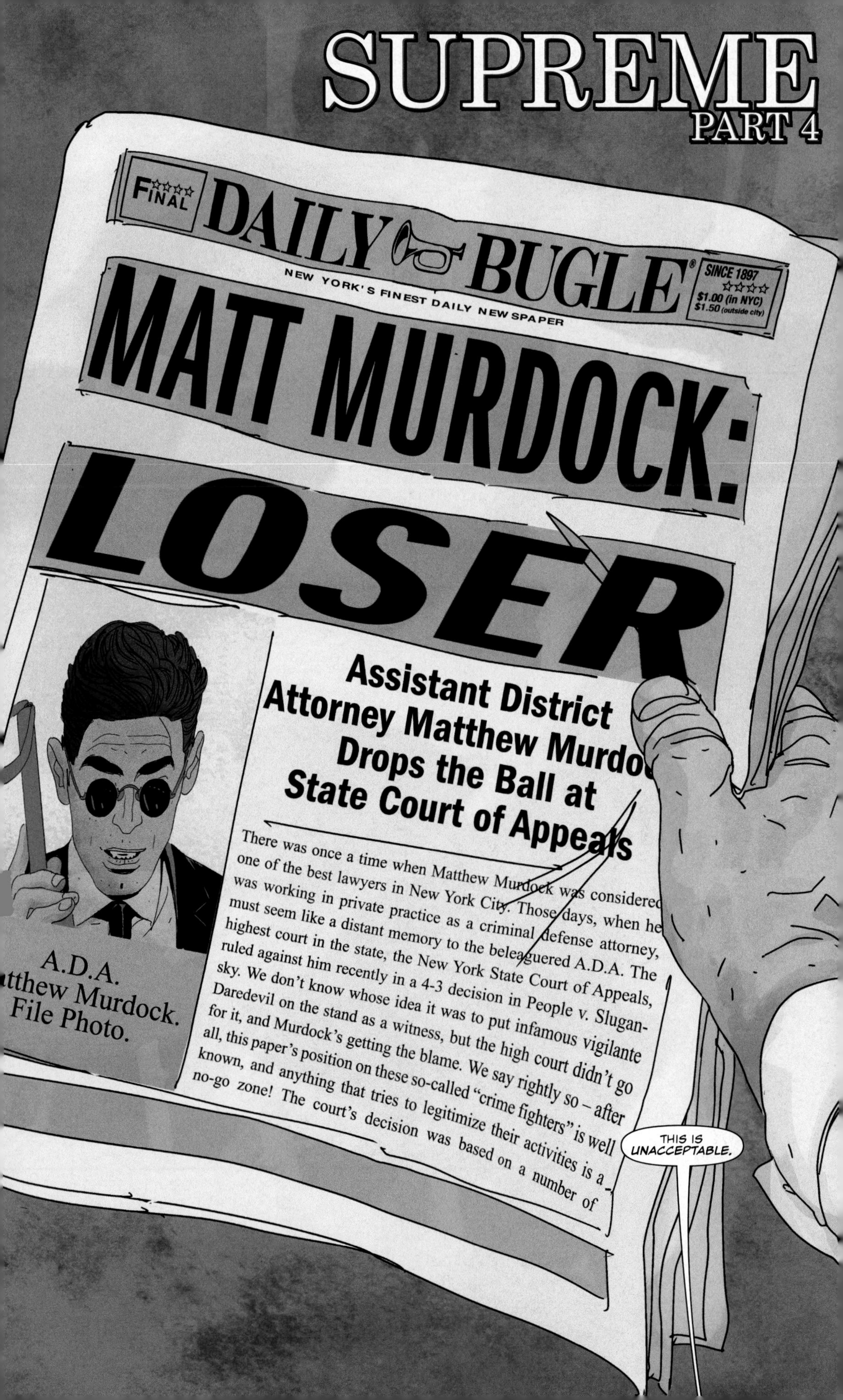
SUPREME
PART 4
FINAL
DAILY BUGLE
NEW YORK'S FINEST DAILY NEWSPAPER
SINCE 1897
$1.00 (in NYC)
$1.50 (outside city)
MATT MURDOCK:
LOSER
Assistant District Attorney Matthew Murdo
Drops the Ball at State Court of Appeals
There was once a time when Matthew Murdock was considered one of the best lawyers in New York City. Those days, when he was working in private practice as a criminal defense attorney, must seem like a distant memory to the beleaguered A.D.A. The highest court in the state, the New York State Court of Appeals, ruled against him recently in a 4-3 decision in People v. Slugan-sky. We don't know whose idea it was to put infamous vigilante Daredevil on the stand as a witness, but the high court didn't go for it, and Murdock's getting the blame. We say rightly so – after all, this paper's position on these so-called "crime fighters" is well known, and anything that tries to legitimize their activities is a no-go zone! The court's decision was based on a number of
A.D.A.
tthew Murdock.
File Photo.
THIS IS UNACCEPTABLE.

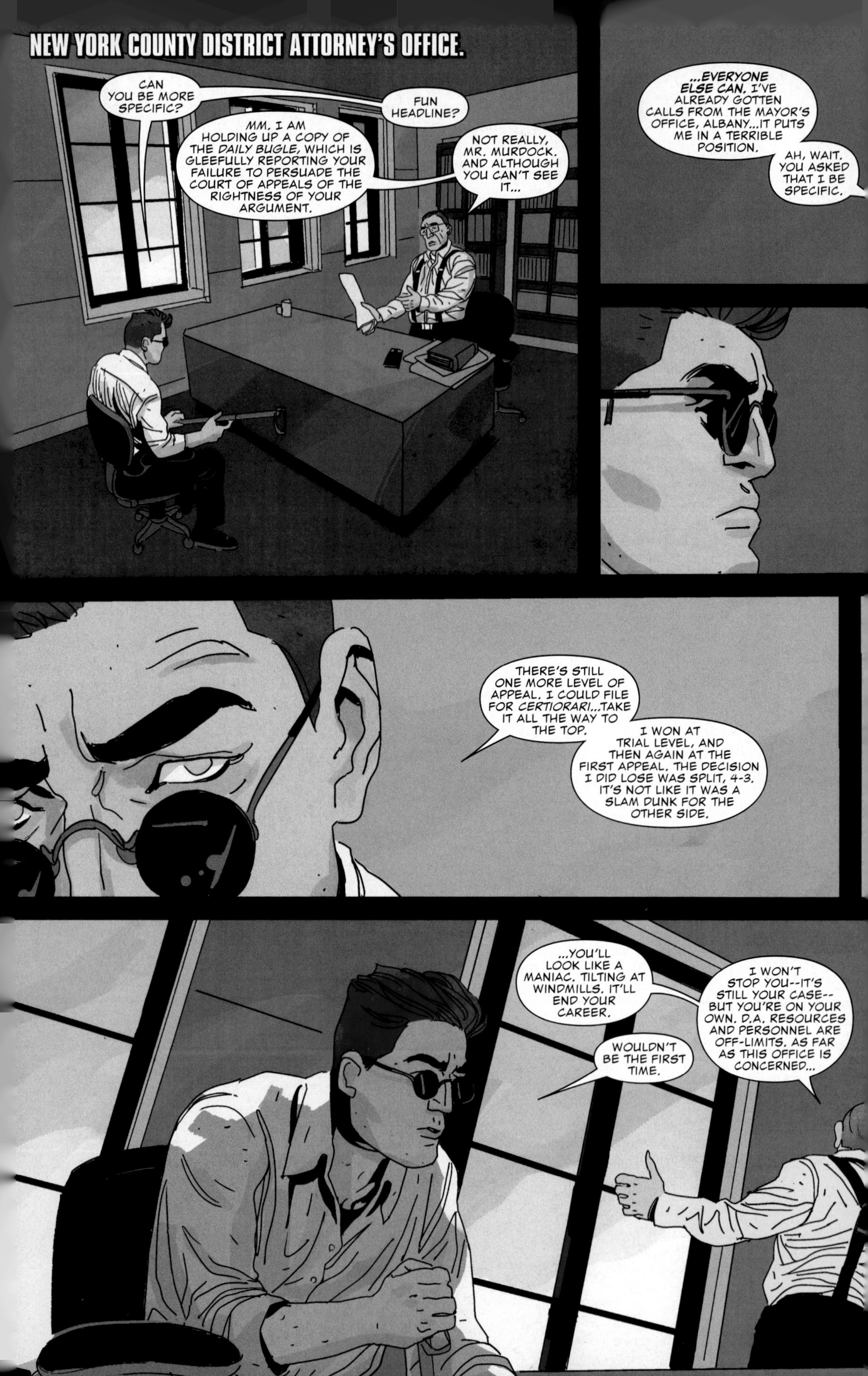
NEW YORK COUNTY DISTRICT ATTORNEY'S OFFICE.
MM. I AM HOLDING UP A COPY OF THE DAILY BUGLE, WHICH IS GLEEFULLY REPORTING YOUR FAILURE TO PERSUADE THE COURT OF APPEALS OF THE RIGHTNESS OF YOUR ARGUMENT.
CAN YOU BE MORE SPECIFIC?
FUN HEADLINE?
NOT REALLY, MR. MURDOCK. AND ALTHOUGH YOU CAN'T SEE IT...
...EVERYONE ELSE CAN. I'VE ALREADY GOTTEN CALLS FROM THE MAYOR'S OFFICE, ALBANY...IT PUTS ME IN A TERRIBLE POSITION.
AH, WAIT. YOU ASKED THAT I BE SPECIFIC.
THERE'S STILL ONE MORE LEVEL OF APPEAL. I COULD FILE FOR CERTIORARI...TAKE IT ALL THE WAY TO THE TOP.
I WON AT TRIAL LEVEL, AND THEN AGAIN AT THE FIRST APPEAL. THE DECISION I DID LOSE WAS SPLIT, 4-3. IT'S NOT LIKE IT WAS A SLAM DUNK FOR THE OTHER SIDE.
...YOU'LL LOOK LIKE A MANIAC. TILTING AT WINDMILLS. IT'LL END YOUR CAREER.
WOULDN'T BE THE FIRST TIME.
I WON'T STOP YOU--IT'S STILL YOUR CASE--BUT YOU'RE ON YOUR OWN. D.A. RESOURCES AND PERSONNEL ARE OFF-LIMITS, AS FAR AS THIS OFFICE IS CONCERNED...

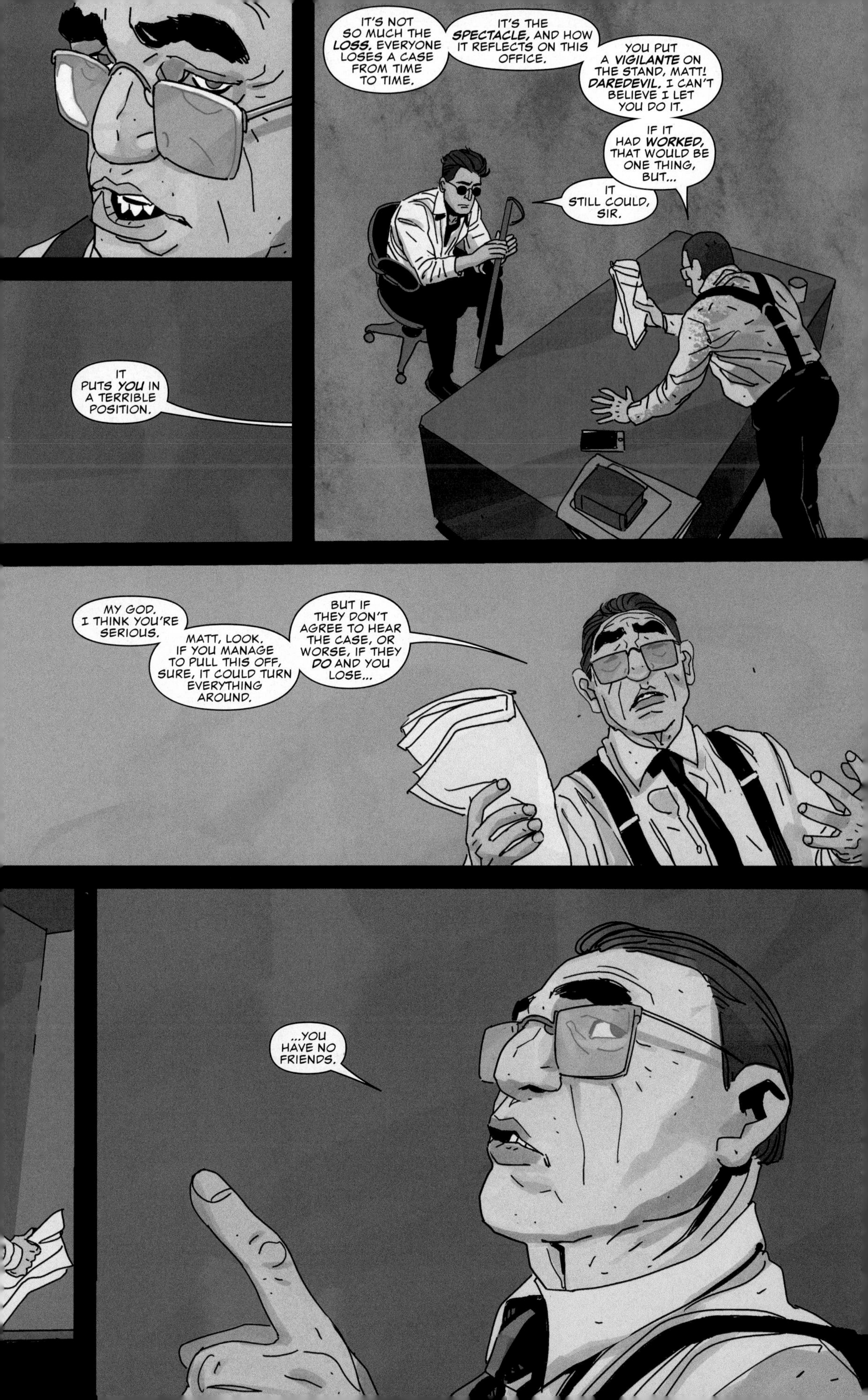

IT'S NOT SO MUCH THE LOSS. EVERYONE LOSES A CASE FROM TIME TO TIME.
IT'S THE SPECTACLE, AND HOW IT REFLECTS ON THIS OFFICE.
YOU PUT A VIGILANTE ON THE STAND, MATT! DAREDEVIL. I CAN'T BELIEVE I LET YOU DO IT.
IF IT HAD WORKED, THAT WOULD BE ONE THING, BUT...
IT STILL COULD, SIR.
IT PUTS YOU IN A TERRIBLE POSITION.
MY GOD. I THINK YOU'RE SERIOUS.
MATT, LOOK. IF YOU MANAGE TO PULL THIS OFF, SURE, IT COULD TURN EVERYTHING AROUND.
BUT IF THEY DON'T AGREE TO HEAR THE CASE, OR WORSE, IF THEY DO AND YOU LOSE...
...YOU HAVE NO FRIENDS.

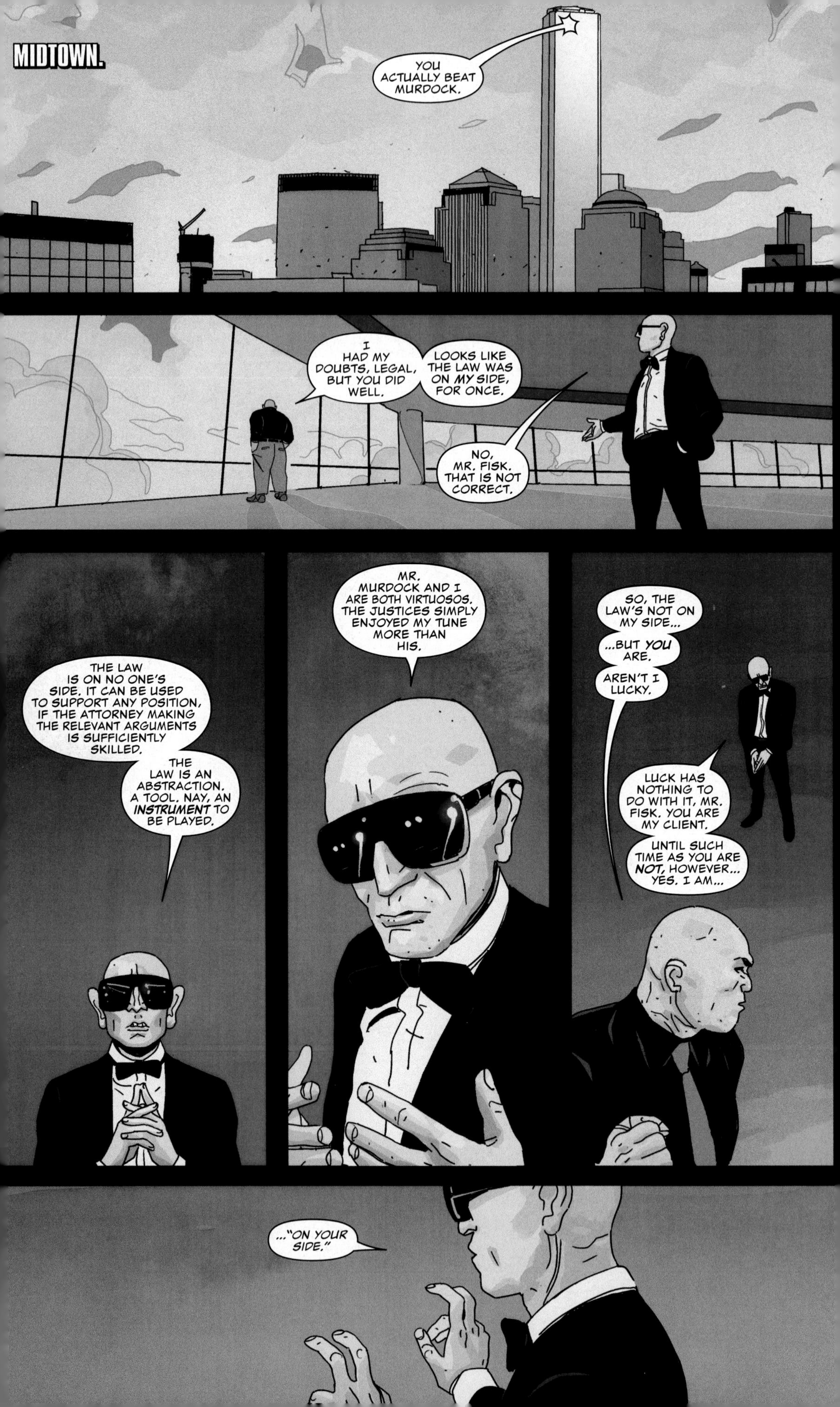
MIDTOWN.
YOU ACTUALLY BEAT MURDOCK.
I HAD MY DOUBTS, LEGAL, BUT YOU DID WELL.
LOOKS LIKE THE LAW WAS ON MY SIDE, FOR ONCE.
NO, MR. FISK. THAT IS NOT CORRECT.
THE LAW IS ON NO ONE'S SIDE. IT CAN BE USED TO SUPPORT ANY POSITION, IF THE ATTORNEY MAKING THE RELEVANT ARGUMENTS IS SUFFICIENTLY SKILLED.
THE LAW IS AN ABSTRACTION. A TOOL. NAY, AN INSTRUMENT TO BE PLAYED.
MR. MURDOCK AND I ARE BOTH VIRTUOSOS. THE JUSTICES SIMPLY ENJOYED MY TUNE MORE THAN HIS.
SO, THE LAW'S NOT ON MY SIDE...
...BUT YOU ARE.
AREN'T I LUCKY.
LUCK HAS NOTHING TO DO WITH IT, MR. FISK. YOU ARE MY CLIENT.
UNTIL SUCH TIME AS YOU ARE NOT, HOWEVER... YES. I AM...
..."ON YOUR SIDE."

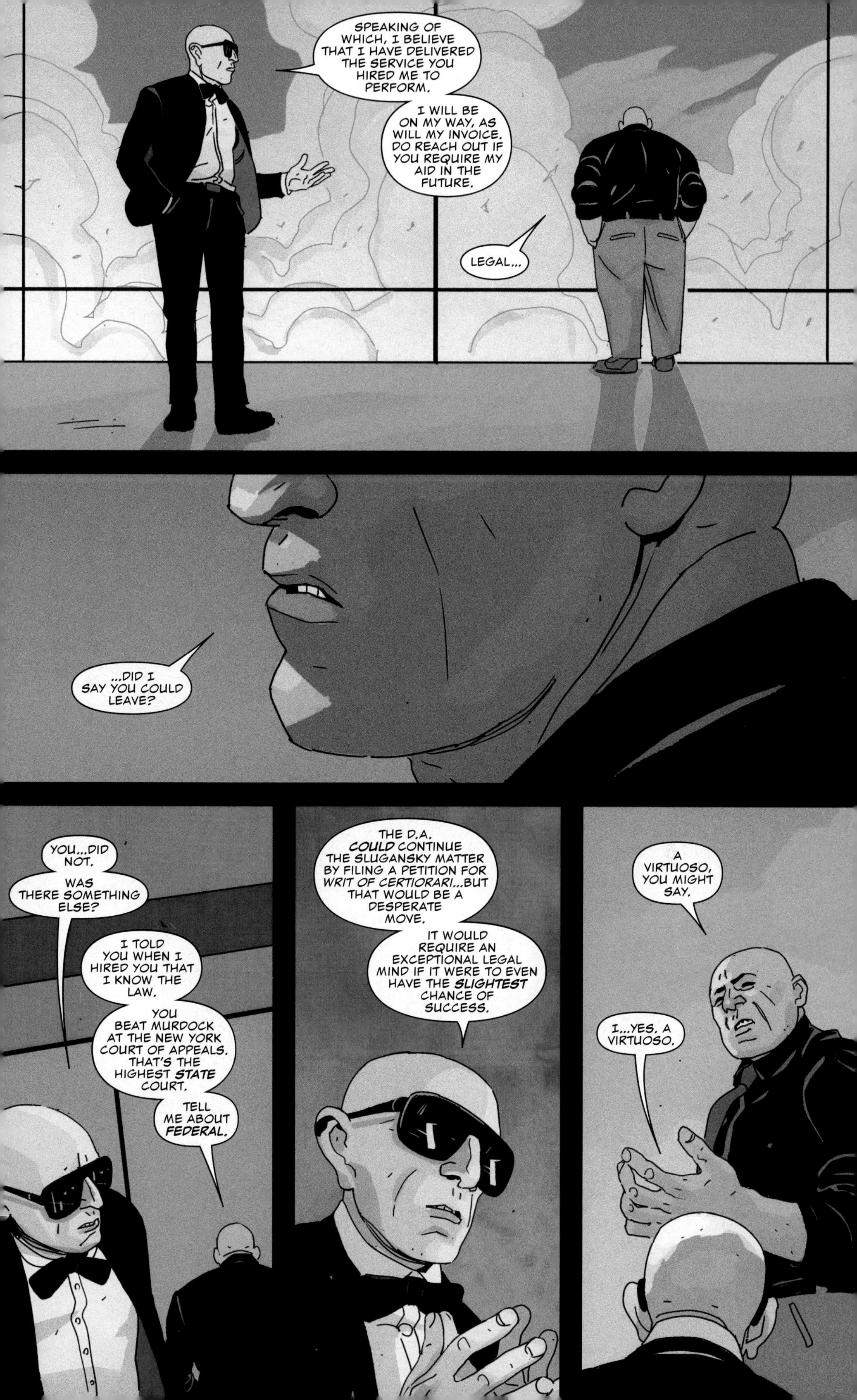

SPEAKING OF WHICH, I BELIEVE THAT I HAVE DELIVERED THE SERVICE YOU HIRED ME TO PERFORM.
I WILL BE ON MY WAY, AS WILL MY INVOICE. DO REACH OUT IF YOU REQUIRE MY AID IN THE FUTURE.
LEGAL...
...DID I SAY YOU COULD LEAVE?
YOU...DID NOT.
WAS THERE SOMETHING ELSE?
I TOLD YOU WHEN I HIRED YOU THAT I KNOW THE LAW.
YOU BEAT MURDOCK AT THE NEW YORK COURT OF APPEALS. THAT'S THE HIGHEST STATE COURT.
TELL ME ABOUT FEDERAL.
THE D.A. COULD CONTINUE THE SLUGANSKY MATTER BY FILING A PETITION FOR WRIT OF CERTIORARI...BUT THAT WOULD BE A DESPERATE MOVE.
IT WOULD REQUIRE AN EXCEPTIONAL LEGAL MIND IF IT WERE TO EVEN HAVE THE SLIGHTEST CHANCE OF SUCCESS.
A VIRTUOSO, YOU MIGHT SAY.
I...YES. A VIRTUOSO.

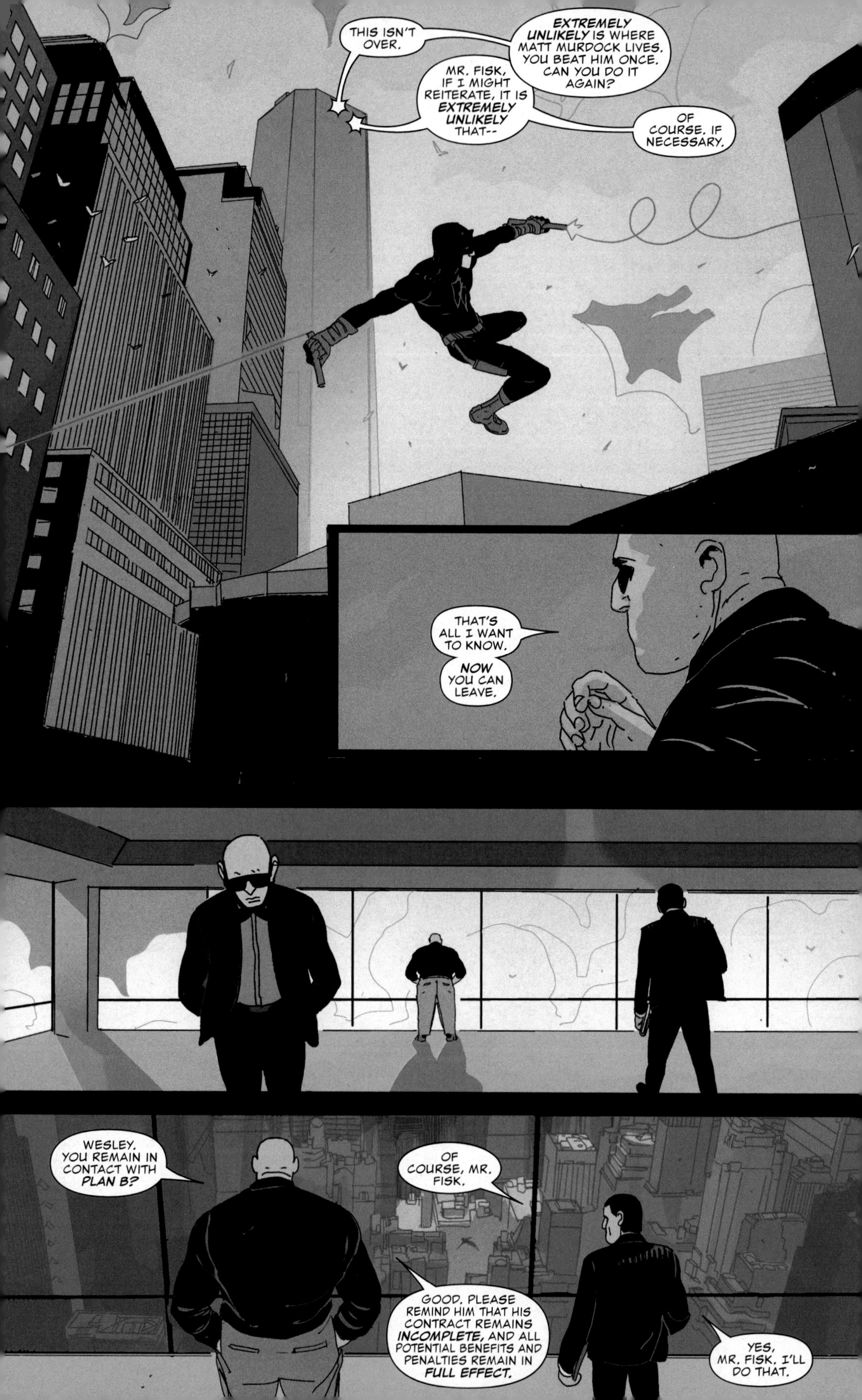
THIS ISN'T OVER.
MR. FISK, IF I MIGHT REITERATE, IT IS EXTREMELY UNLIKELY THAT--
EXTREMELY UNLIKELY IS WHERE MATT MURDOCK LIVES. YOU BEAT HIM ONCE. CAN YOU DO IT AGAIN?
OF COURSE. IF NECESSARY.
THAT'S ALL I WANT TO KNOW.
NOW YOU CAN LEAVE.
WESLEY. YOU REMAIN IN CONTACT WITH PLAN B?
OF COURSE, MR. FISK.
GOOD. PLEASE REMIND HIM THAT HIS CONTRACT REMAINS INCOMPLETE, AND ALL POTENTIAL BENEFITS AND PENALTIES REMAIN IN FULL EFFECT.
YES, MR. FISK. I'LL DO THAT.

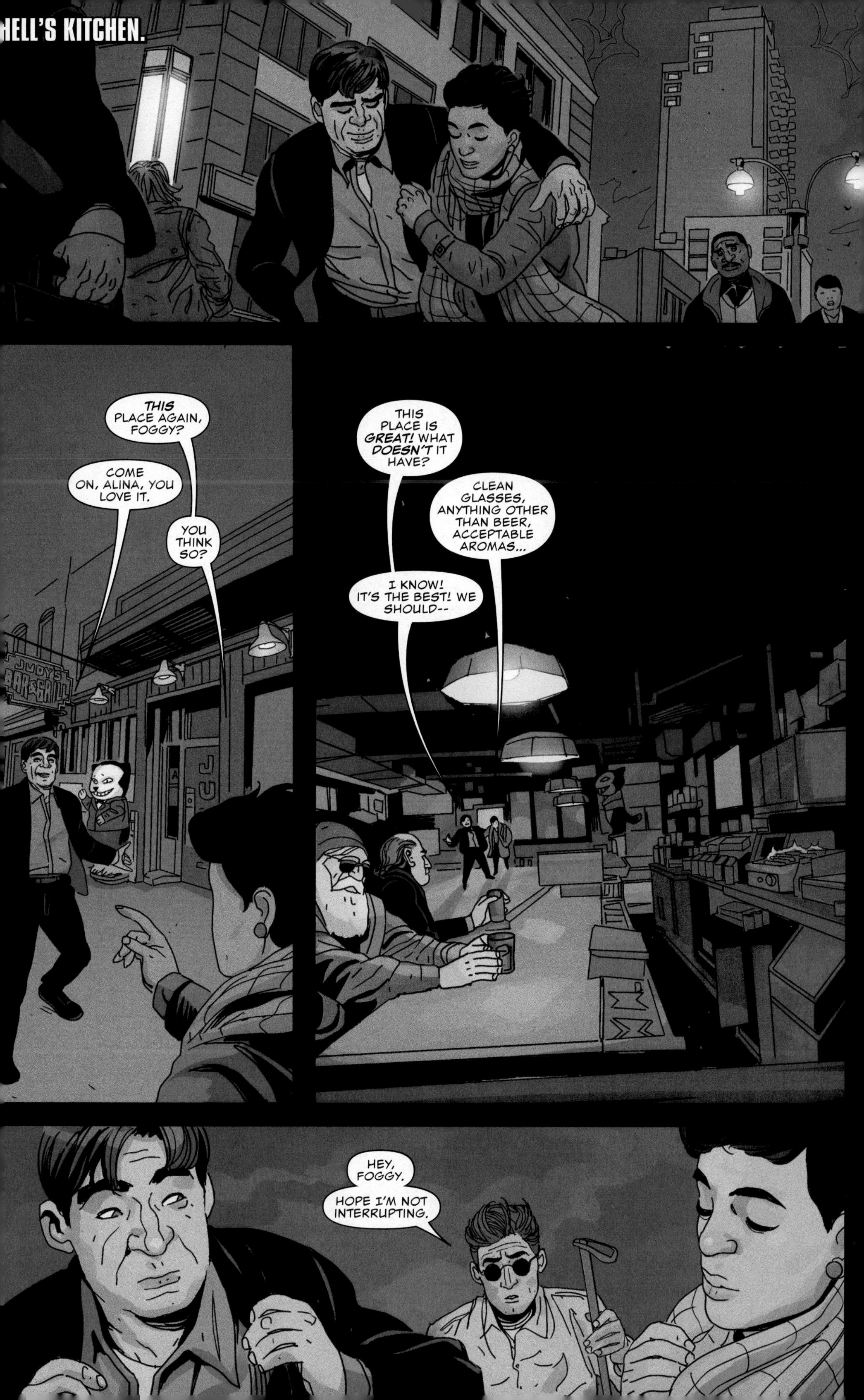
HELL'S KITCHEN.
THIS PLACE AGAIN, FOGGY?
COME ON, ALINA, YOU LOVE IT.
YOU THINK SO?
JUDY'S BAR & GRILL
THIS PLACE IS GREAT! WHAT DOESN'T IT HAVE?
CLEAN GLASSES, ANYTHING OTHER THAN BEER, ACCEPTABLE AROMAS...
I KNOW! IT'S THE BEST! WE SHOULD--
HEY, FOGGY.
HOPE I'M NOT INTERRUPTING.

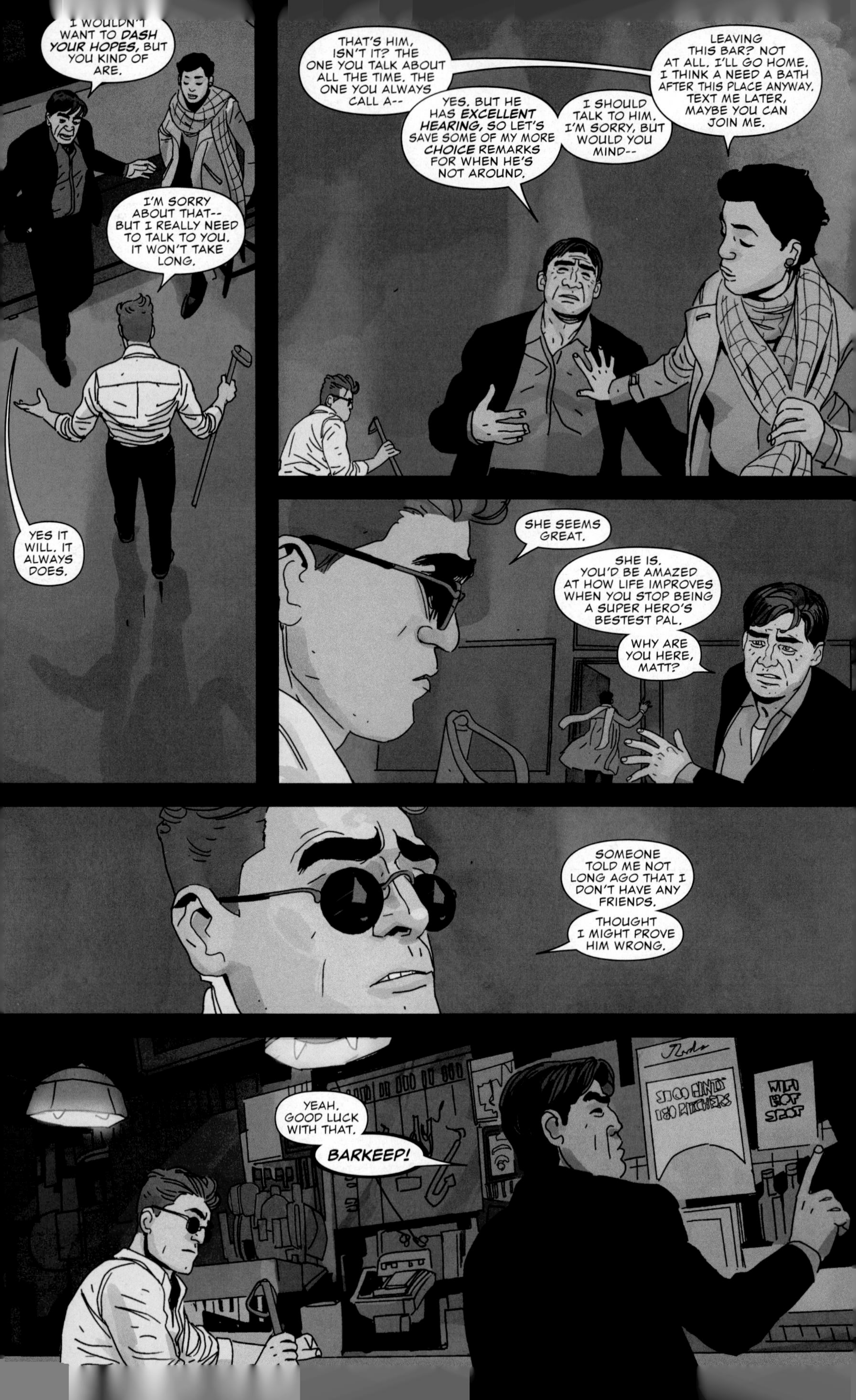
I WOULDN'T WANT TO DASH YOUR HOPES, BUT YOU KIND OF ARE.
I'M SORRY ABOUT THAT-- BUT I REALLY NEED TO TALK TO YOU. IT WON'T TAKE LONG.
YES IT WILL. IT ALWAYS DOES.
THAT'S HIM, ISN'T IT? THE ONE YOU TALK ABOUT ALL THE TIME. THE ONE YOU ALWAYS CALL A--
YES. BUT HE HAS EXCELLENT HEARING, SO LET'S SAVE SOME OF MY MORE CHOICE REMARKS FOR WHEN HE'S NOT AROUND.
I SHOULD TALK TO HIM. I'M SORRY, BUT WOULD YOU MIND--
LEAVING THIS BAR? NOT AT ALL. I'LL GO HOME. I THINK A NEED A BATH AFTER THIS PLACE ANYWAY. TEXT ME LATER, MAYBE YOU CAN JOIN ME.
SHE SEEMS GREAT.
SHE IS. YOU'D BE AMAZED AT HOW LIFE IMPROVES WHEN YOU STOP BEING A SUPER HERO'S BESTEST PAL.
WHY ARE YOU HERE, MATT?
SOMEONE TOLD ME NOT LONG AGO THAT I DON'T HAVE ANY FRIENDS.
THOUGHT I MIGHT PROVE HIM WRONG.
YEAH. GOOD LUCK WITH THAT.
BARKEEP!
WIFI HOT SPOT

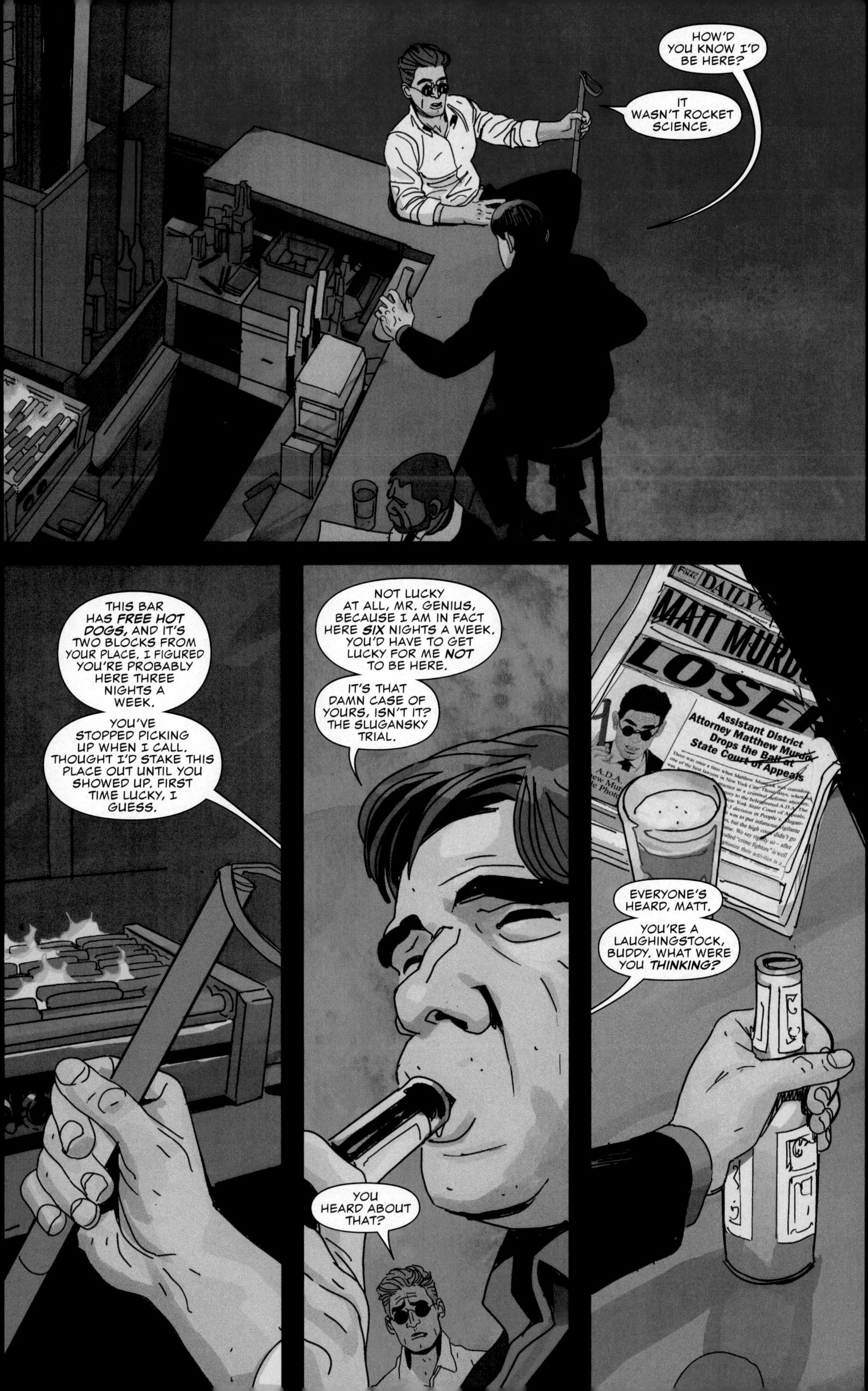
HOW'D YOU KNOW I'D BE HERE?
IT WASN'T ROCKET SCIENCE.
THIS BAR HAS FREE HOT DOGS, AND IT'S TWO BLOCKS FROM YOUR PLACE. I FIGURED YOU'RE PROBABLY HERE THREE NIGHTS A WEEK.
YOU'VE STOPPED PICKING UP WHEN I CALL. THOUGHT I'D STAKE THIS PLACE OUT UNTIL YOU SHOWED UP. FIRST TIME LUCKY, I GUESS.
NOT LUCKY AT ALL, MR. GENIUS, BECAUSE I AM IN FACT HERE SIX NIGHTS A WEEK. YOU'D HAVE TO GET LUCKY FOR ME NOT TO BE HERE.
IT'S THAT DAMN CASE OF YOURS, ISN'T IT? THE SLUGANSKY TRIAL.
YOU HEARD ABOUT THAT?
DAILY
Assistant District Attorney Matthew Murdock Drops the Ball at State Court of Appeals
EVERYONE'S HEARD, MATT.
YOU'RE A LAUGHINGSTOCK, BUDDY. WHAT WERE YOU THINKING?

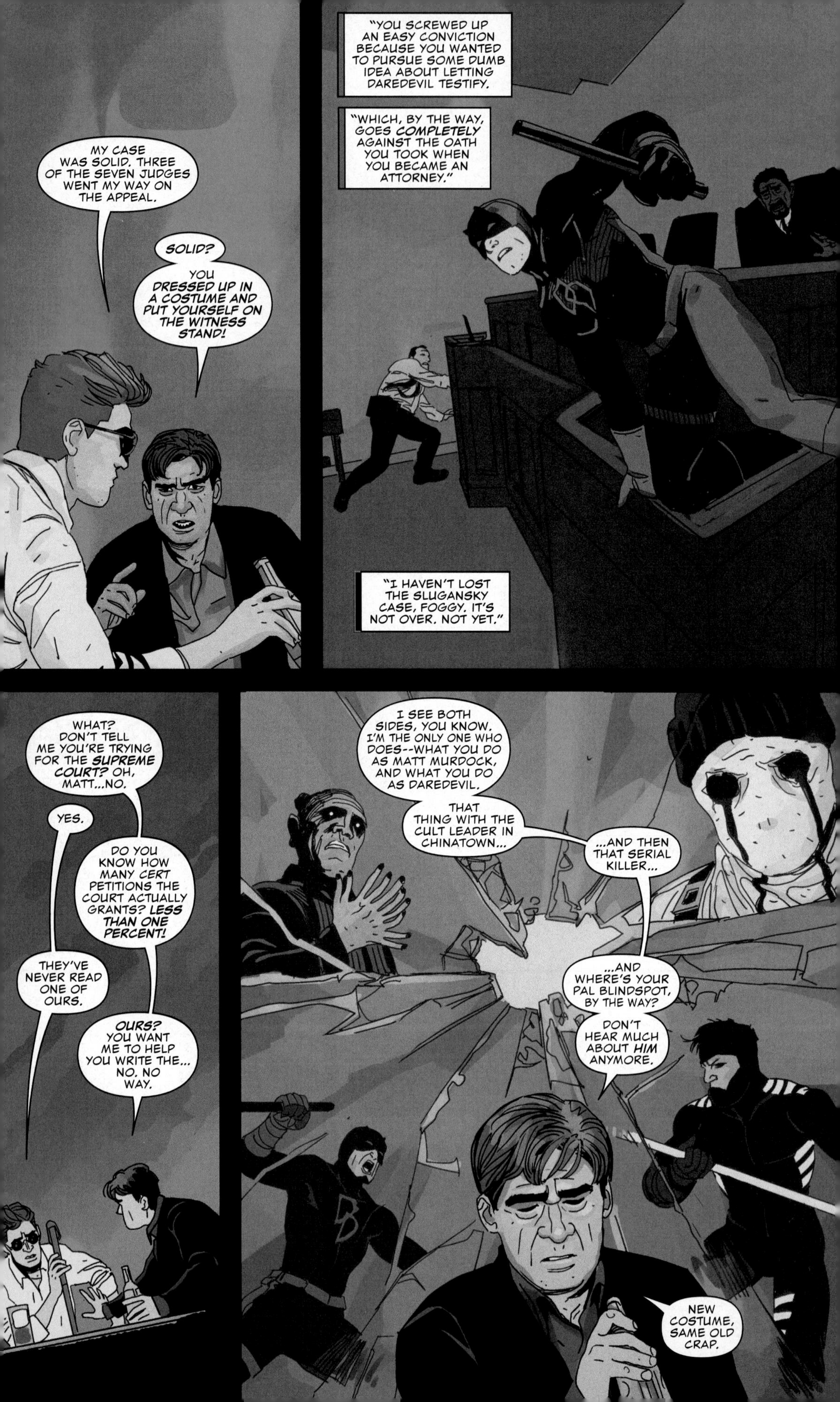
MY CASE WAS SOLID. THREE OF THE SEVEN JUDGES WENT MY WAY ON THE APPEAL.
SOLID?
YOU DRESSED UP IN A COSTUME AND PUT YOURSELF ON THE WITNESS STAND!
"YOU SCREWED UP AN EASY CONVICTION BECAUSE YOU WANTED TO PURSUE SOME DUMB IDEA ABOUT LETTING DAREDEVIL TESTIFY.
"WHICH, BY THE WAY, GOES COMPLETELY AGAINST THE OATH YOU TOOK WHEN YOU BECAME AN ATTORNEY."
"I HAVEN'T LOST THE SLUGANSKY CASE, FOGGY. IT'S NOT OVER. NOT YET."
WHAT? DON'T TELL ME YOU'RE TRYING FOR THE SUPREME COURT? OH, MATT...NO.
YES.
DO YOU KNOW HOW MANY CERT PETITIONS THE COURT ACTUALLY GRANTS? LESS THAN ONE PERCENT!
THEY'VE NEVER READ ONE OF OURS.
OURS? YOU WANT ME TO HELP YOU WRITE THE... NO. NO WAY.
I SEE BOTH SIDES, YOU KNOW. I'M THE ONLY ONE WHO DOES--WHAT YOU DO AS MATT MURDOCK, AND WHAT YOU DO AS DAREDEVIL.
THAT THING WITH THE CULT LEADER IN CHINATOWN...
...AND THEN THAT SERIAL KILLER...
...AND WHERE'S YOUR PAL BLINDSPOT, BY THE WAY?
DON'T HEAR MUCH ABOUT HIM ANYMORE.
NEW COSTUME, SAME OLD CRAP.

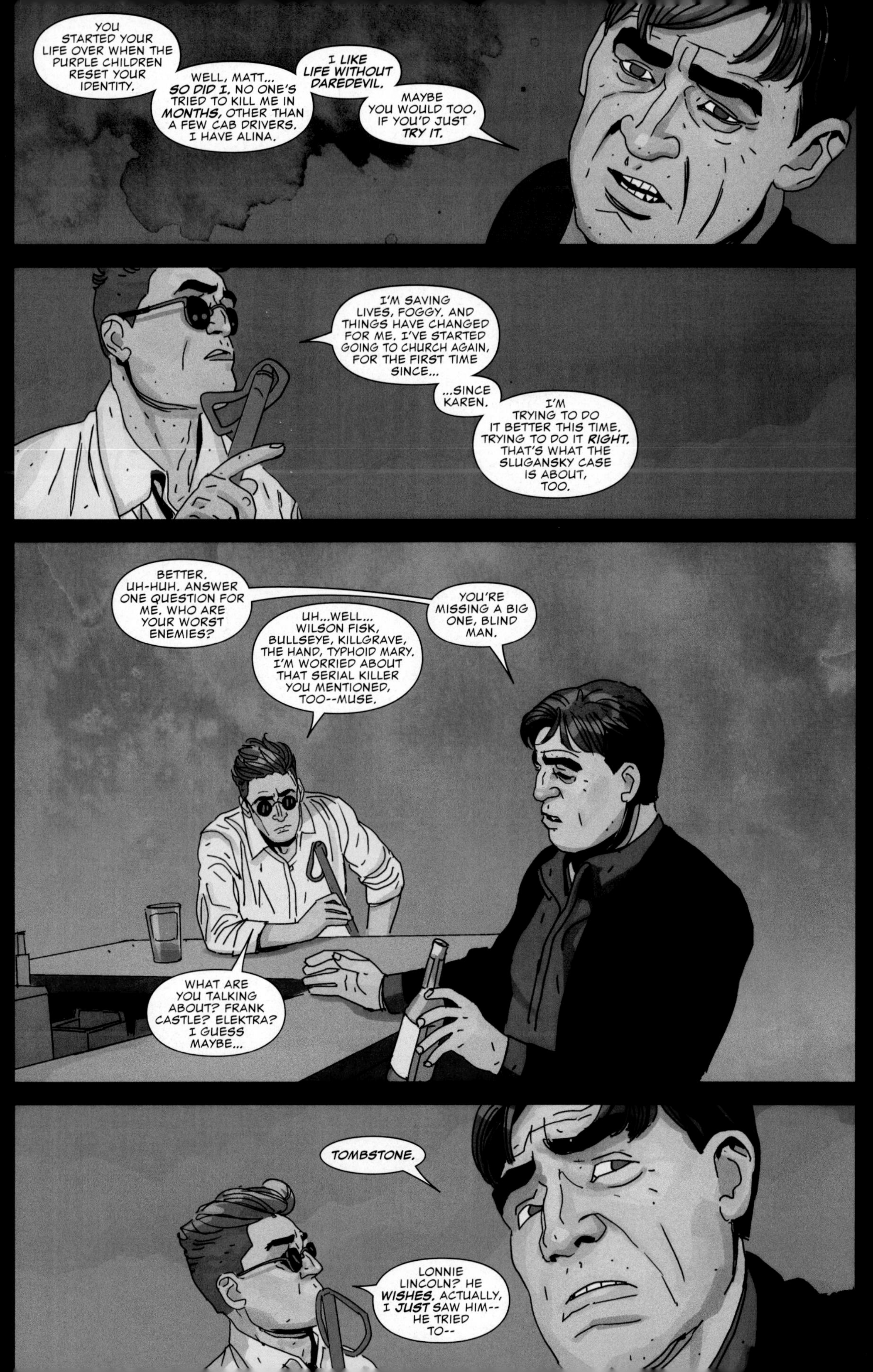
YOU STARTED YOUR LIFE OVER WHEN THE PURPLE CHILDREN RESET YOUR IDENTITY.
WELL, MATT... SO DID I. NO ONE'S TRIED TO KILL ME IN MONTHS, OTHER THAN A FEW CAB DRIVERS. I HAVE ALINA.
I LIKE LIFE WITHOUT DAREDEVIL.
MAYBE YOU WOULD TOO, IF YOU'D JUST TRY IT.
I'M SAVING LIVES, FOGGY. AND THINGS HAVE CHANGED FOR ME. I'VE STARTED GOING TO CHURCH AGAIN, FOR THE FIRST TIME SINCE...
...SINCE KAREN.
I'M TRYING TO DO IT BETTER THIS TIME. TRYING TO DO IT RIGHT. THAT'S WHAT THE SLUGANSKY CASE IS ABOUT, TOO.
BETTER. UH-HUH. ANSWER ONE QUESTION FOR ME. WHO ARE YOUR WORST ENEMIES?
UH...WELL... WILSON FISK, BULLSEYE, KILLGRAVE, THE HAND, TYPHOID MARY. I'M WORRIED ABOUT THAT SERIAL KILLER YOU MENTIONED, TOO--MUSE.
YOU'RE MISSING A BIG ONE, BLIND MAN.
WHAT ARE YOU TALKING ABOUT? FRANK CASTLE? ELEKTRA? I GUESS MAYBE...
TOMBSTONE.
LONNIE LINCOLN? HE WISHES. ACTUALLY, I JUST SAW HIM-- HE TRIED TO--

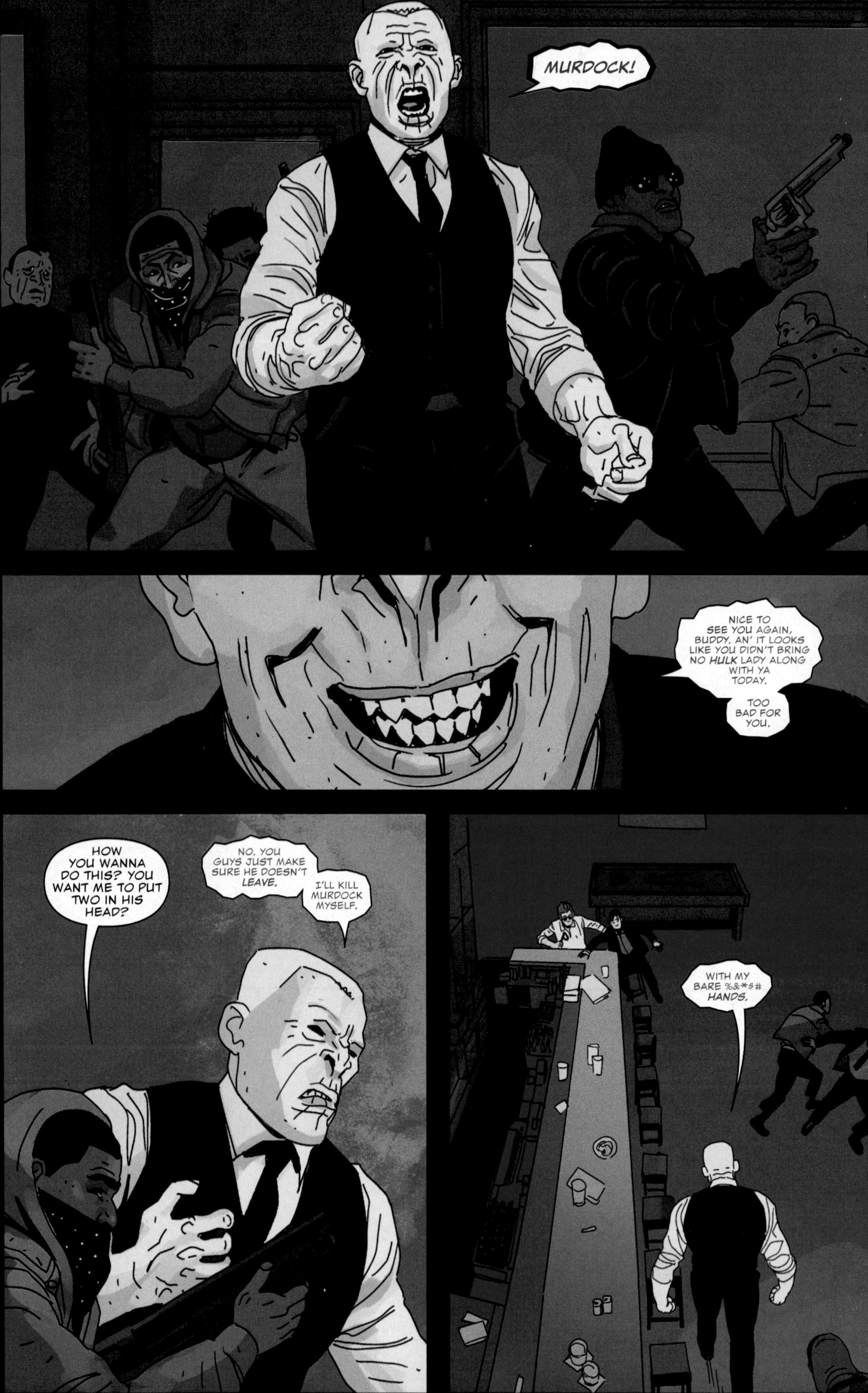
MURDOCK!
NICE TO SEE YOU AGAIN, BUDDY. AN' IT LOOKS LIKE YOU DIDN'T BRING NO HULK LADY ALONG WITH YA TODAY.
TOO BAD FOR YOU.
HOW YOU WANNA DO THIS? YOU WANT ME TO PUT TWO IN HIS HEAD?
NO. YOU GUYS JUST MAKE SURE HE DOESN'T LEAVE.
I'LL KILL MURDOCK MYSELF.
WITH MY BARE %&*$# HANDS.

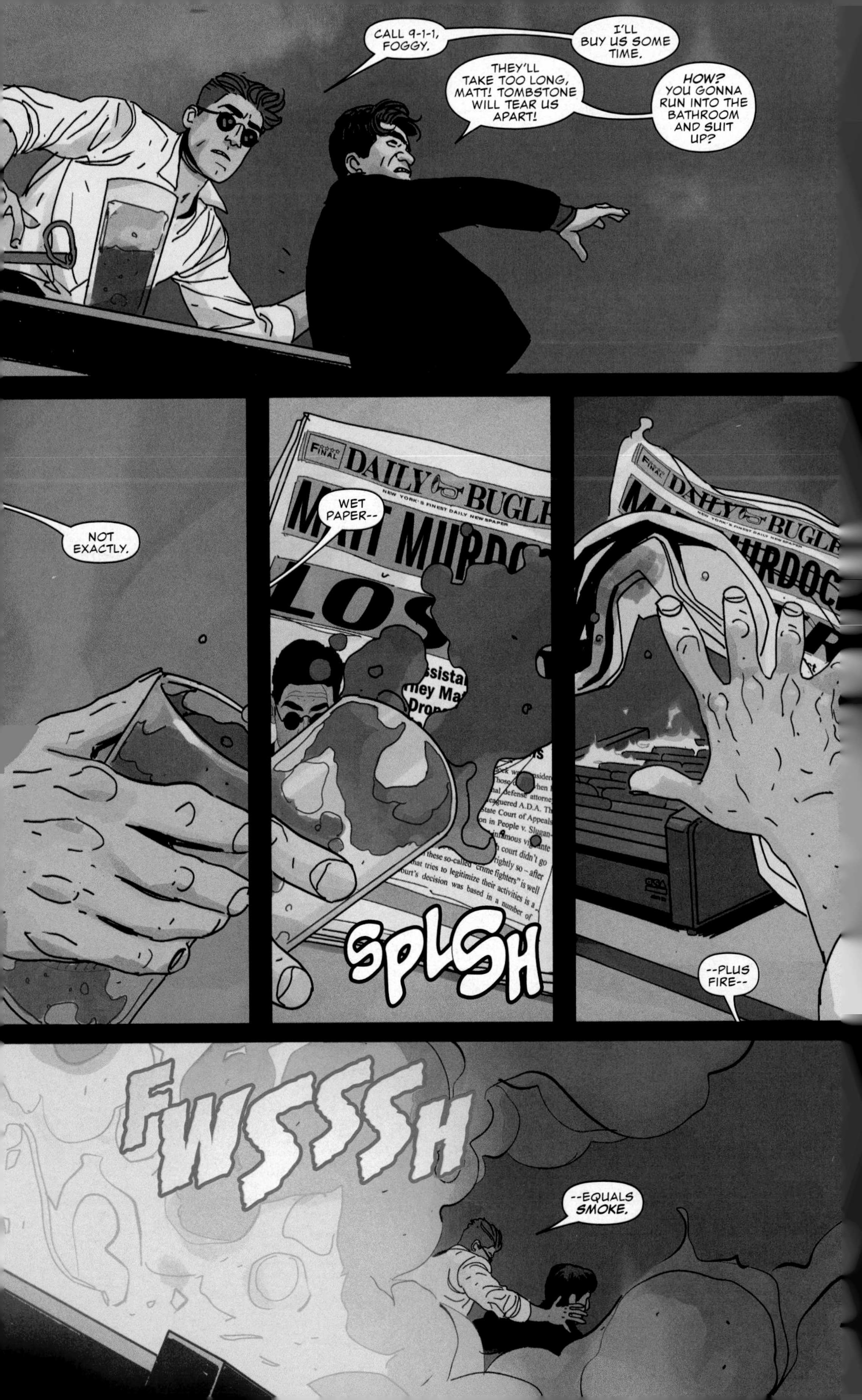
CALL 9-1-1, FOGGY.
I'LL BUY US SOME TIME.
THEY'LL TAKE TOO LONG, MATT! TOMBSTONE WILL TEAR US APART!
HOW? YOU GONNA RUN INTO THE BATHROOM AND SUIT UP?
NOT EXACTLY.
DAILY BUGLE
NEW YORK'S FINEST DAILY NEWSPAPER
WET PAPER--
SPLSH
--PLUS FIRE--
FWSSSH
--EQUALS SMOKE.

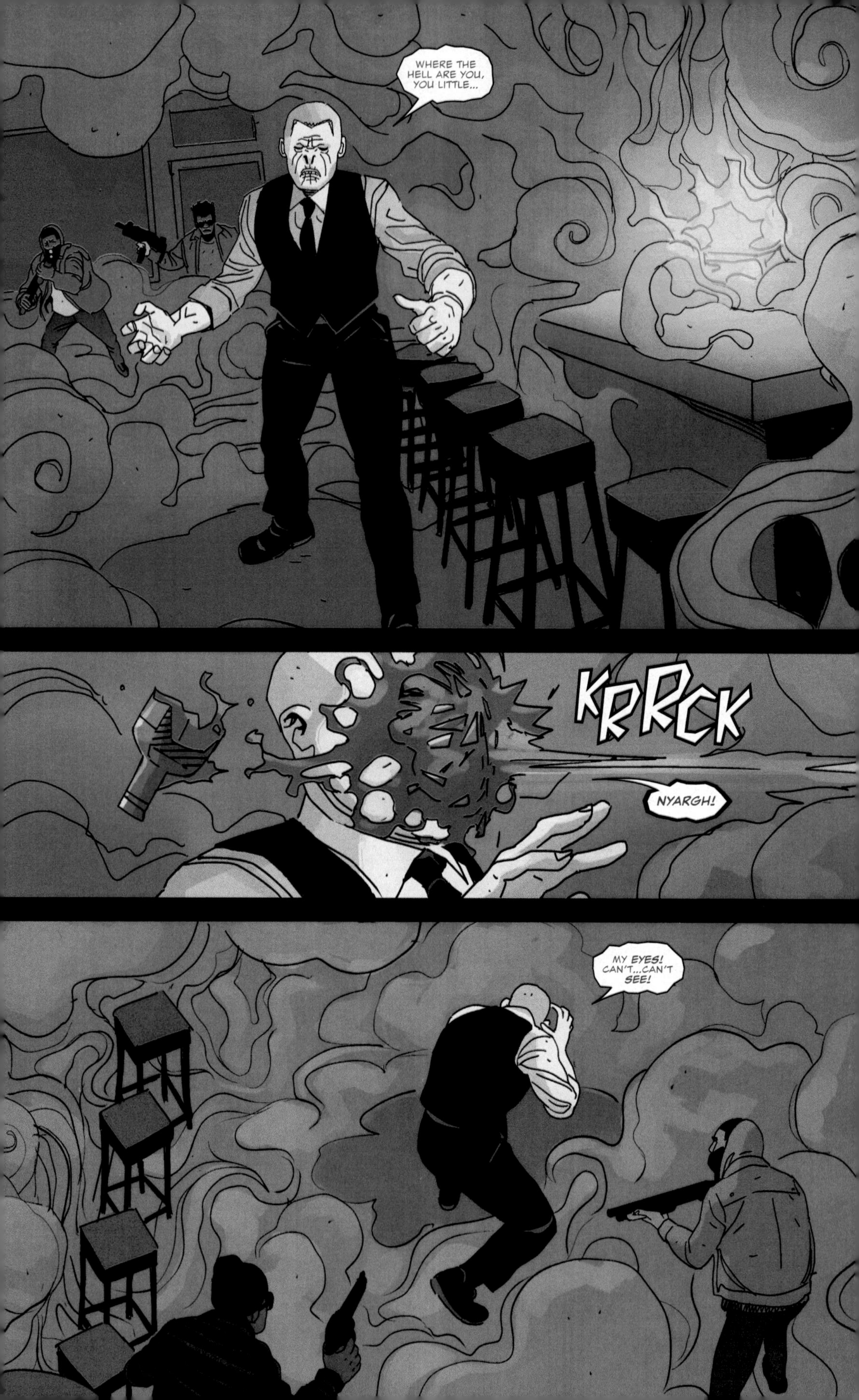
WHERE THE HELL ARE YOU, YOU LITTLE...
KRRCK
NYARGH!
MY EYES! CAN'T...CAN'T SEE!

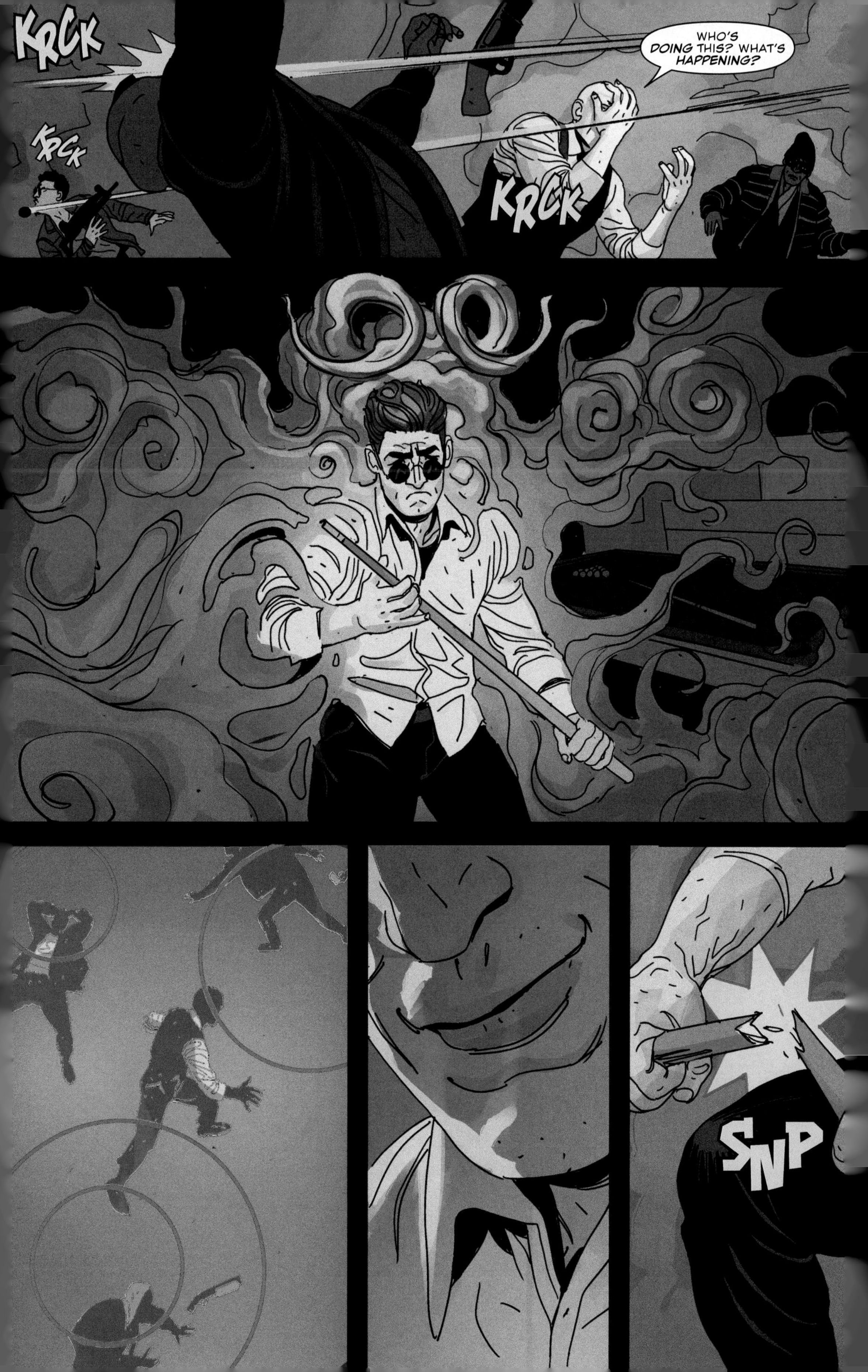
KRCK
KRCK
WHO'S DOING THIS? WHAT'S HAPPENING?
KRCK
SNP

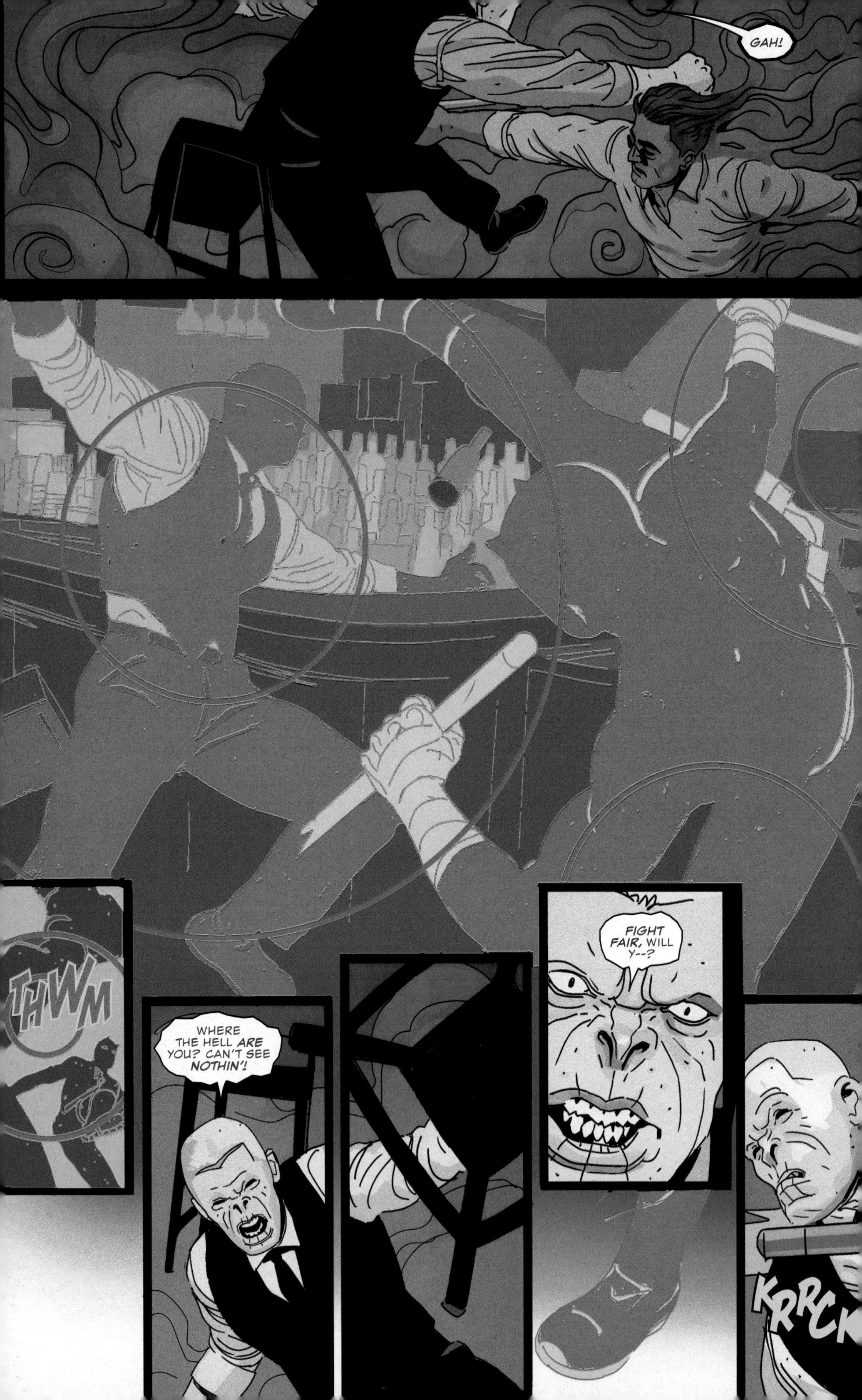
GAH!
THWM
WHERE THE HELL ARE YOU? CAN'T SEE NOTHIN'!
FIGHT FAIR, WILL Y--?
KRRCK

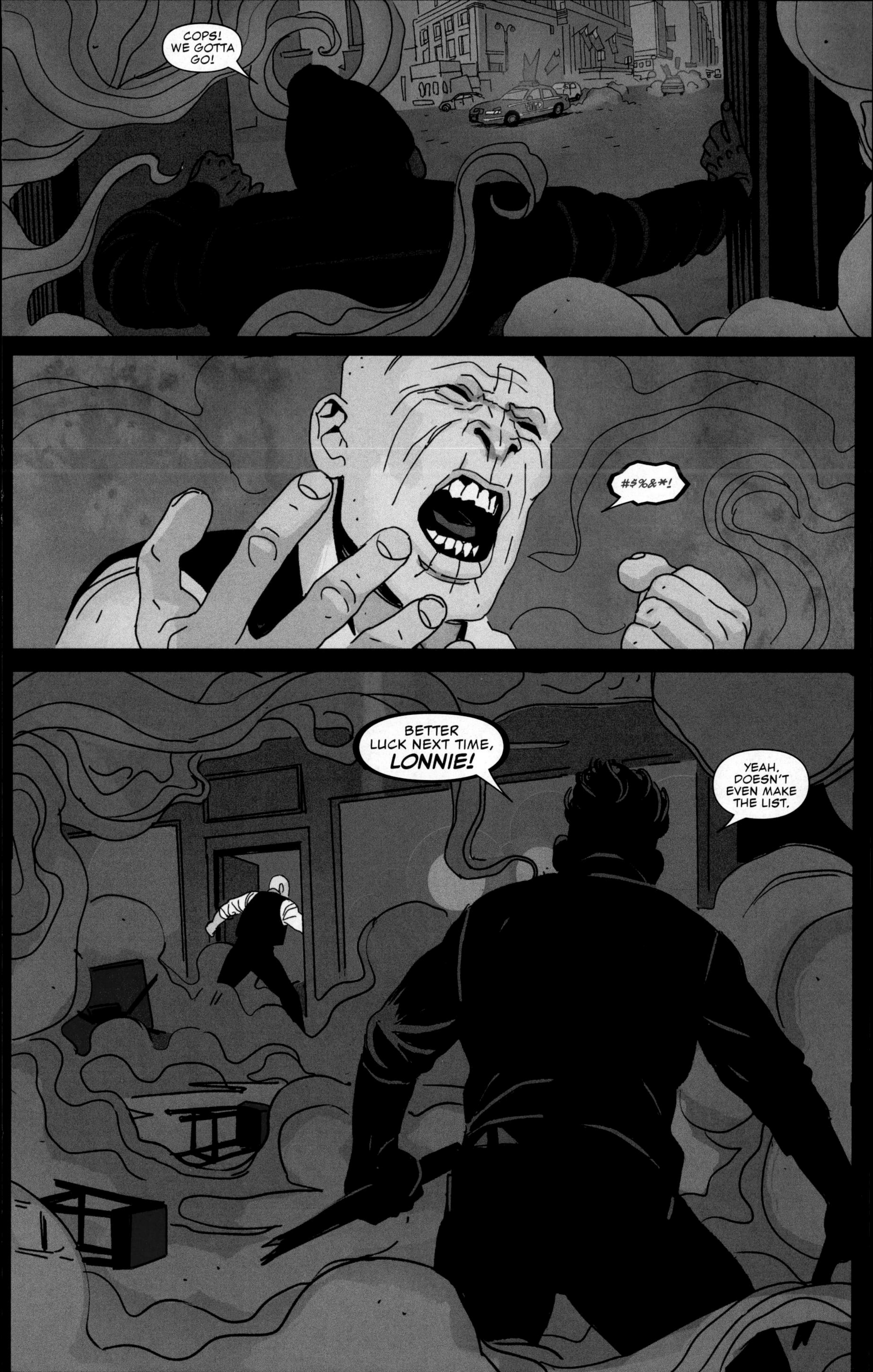
COPS! WE GOTTA GO!
#$%&*!
BETTER LUCK NEXT TIME, LONNIE!
YEAH. DOESN'T EVEN MAKE THE LIST.

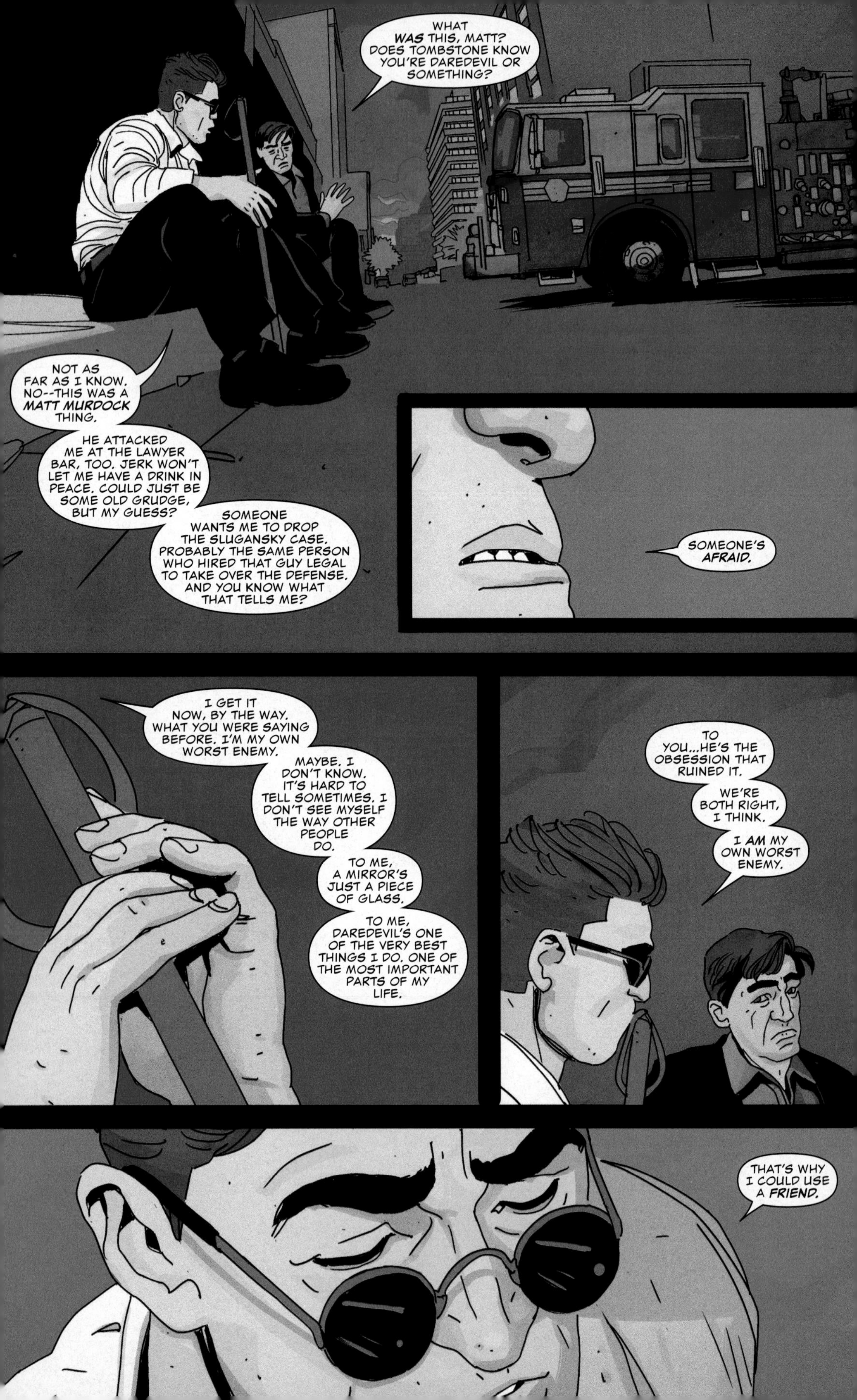
WHAT *WAS* THIS, MATT? DOES TOMBSTONE KNOW YOU'RE DAREDEVIL OR SOMETHING?
NOT AS FAR AS I KNOW. NO--THIS WAS A *MATT MURDOCK* THING.
HE ATTACKED ME AT THE LAWYER BAR, TOO. JERK WON'T LET ME HAVE A DRINK IN PEACE. COULD JUST BE SOME OLD GRUDGE, BUT MY GUESS?
SOMEONE WANTS ME TO DROP THE SLUGANSKY CASE. PROBABLY THE SAME PERSON WHO HIRED THAT GUY LEGAL TO TAKE OVER THE DEFENSE. AND YOU KNOW WHAT THAT TELLS ME?
SOMEONE'S *AFRAID.*
I GET IT NOW, BY THE WAY. WHAT YOU WERE SAYING BEFORE. I'M MY OWN WORST ENEMY.
MAYBE. I DON'T KNOW. IT'S HARD TO TELL SOMETIMES. I DON'T SEE MYSELF THE WAY OTHER PEOPLE DO.
TO ME, A MIRROR'S JUST A PIECE OF GLASS.
TO ME, DAREDEVIL'S ONE OF THE VERY BEST THINGS I DO. ONE OF THE MOST IMPORTANT PARTS OF MY LIFE.
TO YOU...HE'S THE OBSESSION THAT RUINED IT.
WE'RE BOTH RIGHT, I THINK.
I AM MY OWN WORST ENEMY.
THAT'S WHY I COULD USE A *FRIEND.*

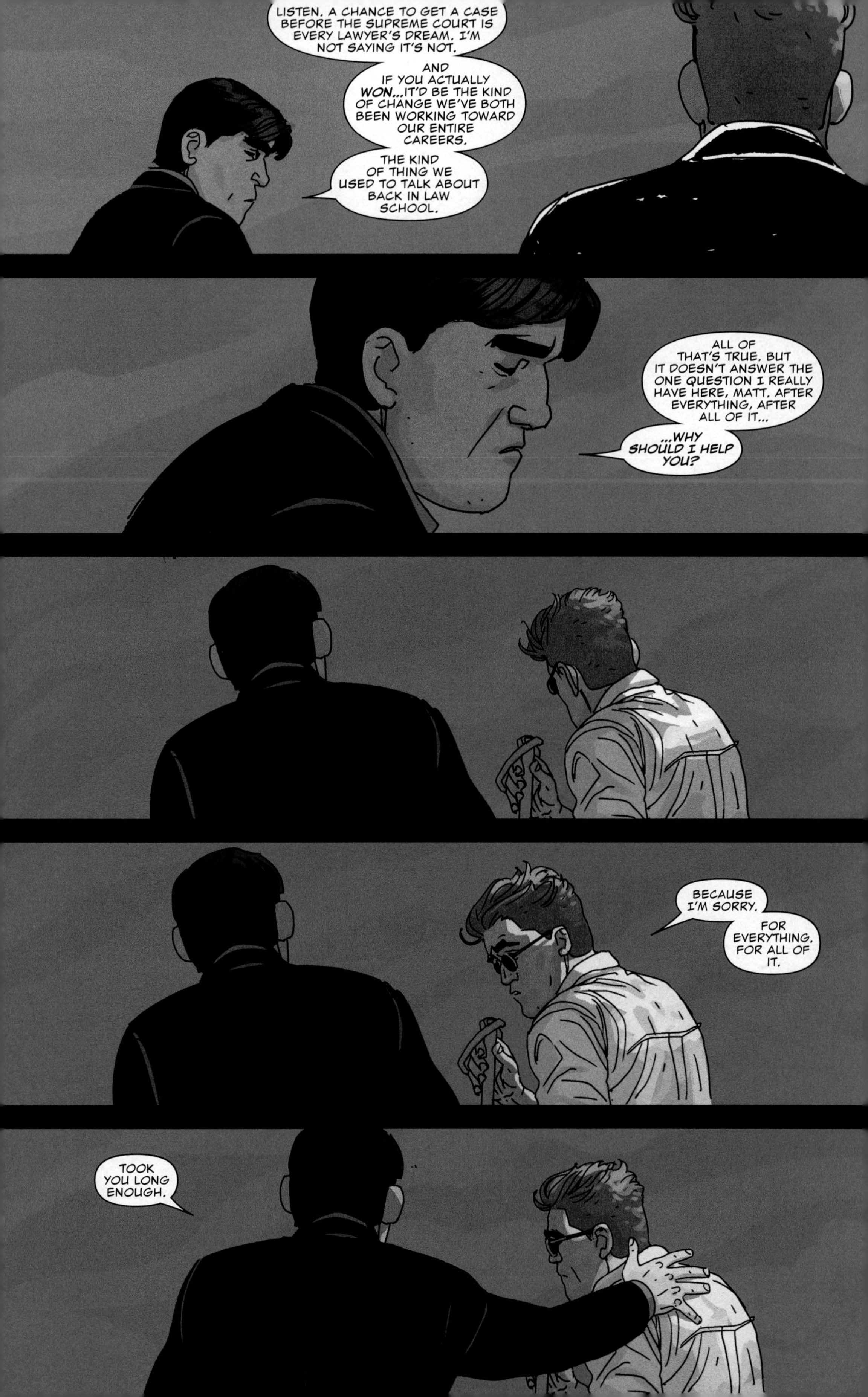
LISTEN. A CHANCE TO GET A CASE BEFORE THE SUPREME COURT IS EVERY LAWYER'S DREAM. I'M NOT SAYING IT'S NOT.
AND IF YOU ACTUALLY WON...IT'D BE THE KIND OF CHANGE WE'VE BOTH BEEN WORKING TOWARD OUR ENTIRE CAREERS.
THE KIND OF THING WE USED TO TALK ABOUT BACK IN LAW SCHOOL.
ALL OF THAT'S TRUE. BUT IT DOESN'T ANSWER THE ONE QUESTION I REALLY HAVE HERE, MATT. AFTER EVERYTHING, AFTER ALL OF IT...
...WHY SHOULD I HELP YOU?
BECAUSE I'M SORRY.
FOR EVERYTHING. FOR ALL OF IT.
TOOK YOU LONG ENOUGH.

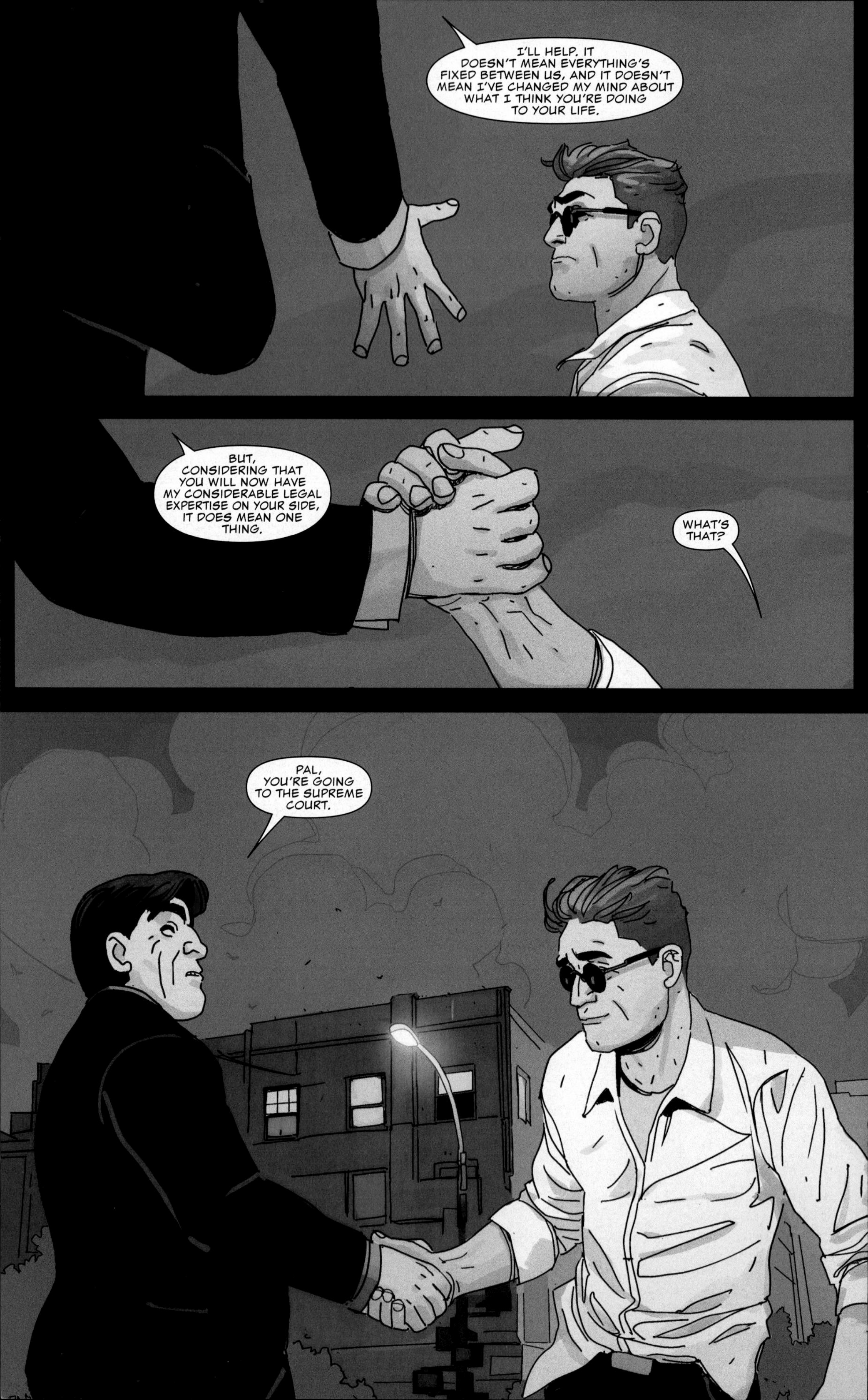
I'LL HELP. IT DOESN'T MEAN EVERYTHING'S FIXED BETWEEN US, AND IT DOESN'T MEAN I'VE CHANGED MY MIND ABOUT WHAT I THINK YOU'RE DOING TO YOUR LIFE.
BUT, CONSIDERING THAT YOU WILL NOW HAVE MY CONSIDERABLE LEGAL EXPERTISE ON YOUR SIDE, IT DOES MEAN ONE THING.
WHAT'S THAT?
PAL, YOU'RE GOING TO THE SUPREME COURT.

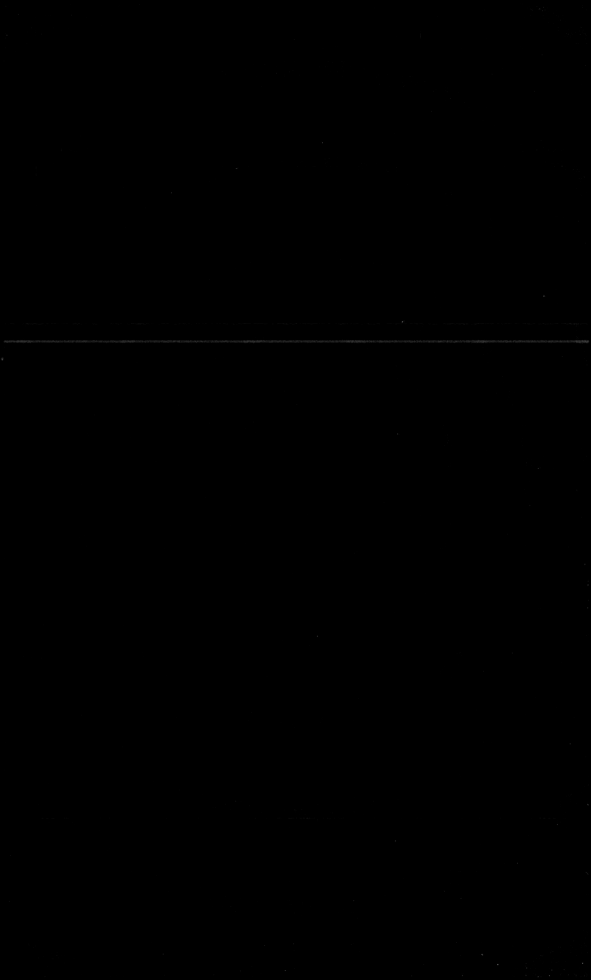

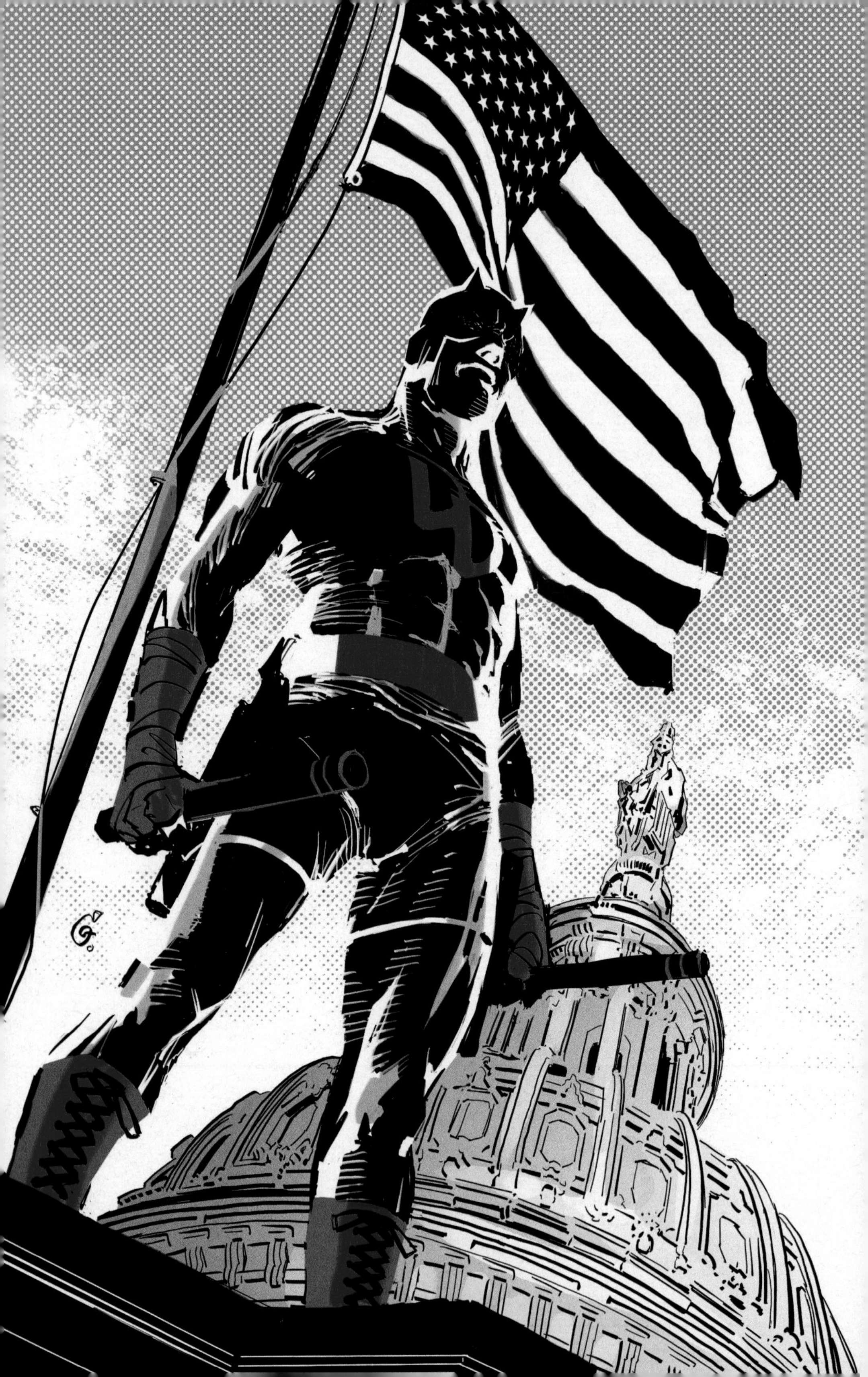

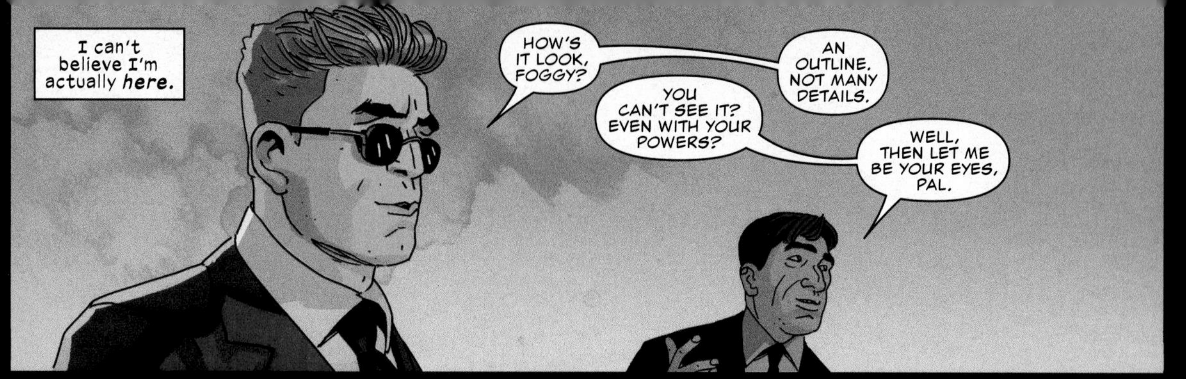
I can't believe I'm actually *here*.
HOW'S IT LOOK, FOGGY?
AN OUTLINE. NOT MANY DETAILS.
YOU CAN'T SEE IT? EVEN WITH YOUR POWERS?
WELL, THEN LET ME BE YOUR EYES, PAL.

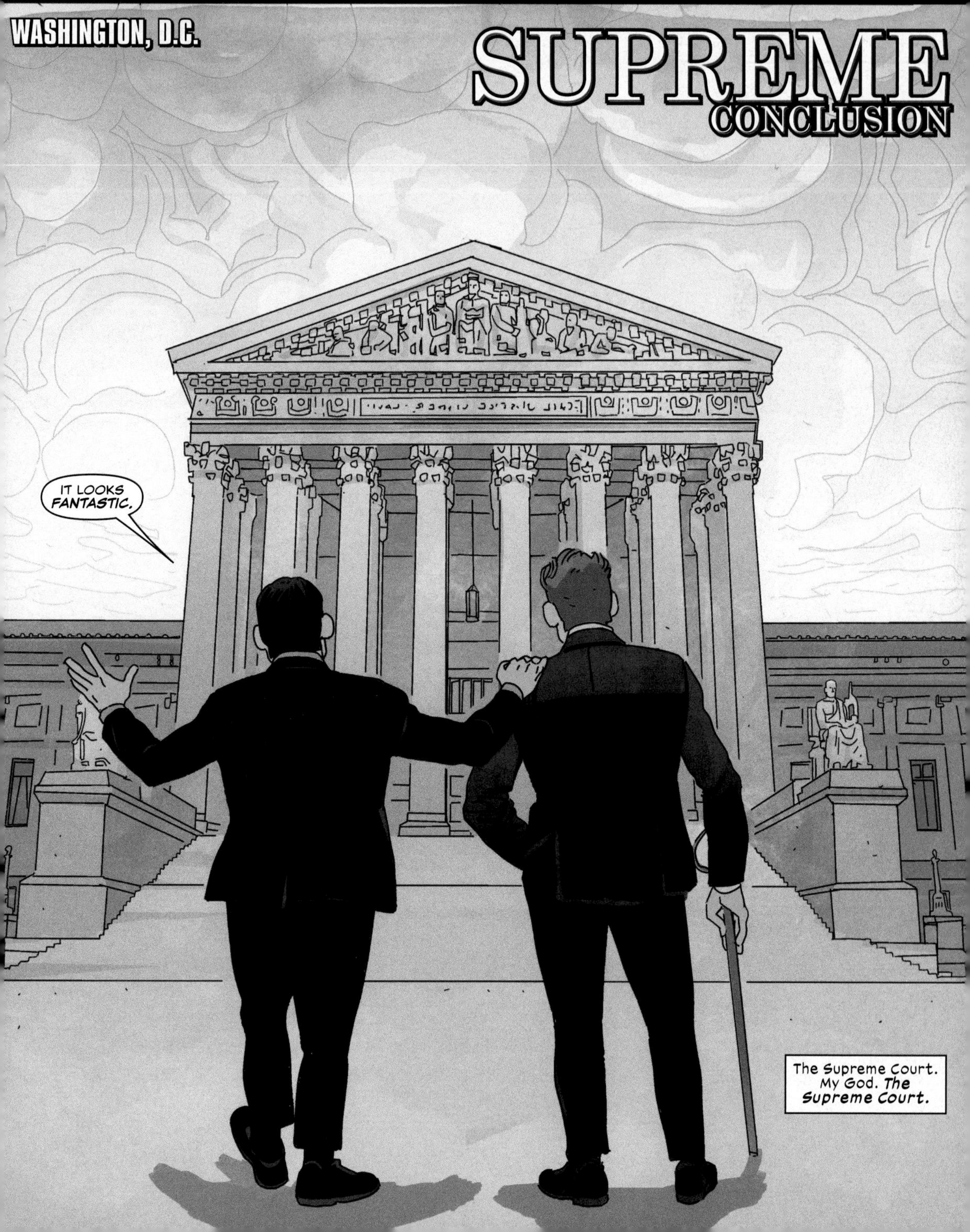
WASHINGTON, D.C.
SUPREME
CONCLUSION
IT LOOKS *FANTASTIC.*
The Supreme Court. My God. *The Supreme Court.*

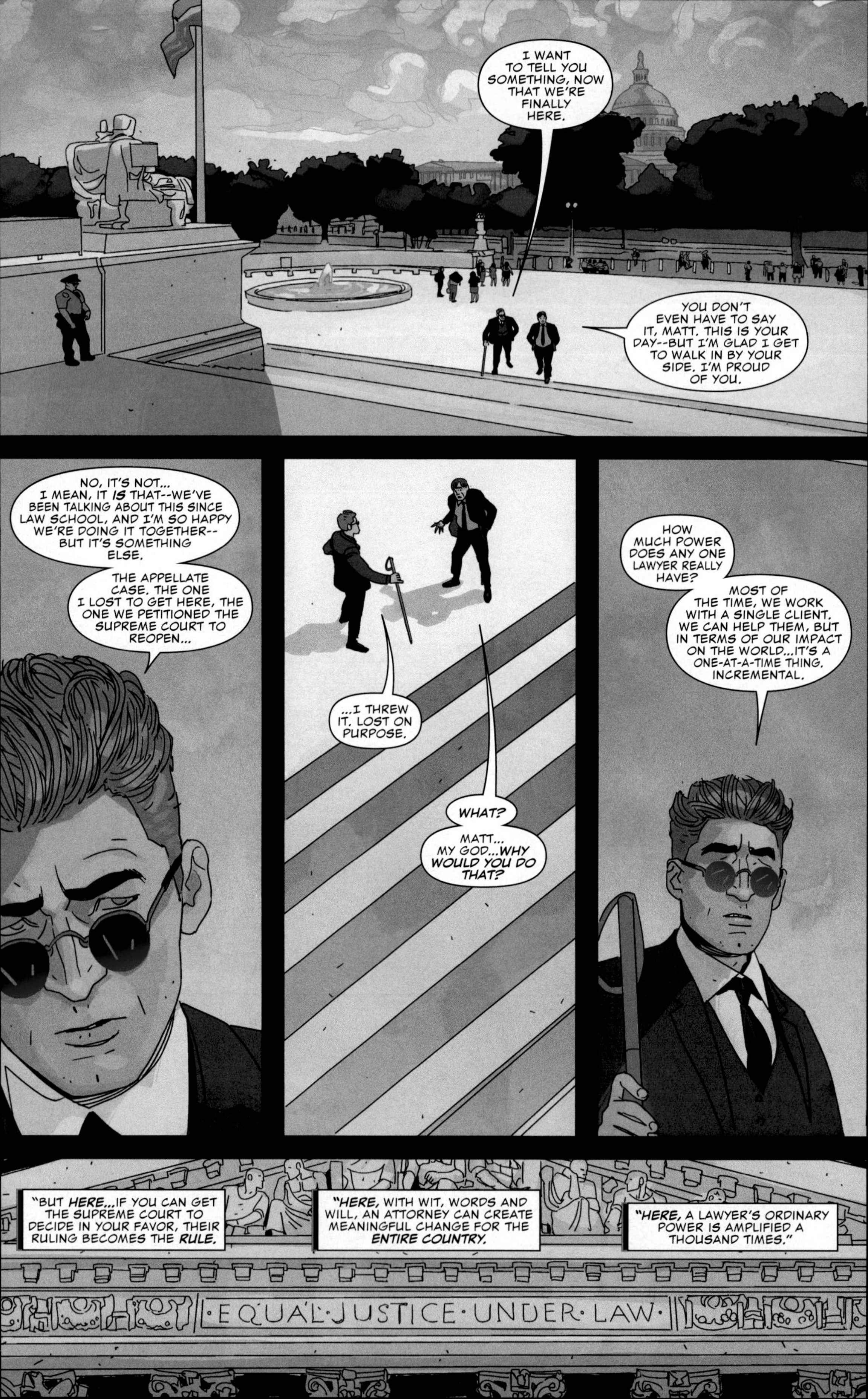

I WANT TO TELL YOU SOMETHING, NOW THAT WE'RE FINALLY HERE.
YOU DON'T EVEN HAVE TO SAY IT, MATT. THIS IS YOUR DAY--BUT I'M GLAD I GET TO WALK IN BY YOUR SIDE. I'M PROUD OF YOU.
NO, IT'S NOT... I MEAN, IT *IS* THAT--WE'VE BEEN TALKING ABOUT THIS SINCE LAW SCHOOL, AND I'M SO HAPPY WE'RE DOING IT TOGETHER-- BUT IT'S SOMETHING ELSE.
THE APPELLATE CASE. THE ONE I LOST TO GET HERE, THE ONE WE PETITIONED THE SUPREME COURT TO REOPEN...
...I THREW IT. LOST ON PURPOSE.
WHAT?
MATT... MY GOD...*WHY WOULD YOU DO THAT?*
HOW MUCH POWER DOES ANY ONE LAWYER REALLY HAVE?
MOST OF THE TIME, WE WORK WITH A SINGLE CLIENT. WE CAN HELP THEM, BUT IN TERMS OF OUR IMPACT ON THE WORLD...IT'S A ONE-AT-A-TIME THING. INCREMENTAL.
"BUT *HERE*...IF YOU CAN GET THE SUPREME COURT TO DECIDE IN YOUR FAVOR, THEIR RULING BECOMES THE *RULE.*
"*HERE,* WITH WIT, WORDS AND WILL, AN ATTORNEY CAN CREATE MEANINGFUL CHANGE FOR THE *ENTIRE COUNTRY.*
"*HERE,* A LAWYER'S ORDINARY POWER IS AMPLIFIED A THOUSAND TIMES."
·EQUAL·JUSTICE·UNDER·LAW·

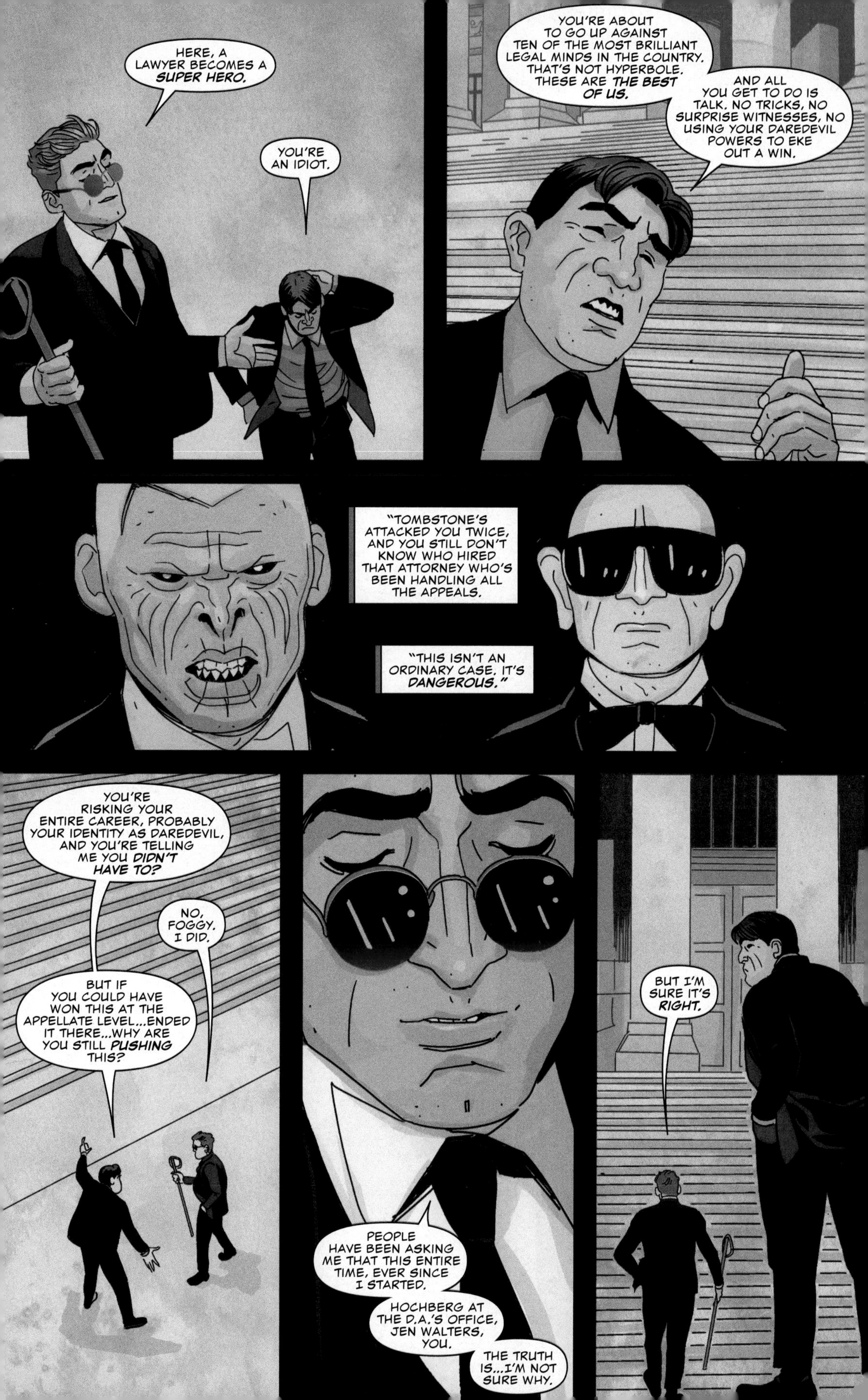
HERE, A LAWYER BECOMES A SUPER HERO.
YOU'RE AN IDIOT.
YOU'RE ABOUT TO GO UP AGAINST TEN OF THE MOST BRILLIANT LEGAL MINDS IN THE COUNTRY. THAT'S NOT HYPERBOLE. THESE ARE THE BEST OF US.
AND ALL YOU GET TO DO IS TALK. NO TRICKS, NO SURPRISE WITNESSES, NO USING YOUR DAREDEVIL POWERS TO EKE OUT A WIN.
"TOMBSTONE'S ATTACKED YOU TWICE, AND YOU STILL DON'T KNOW WHO HIRED THAT ATTORNEY WHO'S BEEN HANDLING ALL THE APPEALS.
"THIS ISN'T AN ORDINARY CASE. IT'S DANGEROUS."
YOU'RE RISKING YOUR ENTIRE CAREER, PROBABLY YOUR IDENTITY AS DAREDEVIL, AND YOU'RE TELLING ME YOU DIDN'T HAVE TO?
NO, FOGGY. I DID.
BUT IF YOU COULD HAVE WON THIS AT THE APPELLATE LEVEL...ENDED IT THERE...WHY ARE YOU STILL PUSHING THIS?
PEOPLE HAVE BEEN ASKING ME THAT THIS ENTIRE TIME, EVER SINCE I STARTED.
HOCHBERG AT THE D.A.'S OFFICE, JEN WALTERS, YOU.
THE TRUTH IS...I'M NOT SURE WHY.
BUT I'M SURE IT'S RIGHT.

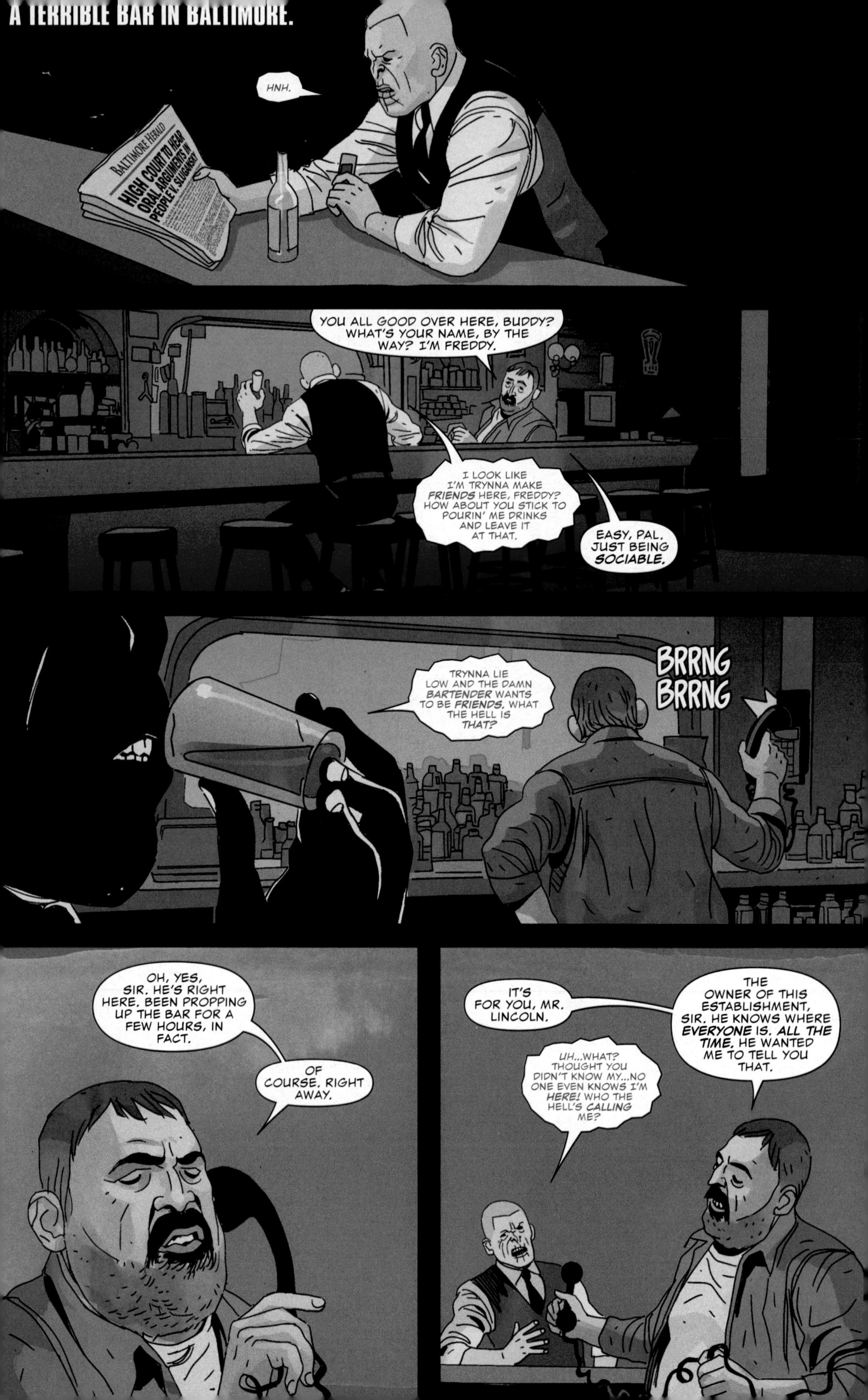
A TERRIBLE BAR IN BALTIMORE.
HNH.
BALTIMORE HERALD
HIGH COURT TO HEAR ORAL ARGUMENTS IN PEOPLE V. SLUGANSKY
YOU ALL GOOD OVER HERE, BUDDY? WHAT'S YOUR NAME, BY THE WAY? I'M FREDDY.
I LOOK LIKE I'M TRYNNA MAKE FRIENDS HERE, FREDDY? HOW ABOUT YOU STICK TO POURIN' ME DRINKS AND LEAVE IT AT THAT.
EASY, PAL. JUST BEING SOCIABLE.
TRYNNA LIE LOW AND THE DAMN BARTENDER WANTS TO BE FRIENDS. WHAT THE HELL IS THAT?
BRRNG BRRNG
OH, YES, SIR. HE'S RIGHT HERE. BEEN PROPPING UP THE BAR FOR A FEW HOURS, IN FACT.
OF COURSE. RIGHT AWAY.
IT'S FOR YOU, MR. LINCOLN.
UH...WHAT? THOUGHT YOU DIDN'T KNOW MY...NO ONE EVEN KNOWS I'M HERE! WHO THE HELL'S CALLING ME?
THE OWNER OF THIS ESTABLISHMENT, SIR. HE KNOWS WHERE EVERYONE IS. ALL THE TIME. HE WANTED ME TO TELL YOU THAT.

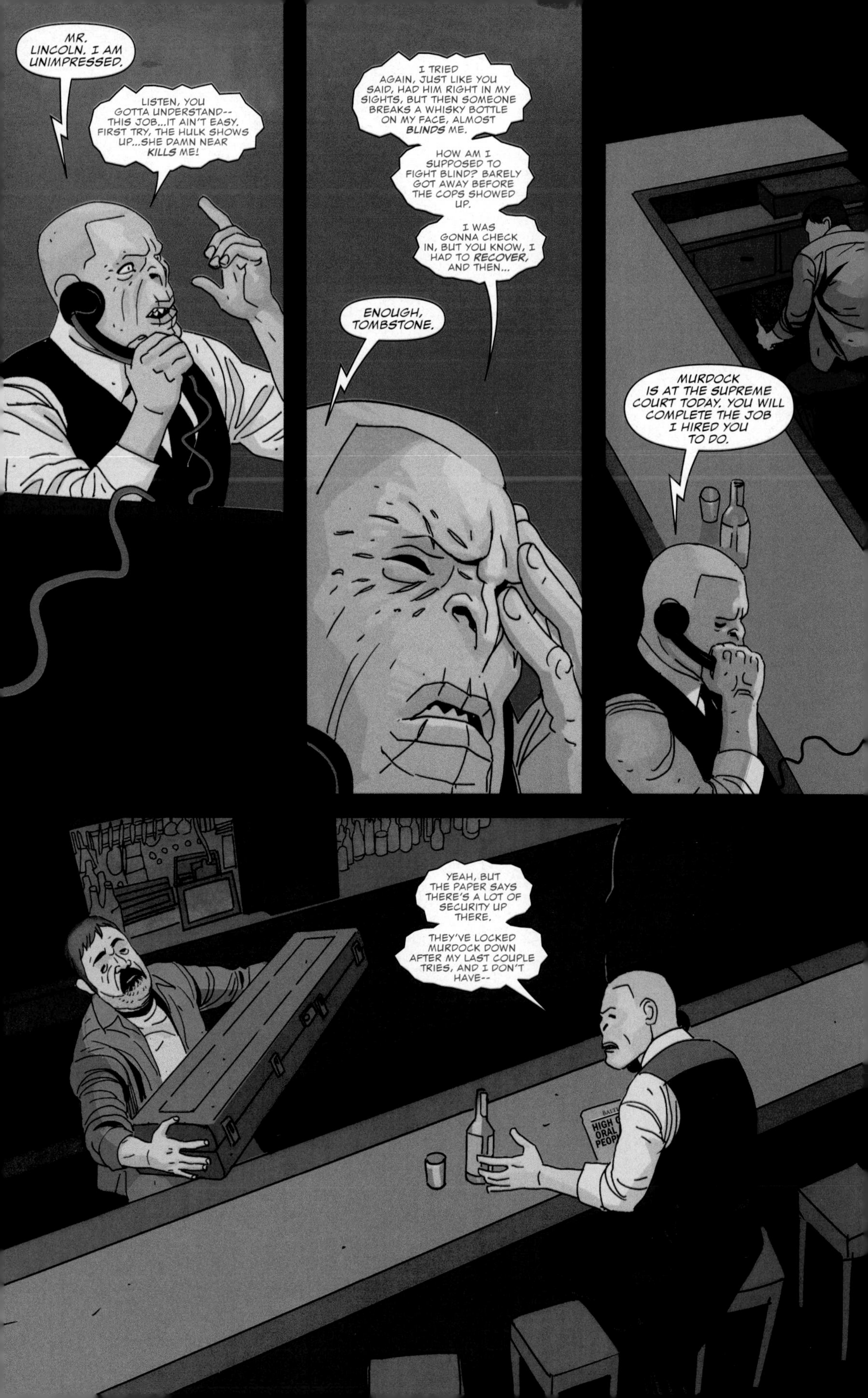

MR. LINCOLN. I AM UNIMPRESSED.
LISTEN, YOU GOTTA UNDERSTAND-- THIS JOB...IT AIN'T EASY. FIRST TRY, THE HULK SHOWS UP...SHE DAMN NEAR KILLS ME!
I TRIED AGAIN, JUST LIKE YOU SAID, HAD HIM RIGHT IN MY SIGHTS, BUT THEN SOMEONE BREAKS A WHISKY BOTTLE ON MY FACE, ALMOST BLINDS ME.
HOW AM I SUPPOSED TO FIGHT BLIND? BARELY GOT AWAY BEFORE THE COPS SHOWED UP.
I WAS GONNA CHECK IN, BUT YOU KNOW, I HAD TO RECOVER, AND THEN...
ENOUGH, TOMBSTONE.
MURDOCK IS AT THE SUPREME COURT TODAY. YOU WILL COMPLETE THE JOB I HIRED YOU TO DO.
YEAH, BUT THE PAPER SAYS THERE'S A LOT OF SECURITY UP THERE.
THEY'VE LOCKED MURDOCK DOWN AFTER MY LAST COUPLE TRIES, AND I DON'T HAVE--

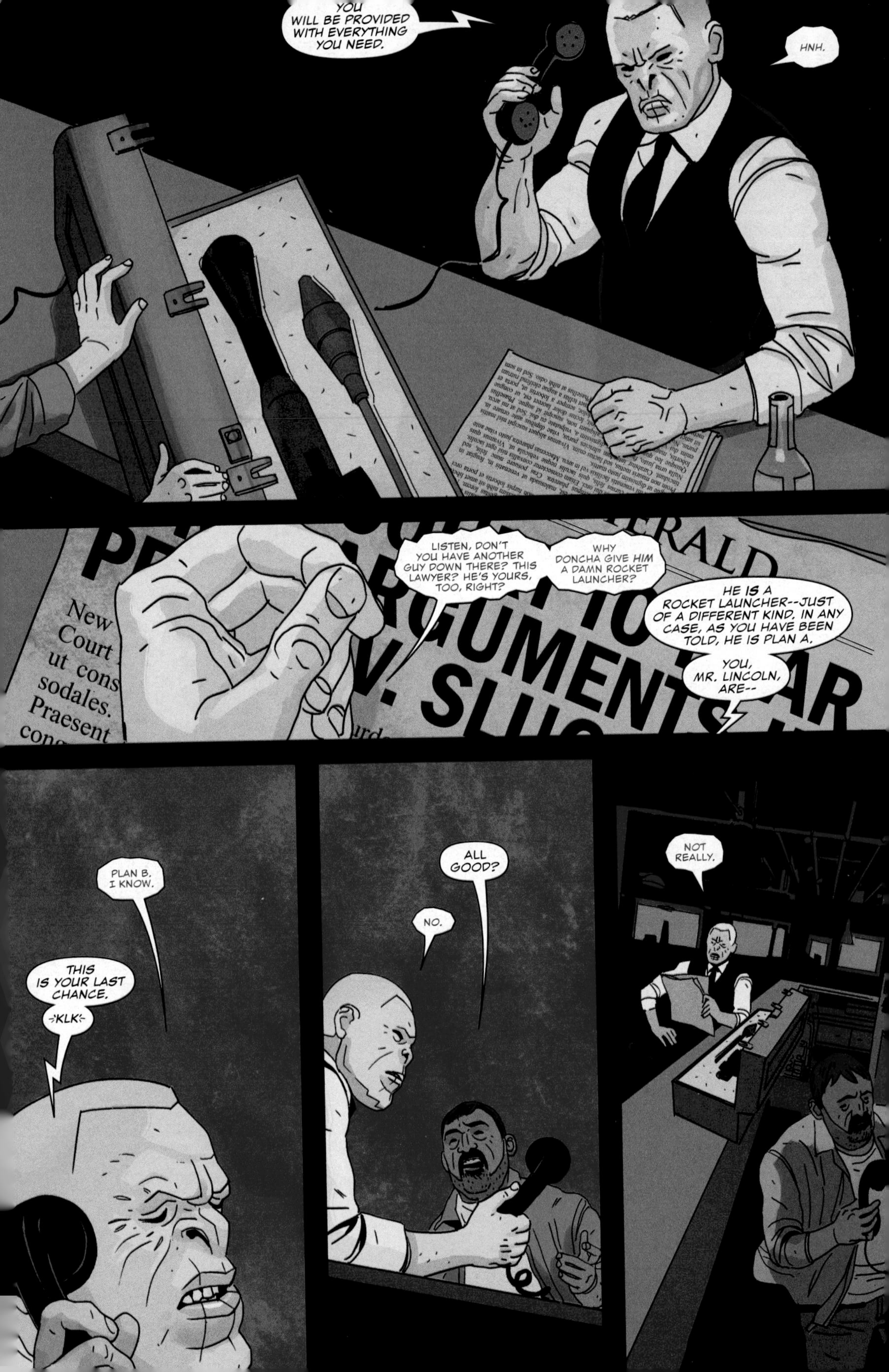
YOU WILL BE PROVIDED WITH EVERYTHING YOU NEED.
HNH.
LISTEN, DON'T YOU HAVE ANOTHER GUY DOWN THERE? THIS LAWYER? HE'S YOURS, TOO, RIGHT?
WHY DONCHA GIVE HIM A DAMN ROCKET LAUNCHER?
HE IS A ROCKET LAUNCHER--JUST OF A DIFFERENT KIND. IN ANY CASE, AS YOU HAVE BEEN TOLD, HE IS PLAN A.
YOU, MR. LINCOLN, ARE--
PLAN B. I KNOW.
THIS IS YOUR LAST CHANCE.
KLK
ALL GOOD?
NO.
NOT REALLY.

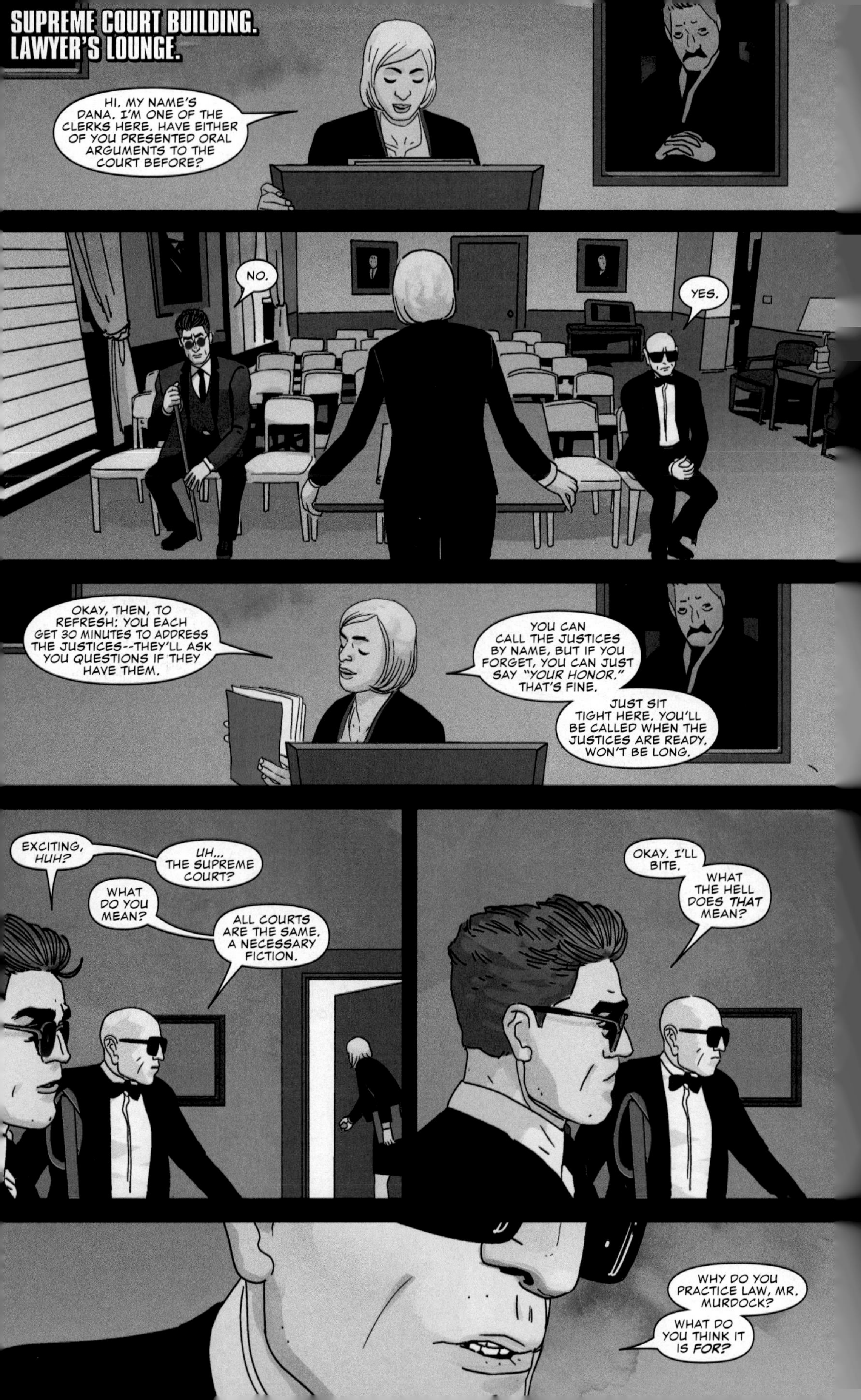
SUPREME COURT BUILDING.
LAWYER'S LOUNGE.
HI. MY NAME'S DANA. I'M ONE OF THE CLERKS HERE. HAVE EITHER OF YOU PRESENTED ORAL ARGUMENTS TO THE COURT BEFORE?
NO.
YES.
OKAY, THEN, TO REFRESH: YOU EACH GET 30 MINUTES TO ADDRESS THE JUSTICES--THEY'LL ASK YOU QUESTIONS IF THEY HAVE THEM.
YOU CAN CALL THE JUSTICES BY NAME, BUT IF YOU FORGET, YOU CAN JUST SAY "YOUR HONOR." THAT'S FINE.
JUST SIT TIGHT HERE. YOU'LL BE CALLED WHEN THE JUSTICES ARE READY. WON'T BE LONG.
EXCITING, HUH?
UH... THE SUPREME COURT?
WHAT DO YOU MEAN?
ALL COURTS ARE THE SAME. A NECESSARY FICTION.
OKAY. I'LL BITE.
WHAT THE HELL DOES THAT MEAN?
WHY DO YOU PRACTICE LAW, MR. MURDOCK?
WHAT DO YOU THINK IT IS FOR?

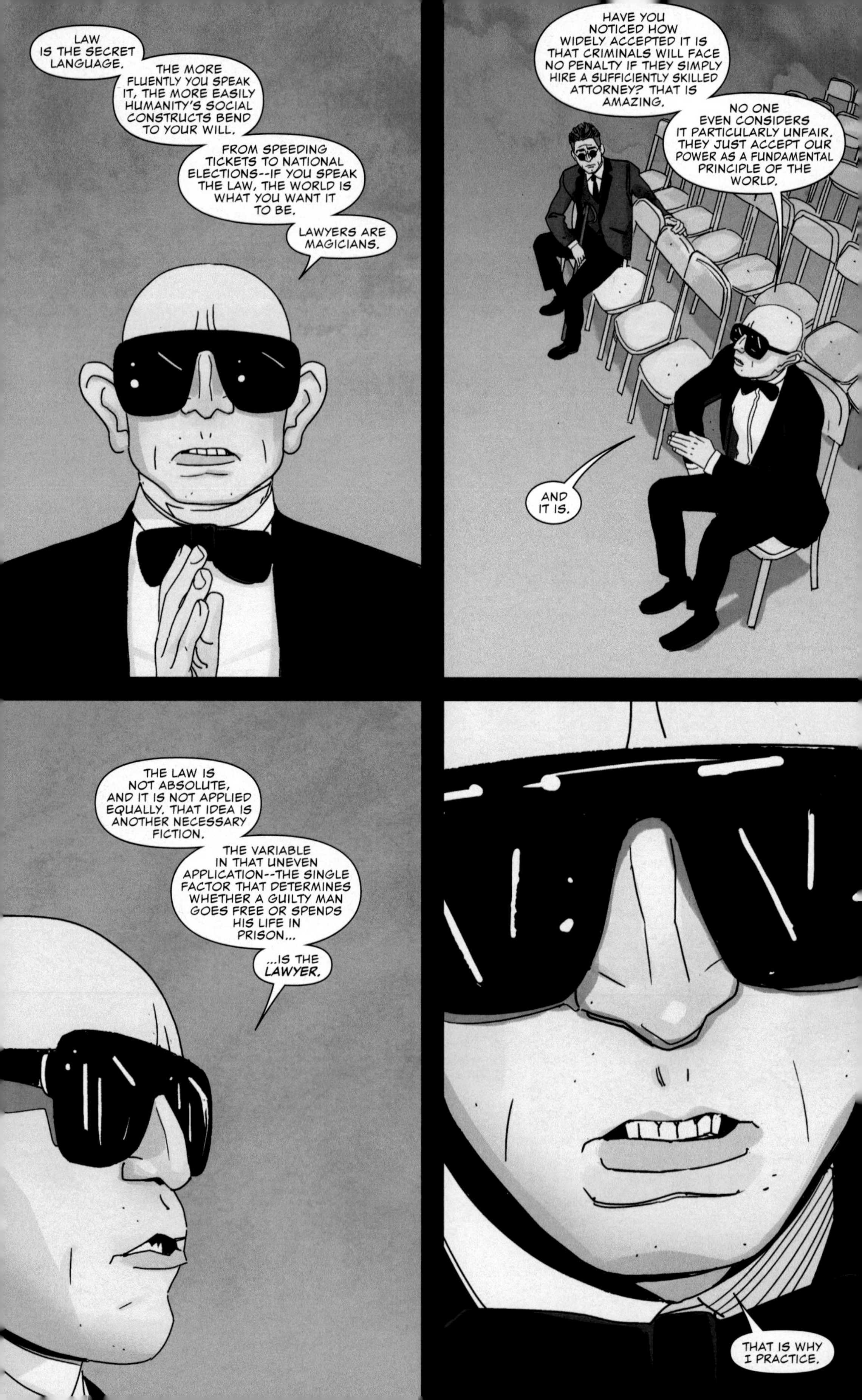
LAW IS THE SECRET LANGUAGE.
THE MORE FLUENTLY YOU SPEAK IT, THE MORE EASILY HUMANITY'S SOCIAL CONSTRUCTS BEND TO YOUR WILL.
FROM SPEEDING TICKETS TO NATIONAL ELECTIONS--IF YOU SPEAK THE LAW, THE WORLD IS WHAT YOU WANT IT TO BE.
LAWYERS ARE MAGICIANS.
HAVE YOU NOTICED HOW WIDELY ACCEPTED IT IS THAT CRIMINALS WILL FACE NO PENALTY IF THEY SIMPLY HIRE A SUFFICIENTLY SKILLED ATTORNEY? THAT IS AMAZING.
NO ONE EVEN CONSIDERS IT PARTICULARLY UNFAIR. THEY JUST ACCEPT OUR POWER AS A FUNDAMENTAL PRINCIPLE OF THE WORLD.
AND IT IS.
THE LAW IS NOT ABSOLUTE, AND IT IS NOT APPLIED EQUALLY. THAT IDEA IS ANOTHER NECESSARY FICTION.
THE VARIABLE IN THAT UNEVEN APPLICATION--THE SINGLE FACTOR THAT DETERMINES WHETHER A GUILTY MAN GOES FREE OR SPENDS HIS LIFE IN PRISON...
...IS THE *LAWYER.*
THAT IS WHY I PRACTICE.

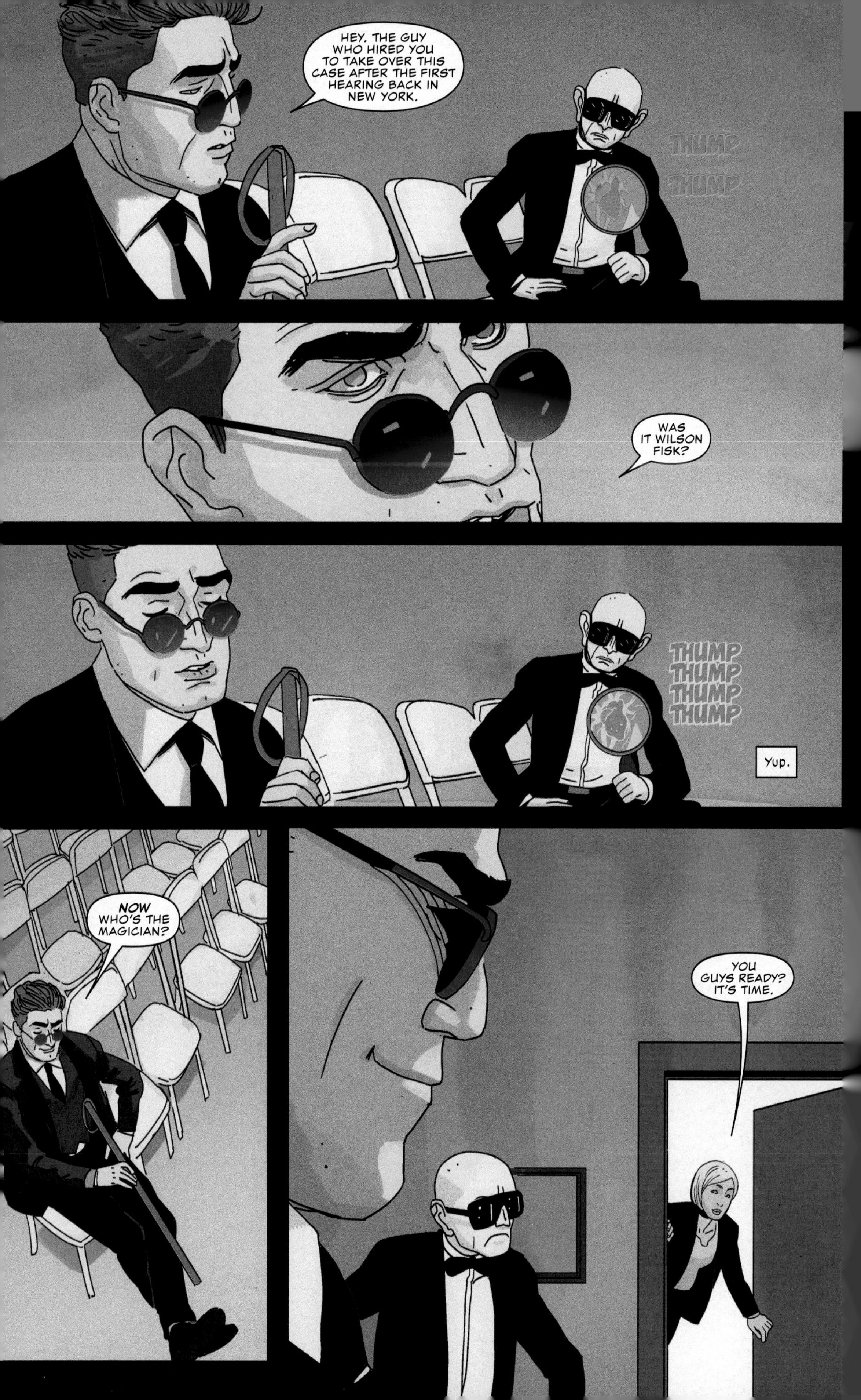
HEY. THE GUY WHO HIRED YOU TO TAKE OVER THIS CASE AFTER THE FIRST HEARING BACK IN NEW YORK.
THUMP
THUMP
WAS IT WILSON FISK?
THUMP THUMP THUMP THUMP
Yup.
NOW WHO'S THE MAGICIAN?
YOU GUYS READY? IT'S TIME.

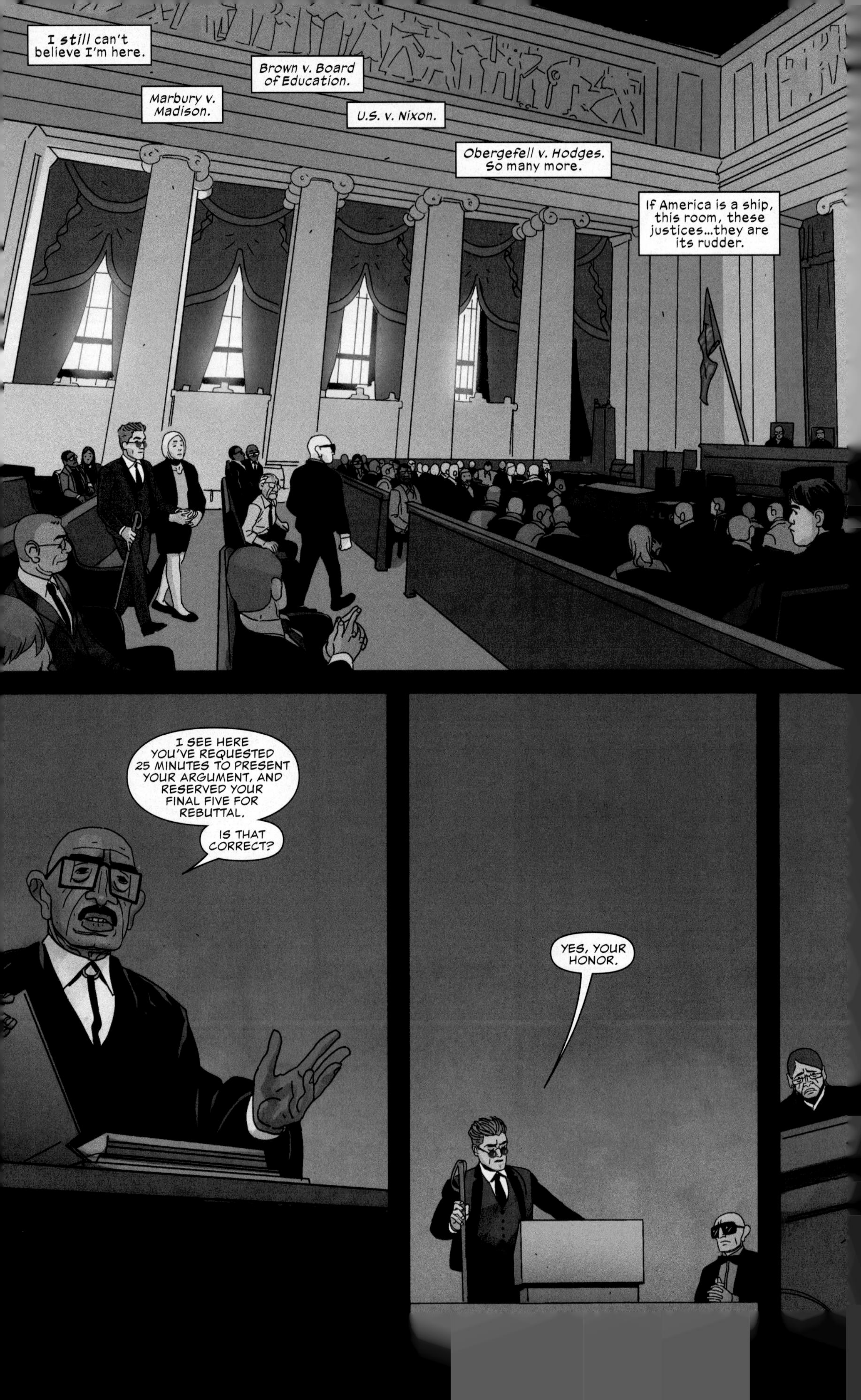
I still can't believe I'm here.
Marbury v. Madison.
Brown v. Board of Education.
U.S. v. Nixon.
Obergefell v. Hodges. So many more.
If America is a ship, this room, these justices...they are its rudder.
I SEE HERE YOU'VE REQUESTED 25 MINUTES TO PRESENT YOUR ARGUMENT, AND RESERVED YOUR FINAL FIVE FOR REBUTTAL.
IS THAT CORRECT?
YES, YOUR HONOR.

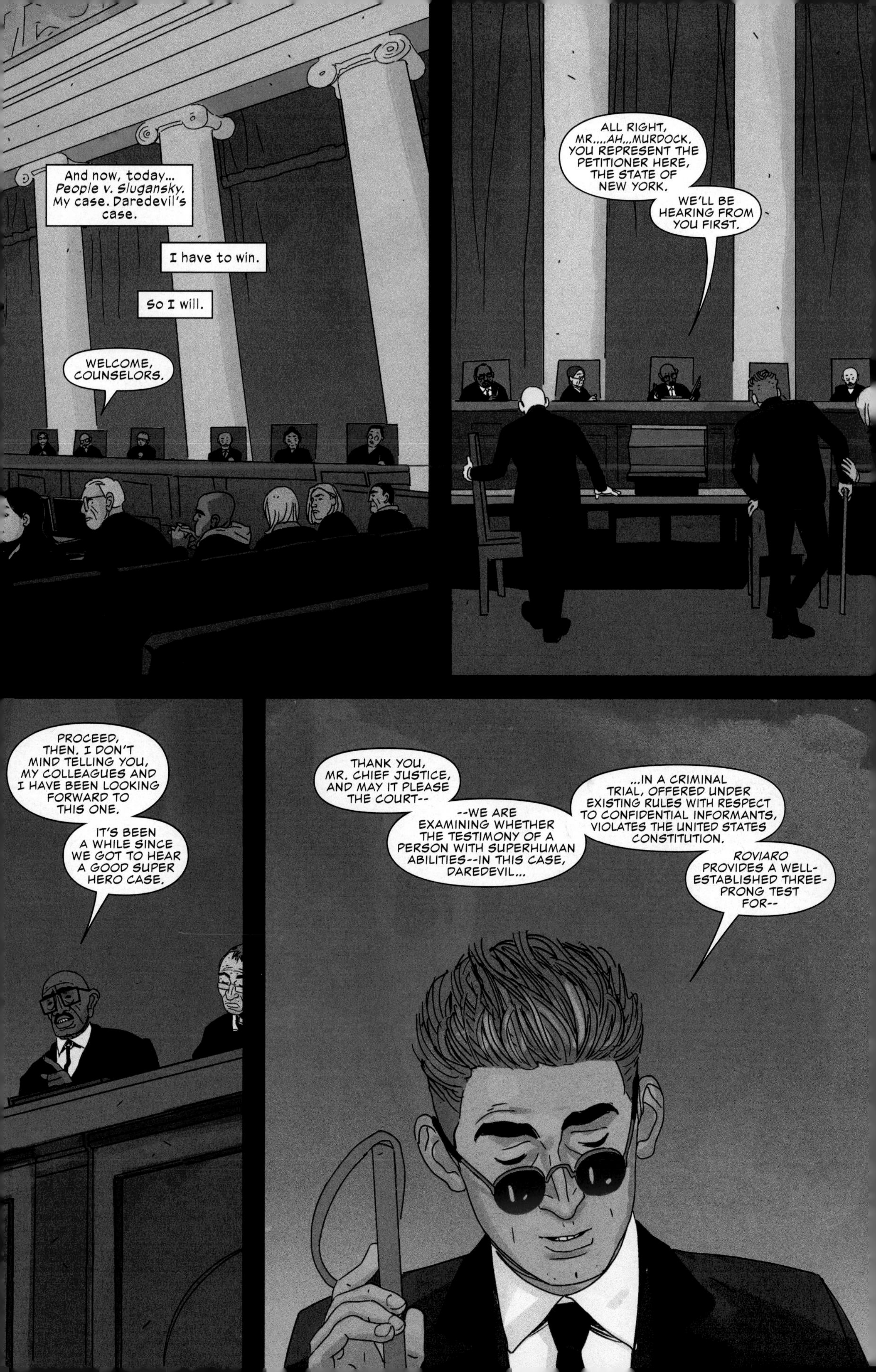

And now, today... *People v. Sluganksy.* My case. Daredevil's case.
I have to win.
So I will.
WELCOME, COUNSELORS.
ALL RIGHT, MR....AH...MURDOCK. YOU REPRESENT THE PETITIONER HERE, THE STATE OF NEW YORK.
WE'LL BE HEARING FROM YOU FIRST.
PROCEED, THEN. I DON'T MIND TELLING YOU, MY COLLEAGUES AND I HAVE BEEN LOOKING FORWARD TO THIS ONE.
IT'S BEEN A WHILE SINCE WE GOT TO HEAR A GOOD SUPER HERO CASE.
THANK YOU, MR. CHIEF JUSTICE, AND MAY IT PLEASE THE COURT--
--WE ARE EXAMINING WHETHER THE TESTIMONY OF A PERSON WITH SUPERHUMAN ABILITIES--IN THIS CASE, DAREDEVIL...
...IN A CRIMINAL TRIAL, OFFERED UNDER EXISTING RULES WITH RESPECT TO CONFIDENTIAL INFORMANTS, VIOLATES THE UNITED STATES CONSTITUTION.
ROVIARO PROVIDES A WELL-ESTABLISHED THREE-PRONG TEST FOR--

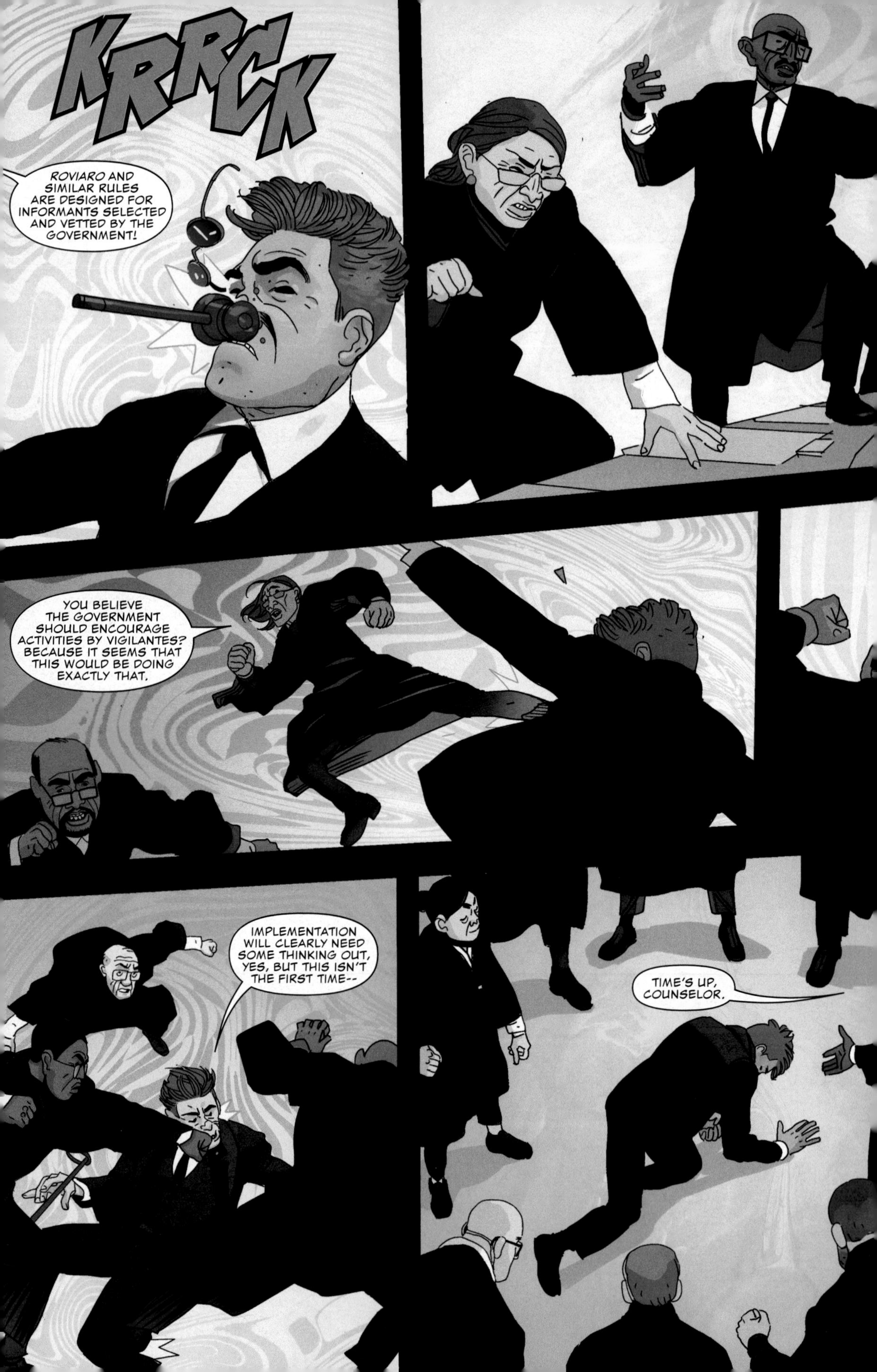
KRRCK
ROVIARO AND SIMILAR RULES ARE DESIGNED FOR INFORMANTS SELECTED AND VETTED BY THE GOVERNMENT!
YOU BELIEVE THE GOVERNMENT SHOULD ENCOURAGE ACTIVITIES BY VIGILANTES? BECAUSE IT SEEMS THAT THIS WOULD BE DOING EXACTLY THAT.
IMPLEMENTATION WILL CLEARLY NEED SOME THINKING OUT, YES, BUT THIS ISN'T THE FIRST TIME--
TIME'S UP, COUNSELOR.

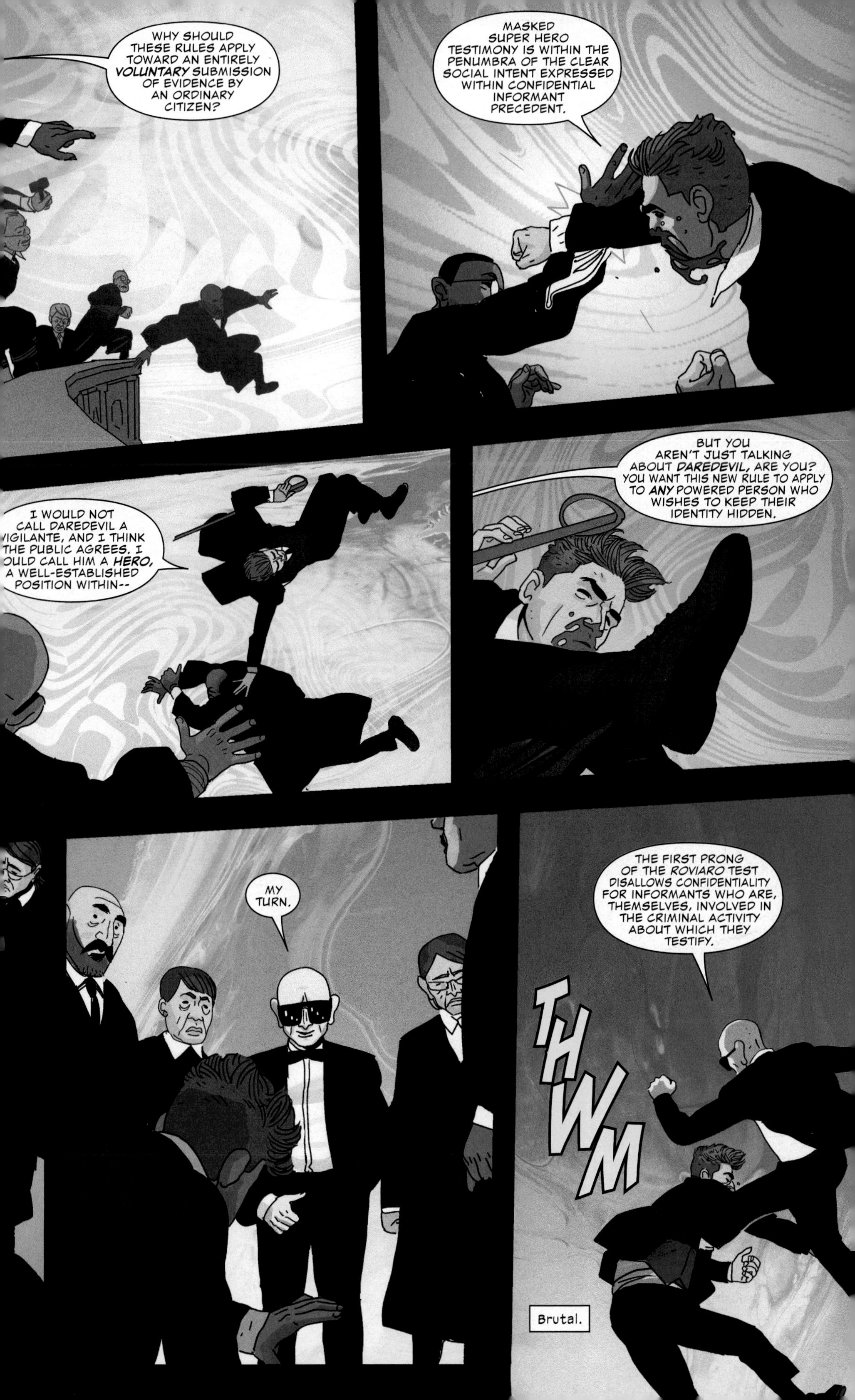
WHY SHOULD THESE RULES APPLY TOWARD AN ENTIRELY VOLUNTARY SUBMISSION OF EVIDENCE BY AN ORDINARY CITIZEN?
MASKED SUPER HERO TESTIMONY IS WITHIN THE PENUMBRA OF THE CLEAR SOCIAL INTENT EXPRESSED WITHIN CONFIDENTIAL INFORMANT PRECEDENT.
I WOULD NOT CALL DAREDEVIL A VIGILANTE, AND I THINK THE PUBLIC AGREES. I OULD CALL HIM A HERO, A WELL-ESTABLISHED POSITION WITHIN--
BUT YOU AREN'T JUST TALKING ABOUT DAREDEVIL, ARE YOU? YOU WANT THIS NEW RULE TO APPLY TO ANY POWERED PERSON WHO WISHES TO KEEP THEIR IDENTITY HIDDEN.
MY TURN.
THE FIRST PRONG OF THE ROVIARO TEST DISALLOWS CONFIDENTIALITY FOR INFORMANTS WHO ARE, THEMSELVES, INVOLVED IN THE CRIMINAL ACTIVITY ABOUT WHICH THEY TESTIFY.
THWM
Brutal.

IT IS THEREFORE WITHIN THE *PENUMBRA* OF THE RULES--TO USE PETITIONER'S COUNSEL'S TERM--TO PREVENT CRIMINALS FROM TESTIFYING ANONYMOUSLY.

Absolutely brutal.

DAREDEVIL AND HIS ILK CAN CALL THEMSELVES WHAT THEY LIKE--BUT THEY ARE *VIGILANTES*. THEY ARE, IN FACT, CRIMINALS.

THE DUE PROCESS ISSUES COULD NOT BE MORE CLEARLY DRAWN, AND OF COURSE THE CONFRONTATION CLAUSE VIOLATION.

I BELIEVE THAT ONCE YOU HAVE GIVEN THESE POINTS DUE CONSIDERATION, YOU WILL AGREE, THANK YOU.

THANK YOU, COUNSELOR.

NOW, MR. MURDOCK--YOU RESERVED FIVE MINUTES FOR REBUTTAL, WE'RE READY WHEN YOU ARE.

Look at that *smile*. Thinks he's got me.

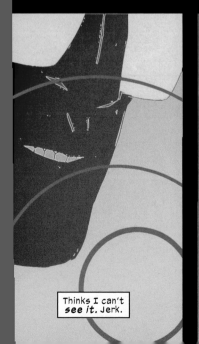

Thinks I can't *see it*. Jerk.

YOU'RE AFRAID, I KNOW THAT.

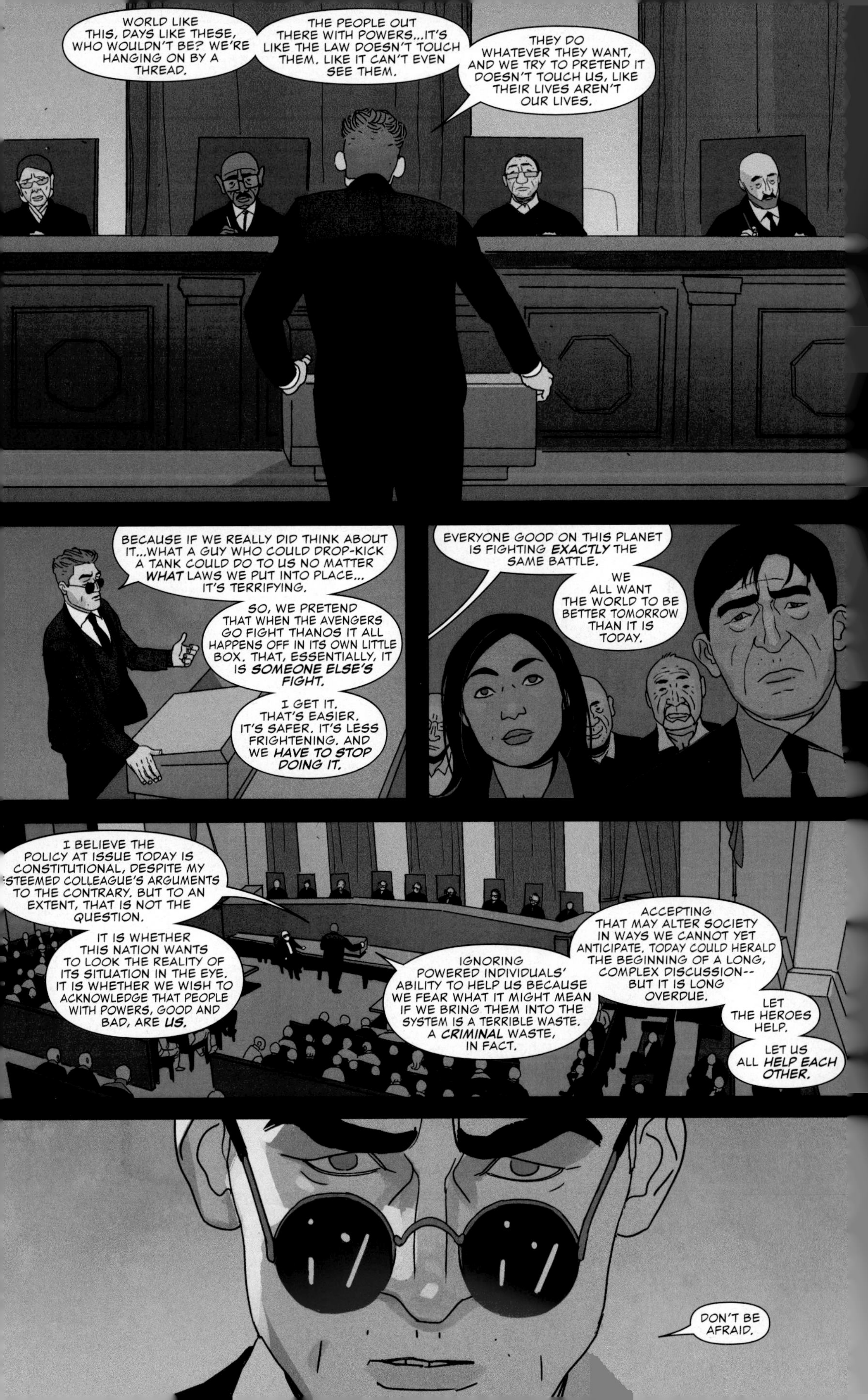
WORLD LIKE THIS, DAYS LIKE THESE, WHO WOULDN'T BE? WE'RE HANGING ON BY A THREAD.
THE PEOPLE OUT THERE WITH POWERS...IT'S LIKE THE LAW DOESN'T TOUCH THEM. LIKE IT CAN'T EVEN SEE THEM.
THEY DO WHATEVER THEY WANT, AND WE TRY TO PRETEND IT DOESN'T TOUCH US, LIKE THEIR LIVES AREN'T OUR LIVES.
BECAUSE IF WE REALLY DID THINK ABOUT IT...WHAT A GUY WHO COULD DROP-KICK A TANK COULD DO TO US NO MATTER WHAT LAWS WE PUT INTO PLACE... IT'S TERRIFYING.
SO, WE PRETEND THAT WHEN THE AVENGERS GO FIGHT THANOS IT ALL HAPPENS OFF IN ITS OWN LITTLE BOX. THAT, ESSENTIALLY, IT IS SOMEONE ELSE'S FIGHT.
I GET IT. THAT'S EASIER. IT'S SAFER. IT'S LESS FRIGHTENING. AND WE HAVE TO STOP DOING IT.
EVERYONE GOOD ON THIS PLANET IS FIGHTING EXACTLY THE SAME BATTLE.
WE ALL WANT THE WORLD TO BE BETTER TOMORROW THAN IT IS TODAY.
I BELIEVE THE POLICY AT ISSUE TODAY IS CONSTITUTIONAL, DESPITE MY ESTEEMED COLLEAGUE'S ARGUMENTS TO THE CONTRARY. BUT TO AN EXTENT, THAT IS NOT THE QUESTION.
IT IS WHETHER THIS NATION WANTS TO LOOK THE REALITY OF ITS SITUATION IN THE EYE. IT IS WHETHER WE WISH TO ACKNOWLEDGE THAT PEOPLE WITH POWERS, GOOD AND BAD, ARE US.
IGNORING POWERED INDIVIDUALS' ABILITY TO HELP US BECAUSE WE FEAR WHAT IT MIGHT MEAN IF WE BRING THEM INTO THE SYSTEM IS A TERRIBLE WASTE. A CRIMINAL WASTE, IN FACT.
ACCEPTING THAT MAY ALTER SOCIETY IN WAYS WE CANNOT YET ANTICIPATE. TODAY COULD HERALD THE BEGINNING OF A LONG, COMPLEX DISCUSSION-- BUT IT IS LONG OVERDUE.
LET THE HEROES HELP.
LET US ALL HELP EACH OTHER.
DON'T BE AFRAID.

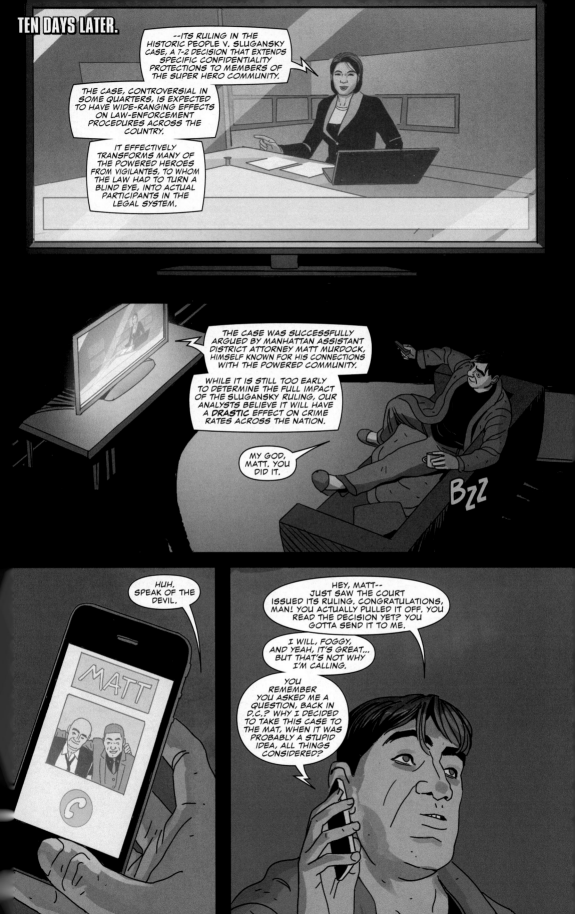

--ITS RULING IN THE HISTORIC PEOPLE V. SLUGANSKY CASE, A 7-2 DECISION THAT EXTENDS SPECIFIC CONFIDENTIALITY PROTECTIONS TO MEMBERS OF THE SUPER HERO COMMUNITY.

THE CASE, CONTROVERSIAL IN SOME QUARTERS, IS EXPECTED TO HAVE WIDE-RANGING EFFECTS ON LAW-ENFORCEMENT PROCEDURES ACROSS THE COUNTRY.

IT EFFECTIVELY TRANSFORMS MANY OF THE POWERED HEROES FROM VIGILANTES, TO WHOM THE LAW HAD TO TURN A BLIND EYE, INTO ACTUAL PARTICIPANTS IN THE LEGAL SYSTEM.

THE CASE WAS SUCCESSFULLY ARGUED BY MANHATTAN ASSISTANT DISTRICT ATTORNEY MATT MURDOCK, HIMSELF KNOWN FOR HIS CONNECTIONS WITH THE POWERED COMMUNITY.

WHILE IT IS STILL TOO EARLY TO DETERMINE THE FULL IMPACT OF THE SLUGANSKY RULING, OUR ANALYSTS BELIEVE IT WILL HAVE A *DRASTIC* EFFECT ON CRIME RATES ACROSS THE NATION.

MY GOD, MATT. YOU DID IT.

BZZ

HUH. SPEAK OF THE DEVIL.

MATT

HEY, MATT-- JUST SAW THE COURT ISSUED ITS RULING. CONGRATULATIONS, MAN! YOU ACTUALLY PULLED IT OFF. YOU READ THE DECISION YET? YOU GOTTA SEND IT TO ME.

I WILL, FOGGY, AND YEAH, IT'S GREAT... BUT THAT'S NOT WHY I'M CALLING.

YOU REMEMBER YOU ASKED ME A QUESTION, BACK IN D.C.? WHY I DECIDED TO TAKE THIS CASE TO THE MAT, WHEN IT WAS PROBABLY A STUPID IDEA, ALL THINGS CONSIDERED?

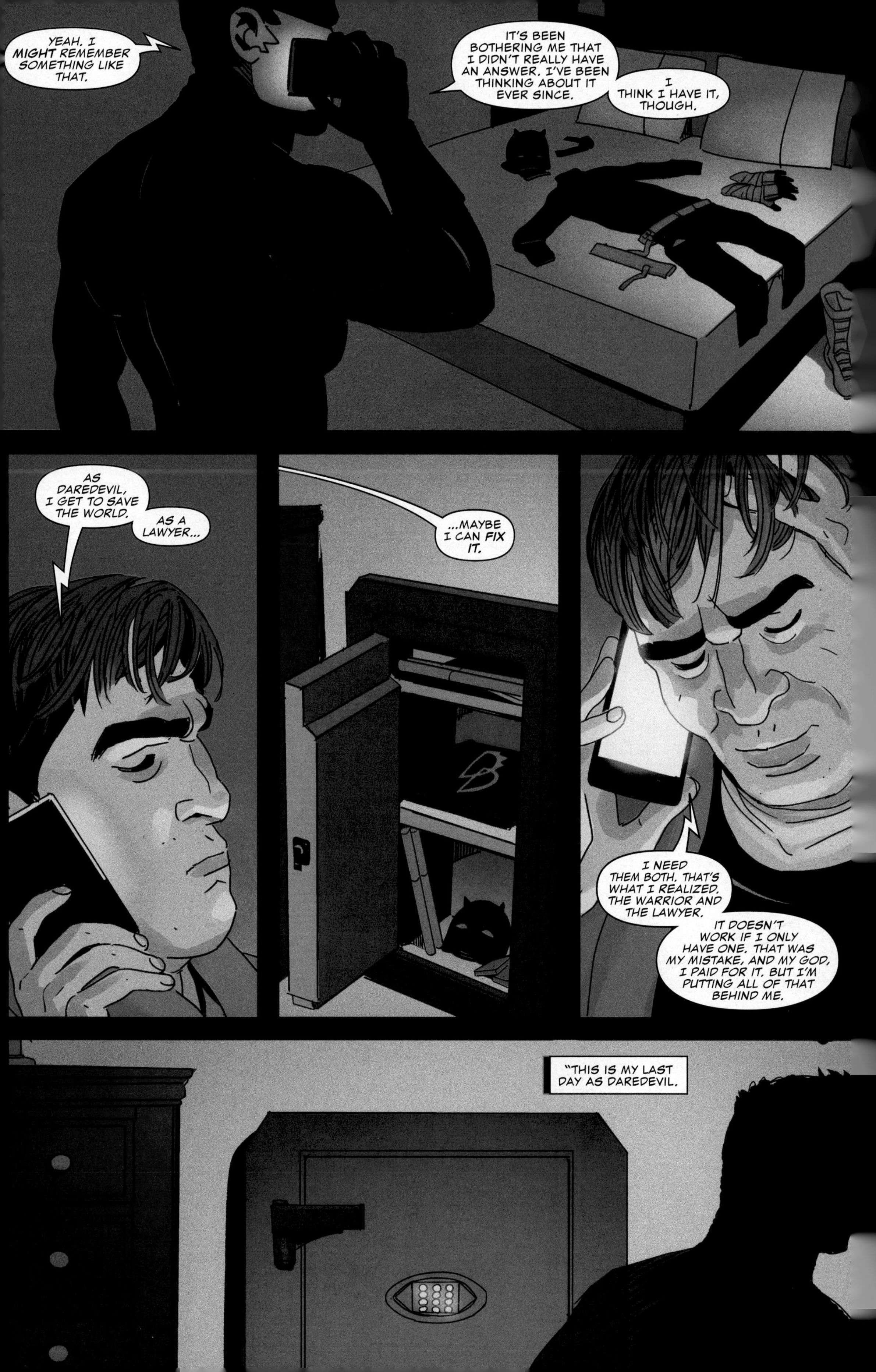
YEAH. I MIGHT REMEMBER SOMETHING LIKE THAT.
IT'S BEEN BOTHERING ME THAT I DIDN'T REALLY HAVE AN ANSWER. I'VE BEEN THINKING ABOUT IT EVER SINCE.
I THINK I HAVE IT, THOUGH.
AS DAREDEVIL, I GET TO SAVE THE WORLD.
AS A LAWYER...
...MAYBE I CAN FIX IT.
I NEED THEM BOTH. THAT'S WHAT I REALIZED. THE WARRIOR AND THE LAWYER.
IT DOESN'T WORK IF I ONLY HAVE ONE. THAT WAS MY MISTAKE, AND MY GOD, I PAID FOR IT. BUT I'M PUTTING ALL OF THAT BEHIND ME.
"THIS IS MY LAST DAY AS DAREDEVIL.

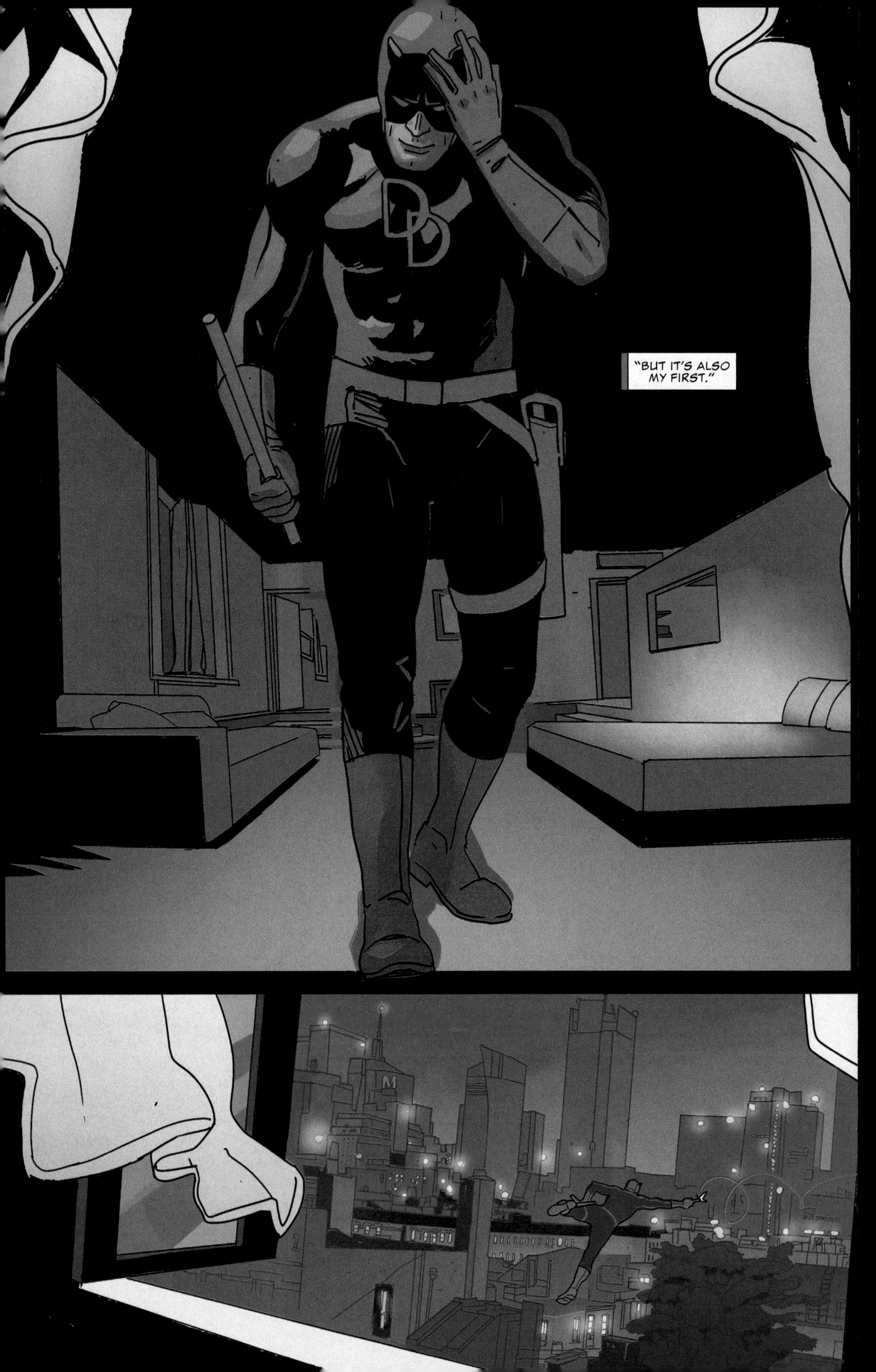
"BUT IT'S ALSO MY FIRST."

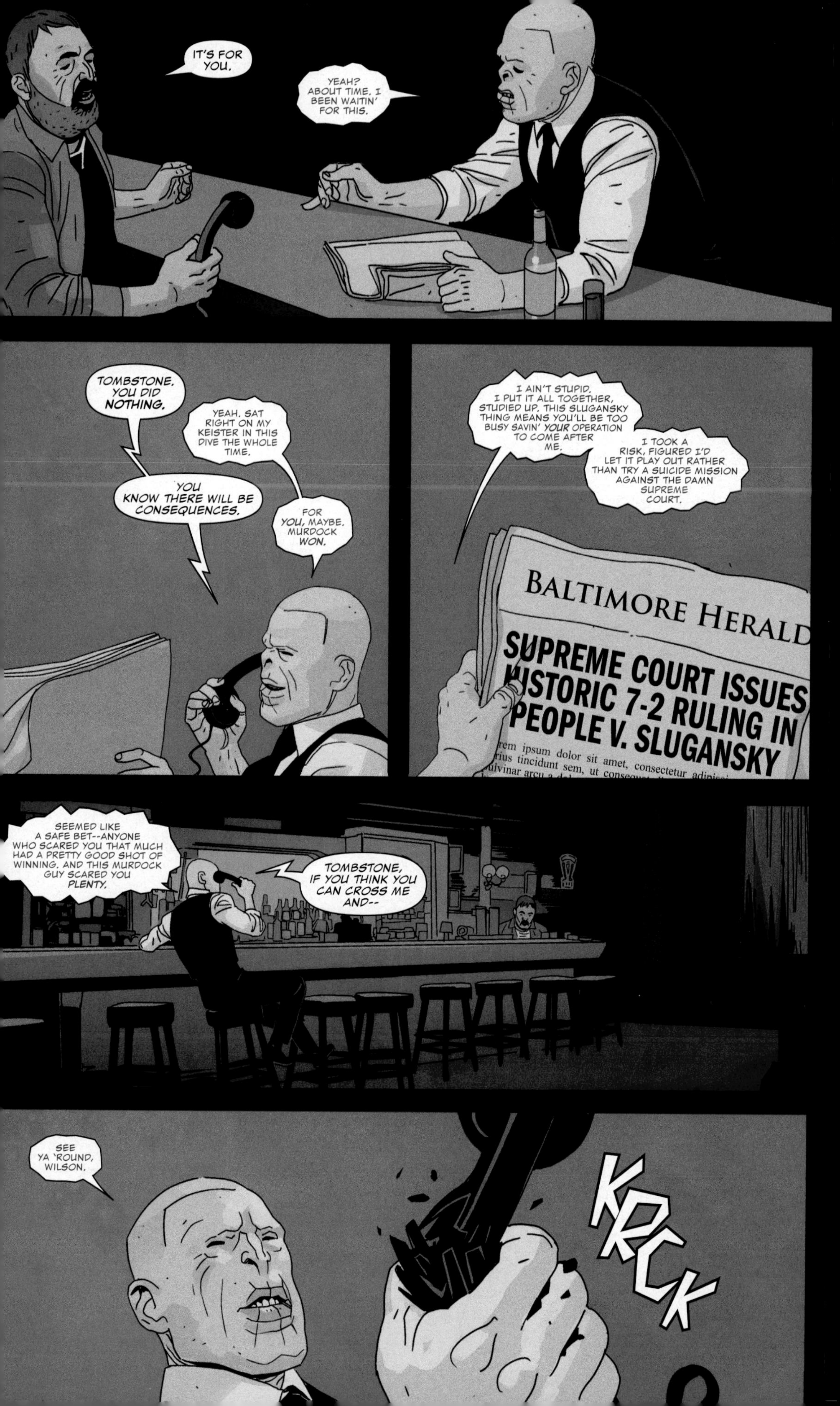
IT'S FOR YOU.
YEAH? ABOUT TIME. I BEEN WAITIN' FOR THIS.
TOMBSTONE. YOU DID NOTHING.
YEAH. SAT RIGHT ON MY KEISTER IN THIS DIVE THE WHOLE TIME.
YOU KNOW THERE WILL BE CONSEQUENCES.
FOR YOU, MAYBE. MURDOCK WON.
I AIN'T STUPID. I PUT IT ALL TOGETHER, STUDIED UP. THIS SLUGANSKY THING MEANS YOU'LL BE TOO BUSY SAVIN' YOUR OPERATION TO COME AFTER ME.
I TOOK A RISK, FIGURED I'D LET IT PLAY OUT RATHER THAN TRY A SUICIDE MISSION AGAINST THE DAMN SUPREME COURT.
BALTIMORE HERALD
SUPREME COURT ISSUES HISTORIC 7-2 RULING IN PEOPLE V. SLUGANSKY
SEEMED LIKE A SAFE BET--ANYONE WHO SCARED YOU THAT MUCH HAD A PRETTY GOOD SHOT OF WINNING. AND THIS MURDOCK GUY SCARED YOU PLENTY.
TOMBSTONE, IF YOU THINK YOU CAN CROSS ME AND--
SEE YA 'ROUND, WILSON.
KRCK

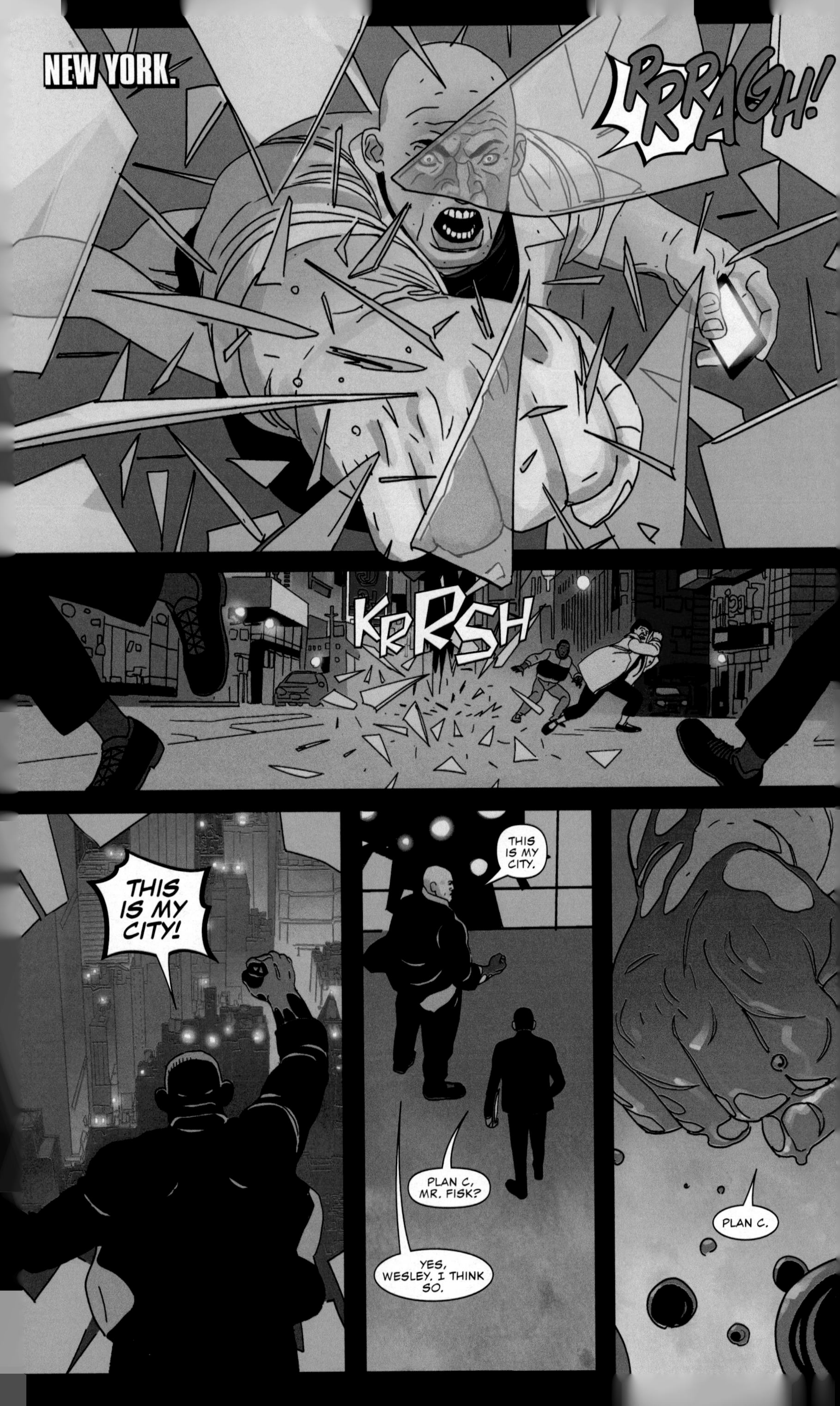
NEW YORK.
RRRAGH!
KRRSH
THIS IS MY CITY!
THIS IS MY CITY.
PLAN C, MR. FISK?
YES, WESLEY. I THINK SO.
PLAN C.

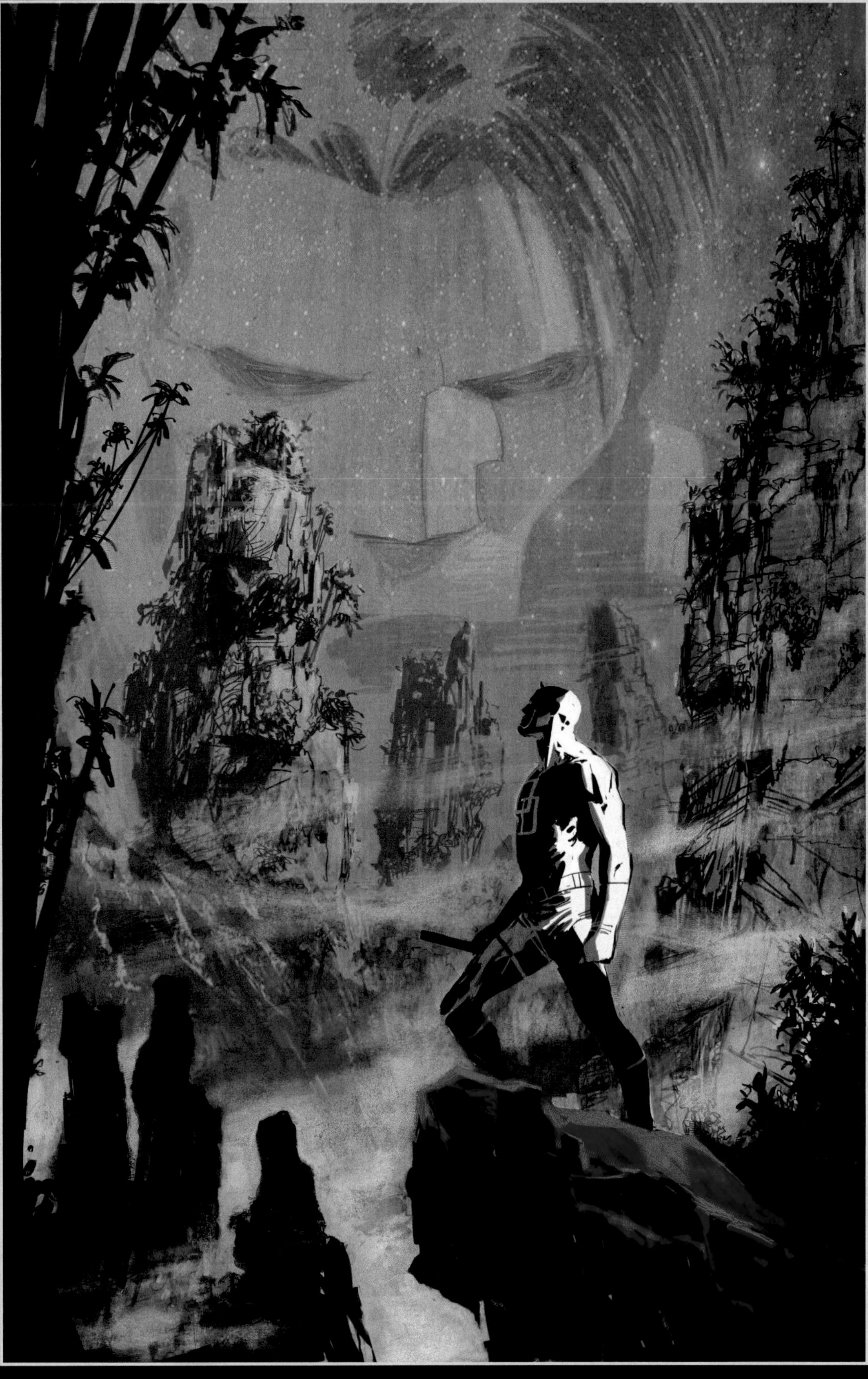

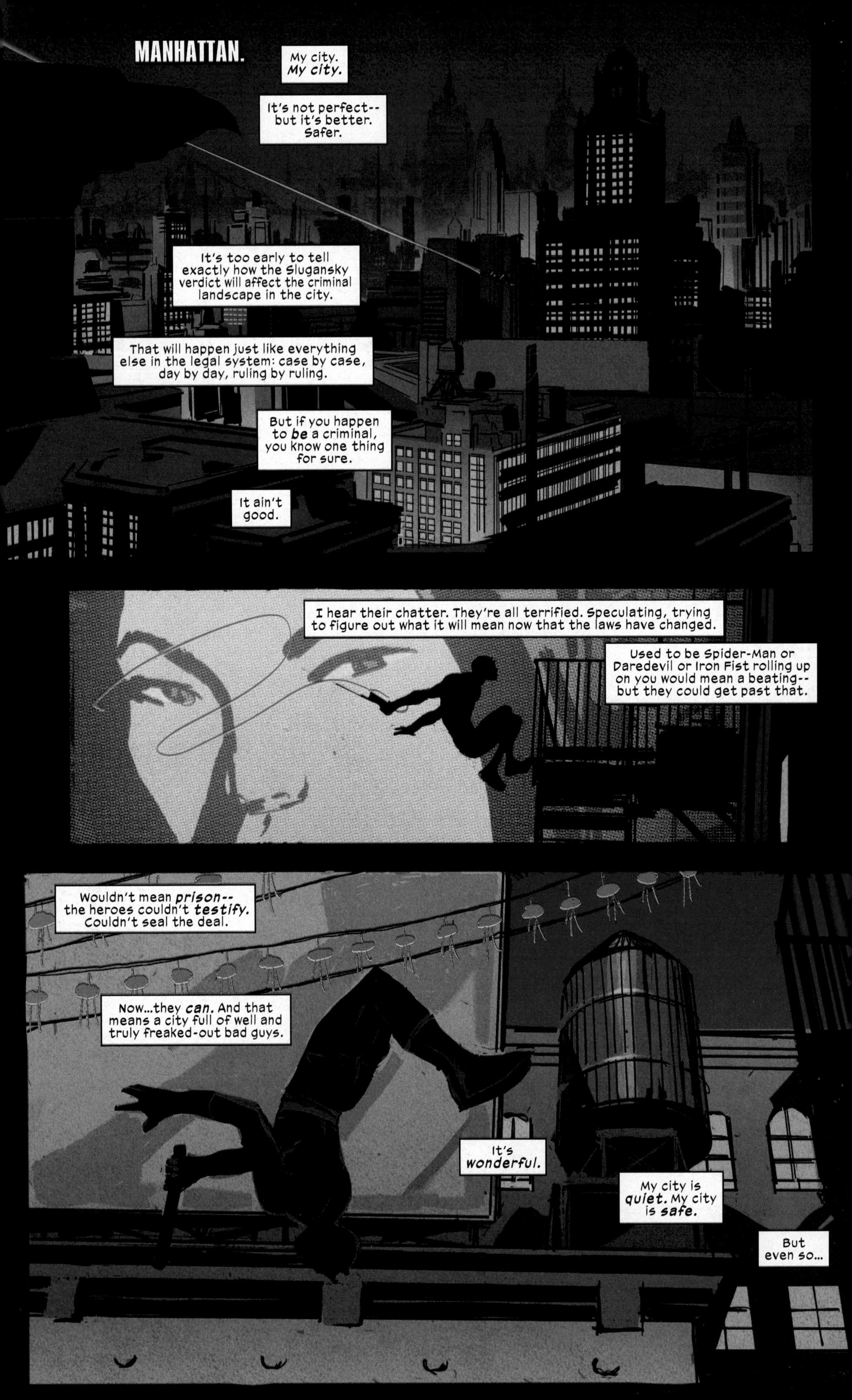
MANHATTAN.
My city. My city.
It's not perfect--but it's better. Safer.
It's too early to tell exactly how the Sluganksy verdict will affect the criminal landscape in the city.
That will happen just like everything else in the legal system: case by case, day by day, ruling by ruling.
But if you happen to be a criminal, you know one thing for sure.
It ain't good.
I hear their chatter. They're all terrified. Speculating, trying to figure out what it will mean now that the laws have changed.
Used to be Spider-Man or Daredevil or Iron Fist rolling up on you would mean a beating--but they could get past that.
Wouldn't mean prison--the heroes couldn't testify. Couldn't seal the deal.
Now...they can. And that means a city full of well and truly freaked-out bad guys.
It's wonderful.
My city is quiet. My city is safe.
But even so...

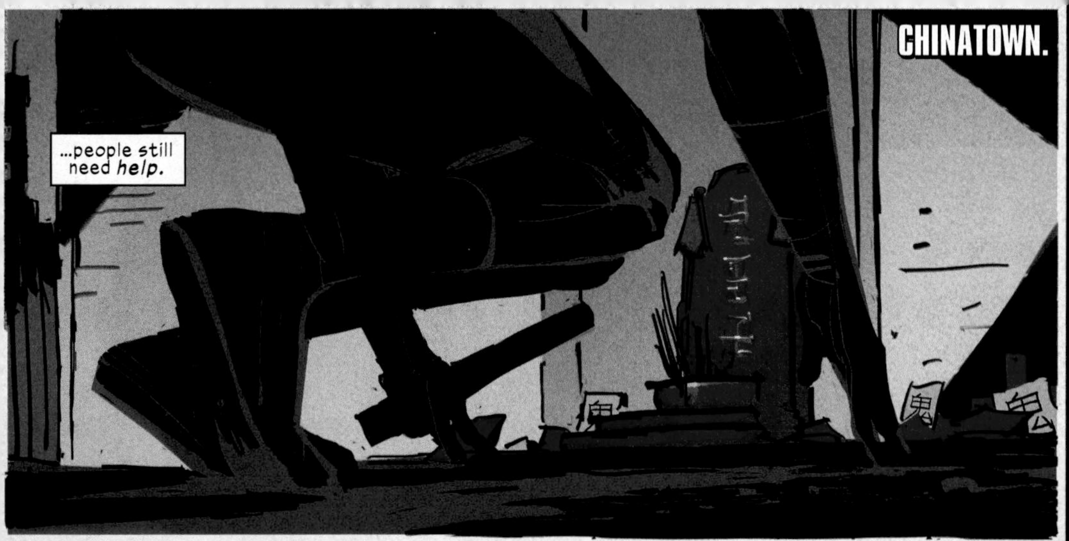
CHINATOWN.
...people still need *help.*
鬼
鬼
鬼

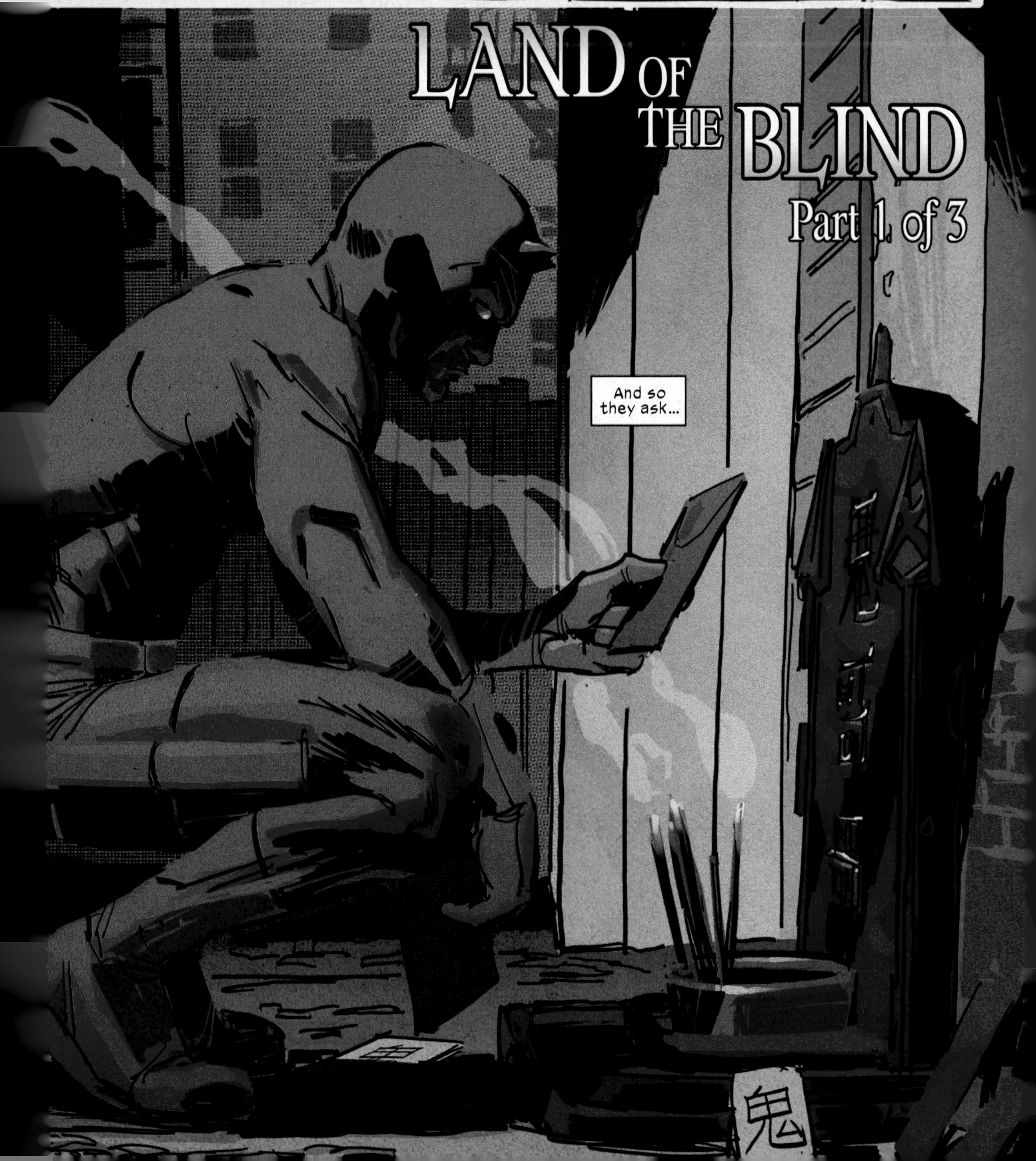
LAND OF THE BLIND
Part 1 of 3
And so they ask...
鬼
鬼

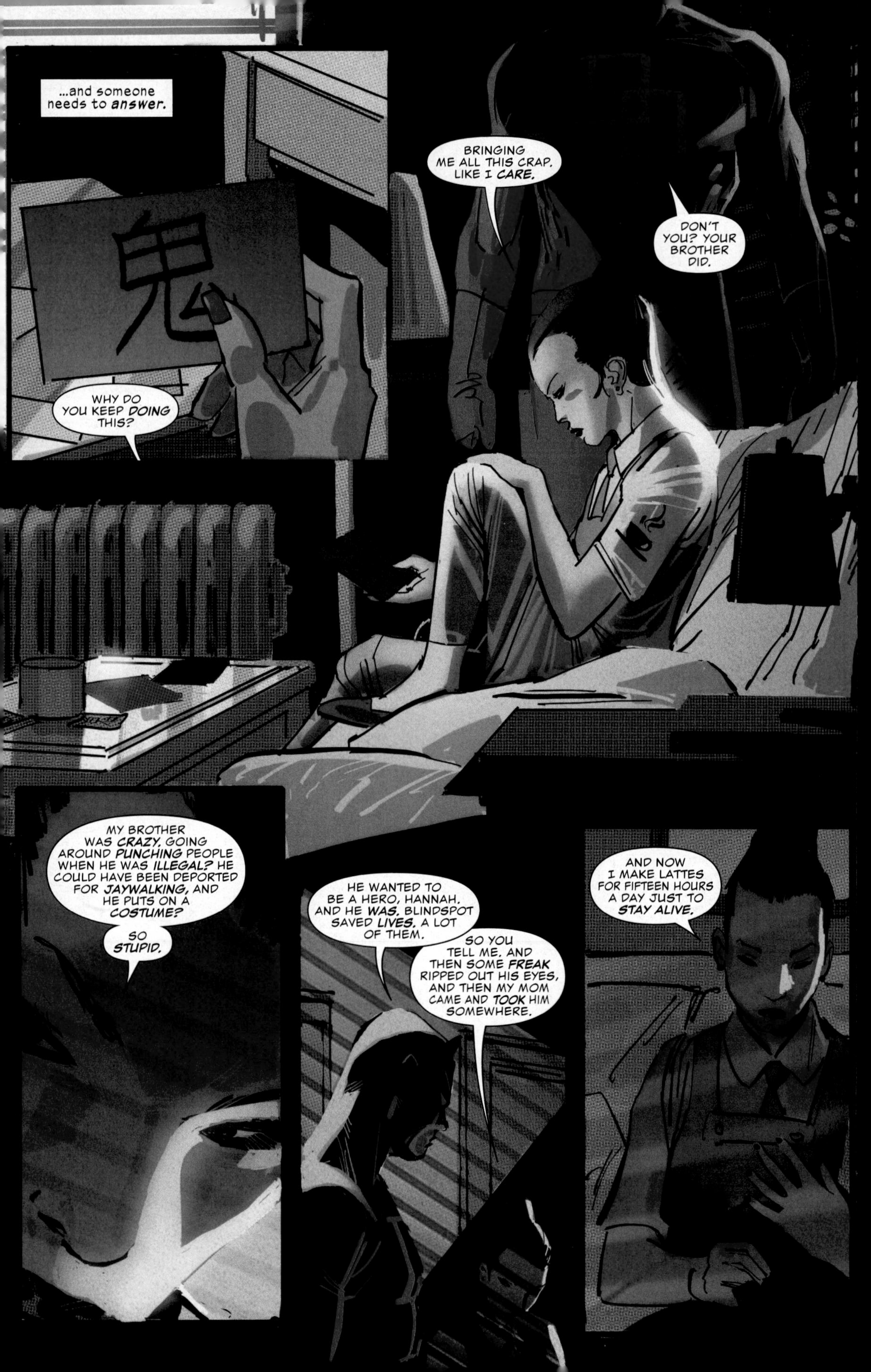
...and someone needs to answer.
BRINGING ME ALL THIS CRAP. LIKE I CARE.
DON'T YOU? YOUR BROTHER DID.
鬼
WHY DO YOU KEEP DOING THIS?
MY BROTHER WAS CRAZY, GOING AROUND PUNCHING PEOPLE WHEN HE WAS ILLEGAL? HE COULD HAVE BEEN DEPORTED FOR JAYWALKING, AND HE PUTS ON A COSTUME?
SO STUPID.
HE WANTED TO BE A HERO, HANNAH, AND HE WAS. BLINDSPOT SAVED LIVES. A LOT OF THEM.
SO YOU TELL ME. AND THEN SOME FREAK RIPPED OUT HIS EYES, AND THEN MY MOM CAME AND TOOK HIM SOMEWHERE.
AND NOW I MAKE LATTES FOR FIFTEEN HOURS A DAY JUST TO STAY ALIVE.

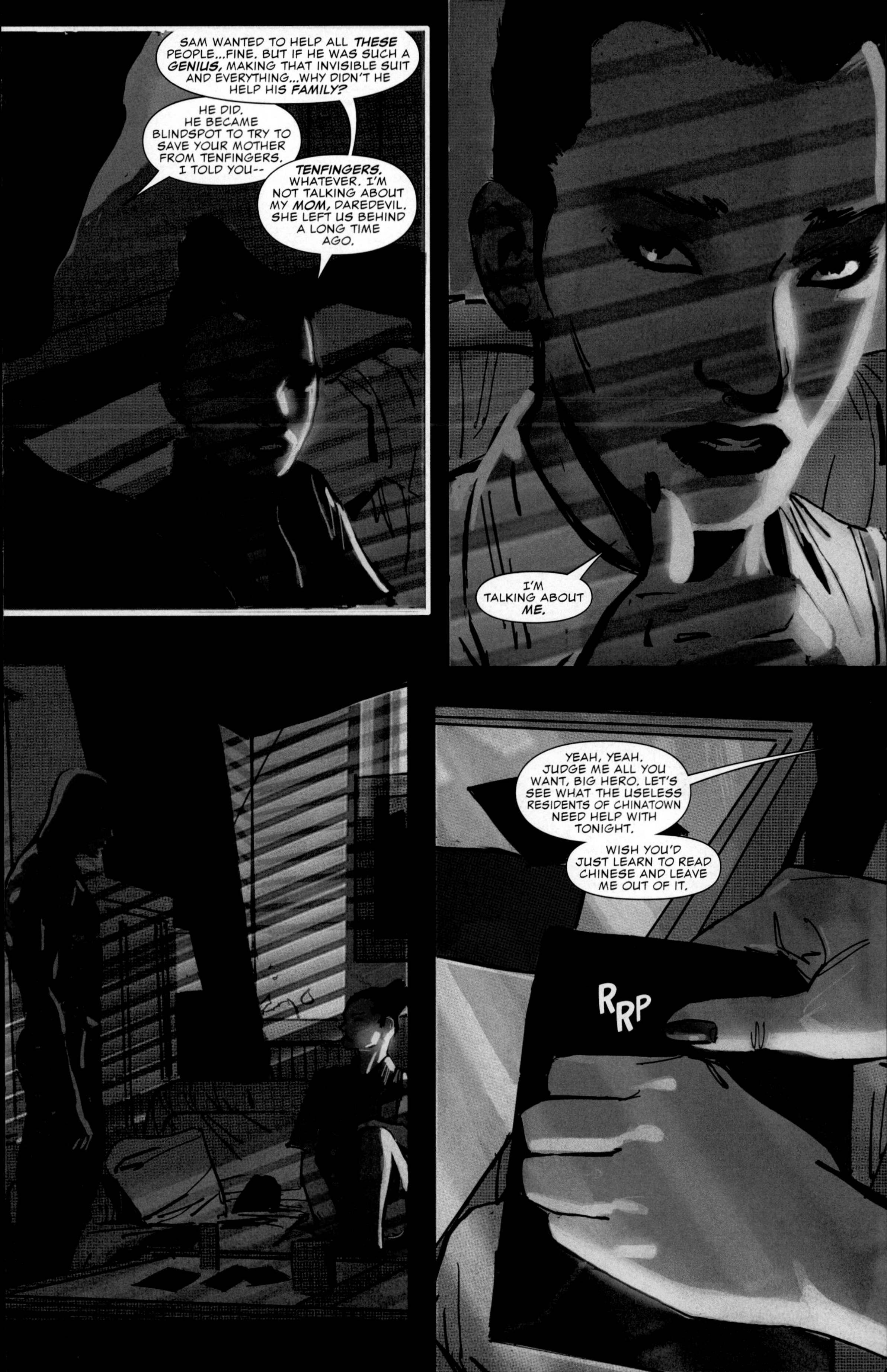

SAM WANTED TO HELP ALL THESE PEOPLE...FINE. BUT IF HE WAS SUCH A GENIUS, MAKING THAT INVISIBLE SUIT AND EVERYTHING...WHY DIDN'T HE HELP HIS FAMILY?
HE DID. HE BECAME BLINDSPOT TO TRY TO SAVE YOUR MOTHER FROM TENFINGERS. I TOLD YOU--
TENFINGERS. WHATEVER. I'M NOT TALKING ABOUT MY MOM, DAREDEVIL. SHE LEFT US BEHIND A LONG TIME AGO.
I'M TALKING ABOUT ME.
YEAH, YEAH. JUDGE ME ALL YOU WANT, BIG HERO. LET'S SEE WHAT THE USELESS RESIDENTS OF CHINATOWN NEED HELP WITH TONIGHT.
WISH YOU'D JUST LEARN TO READ CHINESE AND LEAVE ME OUT OF IT.
RRP

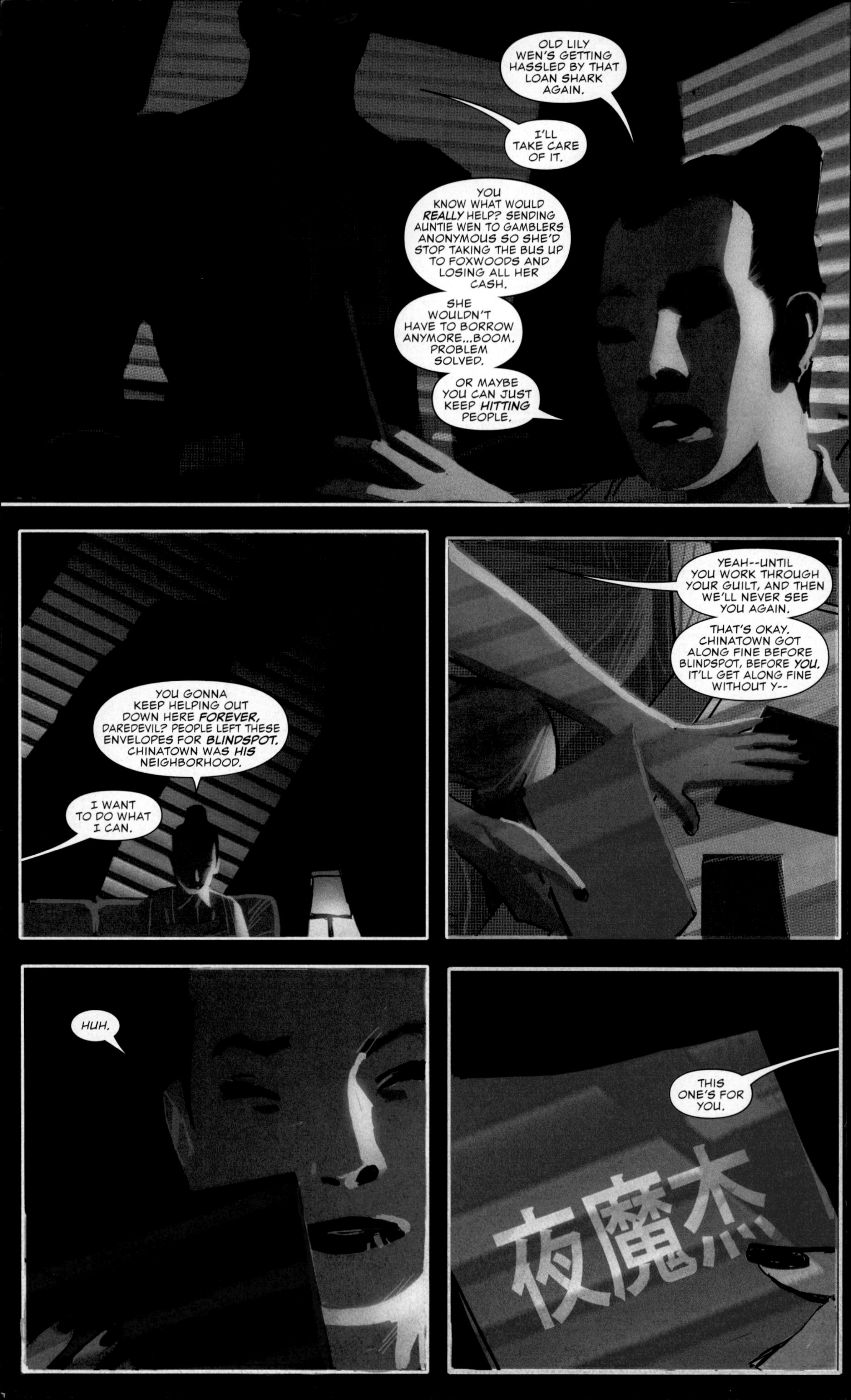
OLD LILY WEN'S GETTING HASSLED BY THAT LOAN SHARK AGAIN.
I'LL TAKE CARE OF IT.
YOU KNOW WHAT WOULD REALLY HELP? SENDING AUNTIE WEN TO GAMBLERS ANONYMOUS SO SHE'D STOP TAKING THE BUS UP TO FOXWOODS AND LOSING ALL HER CASH.
SHE WOULDN'T HAVE TO BORROW ANYMORE...BOOM. PROBLEM SOLVED.
OR MAYBE YOU CAN JUST KEEP HITTING PEOPLE.
YOU GONNA KEEP HELPING OUT DOWN HERE FOREVER, DAREDEVIL? PEOPLE LEFT THESE ENVELOPES FOR BLINDSPOT. CHINATOWN WAS HIS NEIGHBORHOOD.
I WANT TO DO WHAT I CAN.
YEAH--UNTIL YOU WORK THROUGH YOUR GUILT, AND THEN WE'LL NEVER SEE YOU AGAIN.
THAT'S OKAY. CHINATOWN GOT ALONG FINE BEFORE BLINDSPOT, BEFORE YOU. IT'LL GET ALONG FINE WITHOUT Y--
HUH.
THIS ONE'S FOR YOU.
夜魔杰

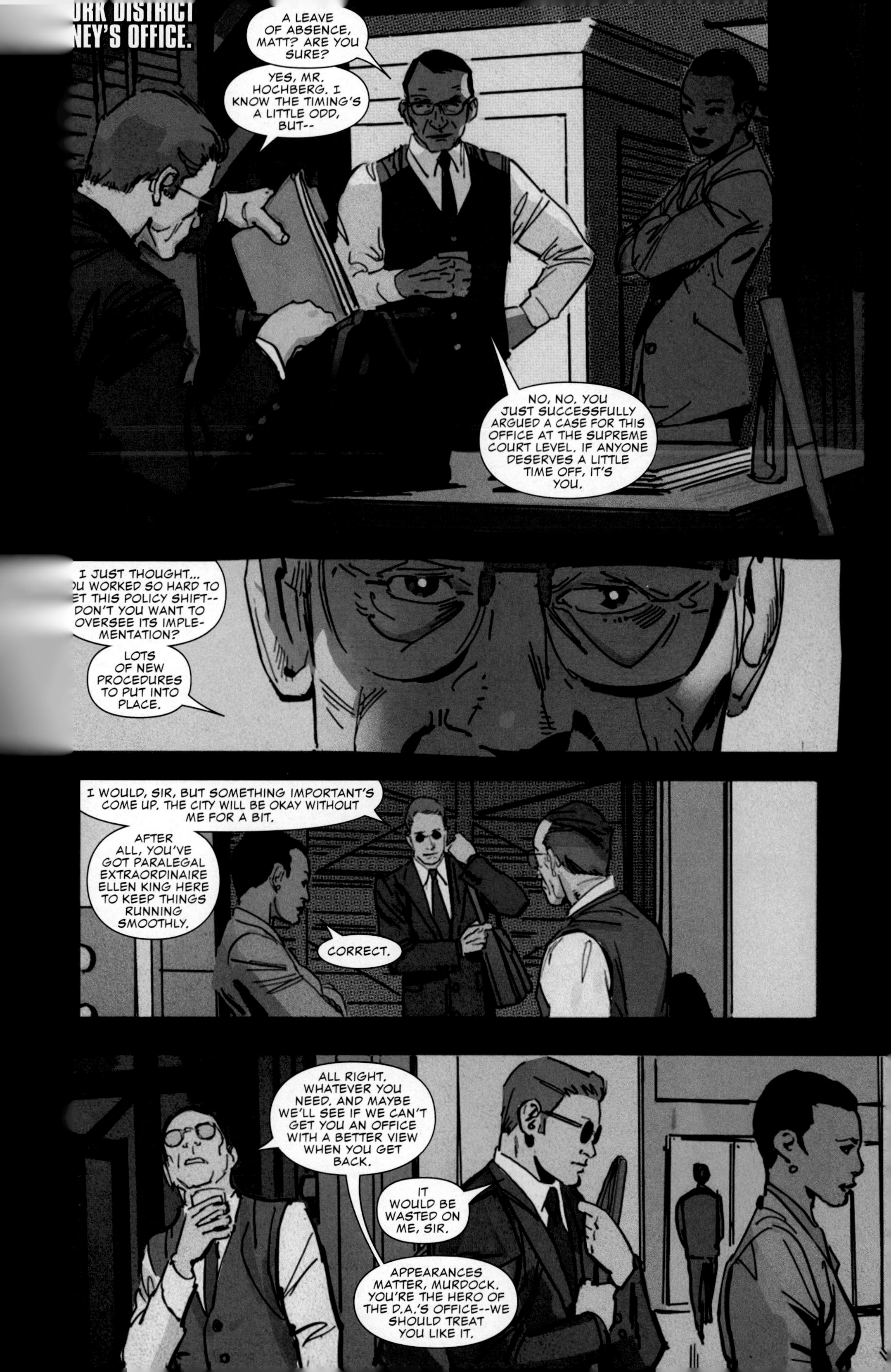
ORK DISTRICT
NEY'S OFFICE.
A LEAVE OF ABSENCE, MATT? ARE YOU SURE?
YES, MR. HOCHBERG. I KNOW THE TIMING'S A LITTLE ODD, BUT--
NO, NO. YOU JUST SUCCESSFULLY ARGUED A CASE FOR THIS OFFICE AT THE SUPREME COURT LEVEL. IF ANYONE DESERVES A LITTLE TIME OFF, IT'S YOU.
I JUST THOUGHT... OU WORKED SO HARD TO ET THIS POLICY SHIFT-- DON'T YOU WANT TO OVERSEE ITS IMPLEMENTATION?
LOTS OF NEW PROCEDURES TO PUT INTO PLACE.
I WOULD, SIR, BUT SOMETHING IMPORTANT'S COME UP. THE CITY WILL BE OKAY WITHOUT ME FOR A BIT.
AFTER ALL, YOU'VE GOT PARALEGAL EXTRAORDINAIRE ELLEN KING HERE TO KEEP THINGS RUNNING SMOOTHLY.
CORRECT.
ALL RIGHT. WHATEVER YOU NEED. AND MAYBE WE'LL SEE IF WE CAN'T GET YOU AN OFFICE WITH A BETTER VIEW WHEN YOU GET BACK.
IT WOULD BE WASTED ON ME, SIR.
APPEARANCES MATTER, MURDOCK. YOU'RE THE HERO OF THE D.A.'S OFFICE--WE SHOULD TREAT YOU LIKE IT.

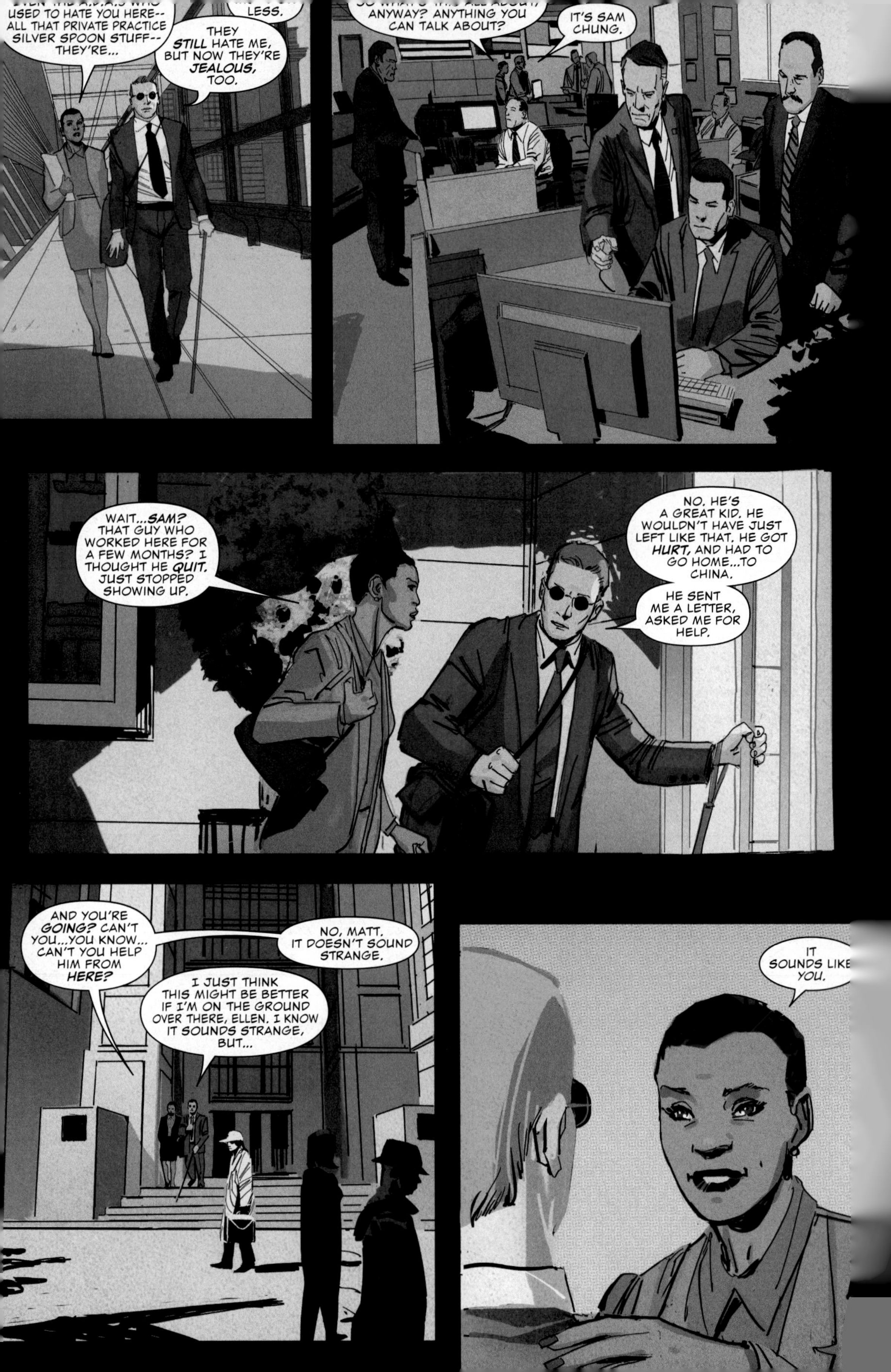
USED TO HATE YOU HERE-- ALL THAT PRIVATE PRACTICE SILVER SPOON STUFF-- THEY'RE...
LESS.
THEY STILL HATE ME, BUT NOW THEY'RE JEALOUS, TOO.
ANYWAY? ANYTHING YOU CAN TALK ABOUT?
IT'S SAM CHUNG.
WAIT...SAM? THAT GUY WHO WORKED HERE FOR A FEW MONTHS? I THOUGHT HE QUIT. JUST STOPPED SHOWING UP.
NO. HE'S A GREAT KID. HE WOULDN'T HAVE JUST LEFT LIKE THAT. HE GOT HURT, AND HAD TO GO HOME...TO CHINA.
HE SENT ME A LETTER, ASKED ME FOR HELP.
AND YOU'RE GOING? CAN'T YOU...YOU KNOW... CAN'T YOU HELP HIM FROM HERE?
I JUST THINK THIS MIGHT BE BETTER IF I'M ON THE GROUND OVER THERE, ELLEN. I KNOW IT SOUNDS STRANGE, BUT...
NO, MATT. IT DOESN'T SOUND STRANGE.
IT SOUNDS LIKE YOU.

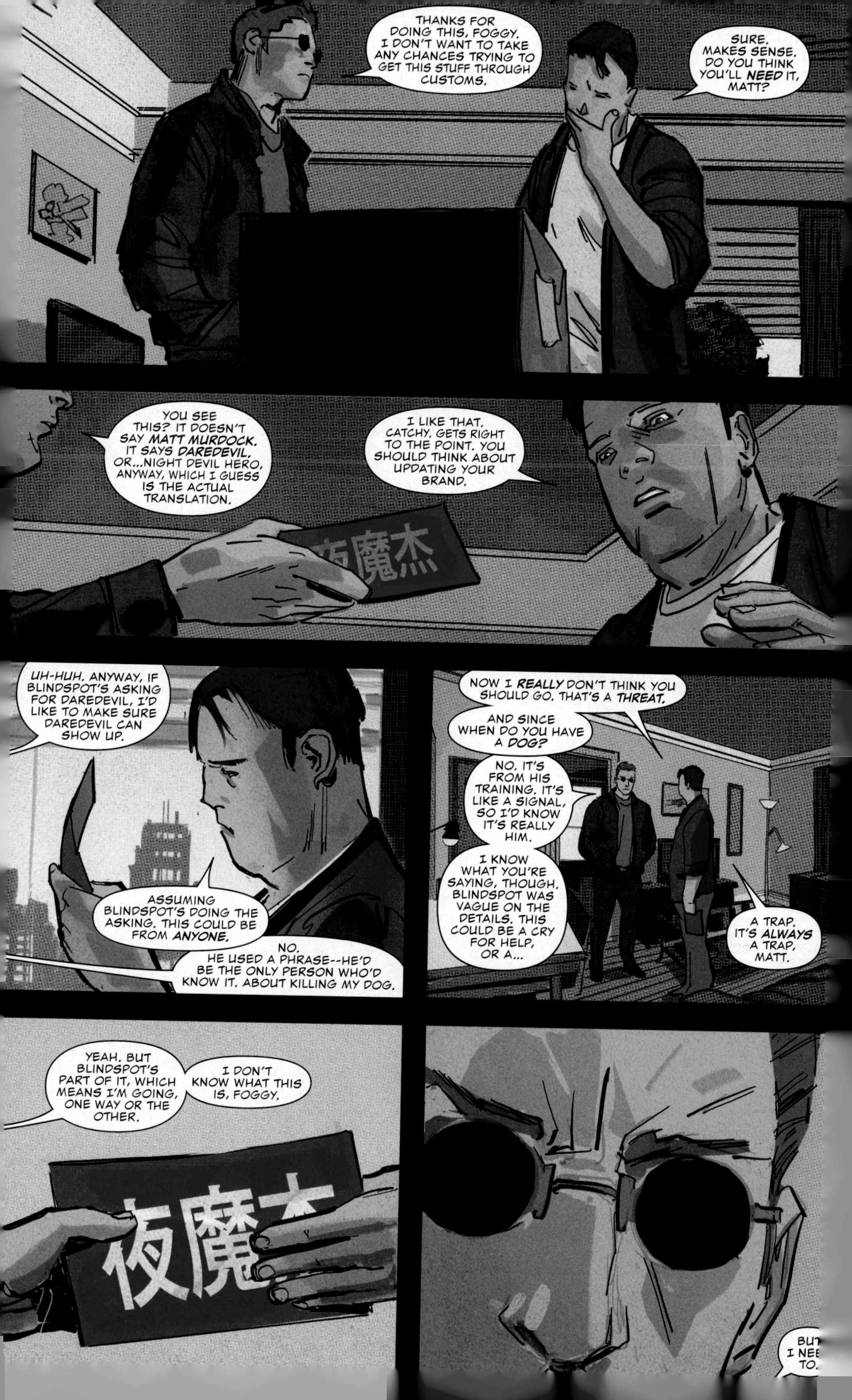
THANKS FOR DOING THIS, FOGGY. I DON'T WANT TO TAKE ANY CHANCES TRYING TO GET THIS STUFF THROUGH CUSTOMS.
SURE. MAKES SENSE. DO YOU THINK YOU'LL NEED IT, MATT?
YOU SEE THIS? IT DOESN'T SAY MATT MURDOCK. IT SAYS DAREDEVIL. OR...NIGHT DEVIL HERO, ANYWAY, WHICH I GUESS IS THE ACTUAL TRANSLATION.
I LIKE THAT. CATCHY. GETS RIGHT TO THE POINT. YOU SHOULD THINK ABOUT UPDATING YOUR BRAND.
夜魔杰
UH-HUH. ANYWAY, IF BLINDSPOT'S ASKING FOR DAREDEVIL, I'D LIKE TO MAKE SURE DAREDEVIL CAN SHOW UP.
ASSUMING BLINDSPOT'S DOING THE ASKING. THIS COULD BE FROM ANYONE.
NO. HE USED A PHRASE--HE'D BE THE ONLY PERSON WHO'D KNOW IT. ABOUT KILLING MY DOG.
NOW I REALLY DON'T THINK YOU SHOULD GO. THAT'S A THREAT.
AND SINCE WHEN DO YOU HAVE A DOG?
NO, IT'S FROM HIS TRAINING. IT'S LIKE A SIGNAL, SO I'D KNOW IT'S REALLY HIM.
I KNOW WHAT YOU'RE SAYING, THOUGH. BLINDSPOT WAS VAGUE ON THE DETAILS. THIS COULD BE A CRY FOR HELP, OR A...
A TRAP. IT'S ALWAYS A TRAP, MATT.
I DON'T KNOW WHAT THIS IS, FOGGY.
YEAH. BUT BLINDSPOT'S PART OF IT, WHICH MEANS I'M GOING, ONE WAY OR THE OTHER.
夜魔

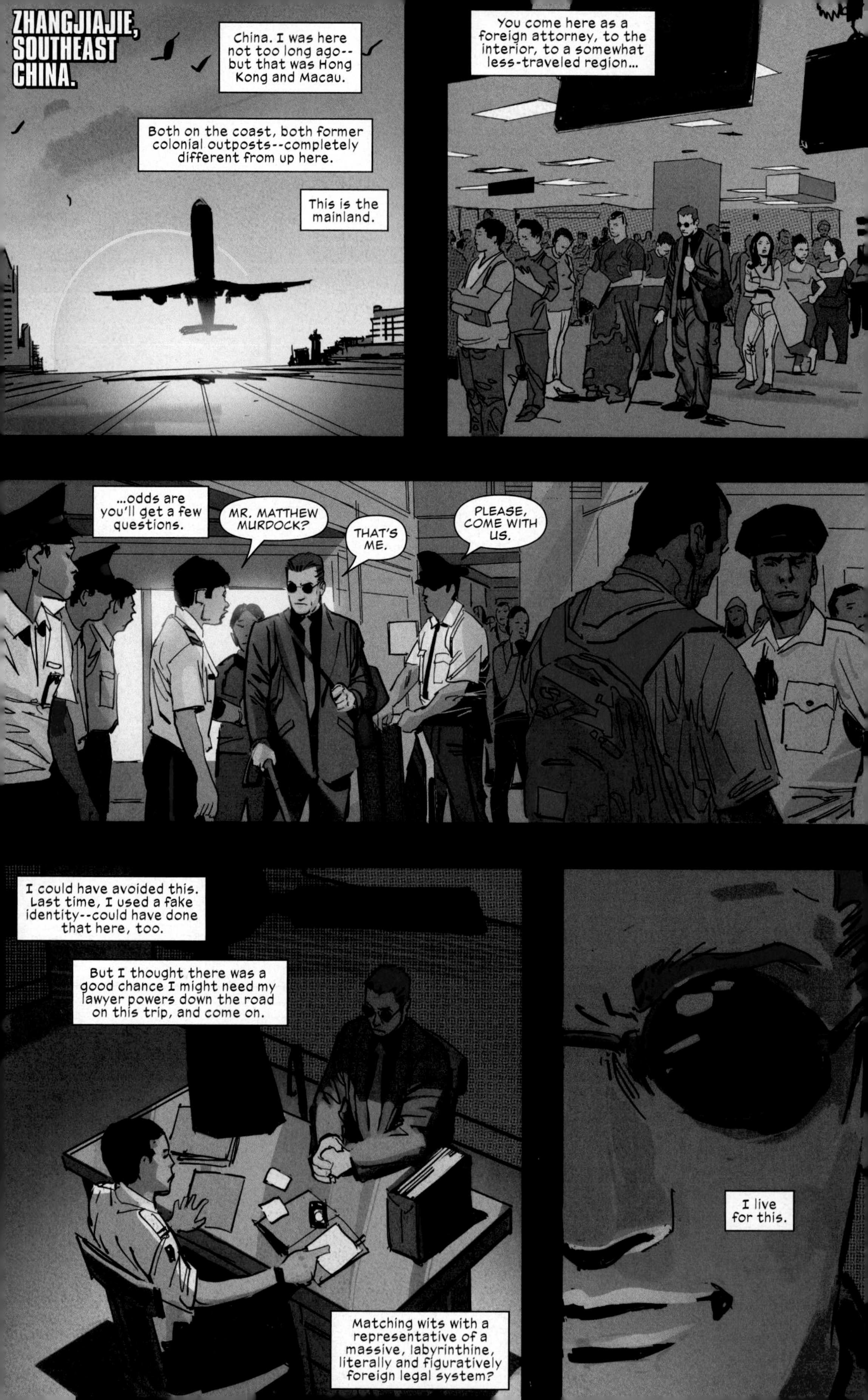
ZHANGJIAJIE, SOUTHEAST CHINA.
China. I was here not too long ago--but that was Hong Kong and Macau.
Both on the coast, both former colonial outposts--completely different from up here.
This is the mainland.
You come here as a foreign attorney, to the interior, to a somewhat less-traveled region...
...odds are you'll get a few questions.
MR. MATTHEW MURDOCK?
THAT'S ME.
PLEASE, COME WITH US.
I could have avoided this. Last time, I used a fake identity--could have done that here, too.
But I thought there was a good chance I might need my lawyer powers down the road on this trip, and come on.
Matching wits with a representative of a massive, labyrinthine, literally and figuratively foreign legal system?
I live for this.

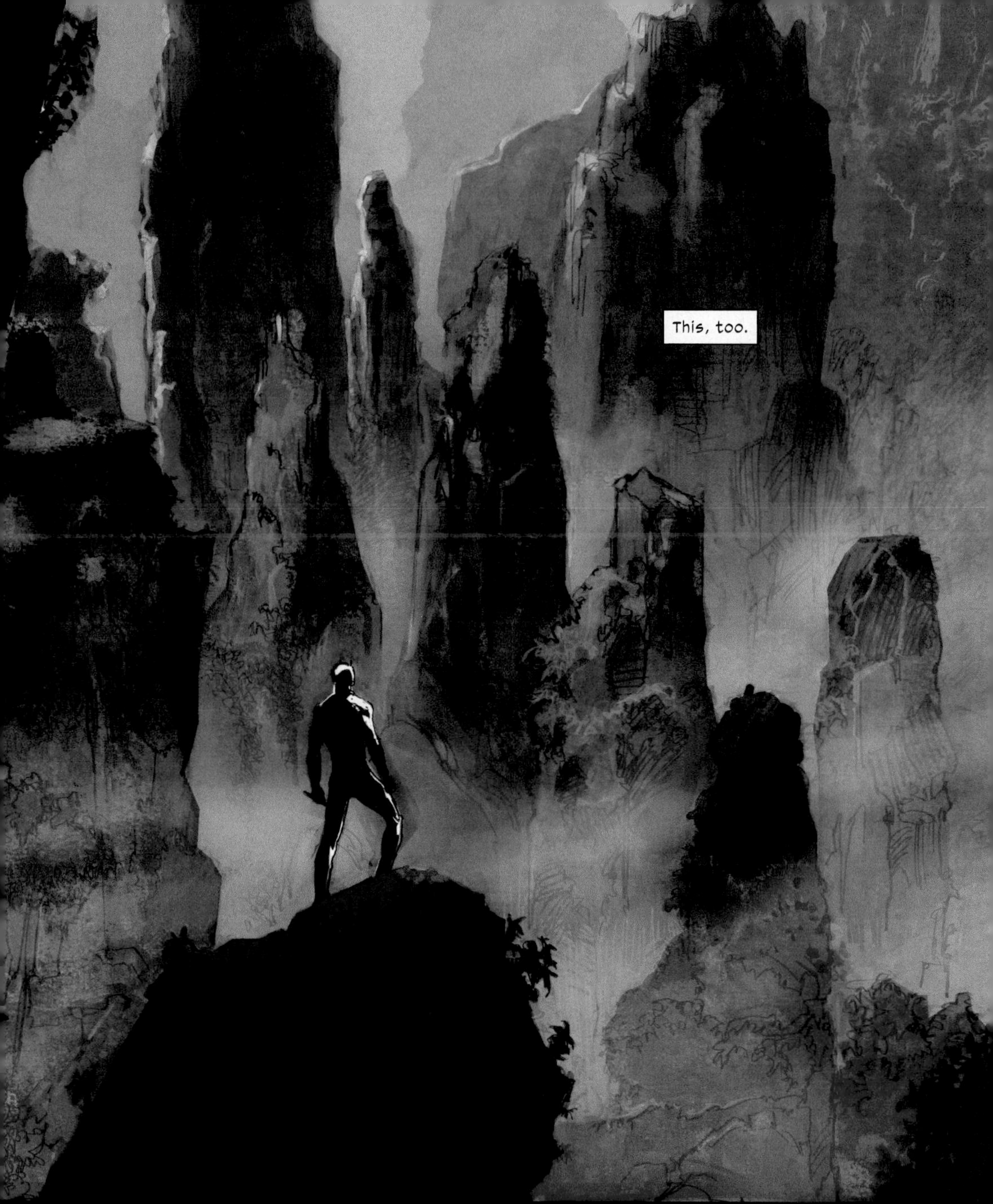
This, too.

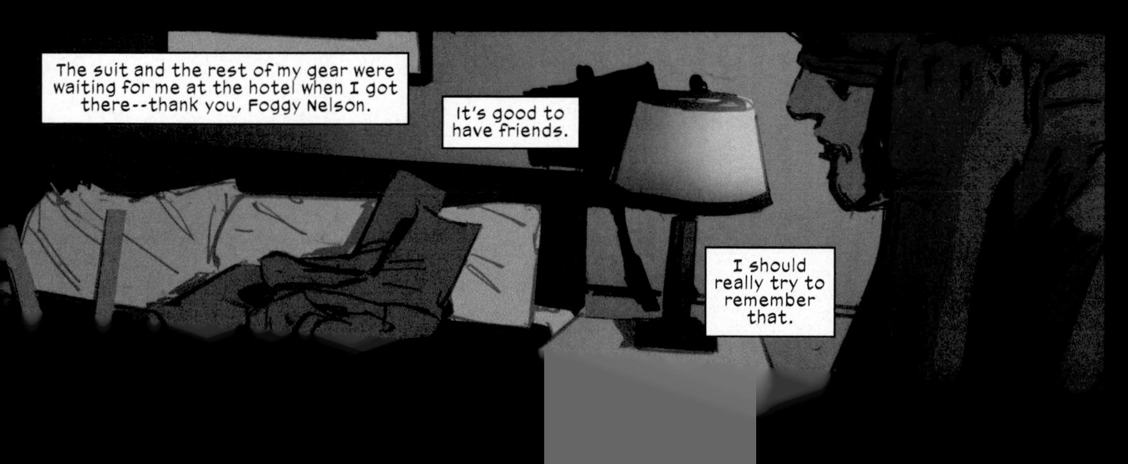
The suit and the rest of my gear were waiting for me at the hotel when I got there--thank you, Foggy Nelson.
It's good to have friends.
I should really try to remember that.

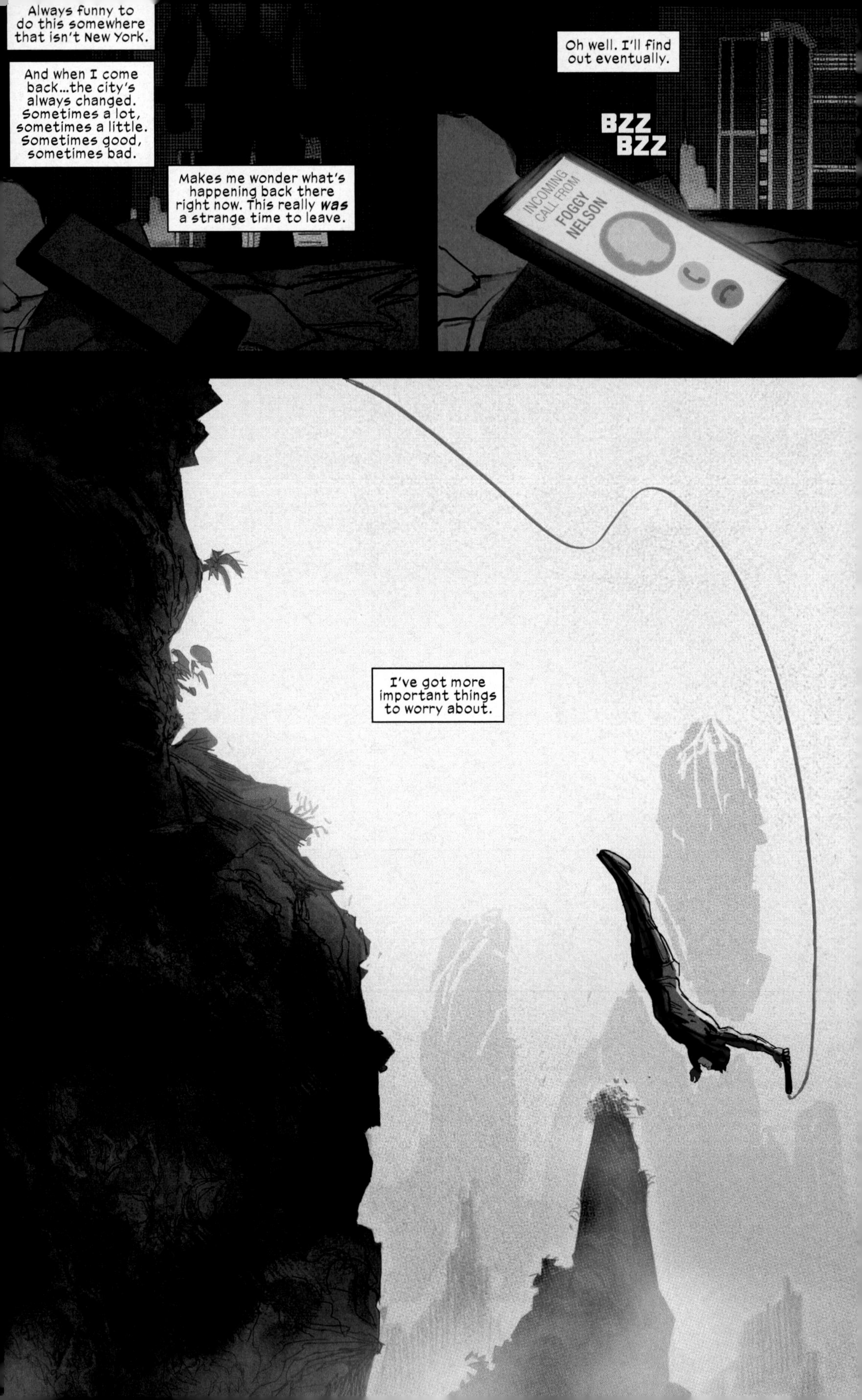
Always funny to do this somewhere that isn't New York.
And when I come back...the city's always changed. Sometimes a lot, sometimes a little. Sometimes good, sometimes bad.
Makes me wonder what's happening back there right now. This really *was* a strange time to leave.
Oh well. I'll find out eventually.
BZZ BZZ
INCOMING CALL FROM
FOGGY NELSON
I've got more important things to worry about.

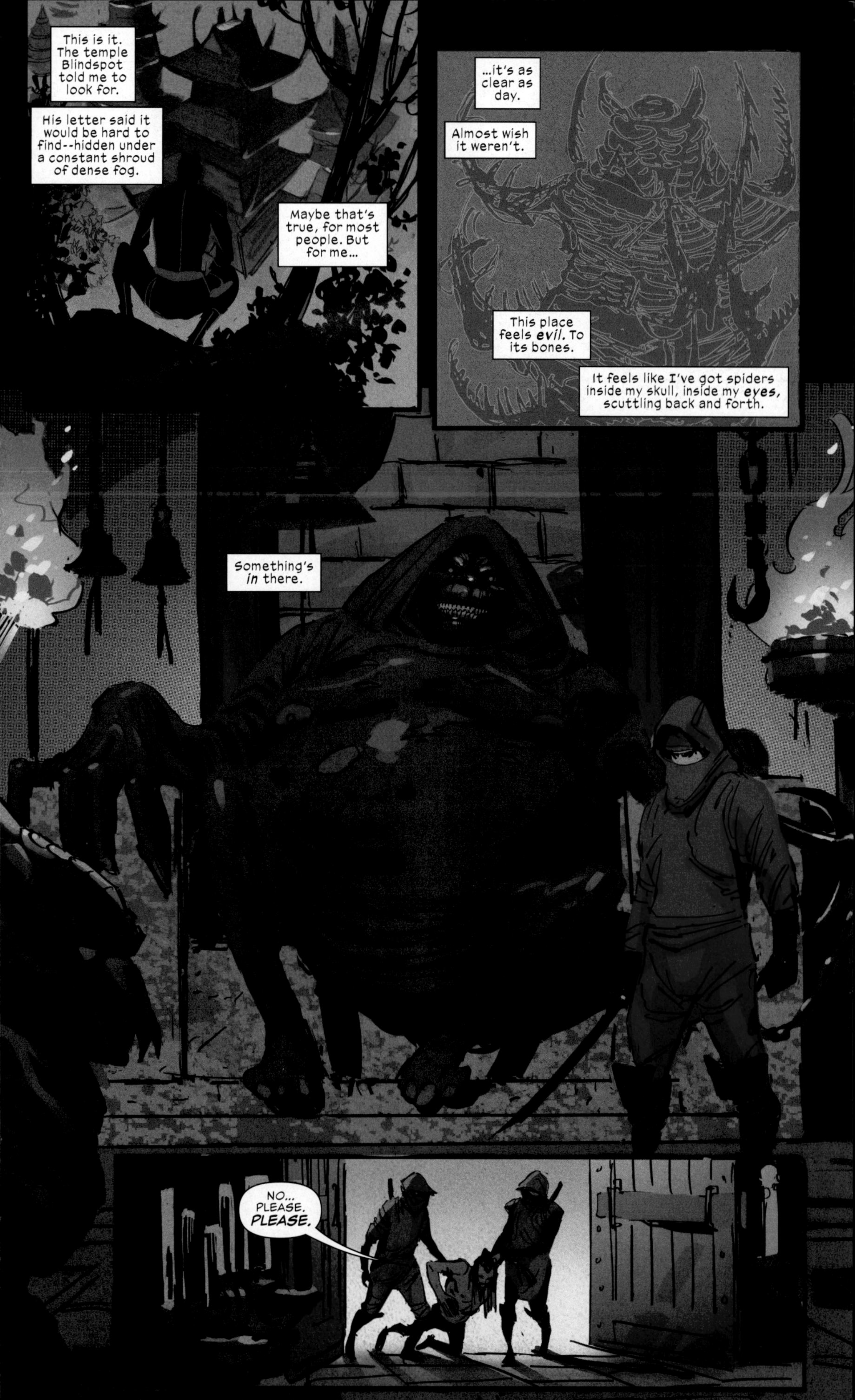
This is it. The temple Blindspot told me to look for.
His letter said it would be hard to find--hidden under a constant shroud of dense fog.
Maybe that's true, for most people. But for me...
...it's as clear as day.
Almost wish it weren't.
This place feels *evil.* To its bones.
It feels like I've got spiders inside my skull, inside my *eyes,* scuttling back and forth.
Something's *in* there.
NO... PLEASE. **PLEASE.**

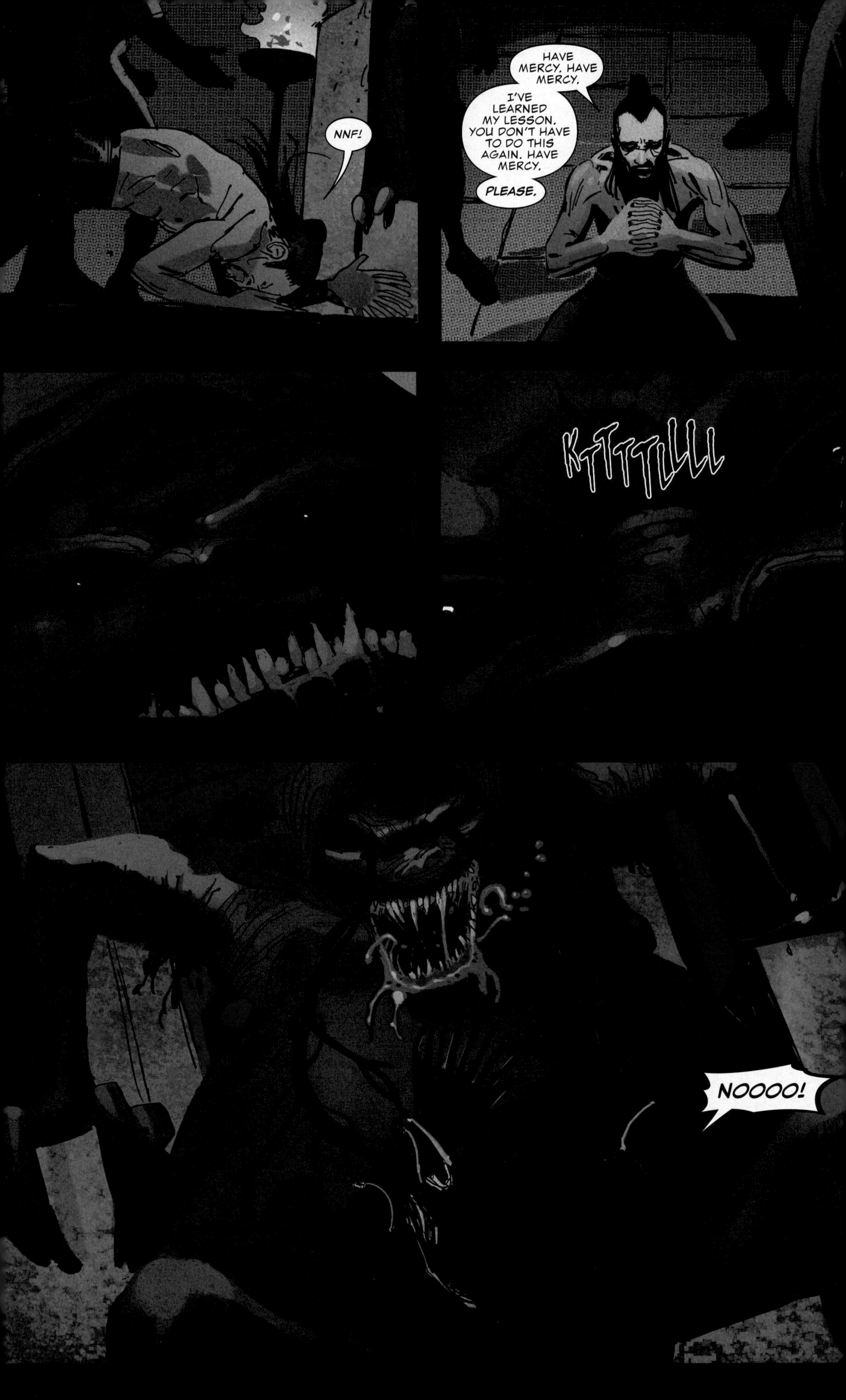
NNF!
HAVE MERCY. HAVE MERCY.
I'VE LEARNED MY LESSON. YOU DON'T HAVE TO DO THIS AGAIN. HAVE MERCY.
PLEASE.
KTTTTLLLL
NOOOO!

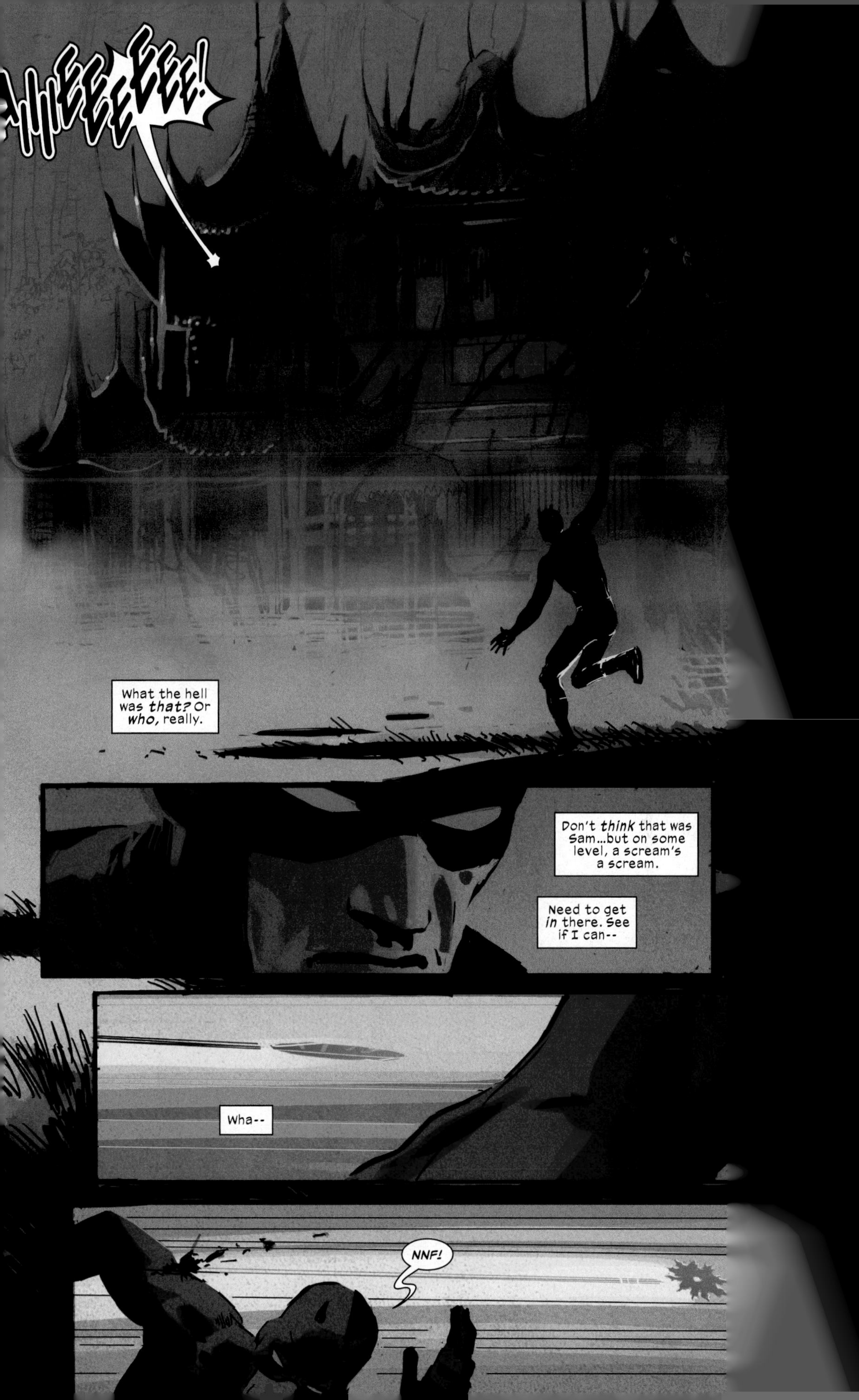
WHEEEEEEE!
What the hell was *that?* Or *who,* really.
Don't *think* that was Sam...but on some level, a scream's a scream.
Need to get *in* there. See if I can--
Wha--
NNF!

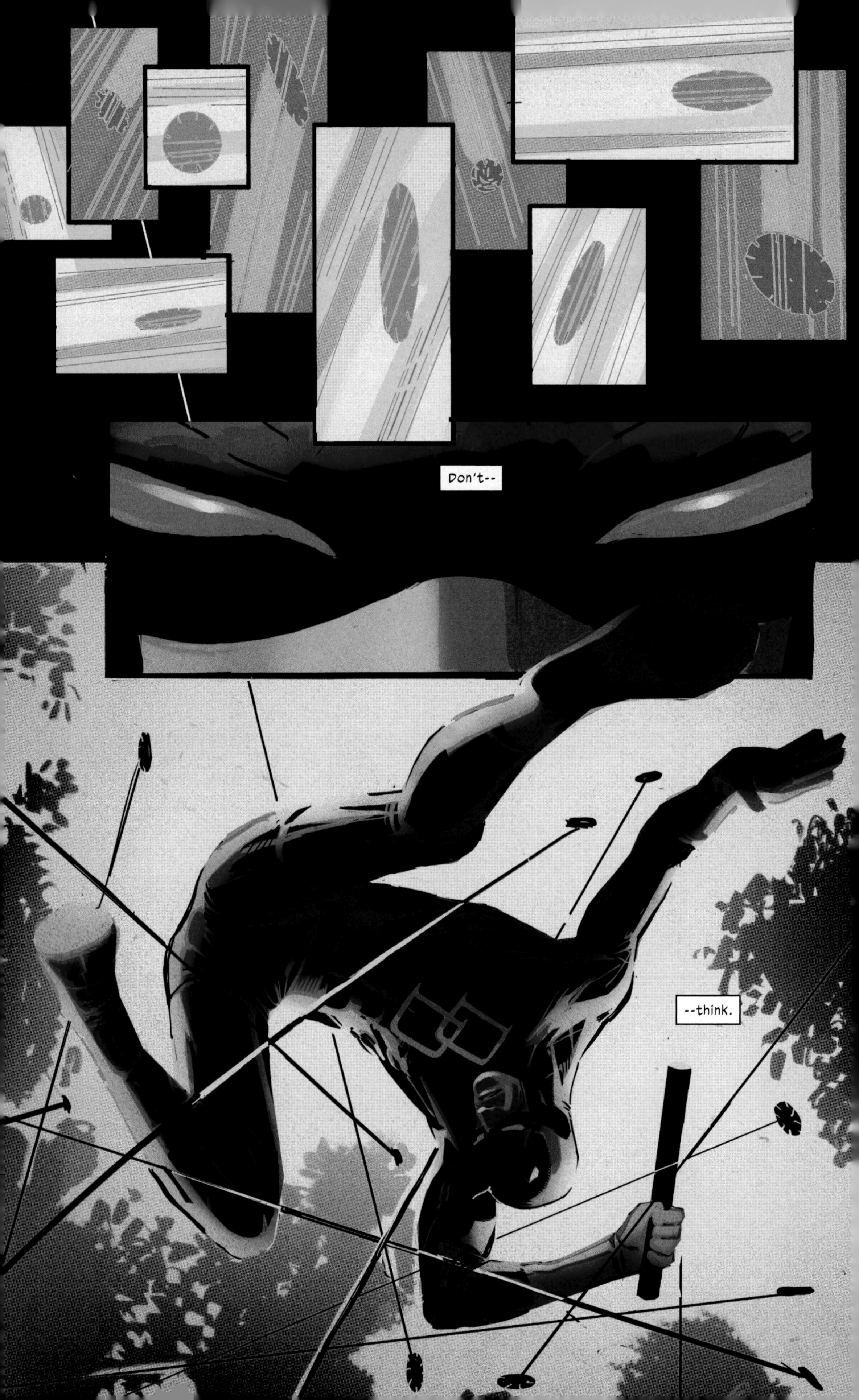
Don't--
--think.

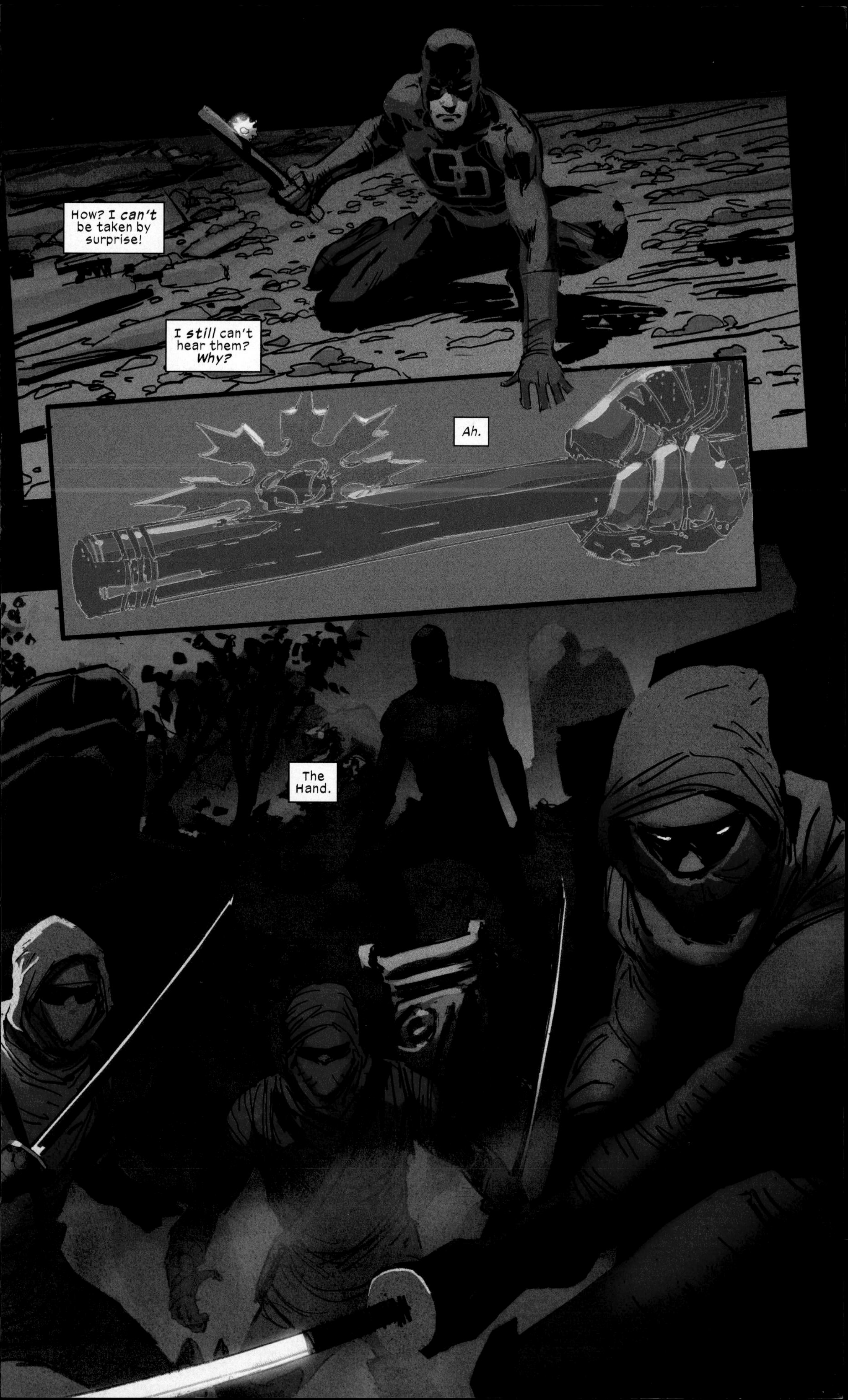
How? I *can't* be taken by surprise!
I *still* can't hear them? *Why?*
Ah.
The Hand.

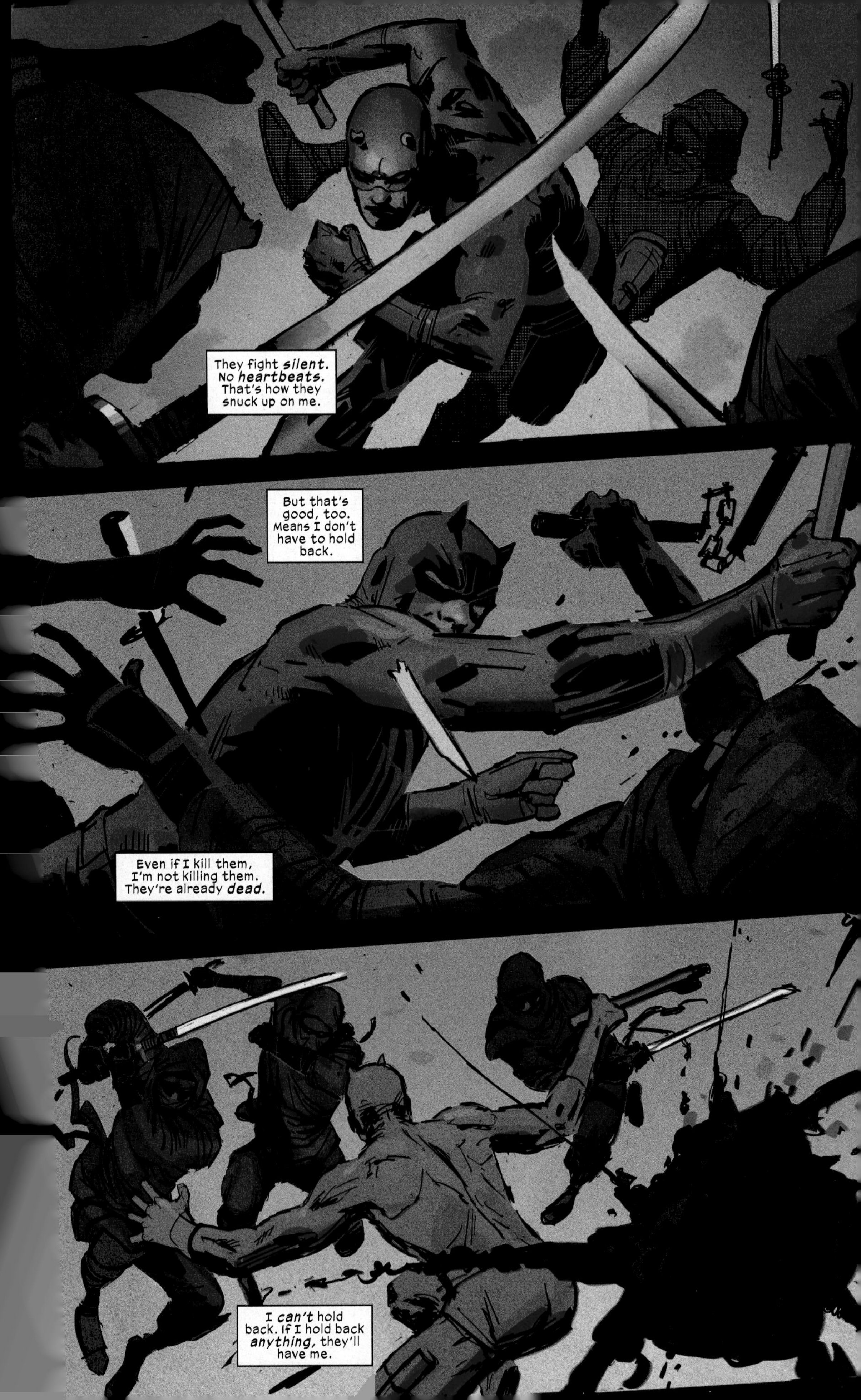
They fight *silent.* No *heartbeats.* That's how they snuck up on me.
But that's good, too. Means I don't have to hold back.
Even if I kill them, I'm not killing them. They're already *dead.*
I *can't* hold back. If I hold back *anything,* they'll have me.

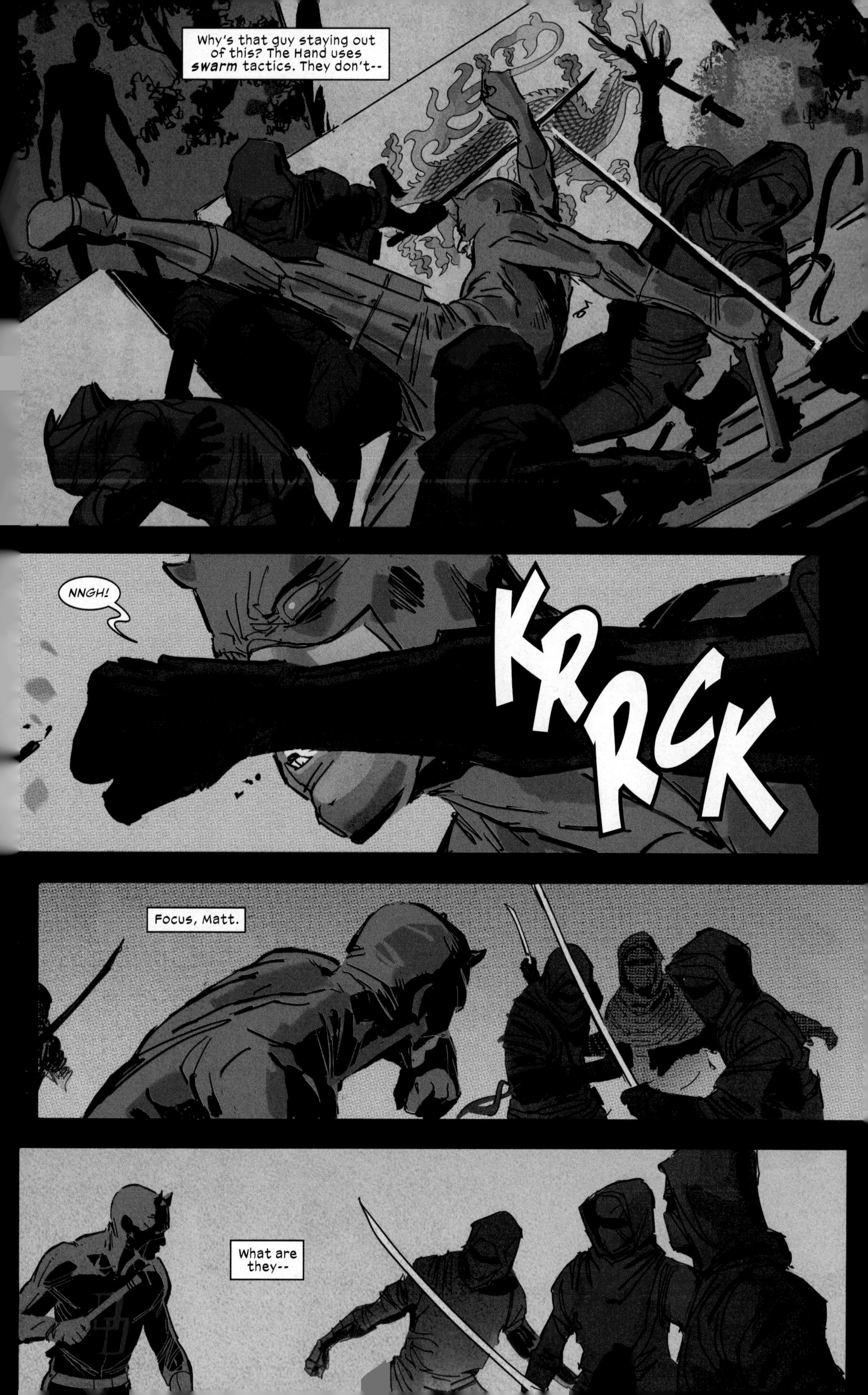
Why's that guy staying out of this? The Hand uses *swarm* tactics. They don't--
NNGH!
KRRCK
Focus, Matt.
What are they--

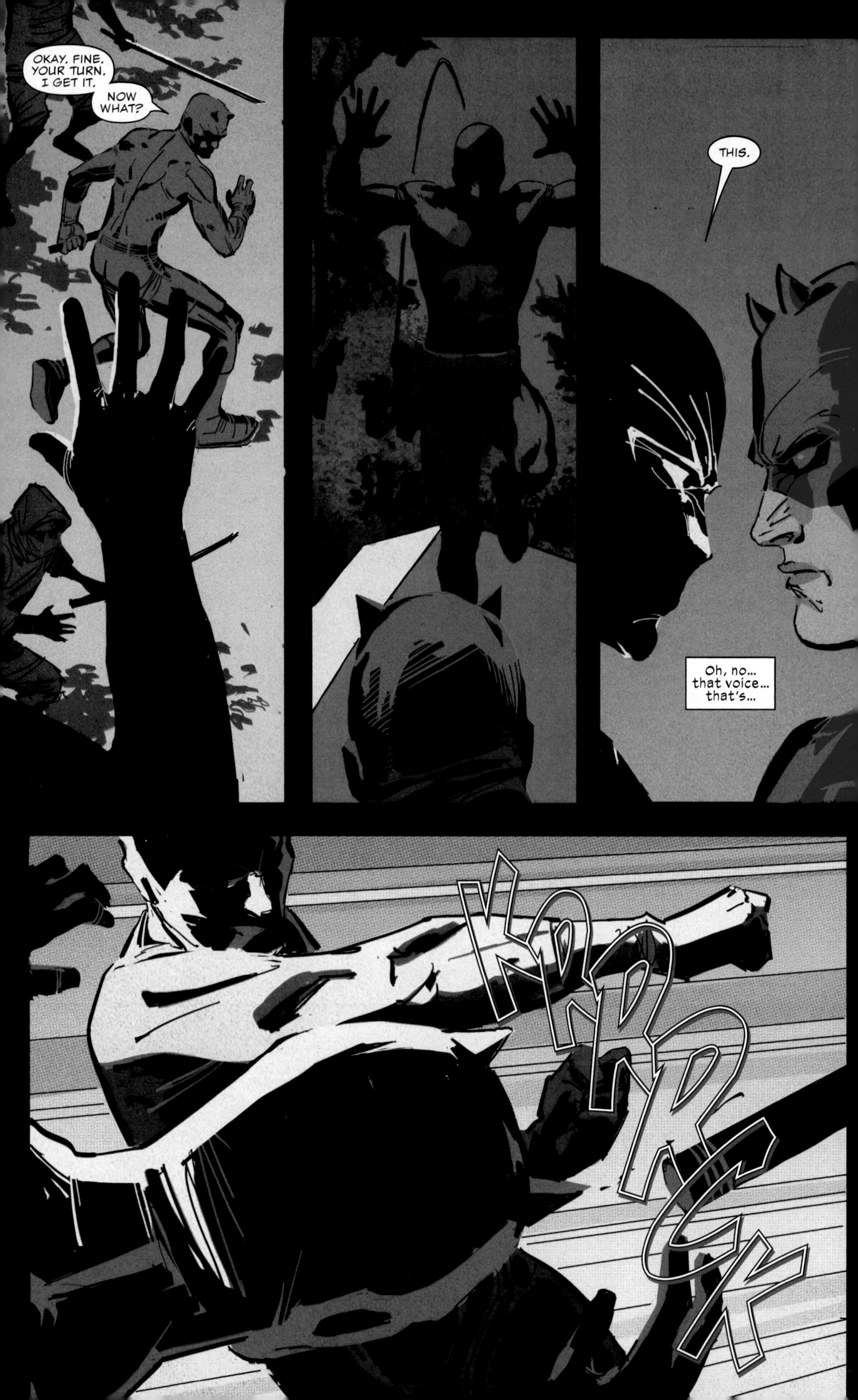
OKAY, FINE. YOUR TURN. I GET IT.
NOW WHAT?
THIS.
Oh, no... that voice... that's...
KRRRACK

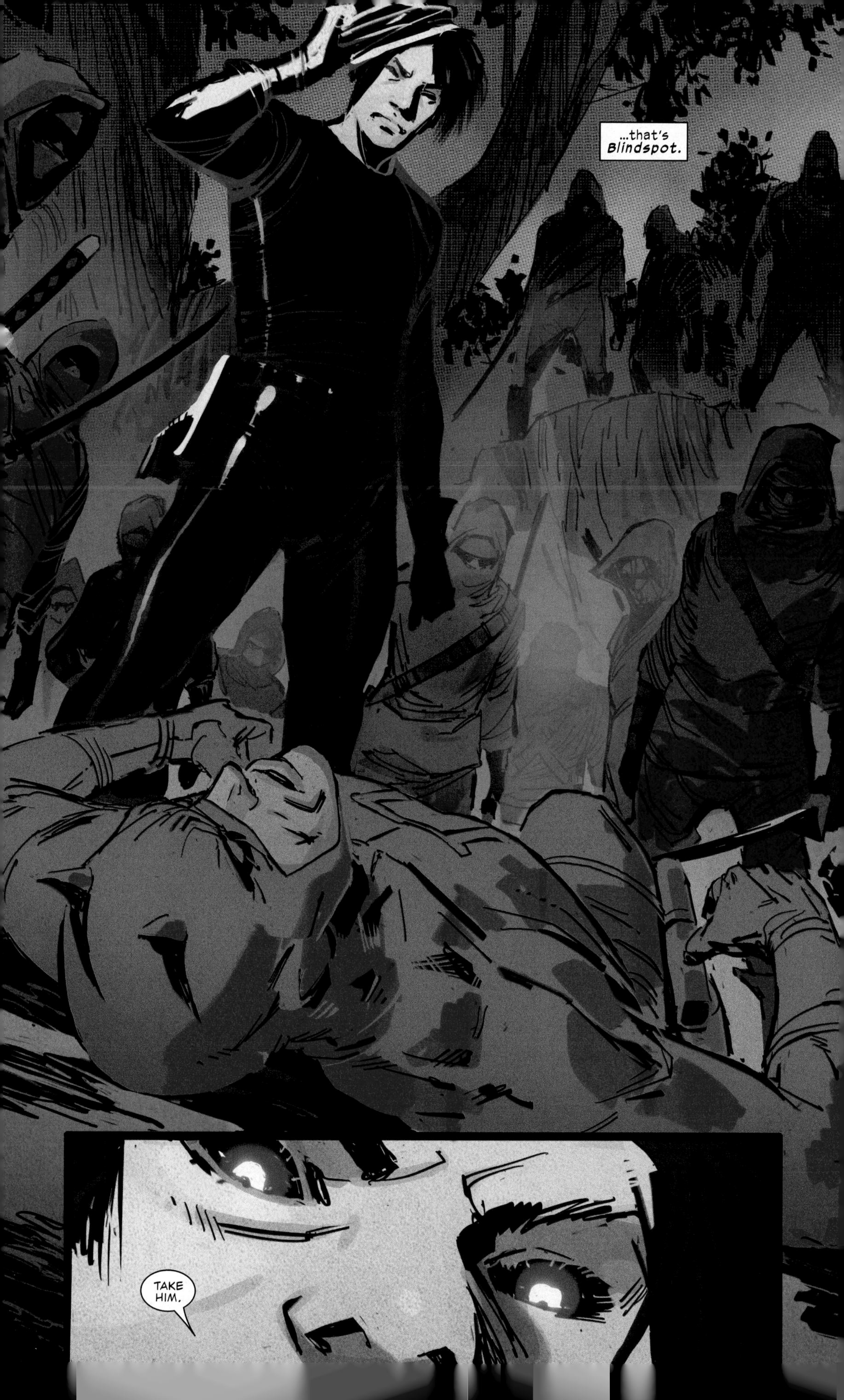
...that's Blindspot.
TAKE HIM.

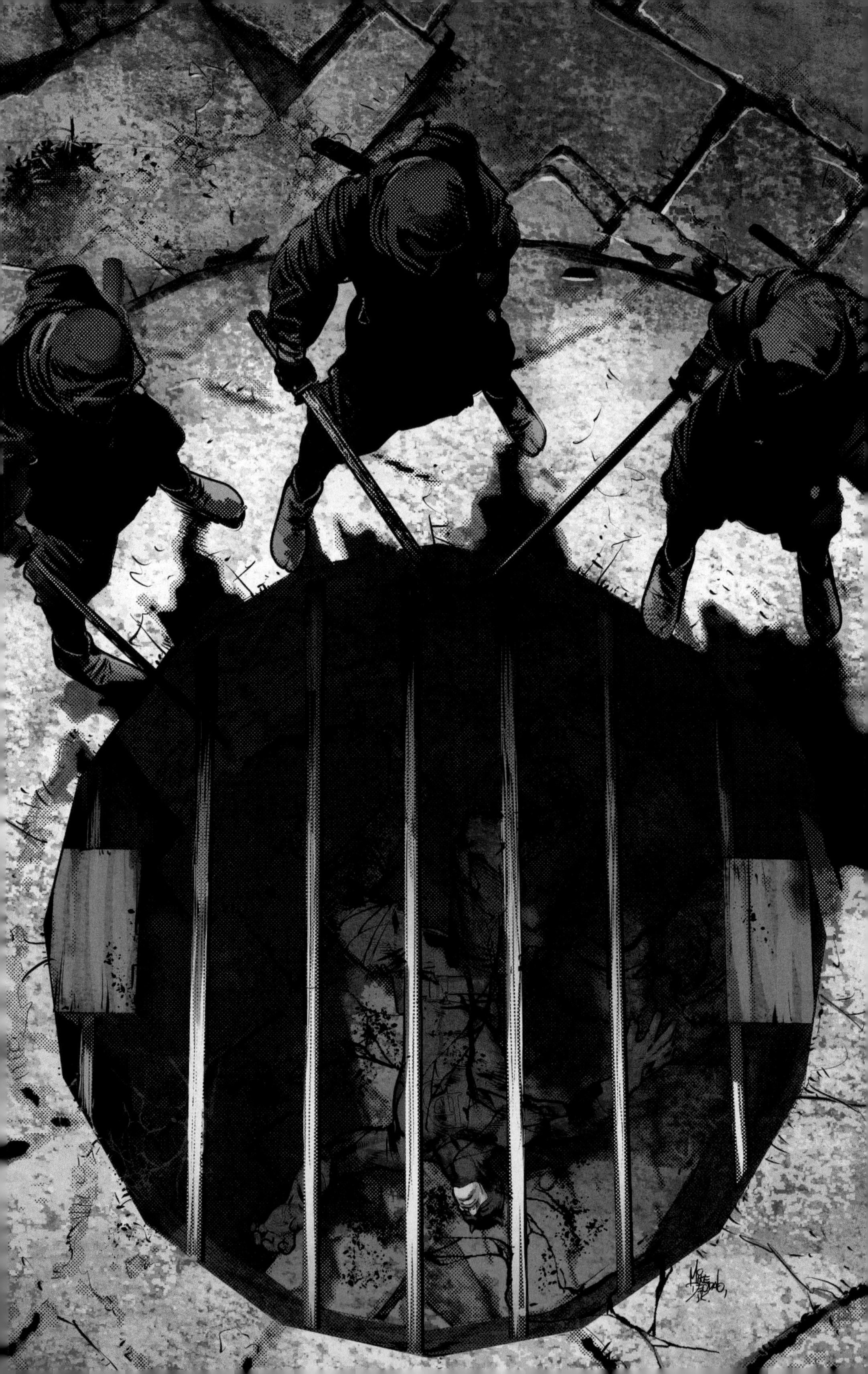

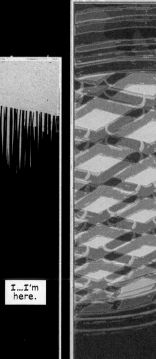

I....I'm here.

...Where?

My mask.

I remember... that voice.

TAKE HIM.

That voice.

YOU'RE MATT MURDOCK.

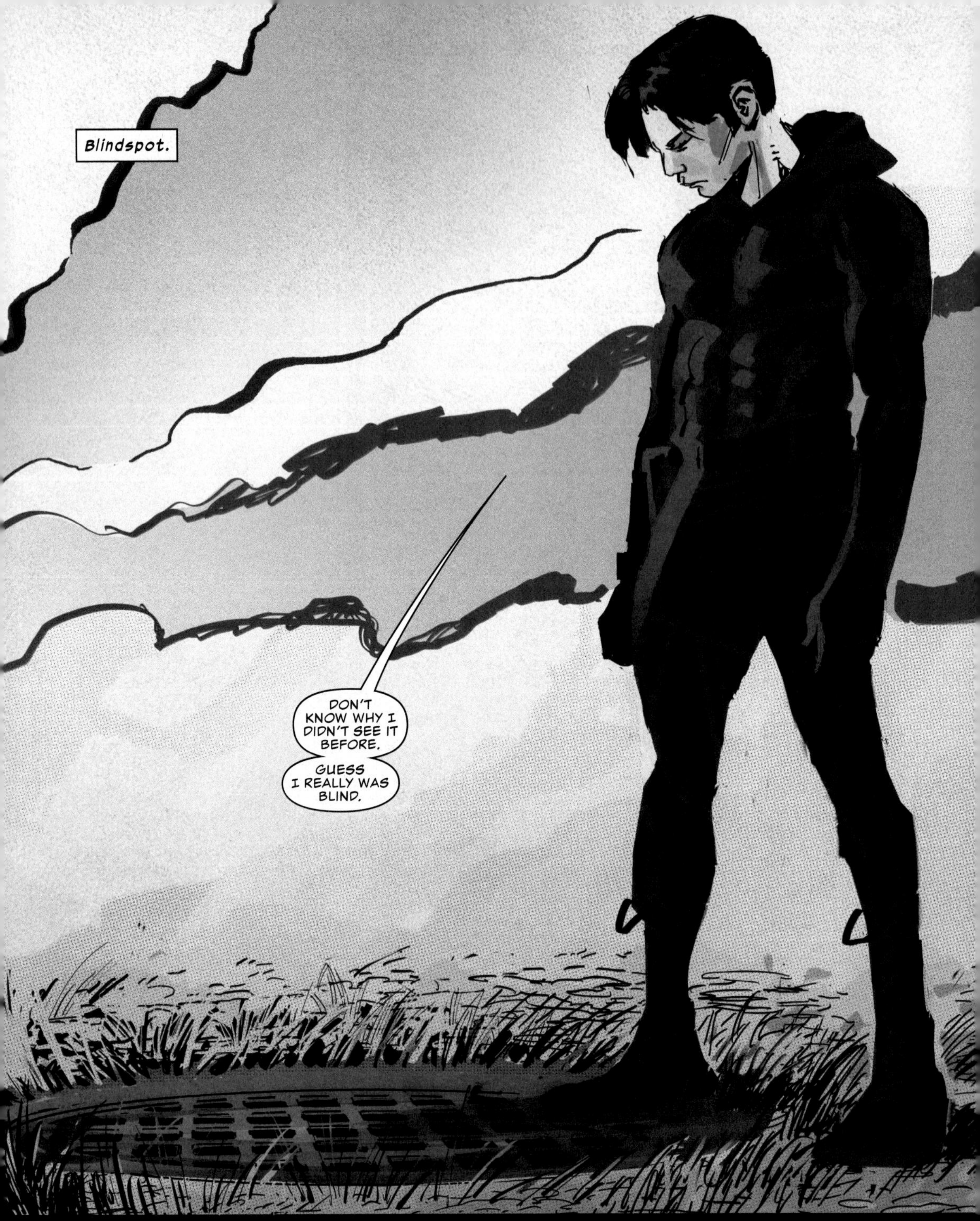
Blindspot.
DON'T KNOW WHY I DIDN'T SEE IT BEFORE.
GUESS I REALLY WAS BLIND.

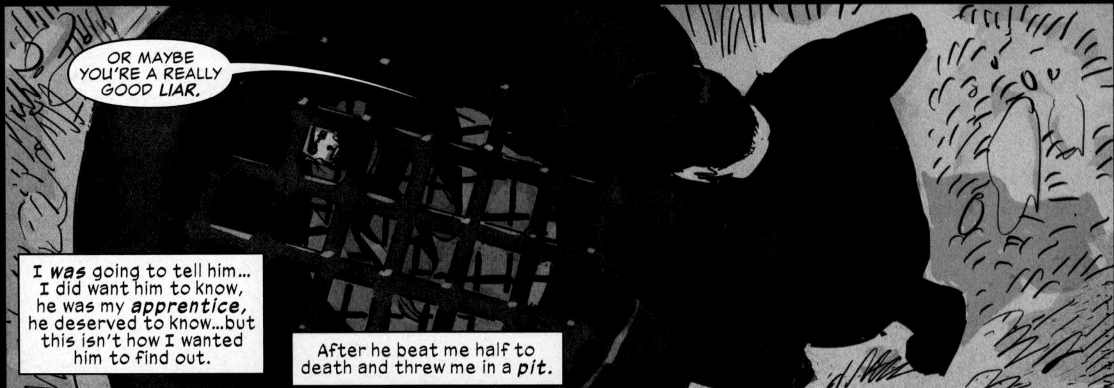
OR MAYBE YOU'RE A REALLY GOOD *LIAR.*
I *was* going to tell him... I did want him to know, he was my *apprentice,* he deserved to know...but this isn't how I wanted him to find out.
After he beat me half to death and threw me in a *pit.*

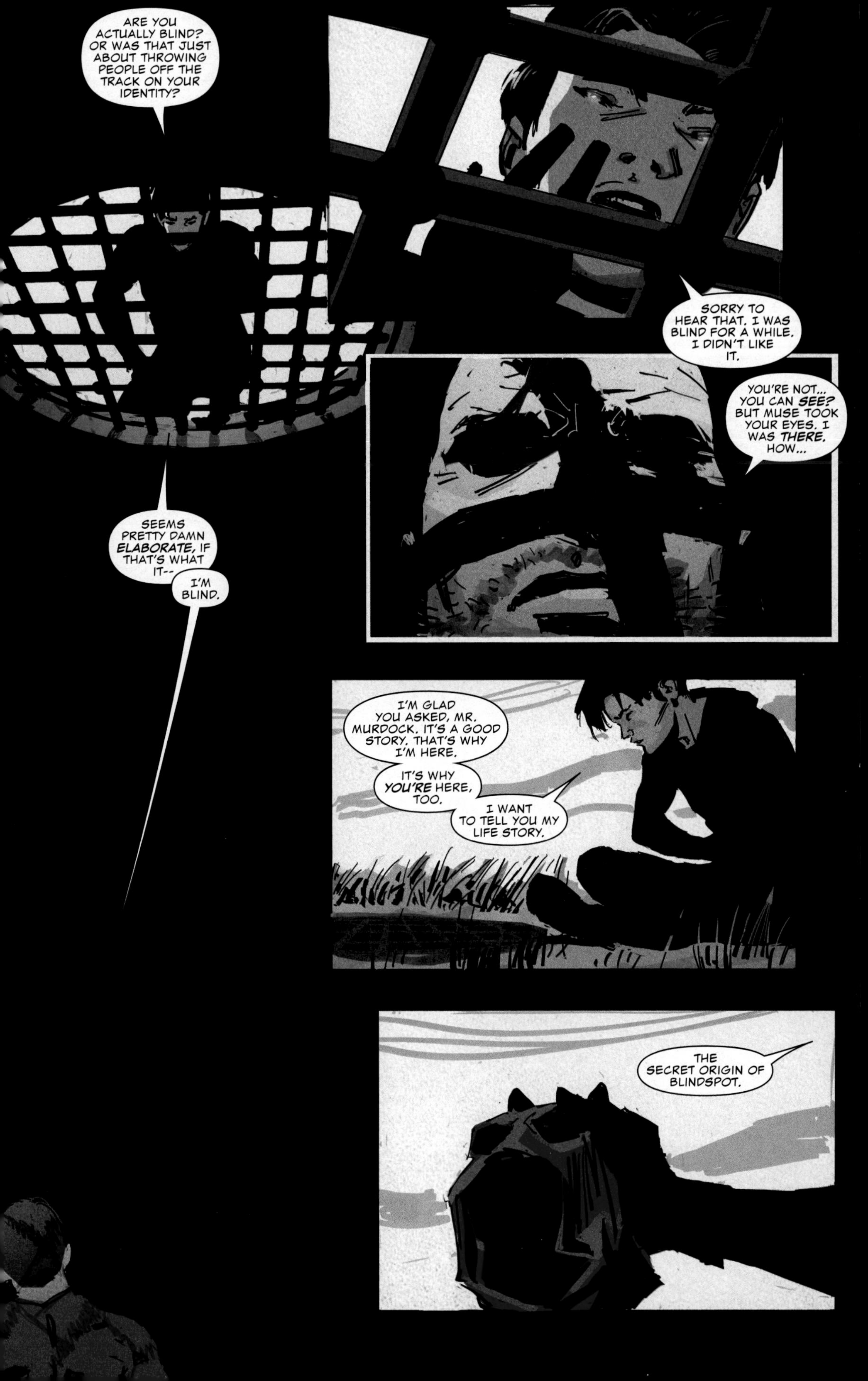
ARE YOU ACTUALLY BLIND? OR WAS THAT JUST ABOUT THROWING PEOPLE OFF THE TRACK ON YOUR IDENTITY?
SEEMS PRETTY DAMN ELABORATE, IF THAT'S WHAT IT--
I'M BLIND.
SORRY TO HEAR THAT. I WAS BLIND FOR A WHILE. I DIDN'T LIKE IT.
YOU'RE NOT... YOU CAN SEE? BUT MUSE TOOK YOUR EYES. I WAS THERE. HOW...
I'M GLAD YOU ASKED, MR. MURDOCK. IT'S A GOOD STORY. THAT'S WHY I'M HERE.
IT'S WHY YOU'RE HERE, TOO.
I WANT TO TELL YOU MY LIFE STORY.
THE SECRET ORIGIN OF BLINDSPOT.

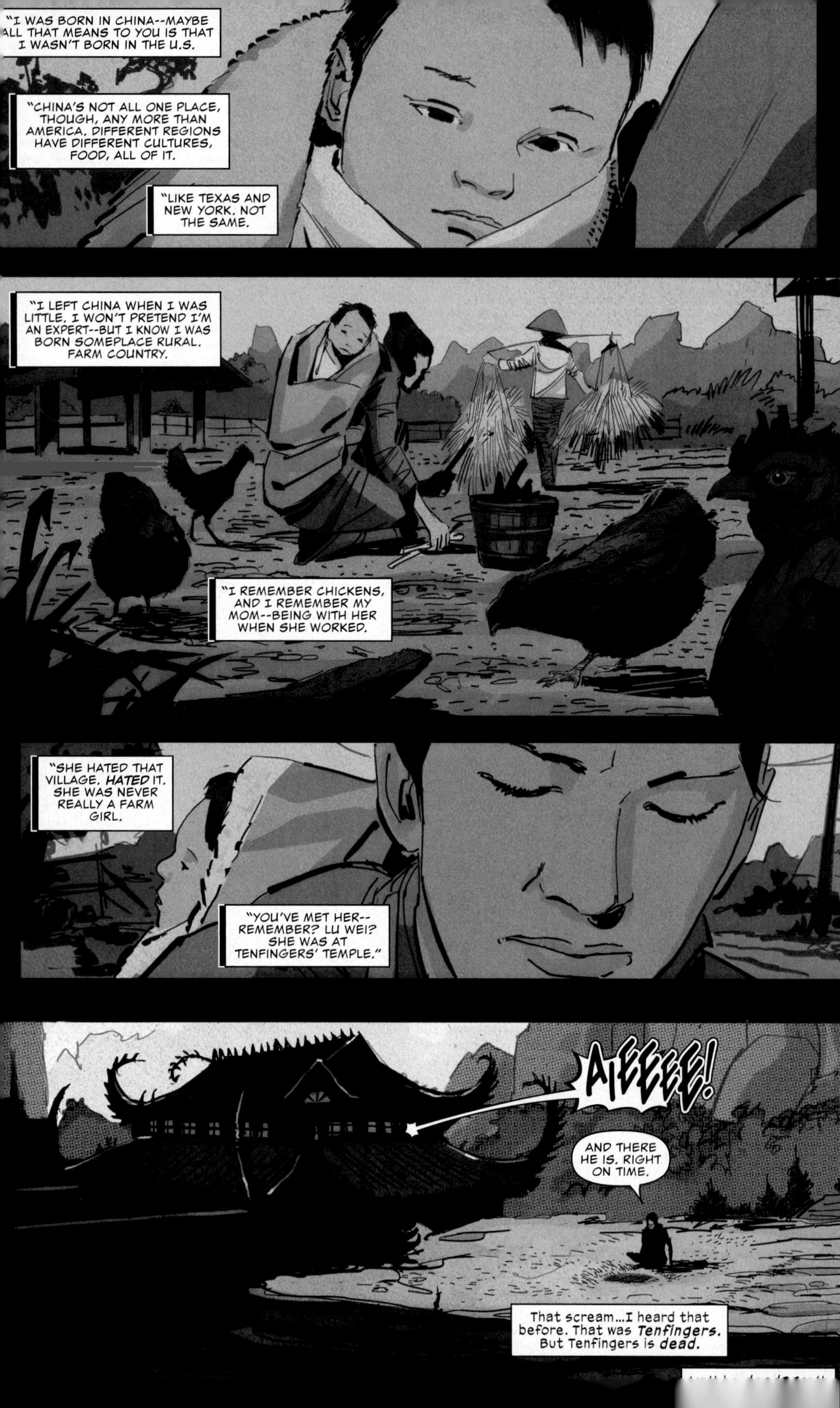
"I WAS BORN IN CHINA--MAYBE ALL THAT MEANS TO YOU IS THAT I WASN'T BORN IN THE U.S.
"CHINA'S NOT ALL ONE PLACE, THOUGH, ANY MORE THAN AMERICA. DIFFERENT REGIONS HAVE DIFFERENT CULTURES, FOOD, ALL OF IT.
"LIKE TEXAS AND NEW YORK. NOT THE SAME.
"I LEFT CHINA WHEN I WAS LITTLE. I WON'T PRETEND I'M AN EXPERT--BUT I KNOW I WAS BORN SOMEPLACE RURAL. FARM COUNTRY.
"I REMEMBER CHICKENS, AND I REMEMBER MY MOM--BEING WITH HER WHEN SHE WORKED.
"SHE HATED THAT VILLAGE. *HATED* IT. SHE WAS NEVER REALLY A FARM GIRL.
"YOU'VE MET HER--REMEMBER? LU WEI? SHE WAS AT TENFINGERS' TEMPLE."
AIEEEE!
AND THERE HE IS. RIGHT ON TIME.
That scream...I heard that before. That was *Tenfingers*. But Tenfingers is *dead*.

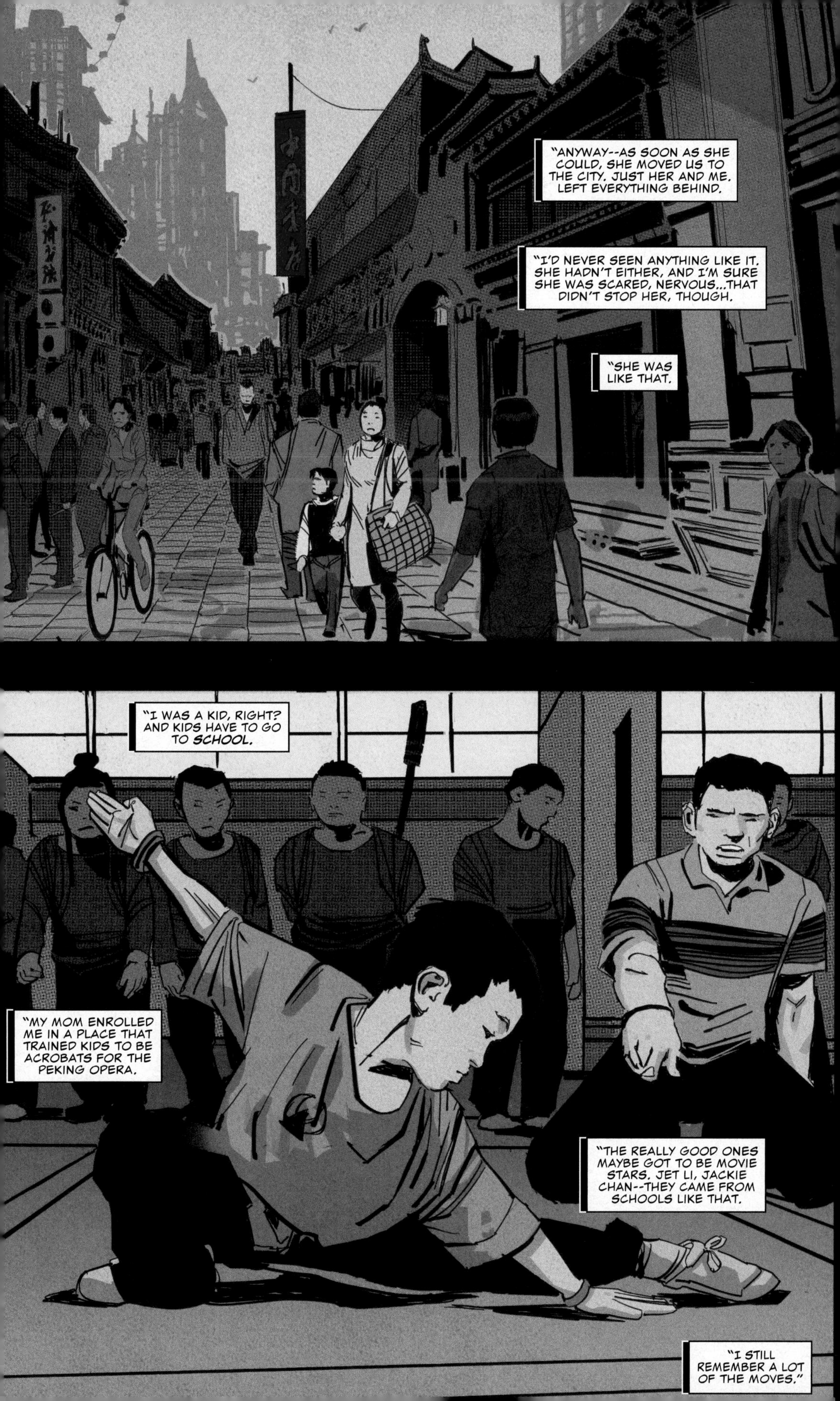
"ANYWAY--AS SOON AS SHE COULD, SHE MOVED US TO THE CITY. JUST HER AND ME. LEFT EVERYTHING BEHIND.
"I'D NEVER SEEN ANYTHING LIKE IT. SHE HADN'T EITHER, AND I'M SURE SHE WAS SCARED, NERVOUS...THAT DIDN'T STOP HER, THOUGH.
"SHE WAS LIKE THAT.
"I WAS A KID, RIGHT? AND KIDS HAVE TO GO TO SCHOOL.
"MY MOM ENROLLED ME IN A PLACE THAT TRAINED KIDS TO BE ACROBATS FOR THE PEKING OPERA.
"THE REALLY GOOD ONES MAYBE GOT TO BE MOVIE STARS. JET LI, JACKIE CHAN--THEY CAME FROM SCHOOLS LIKE THAT.
"I STILL REMEMBER A LOT OF THE MOVES."

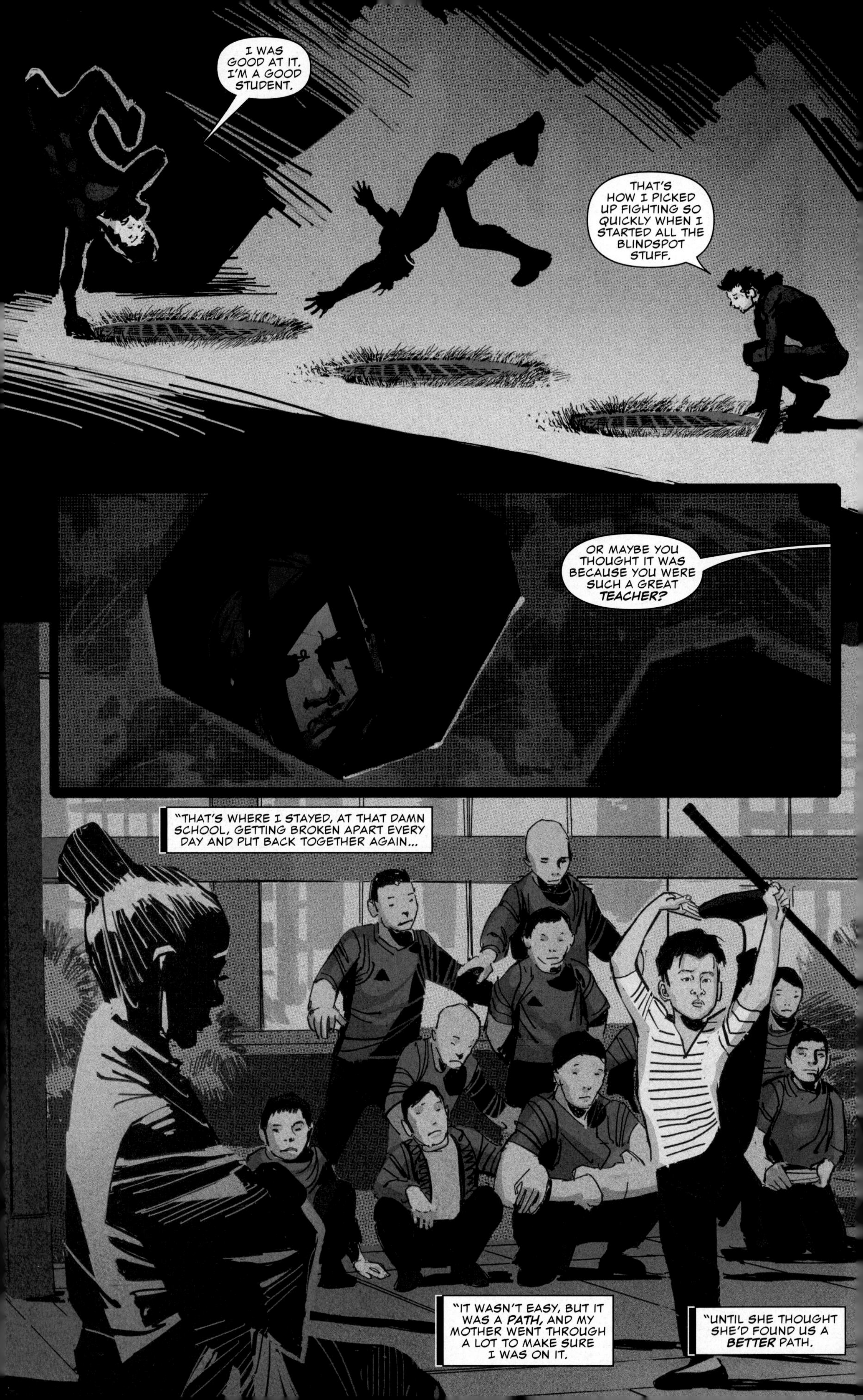
I WAS GOOD AT IT. I'M A GOOD STUDENT.
THAT'S HOW I PICKED UP FIGHTING SO QUICKLY WHEN I STARTED ALL THE BLINDSPOT STUFF.
OR MAYBE YOU THOUGHT IT WAS BECAUSE YOU WERE SUCH A GREAT *TEACHER?*
"THAT'S WHERE I STAYED, AT THAT DAMN SCHOOL, GETTING BROKEN APART EVERY DAY AND PUT BACK TOGETHER AGAIN...
"IT WASN'T EASY, BUT IT WAS A *PATH,* AND MY MOTHER WENT THROUGH A LOT TO MAKE SURE I WAS ON IT.
"UNTIL SHE THOUGHT SHE'D FOUND US A *BETTER* PATH.

"SHE FOUND A SNAKEHEAD-- A PEOPLE-SMUGGLER.

"SHE GAVE HIM EVERY YUAN SHE HAD TO GET US TO THE U.S.

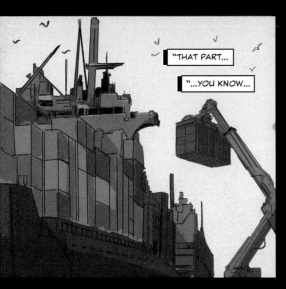
"THAT PART...

"...YOU KNOW...

"...I DON'T REALLY WANT TO TALK ABOUT THAT PART."

That *scent*... what is that? Strong, like evergreen, but there's... something... else...

WE'LL PICK THIS UP LATER. HAVE A GOOD REST, MR. MURDOCK.

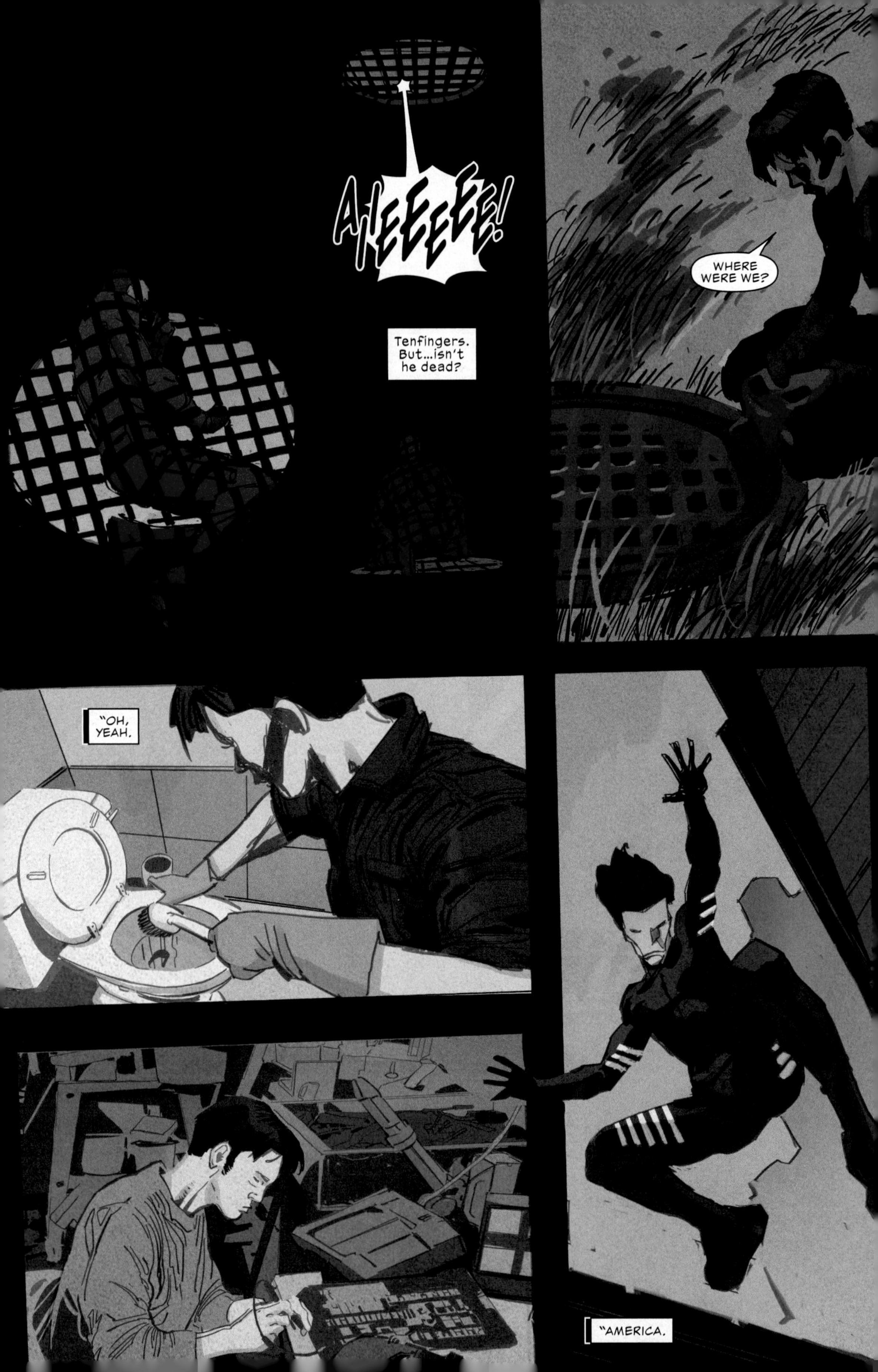
AIEEEEE!
Tenfingers. But...isn't he dead?
WHERE WERE WE?
"OH, YEAH.
"AMERICA.

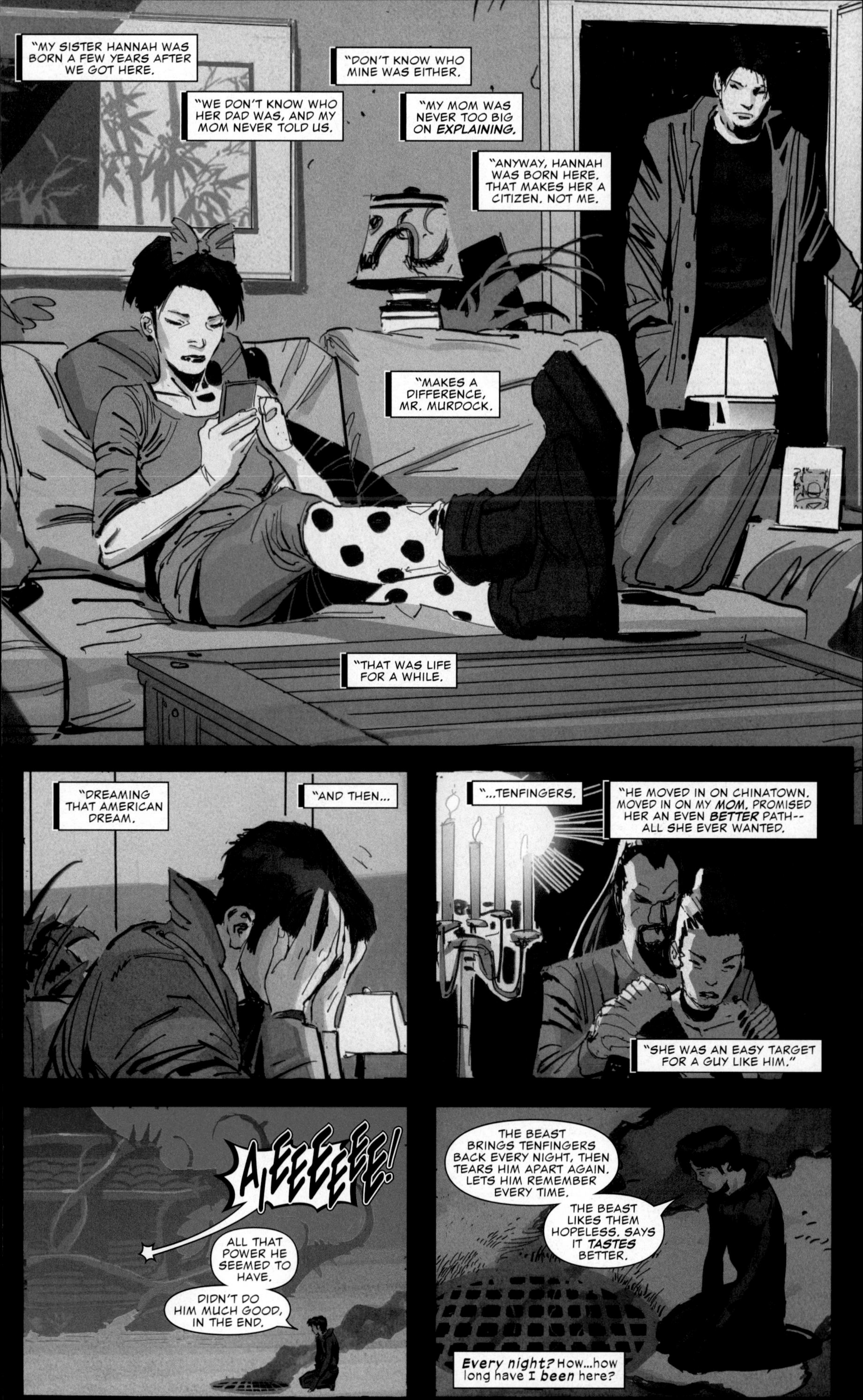
"MY SISTER HANNAH WAS BORN A FEW YEARS AFTER WE GOT HERE.
"WE DON'T KNOW WHO HER DAD WAS, AND MY MOM NEVER TOLD US.
"DON'T KNOW WHO MINE WAS EITHER.
"MY MOM WAS NEVER TOO BIG ON EXPLAINING.
"ANYWAY, HANNAH WAS BORN HERE. THAT MAKES HER A CITIZEN. NOT ME.
"MAKES A DIFFERENCE, MR. MURDOCK.
"THAT WAS LIFE FOR A WHILE.
"DREAMING THAT AMERICAN DREAM.
"AND THEN...
"...TENFINGERS.
"HE MOVED IN ON CHINATOWN. MOVED IN ON MY MOM. PROMISED HER AN EVEN BETTER PATH-- ALL SHE EVER WANTED.
"SHE WAS AN EASY TARGET FOR A GUY LIKE HIM."
AIEEEEEE!
ALL THAT POWER HE SEEMED TO HAVE.
DIDN'T DO HIM MUCH GOOD, IN THE END.
THE BEAST BRINGS TENFINGERS BACK EVERY NIGHT, THEN TEARS HIM APART AGAIN. LETS HIM REMEMBER EVERY TIME.
THE BEAST LIKES THEM HOPELESS. SAYS IT TASTES BETTER.
Every night? How...how long have I been here?

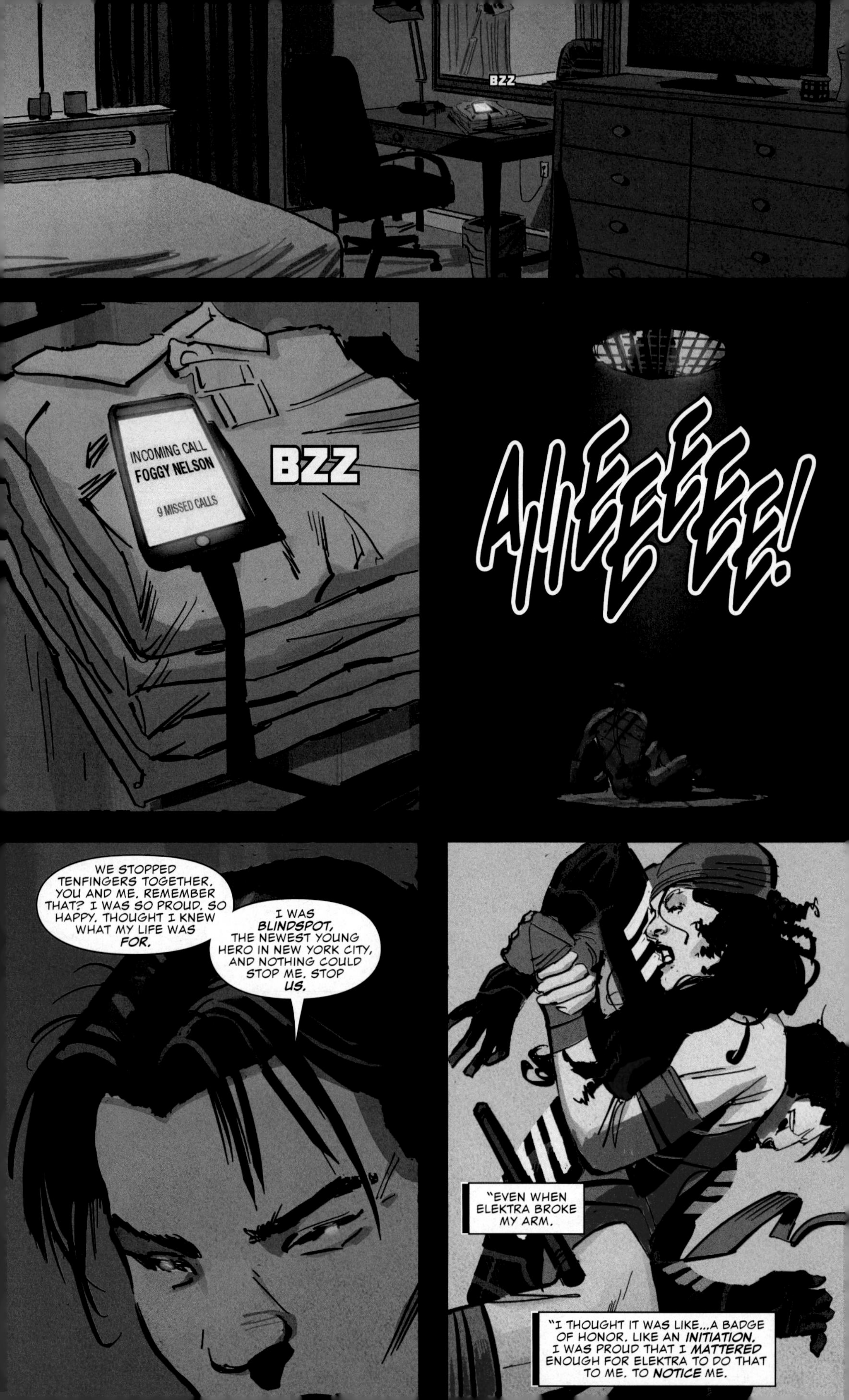
BZZ
INCOMING CALL
FOGGY NELSON
9 MISSED CALLS
BZZ
AIIEEEEE!
WE STOPPED TENFINGERS TOGETHER. YOU AND ME. REMEMBER THAT? I WAS SO PROUD. SO HAPPY. THOUGHT I KNEW WHAT MY LIFE WAS FOR.
I WAS BLINDSPOT, THE NEWEST YOUNG HERO IN NEW YORK CITY, AND NOTHING COULD STOP ME. STOP US.
"EVEN WHEN ELEKTRA BROKE MY ARM.
"I THOUGHT IT WAS LIKE...A BADGE OF HONOR. LIKE AN INITIATION. I WAS PROUD THAT I MATTERED ENOUGH FOR ELEKTRA TO DO THAT TO ME. TO NOTICE ME.

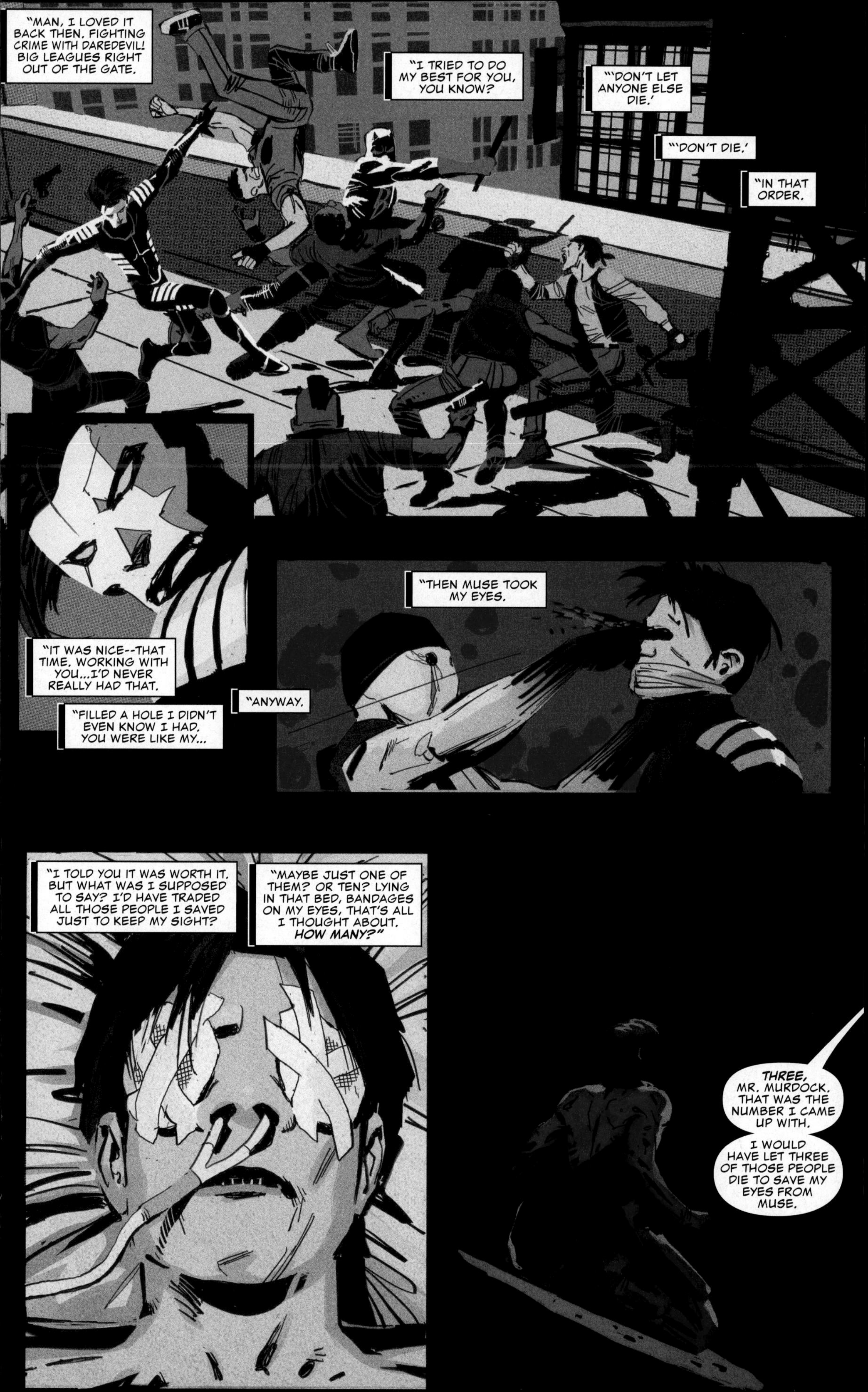
"MAN, I LOVED IT BACK THEN. FIGHTING CRIME WITH DAREDEVIL! BIG LEAGUES RIGHT OUT OF THE GATE.
"I TRIED TO DO MY BEST FOR YOU, YOU KNOW?
"'DON'T LET ANYONE ELSE DIE.'
"'DON'T DIE.'
"IN THAT ORDER.
"IT WAS NICE--THAT TIME, WORKING WITH YOU...I'D NEVER REALLY HAD THAT.
"FILLED A HOLE I DIDN'T EVEN KNOW I HAD. YOU WERE LIKE MY...
"ANYWAY.
"THEN MUSE TOOK MY EYES.
"I TOLD YOU IT WAS WORTH IT. BUT WHAT WAS I SUPPOSED TO SAY? I'D HAVE TRADED ALL THOSE PEOPLE I SAVED JUST TO KEEP MY SIGHT?
"MAYBE JUST ONE OF THEM? OR TEN? LYING IN THAT BED, BANDAGES ON MY EYES, THAT'S ALL I THOUGHT ABOUT. HOW MANY?"
THREE, MR. MURDOCK. THAT WAS THE NUMBER I CAME UP WITH.
I WOULD HAVE LET THREE OF THOSE PEOPLE DIE TO SAVE MY EYES FROM MUSE.

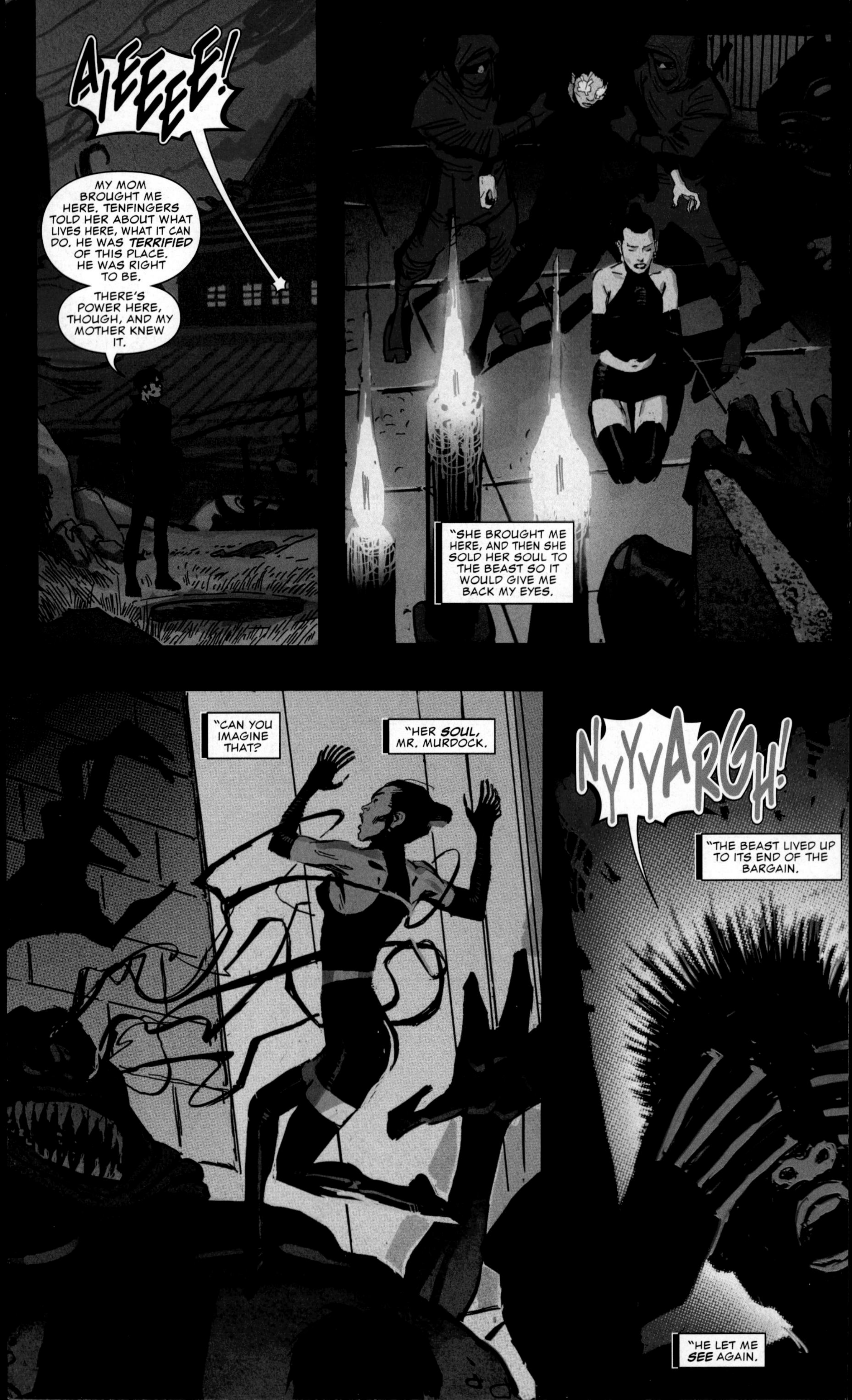
AIEEEE!
MY MOM BROUGHT ME HERE. TENFINGERS TOLD HER ABOUT WHAT LIVES HERE, WHAT IT CAN DO. HE WAS *TERRIFIED* OF THIS PLACE. HE WAS RIGHT TO BE.
THERE'S POWER HERE, THOUGH, AND MY MOTHER KNEW IT.
"SHE BROUGHT ME HERE, AND THEN SHE SOLD HER SOUL TO THE BEAST SO IT WOULD GIVE ME BACK MY EYES.
"CAN YOU IMAGINE THAT?
"HER *SOUL*, MR. MURDOCK.
NYYYARGH!
"THE BEAST LIVED UP TO ITS END OF THE BARGAIN.
"HE LET ME *SEE* AGAIN.

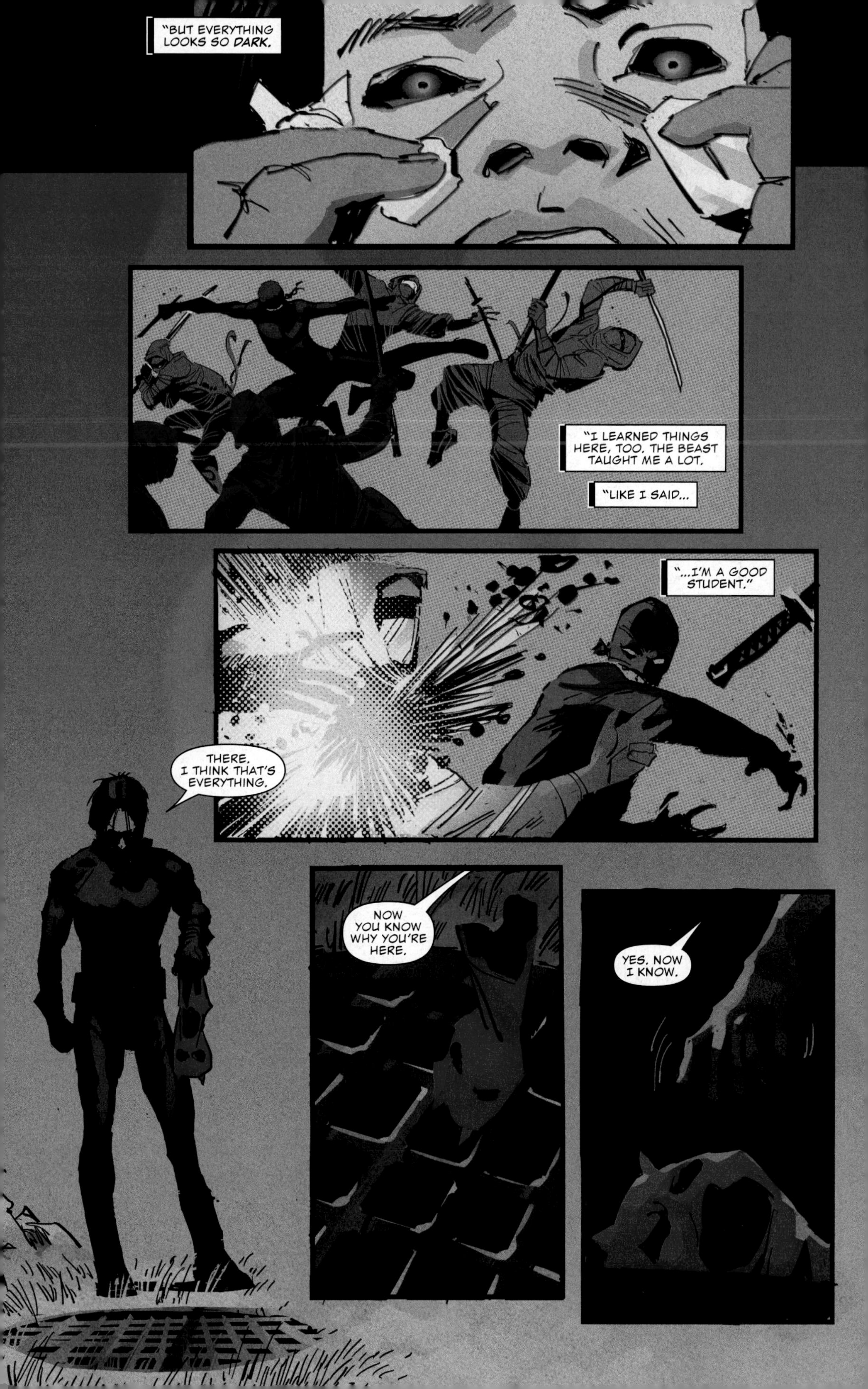
"BUT EVERYTHING LOOKS SO DARK.
"I LEARNED THINGS HERE, TOO. THE BEAST TAUGHT ME A LOT.
"LIKE I SAID...
"...I'M A GOOD STUDENT."
THERE. I THINK THAT'S EVERYTHING.
NOW YOU KNOW WHY YOU'RE HERE.
YES. NOW I KNOW.

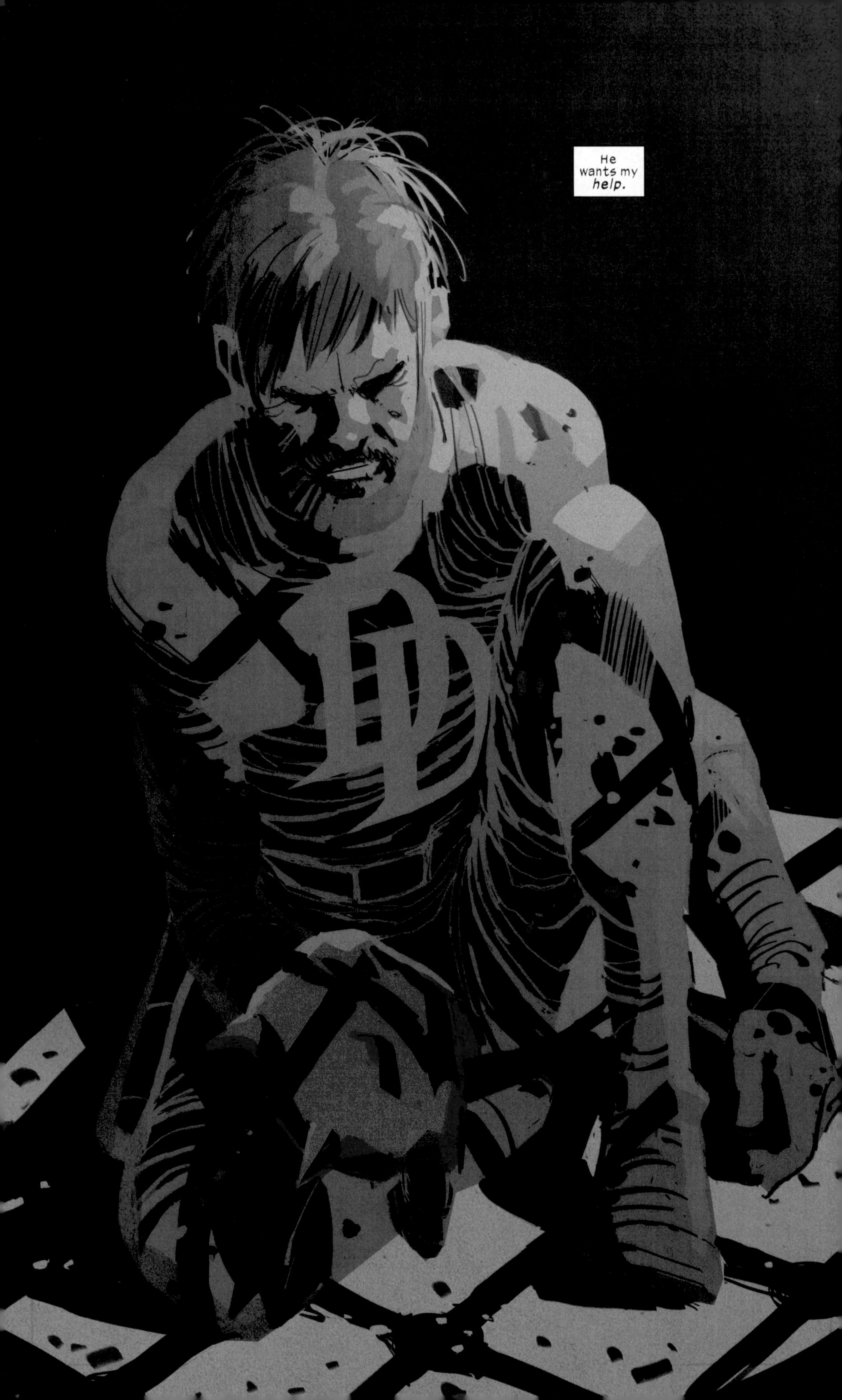
He wants my *help.*

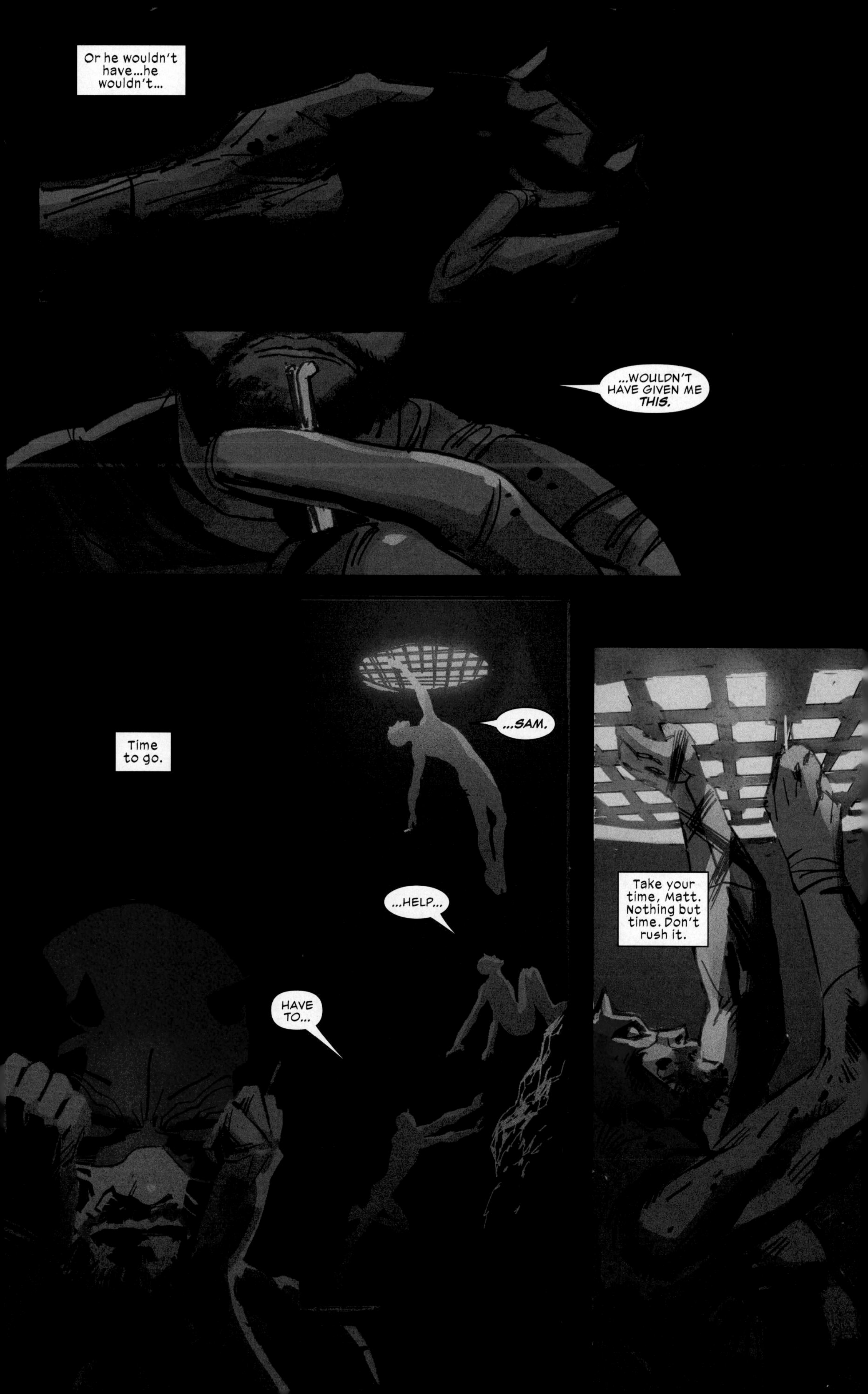
Or he wouldn't have...he wouldn't...
...WOULDN'T HAVE GIVEN ME THIS.
Time to go.
...SAM.
...HELP...
HAVE TO...
Take your time, Matt. Nothing but time. Don't rush it.

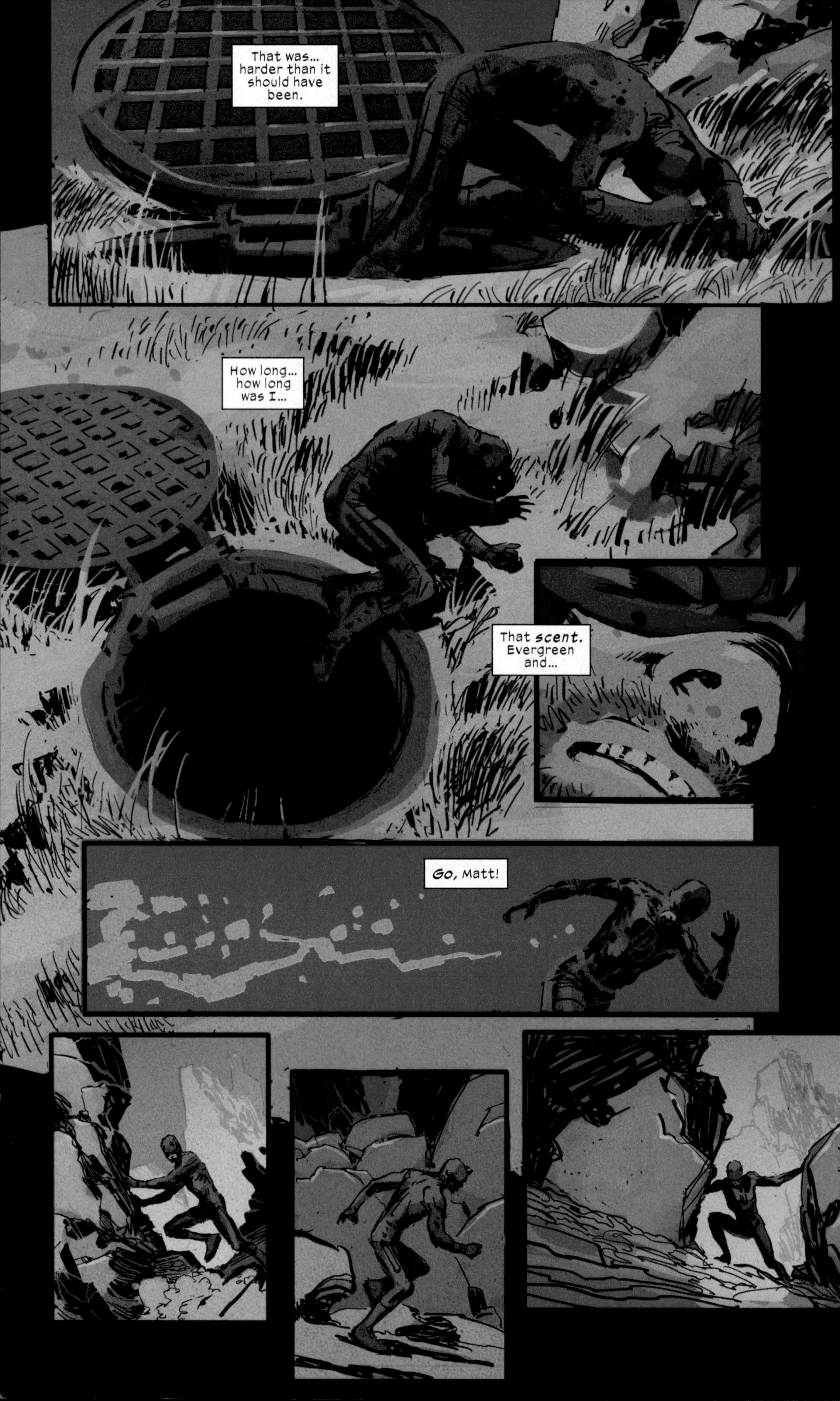
That was... harder than it should have been.
How long... how long was I...
That scent. Evergreen and...
Go, Matt!

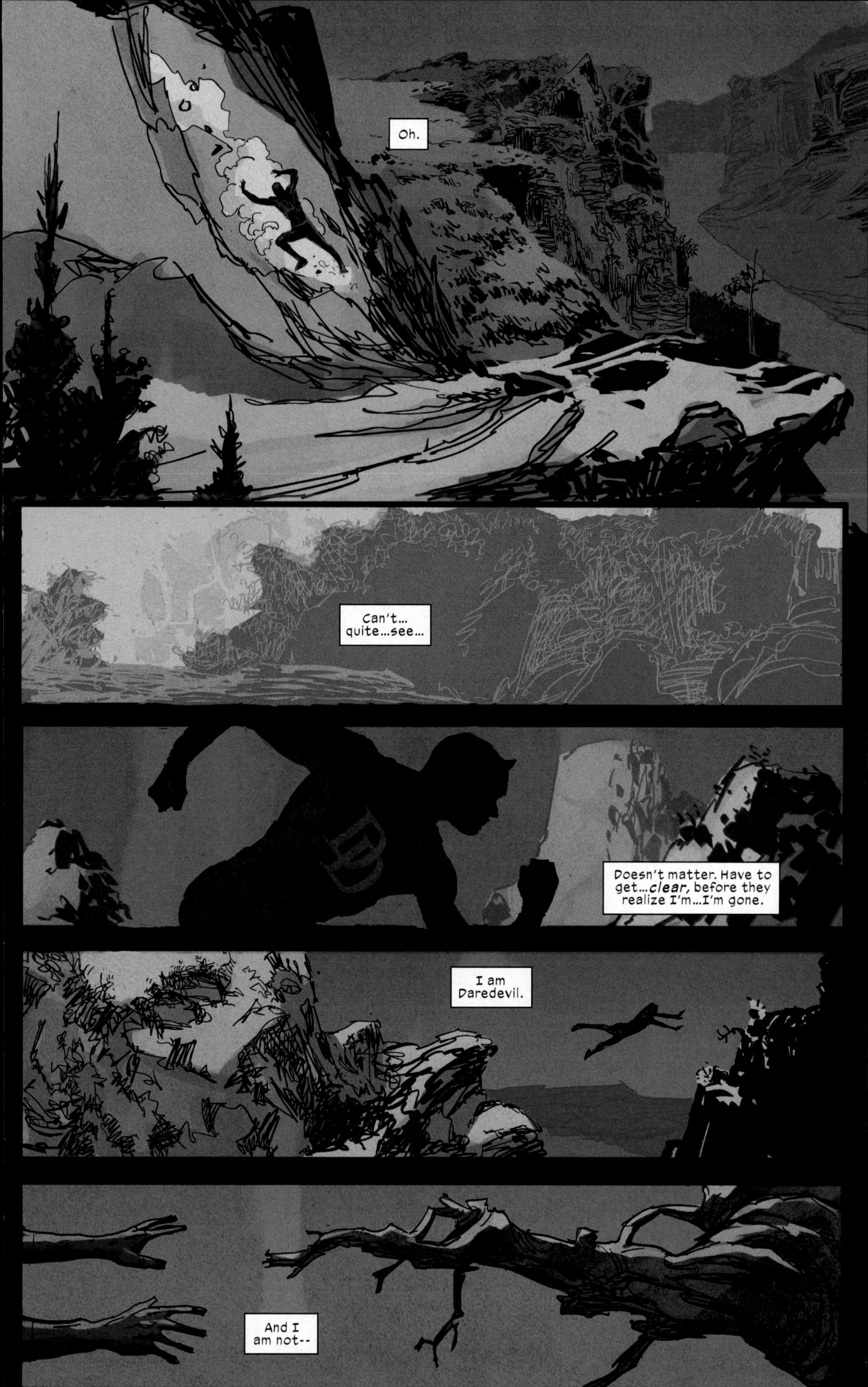
Oh.
Can't... quite...see...
Doesn't matter. Have to get...*clear,* before they realize I'm...I'm gone.
I am Daredevil.
And I am not--

SLAM

NO...
NO...

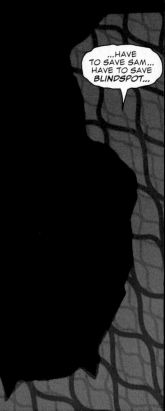

...HAVE
TO SAVE SAM...
HAVE TO SAVE
BLINDSPOT...

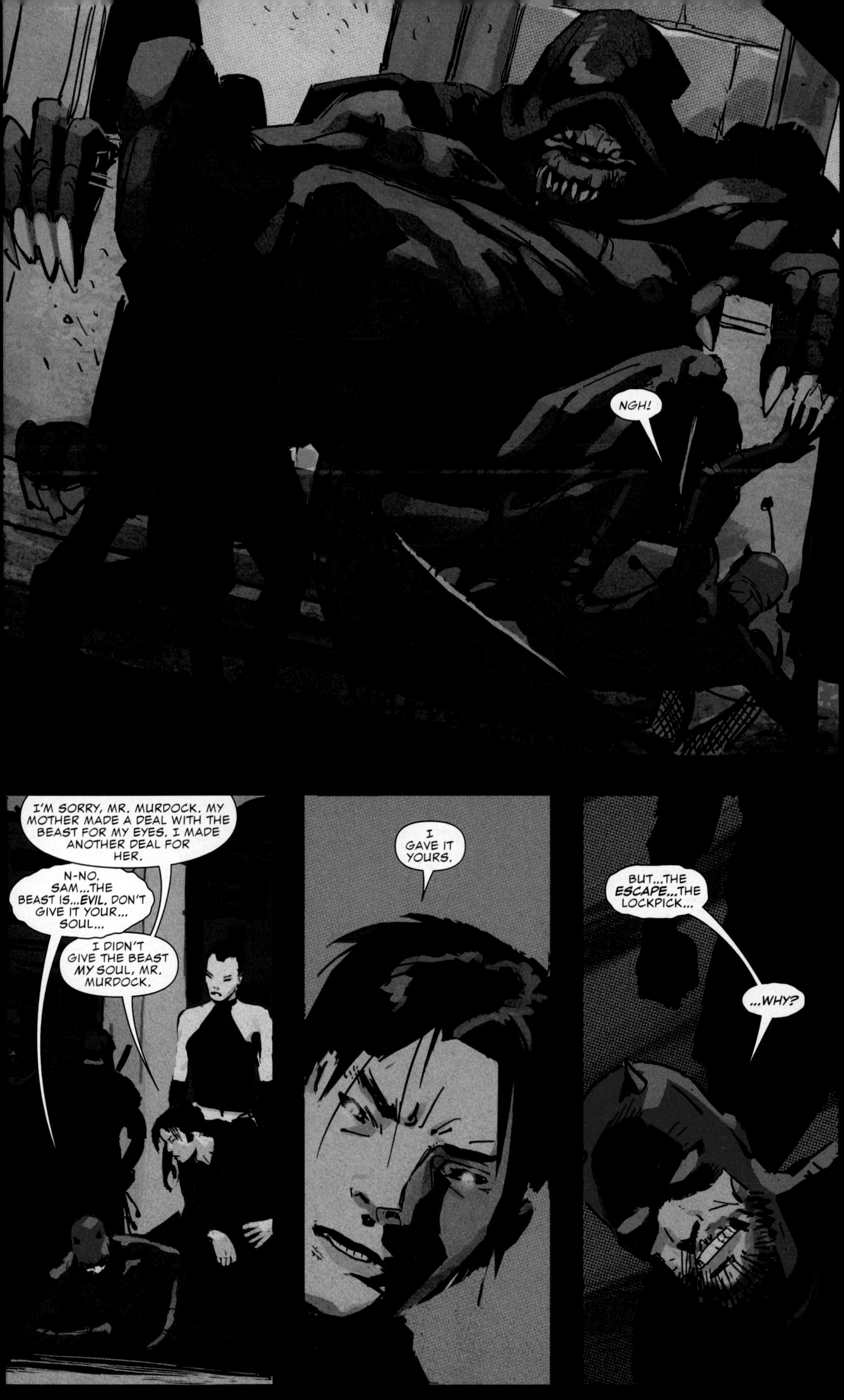
NGH!
I'M SORRY, MR. MURDOCK. MY MOTHER MADE A DEAL WITH THE BEAST FOR MY EYES. I MADE ANOTHER DEAL FOR HER.
N-NO. SAM...THE BEAST IS...EVIL. DON'T GIVE IT YOUR... SOUL...
I DIDN'T GIVE THE BEAST MY SOUL, MR. MURDOCK.
I GAVE IT YOURS.
BUT...THE ESCAPE...THE LOCKPICK...
...WHY?

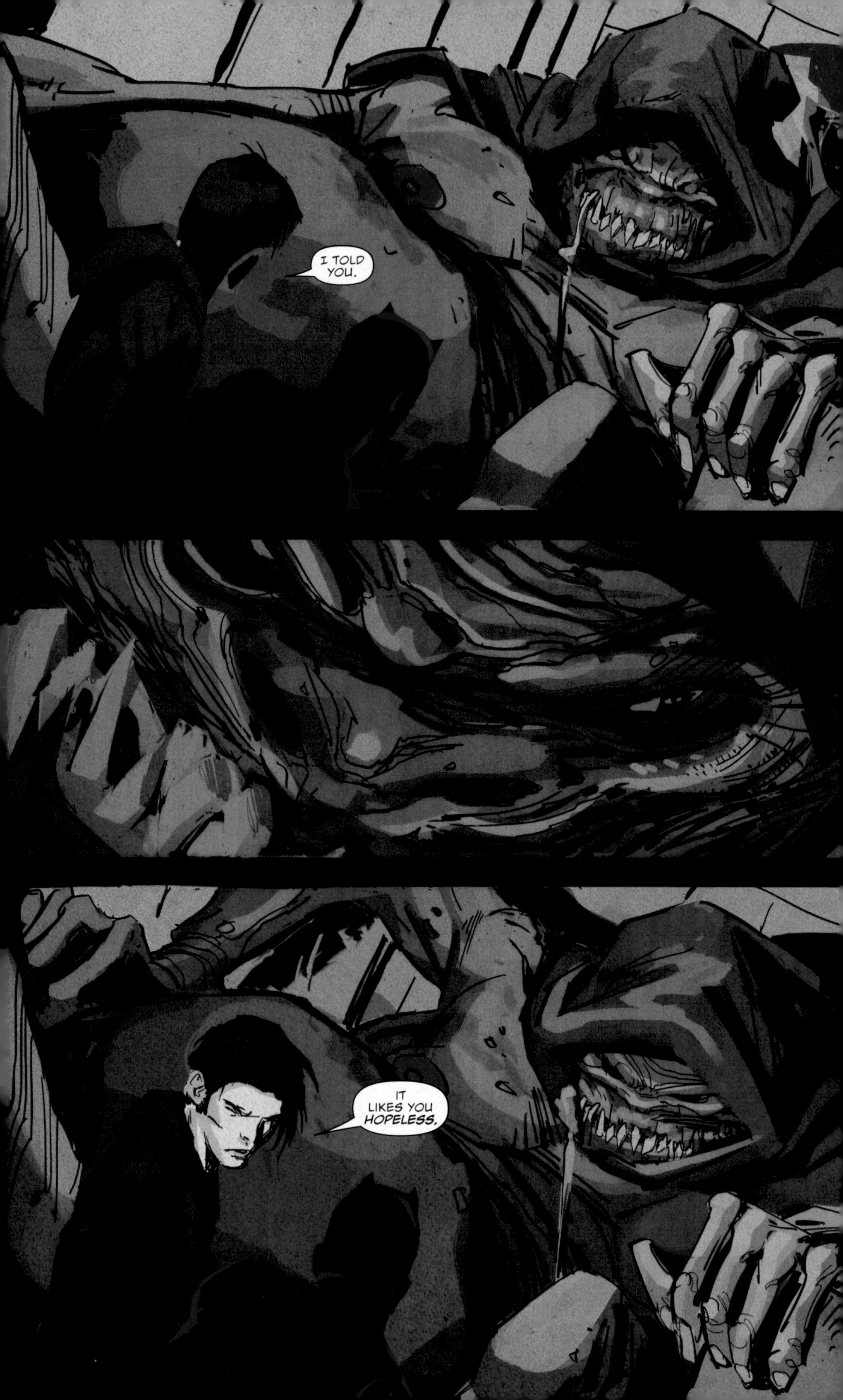
I TOLD YOU.
IT LIKES YOU HOPELESS.

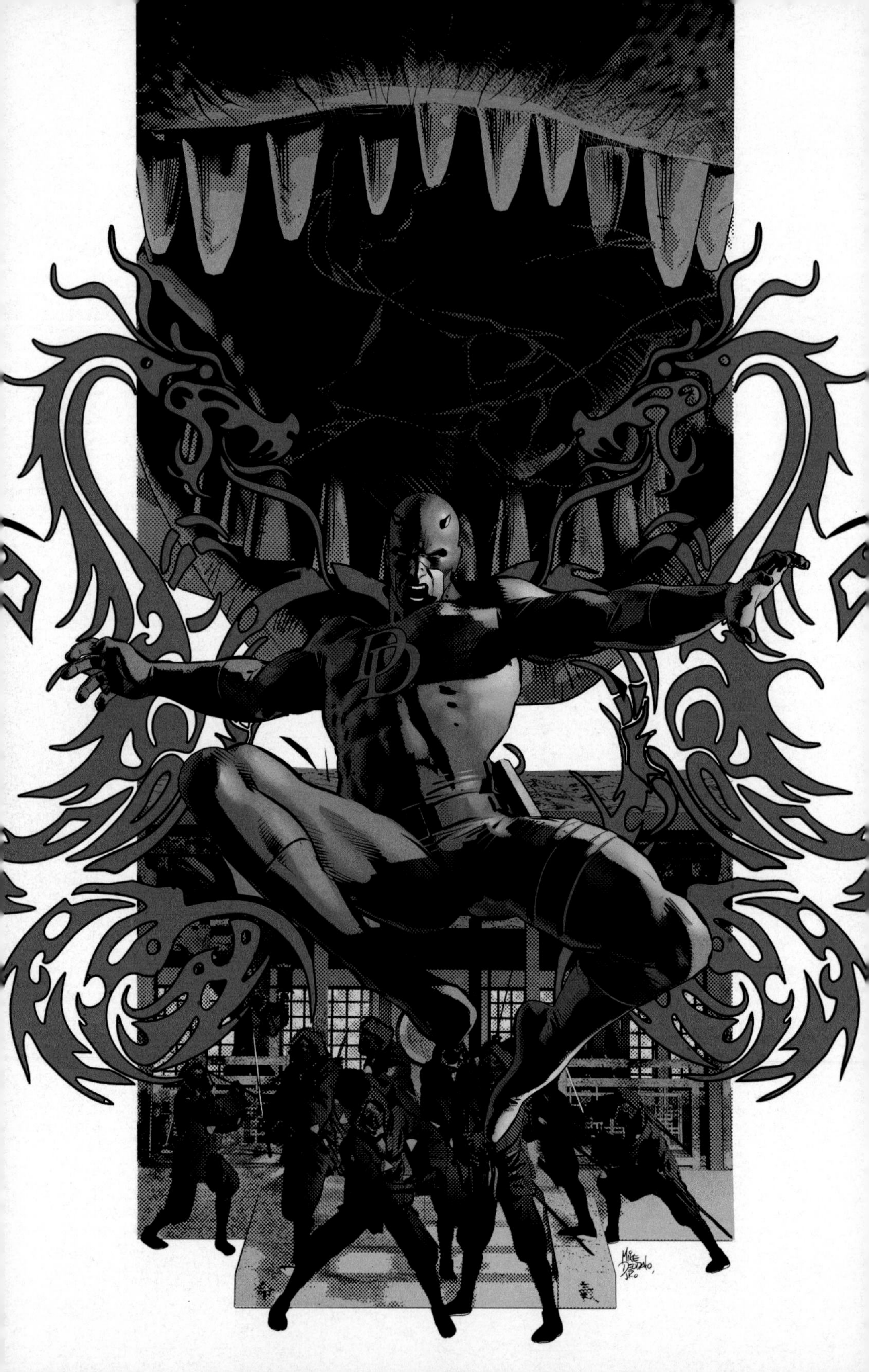

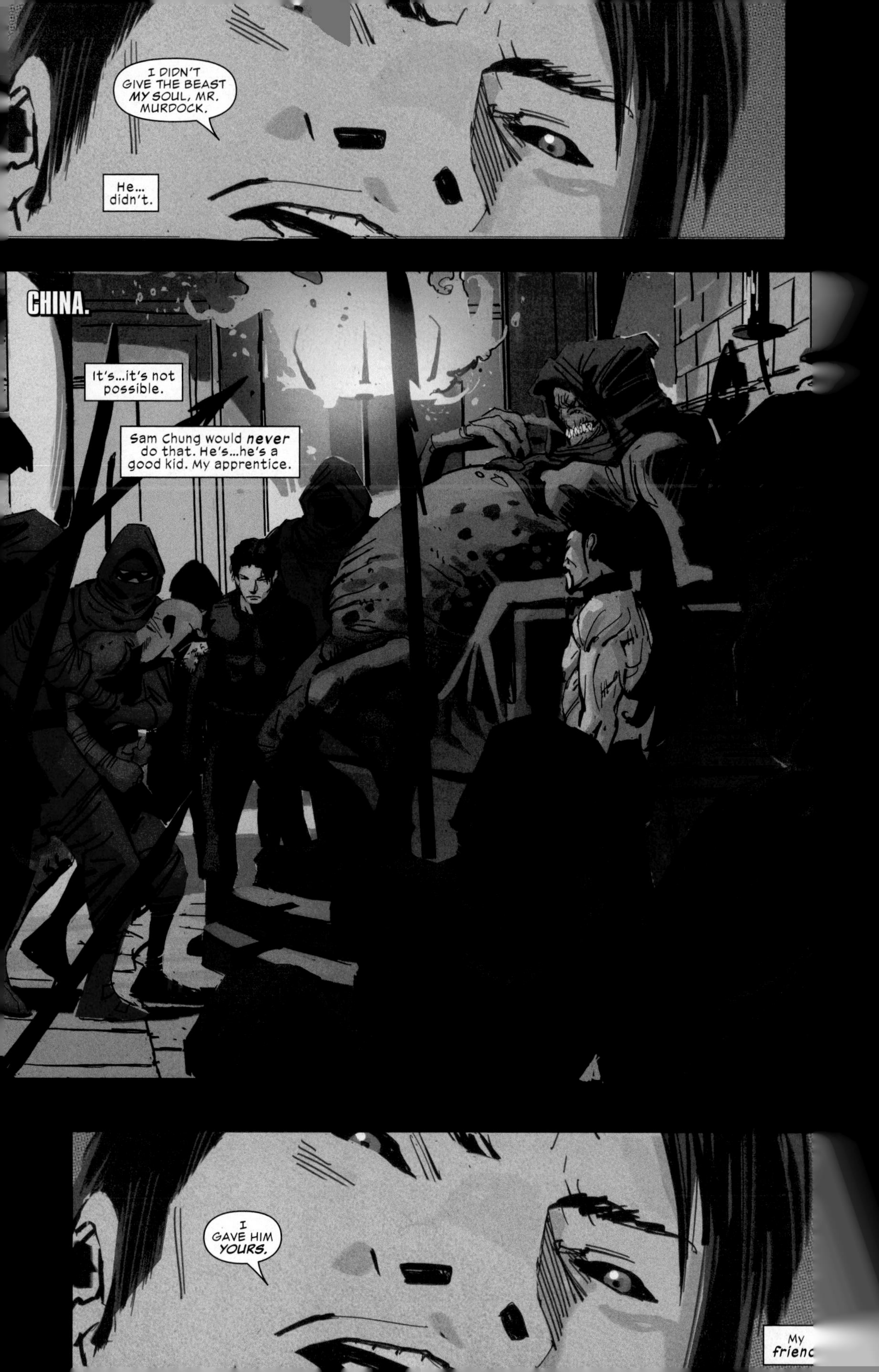
I DIDN'T GIVE THE BEAST MY SOUL, MR. MURDOCK.
He... didn't.
CHINA.
It's...it's not possible.
Sam Chung would never do that. He's...he's a good kid. My apprentice.
I GAVE HIM YOURS.
My frienc

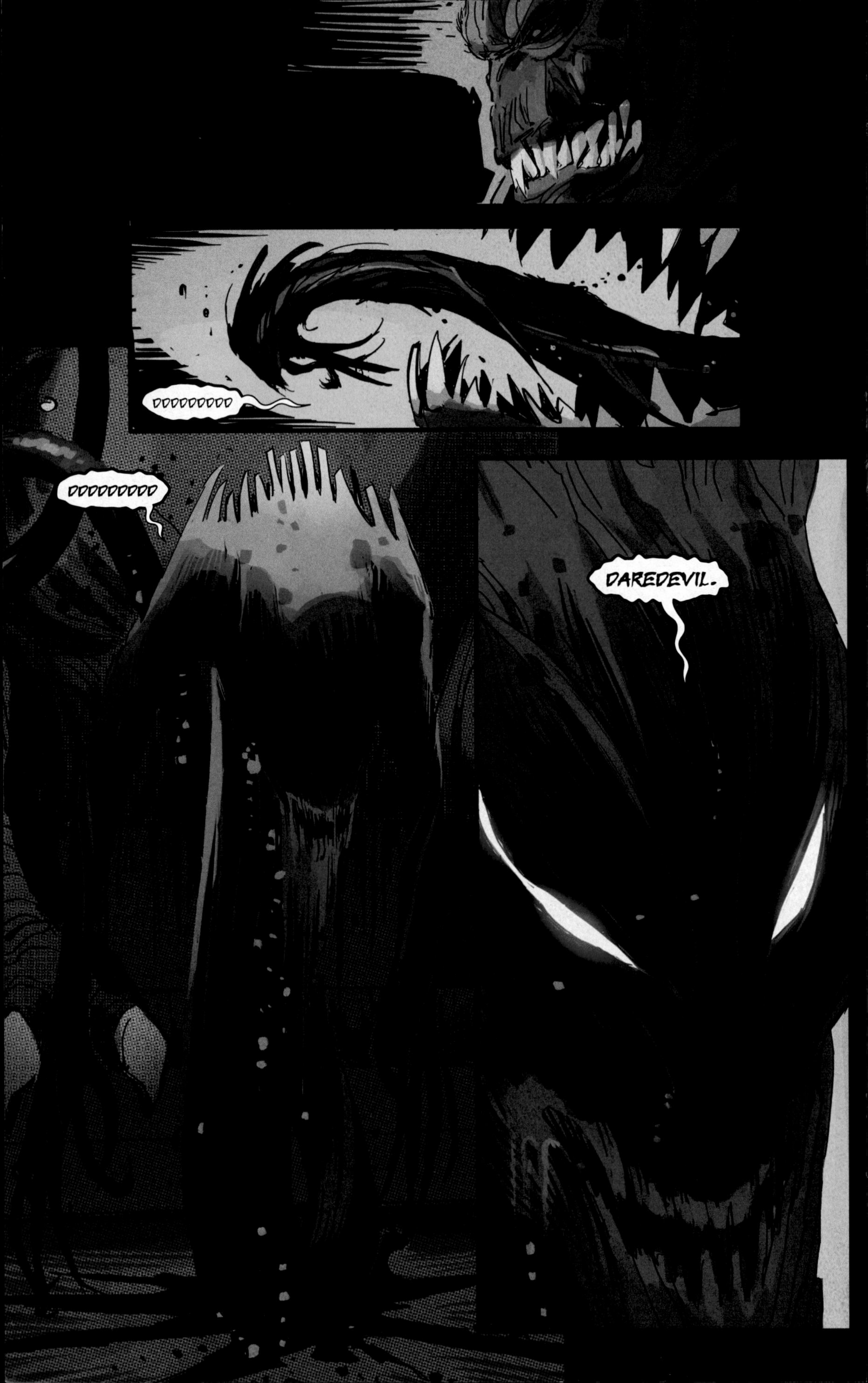
DDDDDDDDD
DDDDDDDDD
DAREDEVIL.

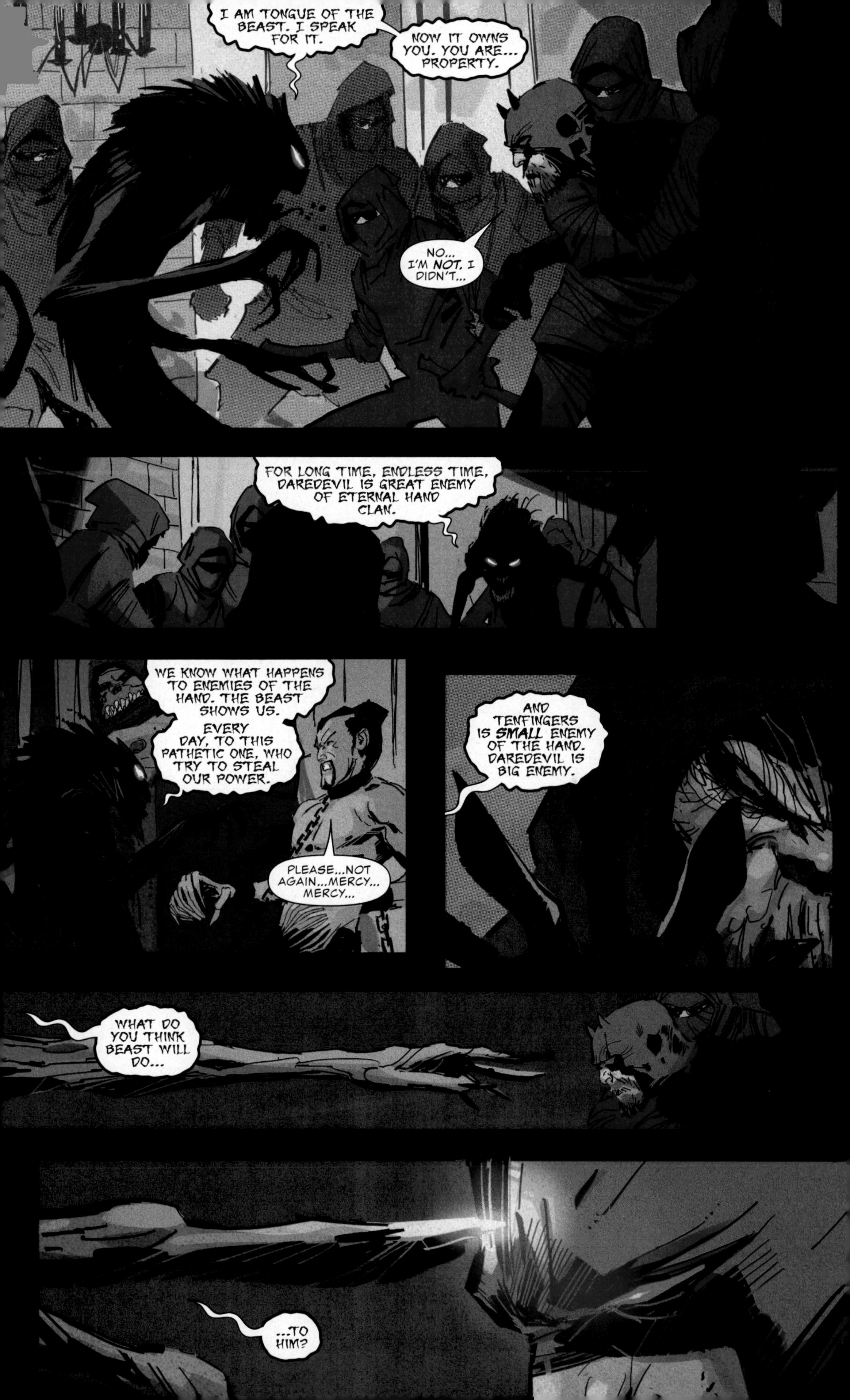
I AM TONGUE OF THE BEAST. I SPEAK FOR IT.
NOW IT OWNS YOU. YOU ARE... PROPERTY.
NO... I'M NOT. I DIDN'T...
FOR LONG TIME, ENDLESS TIME, DAREDEVIL IS GREAT ENEMY OF ETERNAL HAND CLAN.
WE KNOW WHAT HAPPENS TO ENEMIES OF THE HAND. THE BEAST SHOWS US.
EVERY DAY, TO THIS PATHETIC ONE, WHO TRY TO STEAL OUR POWER.
PLEASE...NOT AGAIN...MERCY... MERCY...
AND TENFINGERS IS SMALL ENEMY OF THE HAND. DAREDEVIL IS BIG ENEMY.
WHAT DO YOU THINK BEAST WILL DO...
...TO HIM?

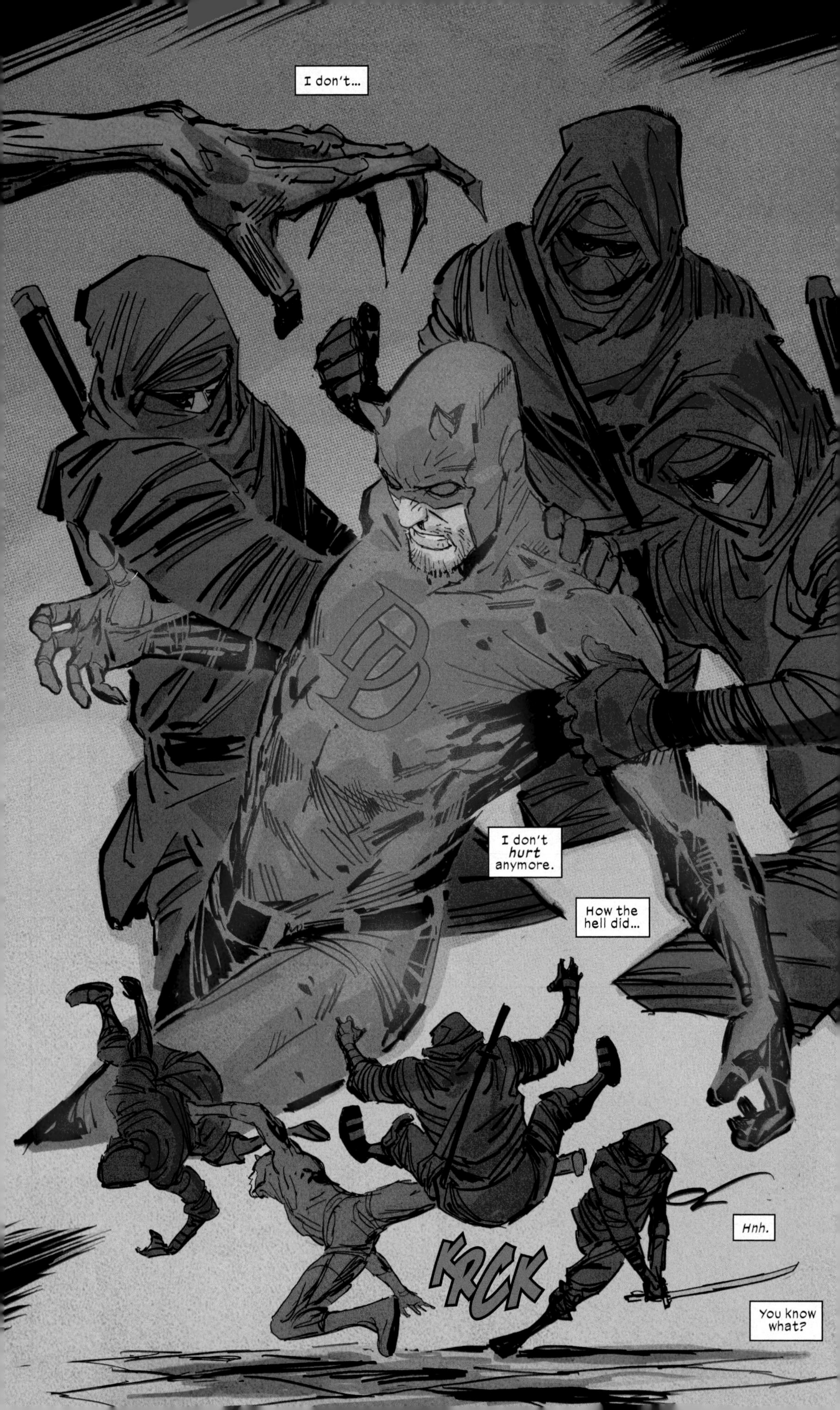
I don't...
I don't *hurt* anymore.
How the hell did...
Hnh.
KRCK
You know what?

...I don't care.

AAAAAGGGHH!

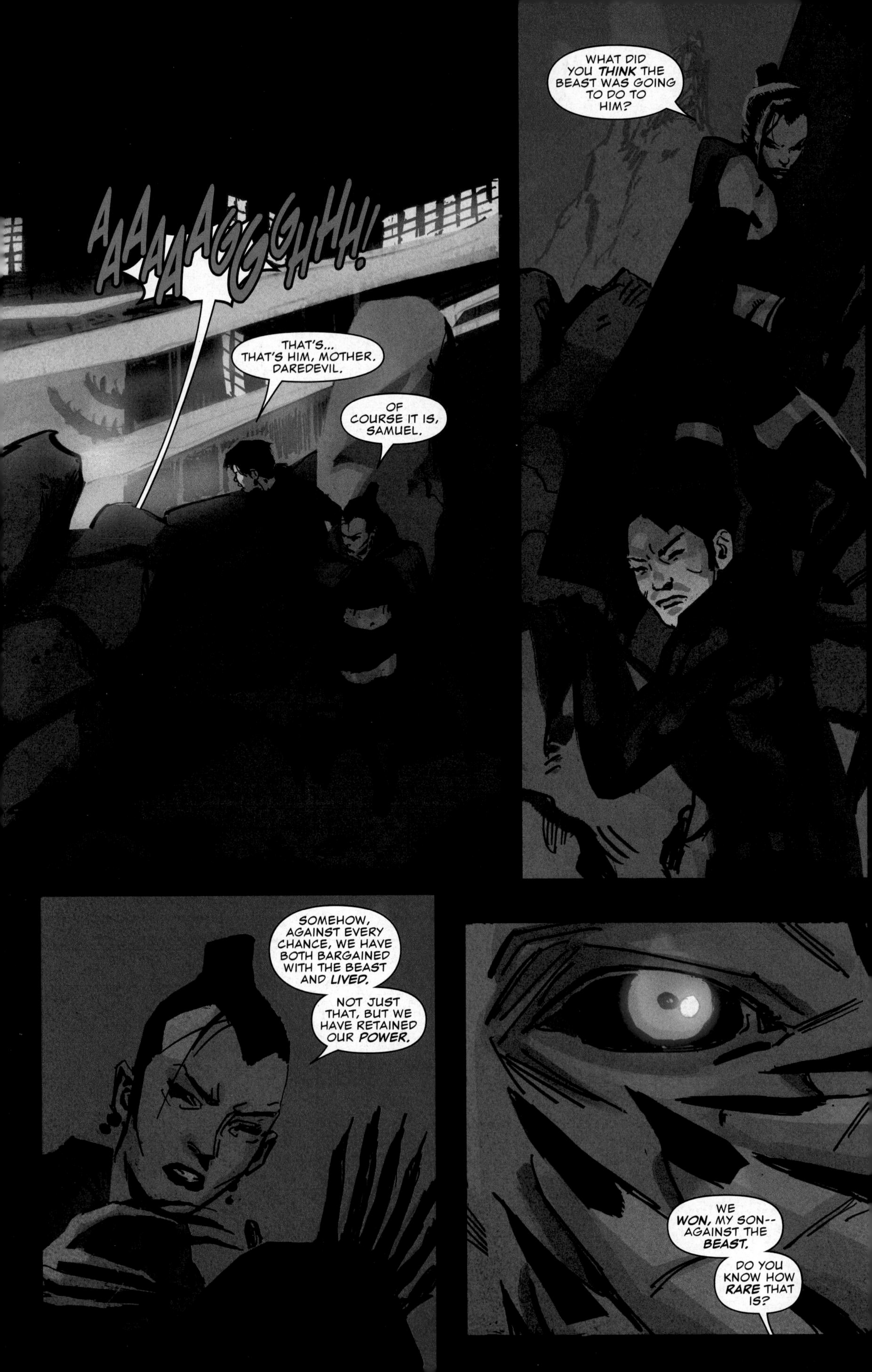
AAAAAAGGGHHH!
THAT'S... THAT'S HIM, MOTHER. DAREDEVIL.
OF COURSE IT IS, SAMUEL.
WHAT DID YOU THINK THE BEAST WAS GOING TO DO TO HIM?
SOMEHOW, AGAINST EVERY CHANCE, WE HAVE BOTH BARGAINED WITH THE BEAST AND LIVED.
NOT JUST THAT, BUT WE HAVE RETAINED OUR POWER.
WE WON, MY SON-- AGAINST THE BEAST.
DO YOU KNOW HOW RARE THAT IS?

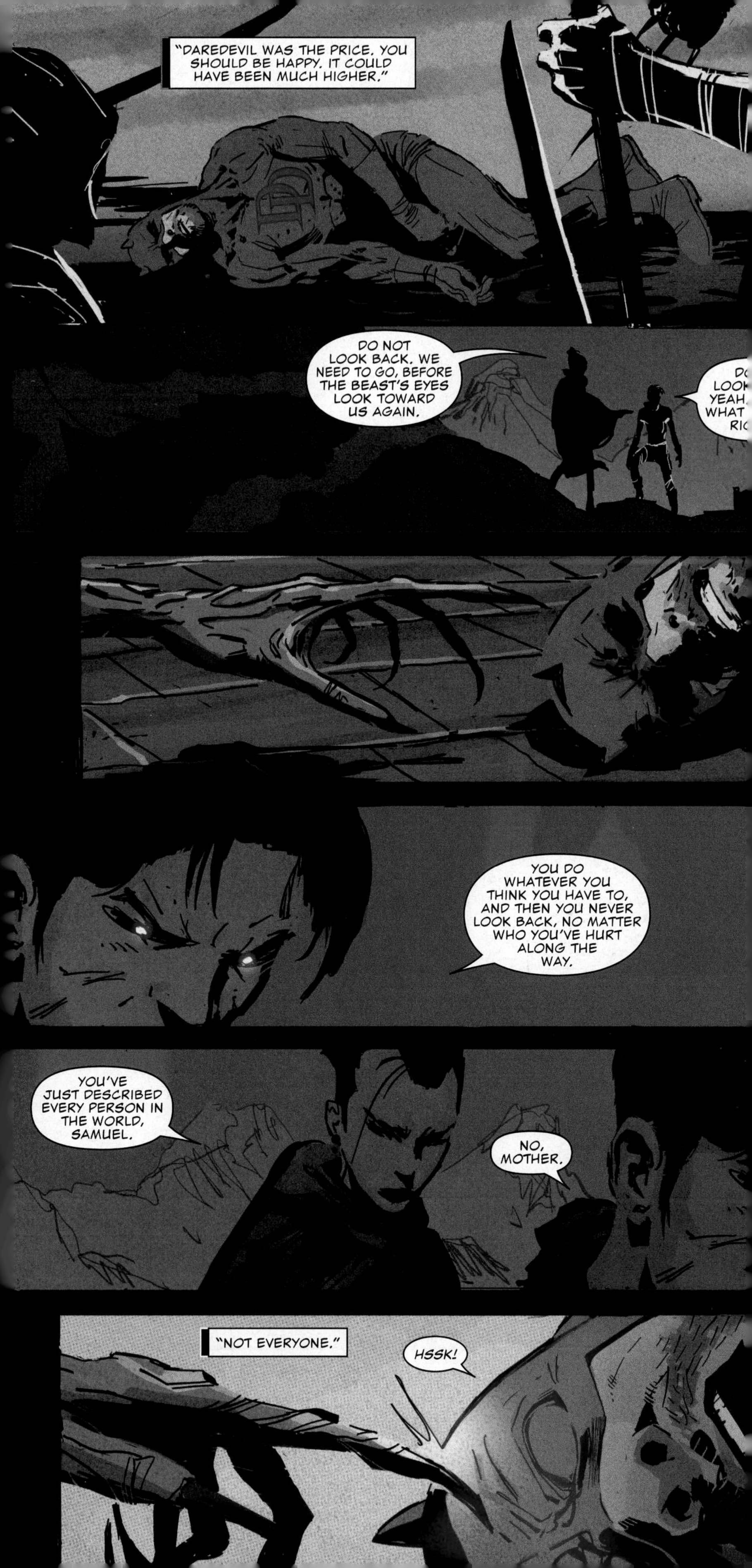
"DAREDEVIL WAS THE PRICE. YOU SHOULD BE HAPPY. IT COULD HAVE BEEN MUCH HIGHER."
DO NOT LOOK BACK. WE NEED TO GO, BEFORE THE BEAST'S EYES LOOK TOWARD US AGAIN.
YOU DO WHATEVER YOU THINK YOU HAVE TO, AND THEN YOU NEVER LOOK BACK, NO MATTER WHO YOU'VE HURT ALONG THE WAY.
YOU'VE JUST DESCRIBED EVERY PERSON IN THE WORLD, SAMUEL.
NO, MOTHER.
"NOT EVERYONE."
HSSK!

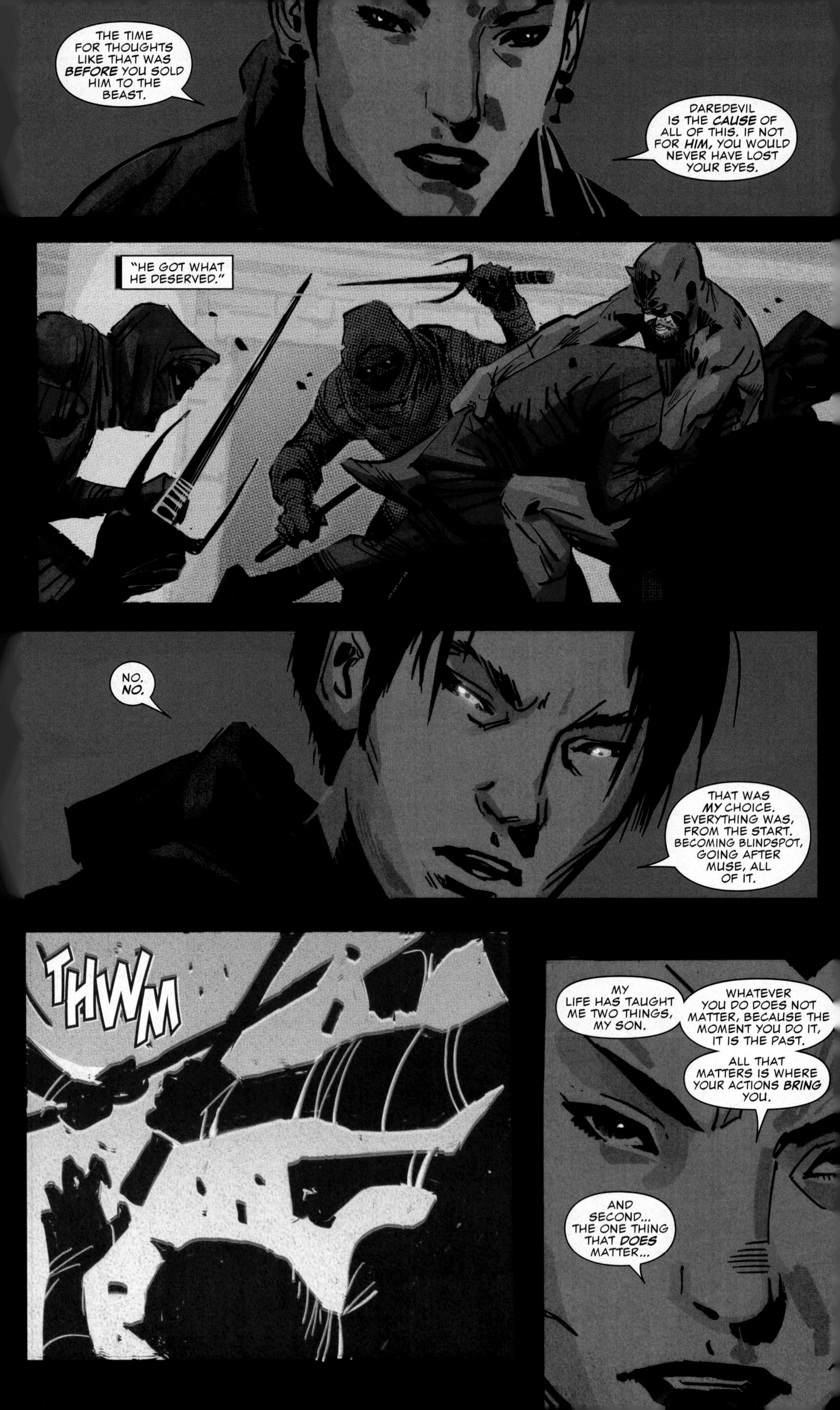

THE TIME FOR THOUGHTS LIKE THAT WAS BEFORE YOU SOLD HIM TO THE BEAST.
DAREDEVIL IS THE CAUSE OF ALL OF THIS. IF NOT FOR HIM, YOU WOULD NEVER HAVE LOST YOUR EYES.
"HE GOT WHAT HE DESERVED."
NO. NO.
THAT WAS MY CHOICE. EVERYTHING WAS, FROM THE START. BECOMING BLINDSPOT, GOING AFTER MUSE, ALL OF IT.
THWM
MY LIFE HAS TAUGHT ME TWO THINGS, MY SON.
WHATEVER YOU DO DOES NOT MATTER, BECAUSE THE MOMENT YOU DO IT, IT IS THE PAST.
ALL THAT MATTERS IS WHERE YOUR ACTIONS BRING YOU.
AND SECOND... THE ONE THING THAT DOES MATTER...

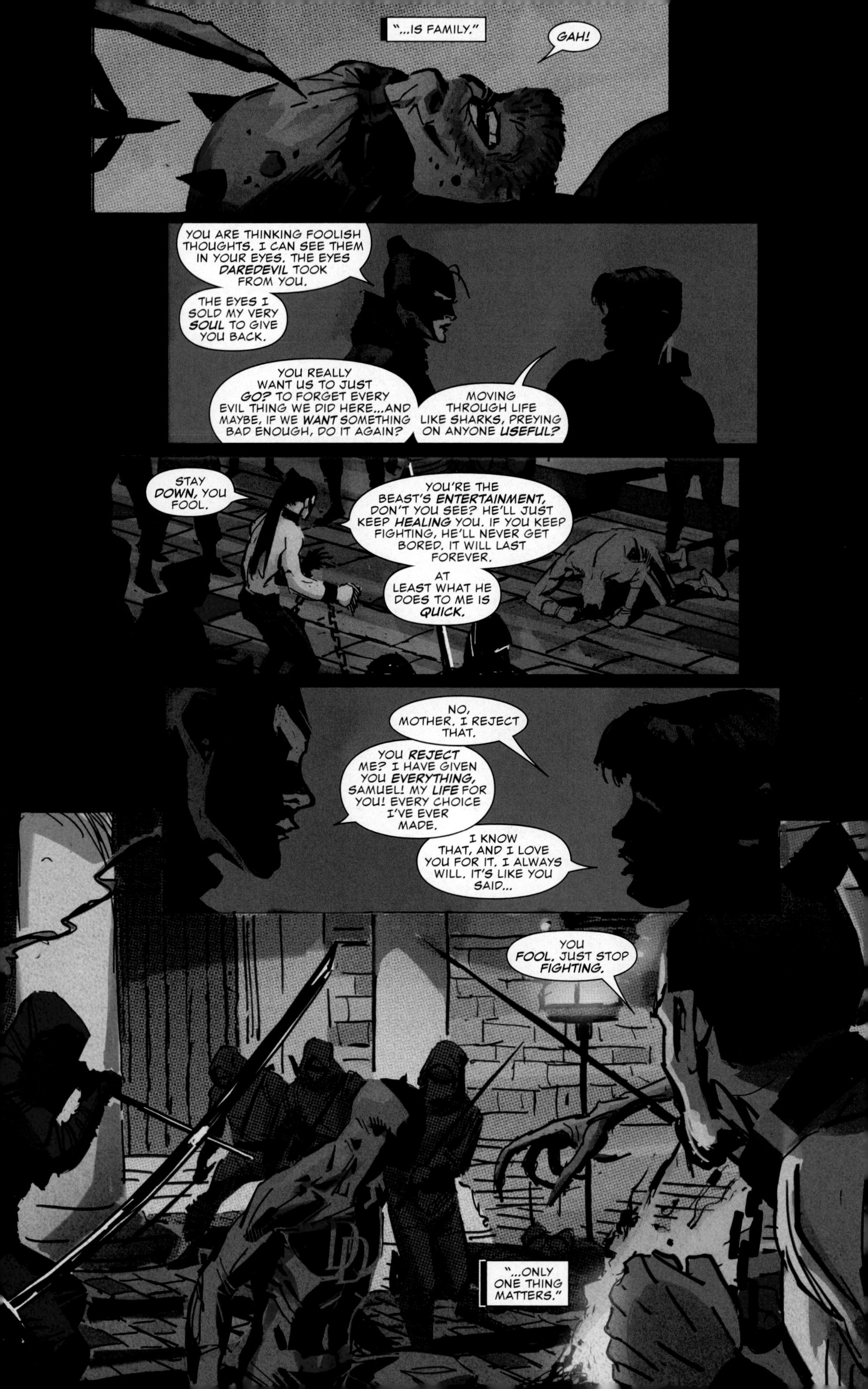
"...IS FAMILY."
GAH!
YOU ARE THINKING FOOLISH THOUGHTS. I CAN SEE THEM IN YOUR EYES. THE EYES DAREDEVIL TOOK FROM YOU.
THE EYES I SOLD MY VERY SOUL TO GIVE YOU BACK.
YOU REALLY WANT US TO JUST GO? TO FORGET EVERY EVIL THING WE DID HERE...AND MAYBE, IF WE WANT SOMETHING BAD ENOUGH, DO IT AGAIN?
MOVING THROUGH LIFE LIKE SHARKS, PREYING ON ANYONE USEFUL?
STAY DOWN, YOU FOOL.
YOU'RE THE BEAST'S ENTERTAINMENT, DON'T YOU SEE? HE'LL JUST KEEP HEALING YOU. IF YOU KEEP FIGHTING, HE'LL NEVER GET BORED. IT WILL LAST FOREVER.
AT LEAST WHAT HE DOES TO ME IS QUICK.
NO, MOTHER. I REJECT THAT.
YOU REJECT ME? I HAVE GIVEN YOU EVERYTHING, SAMUEL! MY LIFE FOR YOU! EVERY CHOICE I'VE EVER MADE.
I KNOW THAT, AND I LOVE YOU FOR IT. I ALWAYS WILL. IT'S LIKE YOU SAID...
YOU FOOL. JUST STOP FIGHTING.
"...ONLY ONE THING MATTERS."

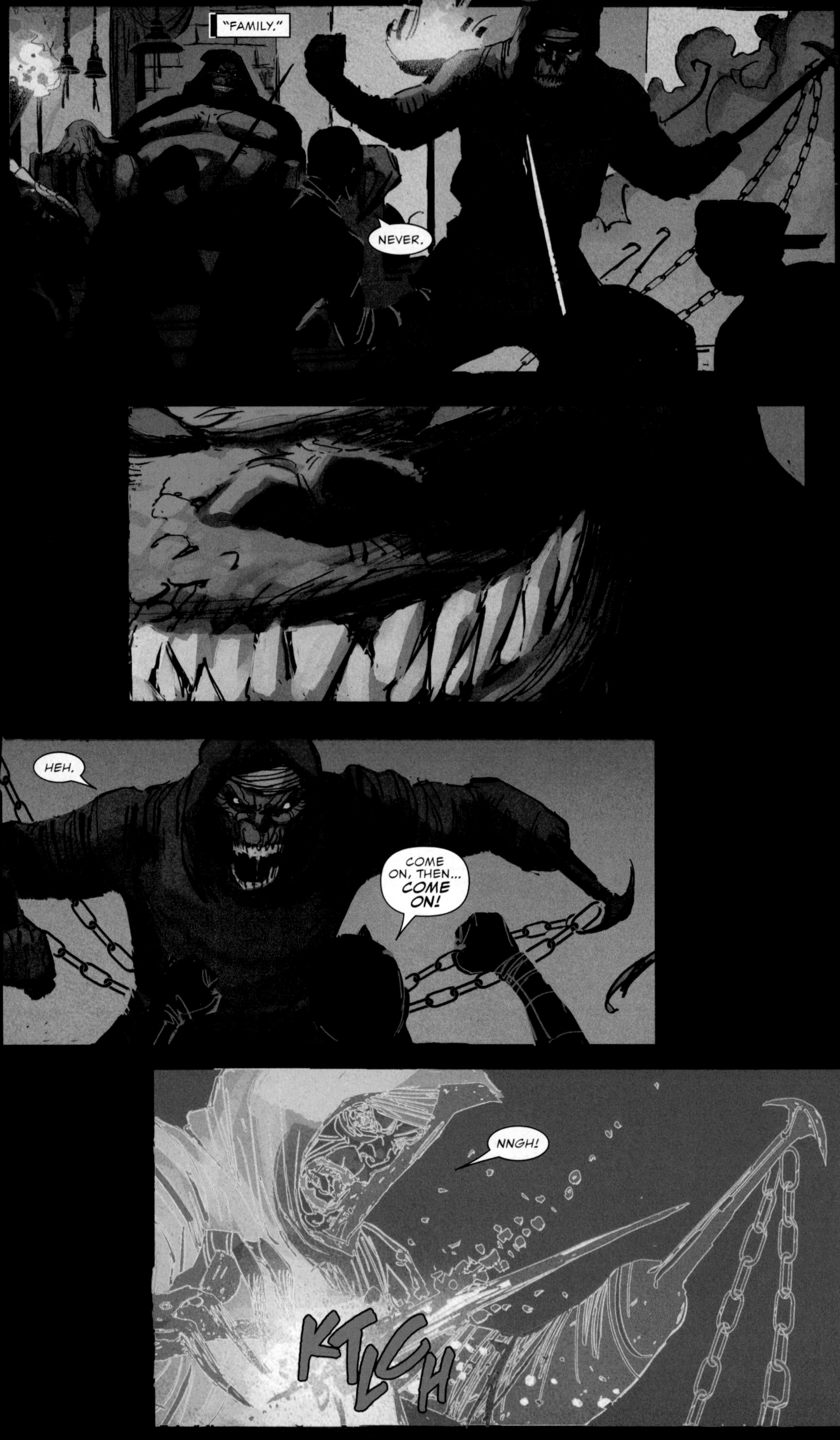
"FAMILY."
NEVER.
HEH.
COME ON, THEN... COME ON!
NNGH!
KTLCH

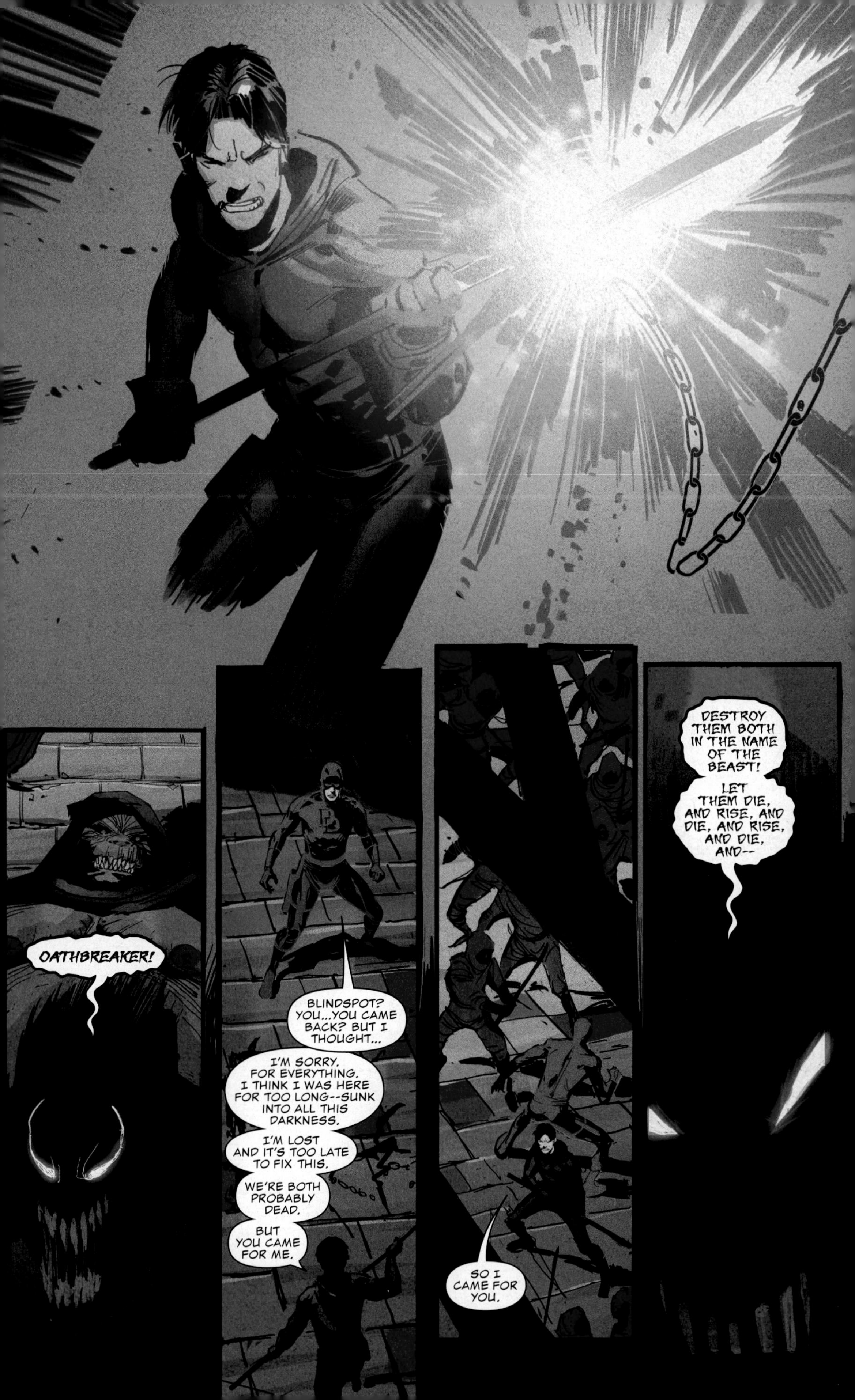
OATHBREAKER!
BLINDSPOT? YOU...YOU CAME BACK? BUT I THOUGHT...
I'M SORRY. FOR EVERYTHING. I THINK I WAS HERE FOR TOO LONG--SUNK INTO ALL THIS DARKNESS.
I'M LOST AND IT'S TOO LATE TO FIX THIS.
WE'RE BOTH PROBABLY DEAD.
BUT YOU CAME FOR ME.
SO I CAME FOR YOU.
DESTROY THEM BOTH IN THE NAME OF THE BEAST!
LET THEM DIE, AND RISE, AND DIE, AND RISE, AND DIE, AND--

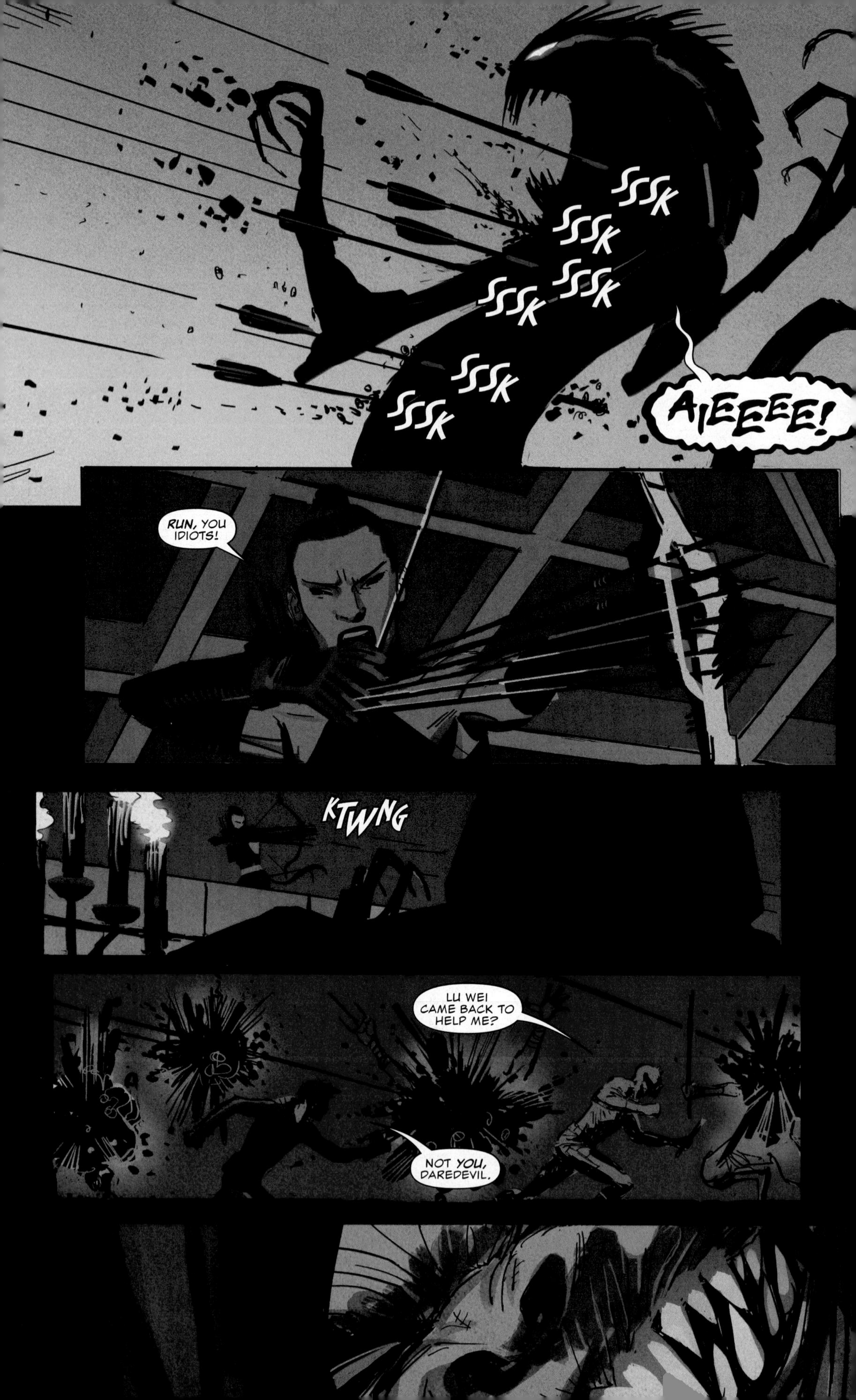
SSSK
SSSK
SSSK
SSSK
SSSK
SSSK
AIEEEEE!
RUN, YOU IDIOTS!
KTWNG
LU WEI CAME BACK TO HELP ME?
NOT YOU, DAREDEVIL.

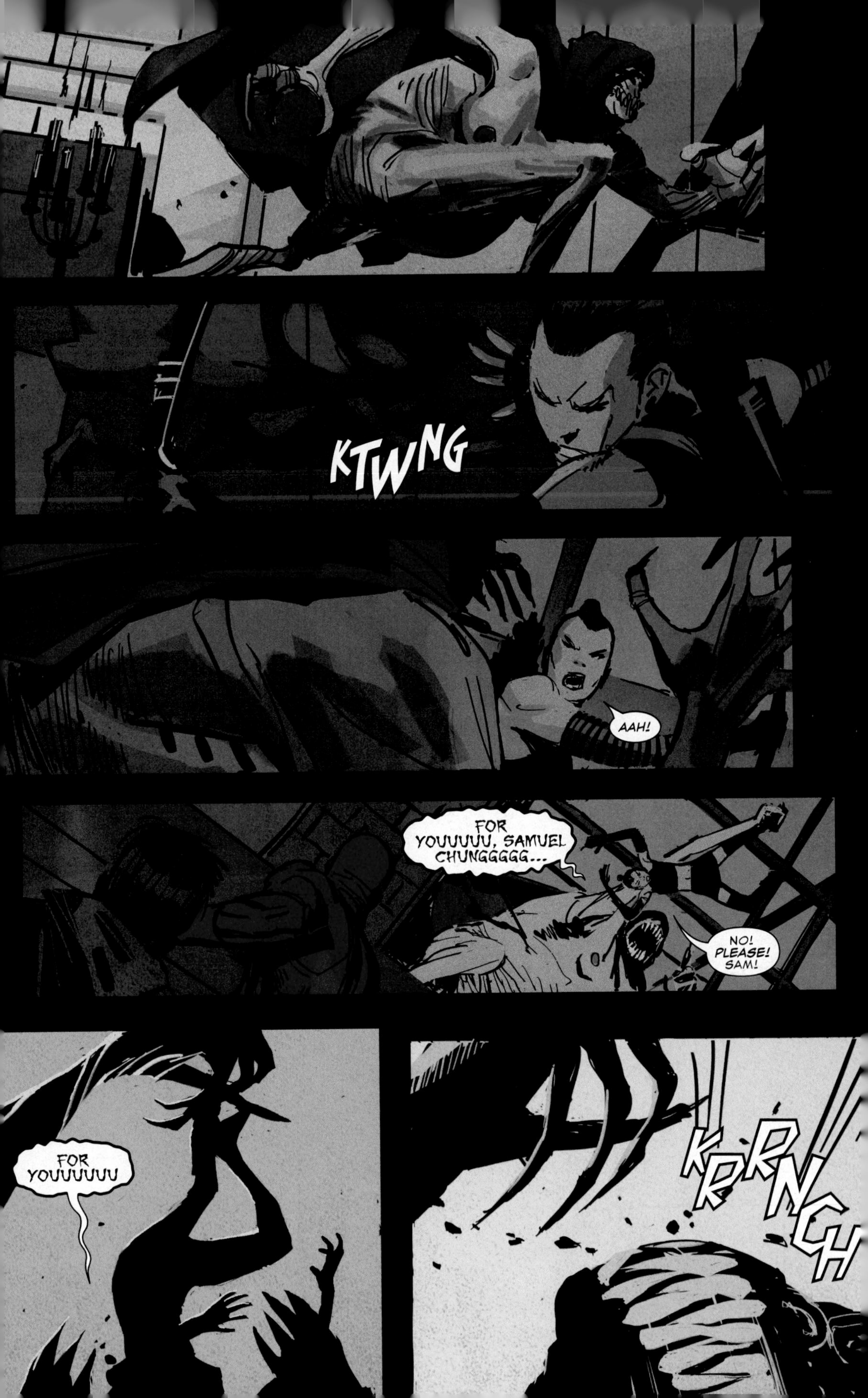
KTWNG
AAH!
FOR YOUUUUU, SAMUEL CHUNGGGGG...
NO! PLEASE! SAM!
FOR YOUUUUUU
KRRNCH

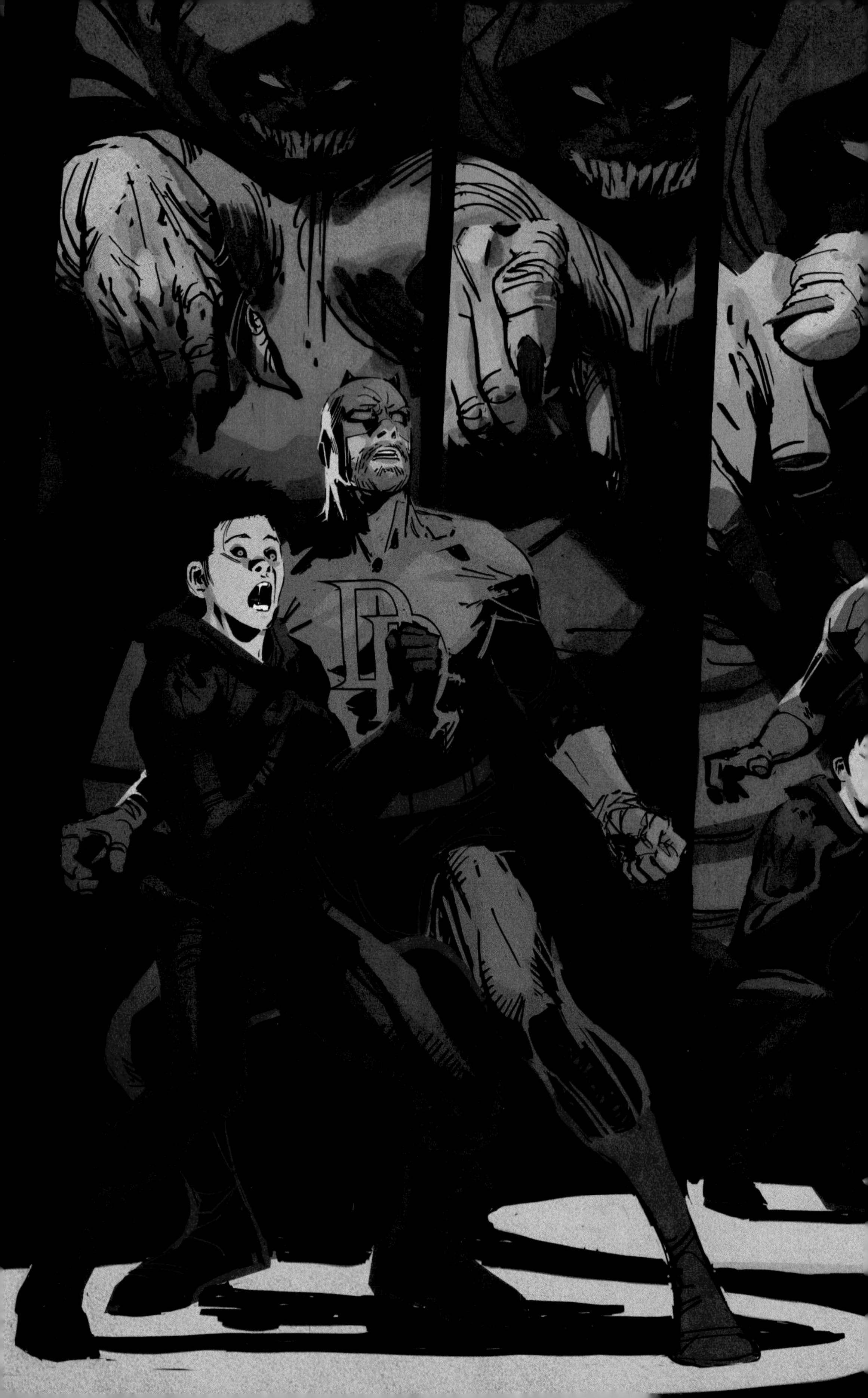

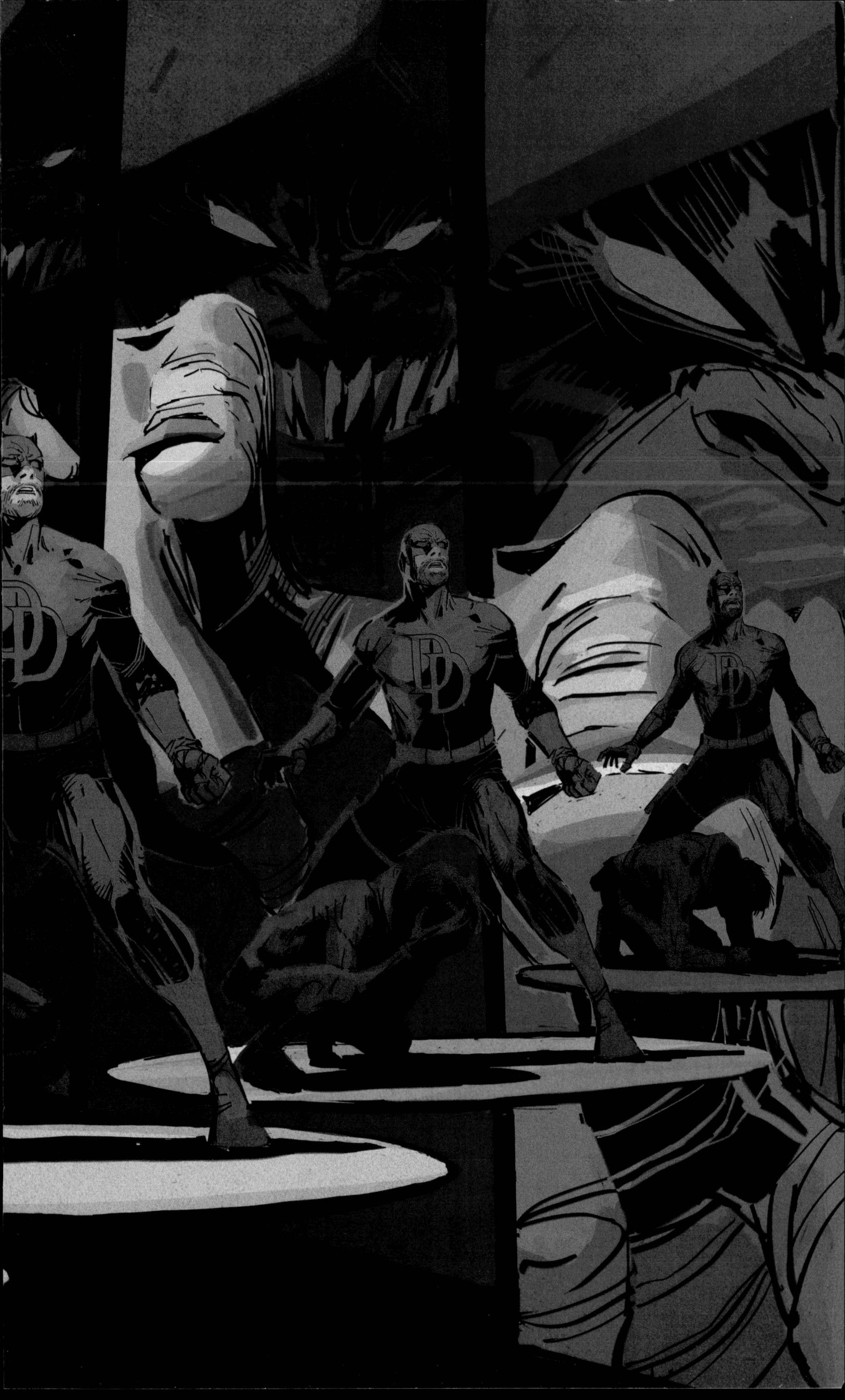

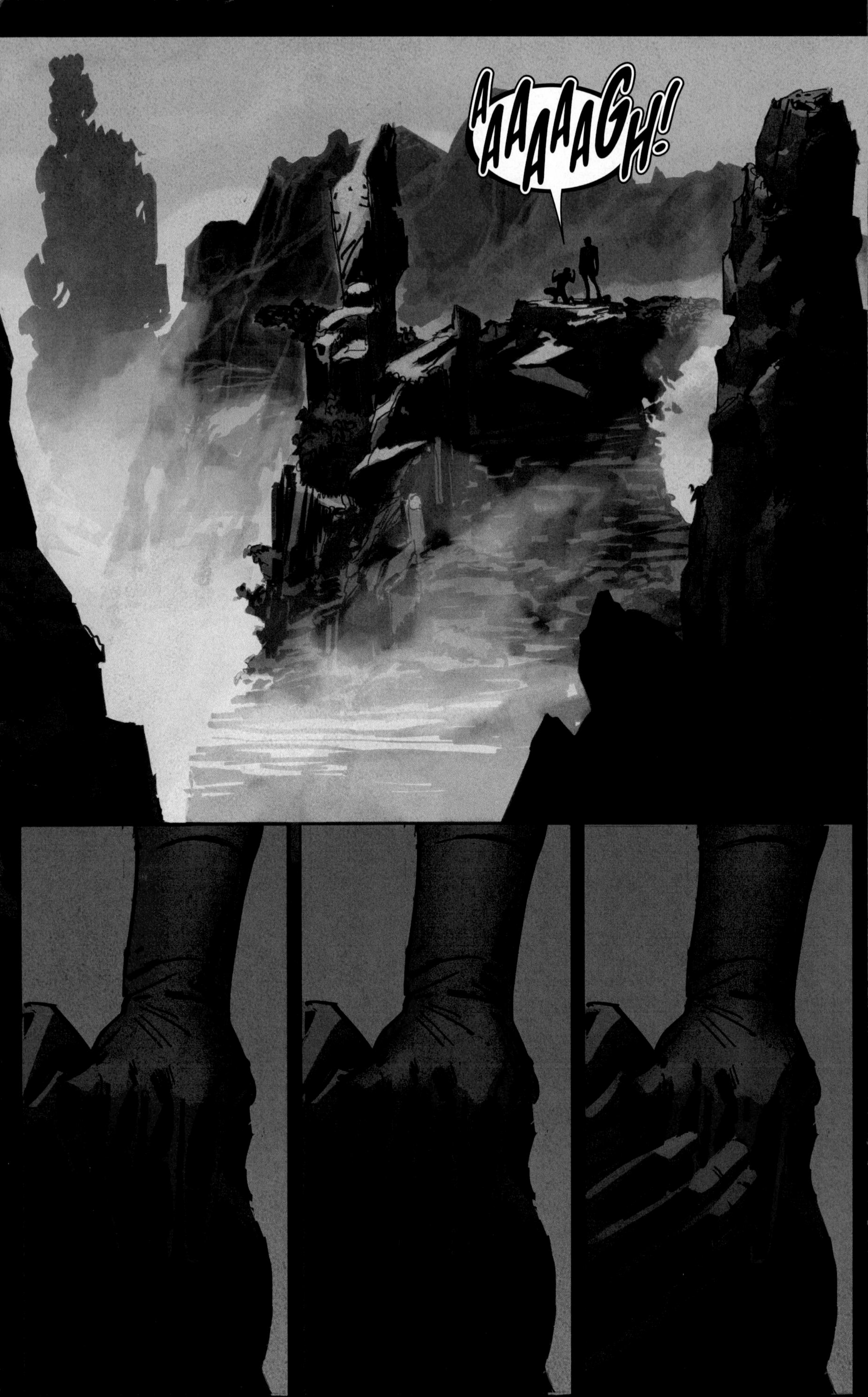
AAAAAAGH!

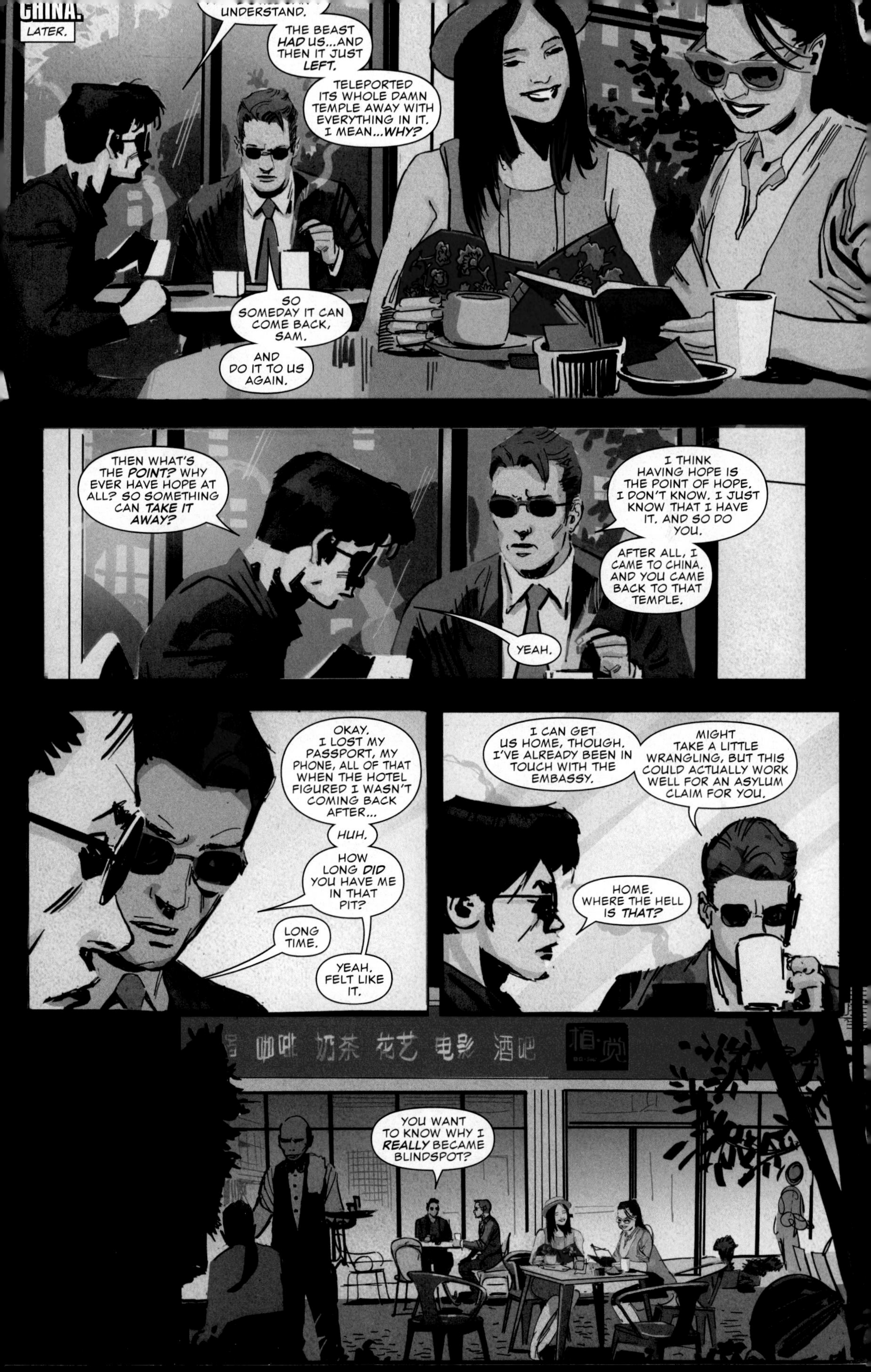
CHINA.
LATER.
UNDERSTAND.
THE BEAST HAD US...AND THEN IT JUST LEFT.
TELEPORTED ITS WHOLE DAMN TEMPLE AWAY WITH EVERYTHING IN IT. I MEAN...WHY?
SO SOMEDAY IT CAN COME BACK, SAM.
AND DO IT TO US AGAIN.
THEN WHAT'S THE POINT? WHY EVER HAVE HOPE AT ALL? SO SOMETHING CAN TAKE IT AWAY?
I THINK HAVING HOPE IS THE POINT OF HOPE. I DON'T KNOW. I JUST KNOW THAT I HAVE IT. AND SO DO YOU.
AFTER ALL, I CAME TO CHINA. AND YOU CAME BACK TO THAT TEMPLE.
YEAH.
OKAY. I LOST MY PASSPORT, MY PHONE, ALL OF THAT WHEN THE HOTEL FIGURED I WASN'T COMING BACK AFTER...
HUH.
HOW LONG DID YOU HAVE ME IN THAT PIT?
LONG TIME.
YEAH. FELT LIKE IT.
I CAN GET US HOME, THOUGH. I'VE ALREADY BEEN IN TOUCH WITH THE EMBASSY.
MIGHT TAKE A LITTLE WRANGLING, BUT THIS COULD ACTUALLY WORK WELL FOR AN ASYLUM CLAIM FOR YOU.
HOME. WHERE THE HELL IS THAT?
咖啡 奶茶 花艺 电影 酒吧
YOU WANT TO KNOW WHY I REALLY BECAME BLINDSPOT?

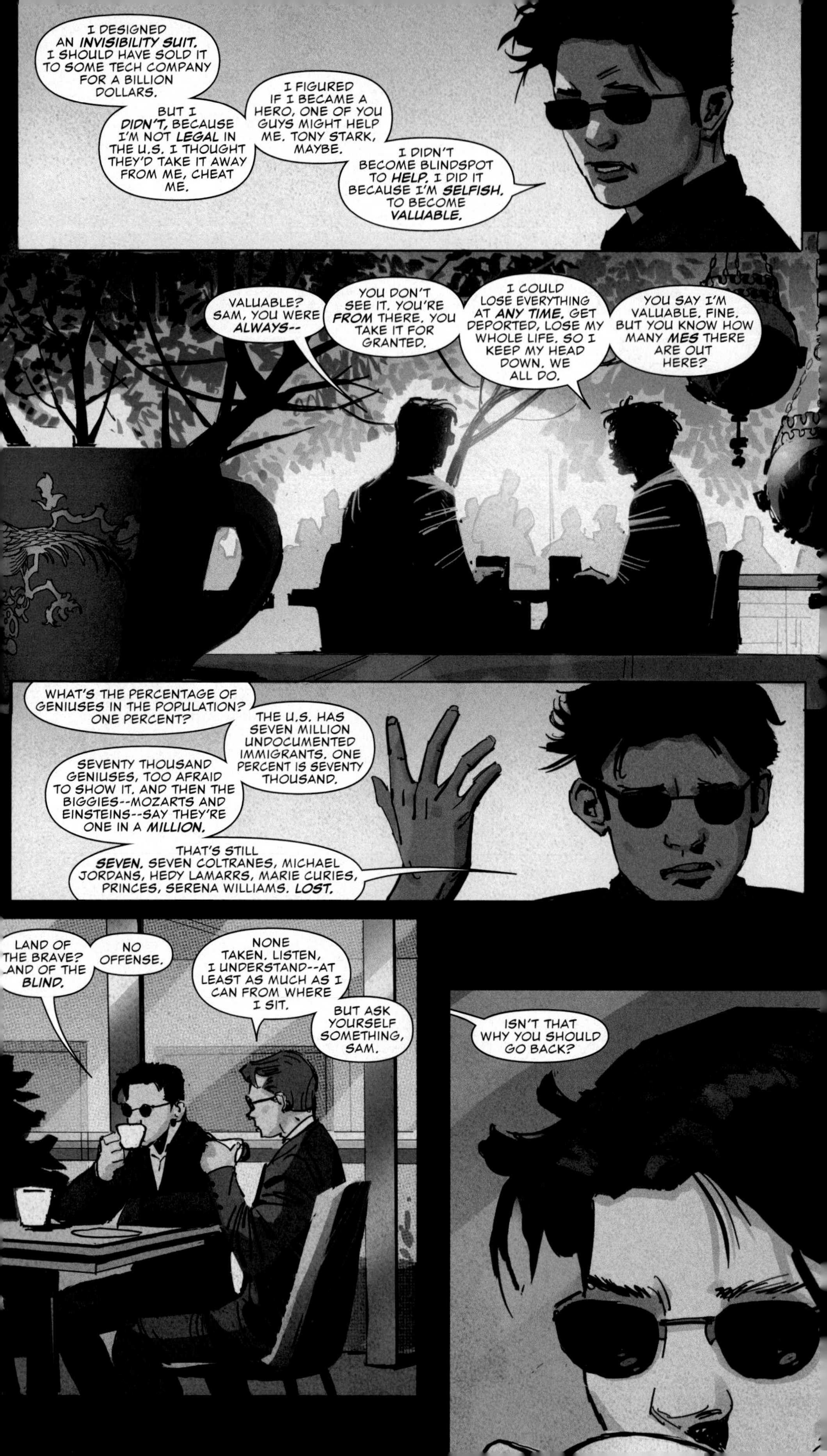

I DESIGNED AN INVISIBILITY SUIT. I SHOULD HAVE SOLD IT TO SOME TECH COMPANY FOR A BILLION DOLLARS.
BUT I DIDN'T, BECAUSE I'M NOT LEGAL IN THE U.S. I THOUGHT THEY'D TAKE IT AWAY FROM ME, CHEAT ME.
I FIGURED IF I BECAME A HERO, ONE OF YOU GUYS MIGHT HELP ME. TONY STARK, MAYBE.
I DIDN'T BECOME BLINDSPOT TO HELP. I DID IT BECAUSE I'M SELFISH. TO BECOME VALUABLE.
VALUABLE? SAM, YOU WERE ALWAYS--
YOU DON'T SEE IT. YOU'RE FROM THERE. YOU TAKE IT FOR GRANTED.
I COULD LOSE EVERYTHING AT ANY TIME. GET DEPORTED, LOSE MY WHOLE LIFE. SO I KEEP MY HEAD DOWN. WE ALL DO.
YOU SAY I'M VALUABLE. FINE. BUT YOU KNOW HOW MANY MES THERE ARE OUT HERE?
WHAT'S THE PERCENTAGE OF GENIUSES IN THE POPULATION? ONE PERCENT?
THE U.S. HAS SEVEN MILLION UNDOCUMENTED IMMIGRANTS. ONE PERCENT IS SEVENTY THOUSAND.
SEVENTY THOUSAND GENIUSES, TOO AFRAID TO SHOW IT. AND THEN THE BIGGIES--MOZARTS AND EINSTEINS--SAY THEY'RE ONE IN A MILLION.
THAT'S STILL SEVEN. SEVEN COLTRANES, MICHAEL JORDANS, HEDY LAMARRS, MARIE CURIES, PRINCES, SERENA WILLIAMS. LOST.
LAND OF THE BRAVE? LAND OF THE BLIND.
NO OFFENSE.
NONE TAKEN. LISTEN, I UNDERSTAND--AT LEAST AS MUCH AS I CAN FROM WHERE I SIT.
BUT ASK YOURSELF SOMETHING, SAM.
ISN'T THAT WHY YOU SHOULD GO BACK?

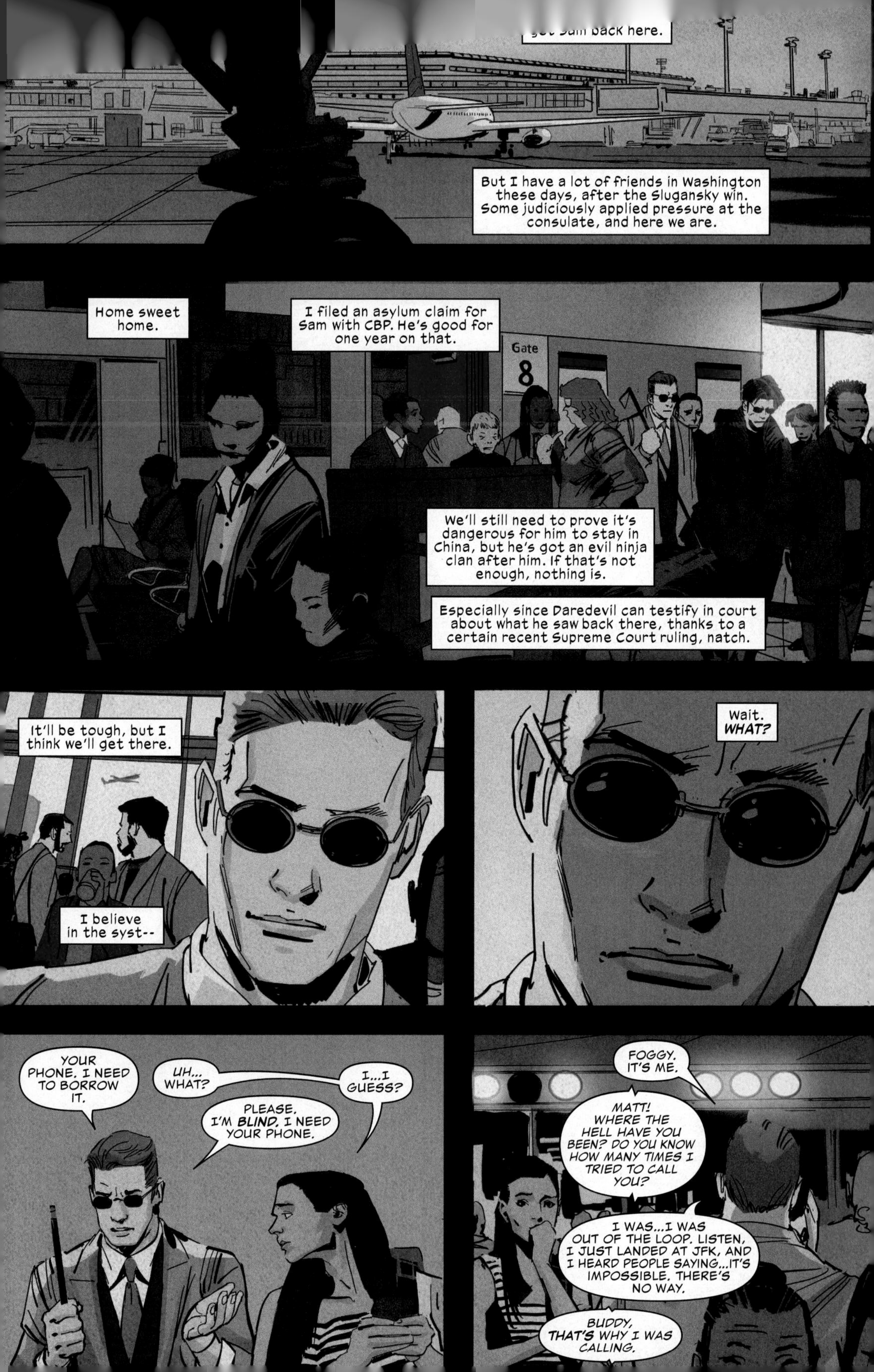
back here.
But I have a lot of friends in Washington these days, after the Slugansky win. Some judiciously applied pressure at the consulate, and here we are.
Home sweet home.
I filed an asylum claim for Sam with CBP. He's good for one year on that.
Gate
8
We'll still need to prove it's dangerous for him to stay in China, but he's got an evil ninja clan after him. If that's not enough, nothing is.
Especially since Daredevil can testify in court about what he saw back there, thanks to a certain recent Supreme Court ruling, natch.
It'll be tough, but I think we'll get there.
I believe in the syst--
Wait. *WHAT?*
YOUR PHONE. I NEED TO BORROW IT.
UH... WHAT?
PLEASE. I'M *BLIND.* I NEED YOUR PHONE.
I...I GUESS?
FOGGY. IT'S ME.
MATT! WHERE THE HELL HAVE YOU BEEN? DO YOU KNOW HOW MANY TIMES I TRIED TO CALL YOU?
I WAS...I WAS OUT OF THE LOOP. LISTEN, I JUST LANDED AT JFK, AND I HEARD PEOPLE SAYING...IT'S IMPOSSIBLE. THERE'S NO WAY.
BUDDY, *THAT'S* WHY I WAS CALLING.

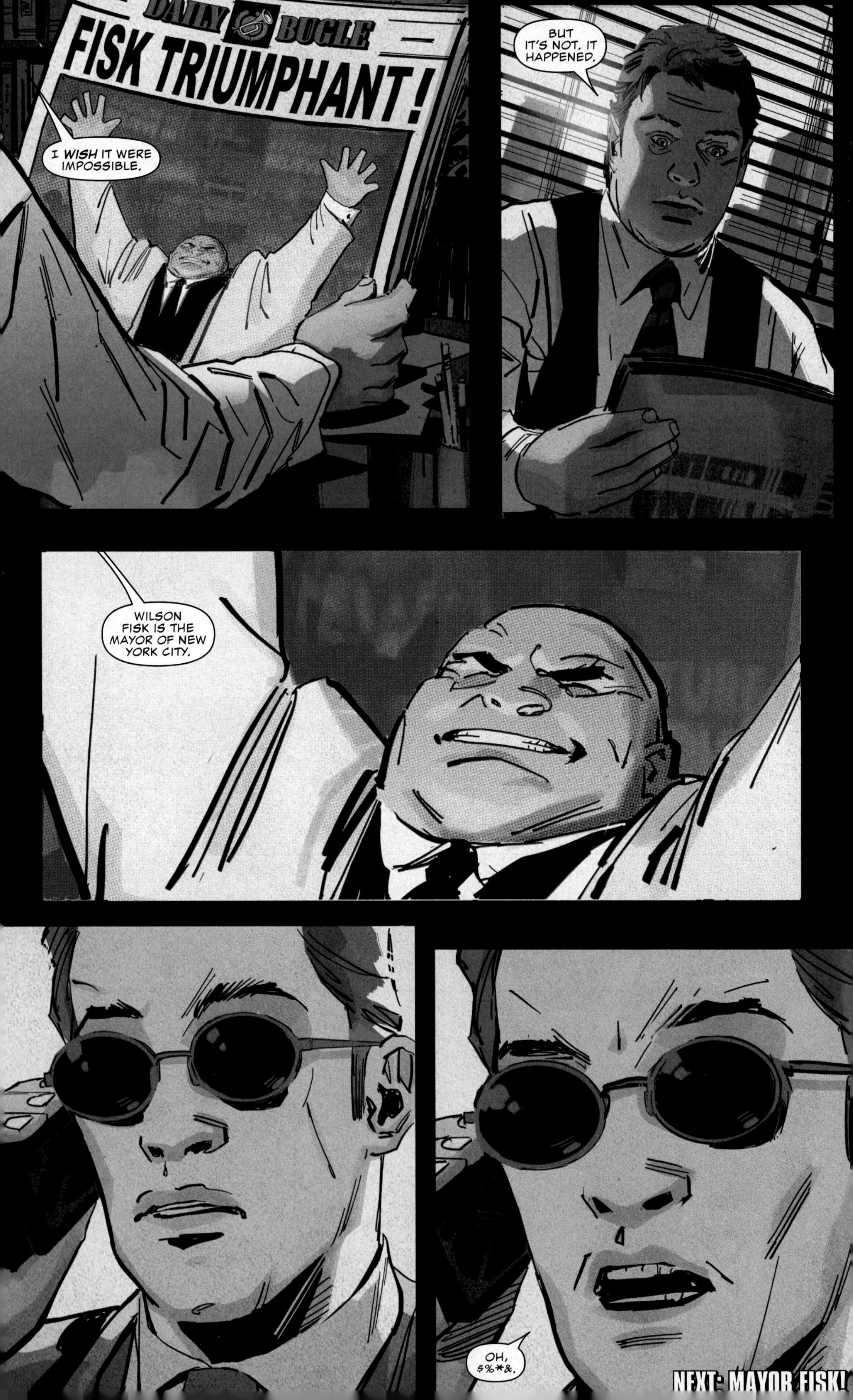

DAILY BUGLE
FISK TRIUMPHANT!
I WISH IT WERE IMPOSSIBLE.
BUT IT'S NOT. IT HAPPENED.
WILSON FISK IS THE MAYOR OF NEW YORK CITY.
OH, $%*&.
NEXT: MAYOR FISK!

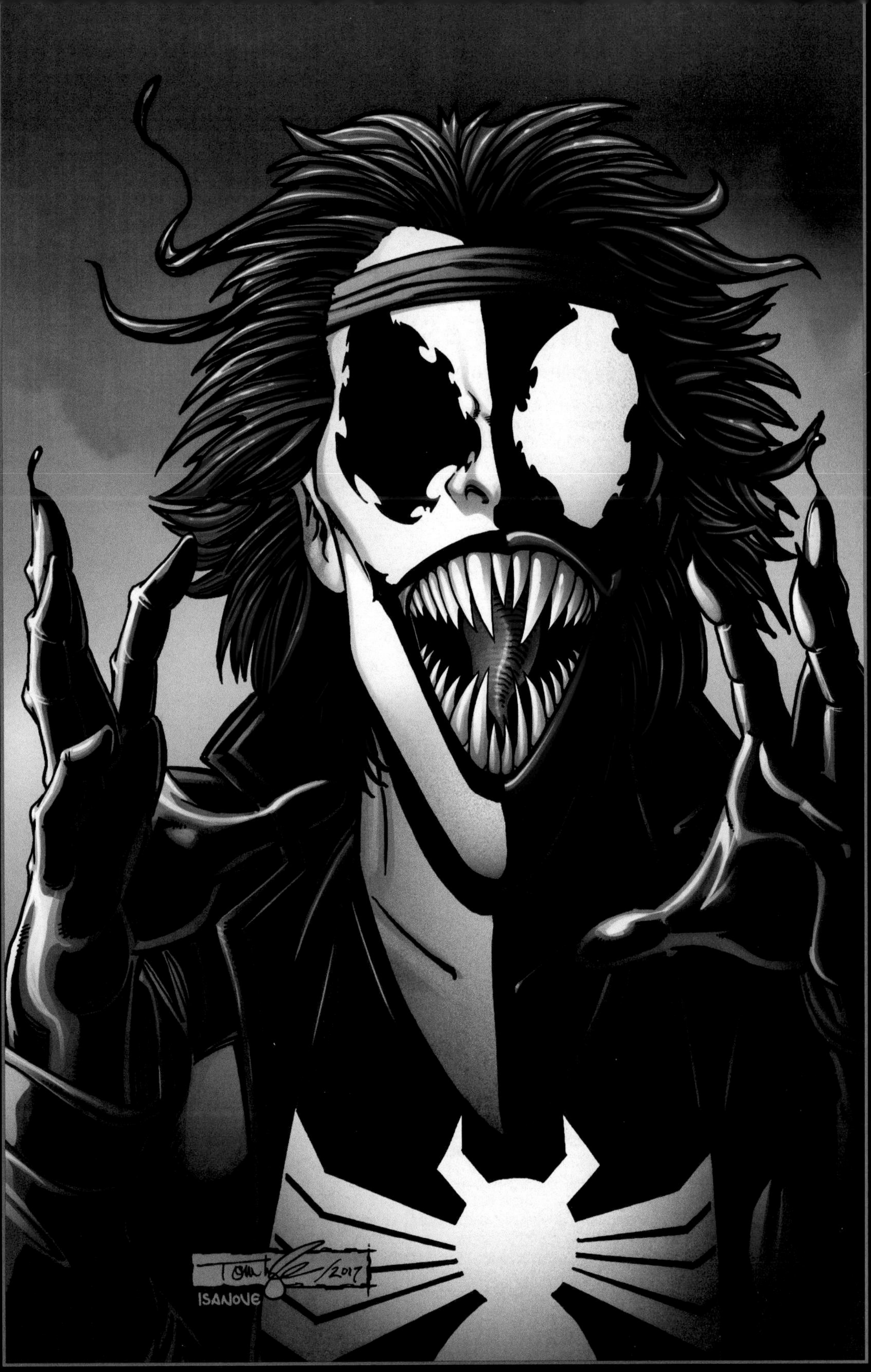
ISANOVE

DAREDEVIL

HOW TO DRAW DAREDEVIL
IN SIX EASY STEPS!
BY CHIP "MAN WITH MANY FEARS" ZDARSKY

Wow! A "sketch variant cover"! Are you a millionaire or something??
To prepare you to draw your very own DEVIL OF HECK'S KITCHEN,
here's a fun and informative step-by-step guide!

1

A lot of comic artists use photo reference when drawing! So, for this one, pull up an image of someone who resembles Daredevil, like popular New York District Attorney Matt Murdock!

2

Use a light blue pencil to rough out the shape of his head and placement of features. Ha! Just noticed that Murdock wears red glasses!

3

As most of you know, Matt Murdock is blind, so he may not even realize that Daredevil's main color of choice is red! Anyway! Sketch out the rest of his features!

4

Now, with a darker pencil, use the blue template to sketch out the shape of Daredevil's head and give him some eyes! How does he see through those tiny red lenses?! Ha ha!

5

Okay! Now you can add all the details that make him Daredevil! I mean, makes the HEAD Daredevil, not Murdock! Though Murdock does have a great knowledge of the law and criminals, and being blind in public would really throw people off your—

6

oh my god.